BURY ME AT THE MARKETPLACE

ES'KIA MPHAHLELE AND COMPANY

LETTERS 1943-2006

Edited by N Chabani Manganyi and David Attwell

Wits University Press
1 Jan Smuts Avenue
Johannesburg
South Africa
http://witspress.wits.ac.za

First published 2010.

ISBN: 978 1 86814 489 1

Edit by Pat Tucker
Design, layout and typesetting by Crazy Cat Designs
Cover image by George Mnyalaza Milwa Pemba, courtesy of N Chabani Manganyi
Printed and bound by Creda Communications

When I die, don't bury me under forest trees.
I fear the dripping water.
Bury me under the great shade trees in the market,
I want to hear the drums beating
I want to feel the dancers' feet.

Taken from the poem 'Death' by Kuba

CONTENTS

The editors have compiled footnotes to place the letters in this volume in context. The footnotes include information about correspondents, information about the historical, political or social context surrounding the time of writing, translations into English from other languages, as well as other useful information. For ease of reading the notes in each letter start at 1 and appear directly below the letter in which they appear.

THE EDITORS

N CHABANI MANGANYI

N Chabani Manganyi is a Senior Research Fellow in the Unit for Advanced Studies at the University of Pretoria. A retired clinical psychologist, his professional writings have appeared in academic journals and in collections of essays such as *Treachery and Innocence: Psychology and Racial Difference in South Africa* (1991). A long-standing interest in life writing dating back to the late 1970s resulted in the publication of the biographies of Es'kia Mphahlele (1983) and the late South African artist, Gerard Sekoto (2004). In 2008 Chabani Manganyi was honoured by the universities of the Witwatersrand, South Africa and Rhodes in recognition of his contribution to psychology and social change in South Africa.

DAVID ATTWELL

South African by birth, David Attwell is Chair of Modern Literature at the University of York (UK), having held positions at the universities of the Western Cape, KwaZulu-Natal and Witwatersrand. He collaborated with J M Coetzee on a series of dialogues which were collected, with Coetzee's non-fiction, as *Doubling the Point* (1992), and later wrote *J M Coetzee: South Africa and the Politics of Writing* (1993). His interest in African literature dates from the late 1970s and has led to essays on Wole Soyinka's uses of Yoruba mythology, on Thomas Mofolo's historical fiction, and on theoretical formations in African criticism. His most recent book is *Rewriting Modernity: Studies in Black South African Literary History* (2005).

ACKNOWLEDGEMENTS

We dedicate our book to the memory of Es'kia Mphahlele, who, in 2005, graciously entrusted us with the task of researching and editing this expanded edition of letters and interviews. We pay homage to him and are grateful to his family, and to South African and international correspondents for enriching our lives and those of future generations of fellow South Africans.

Funding for the Life Writing Project at the Unit for Advanced Study of the University of Pretoria was provided by the university and by the Department of Arts and Culture of the Republic of South Africa.

We are grateful for the cooperation we have received from the staff of the National English Literary Museum in Grahamstown, the Beinecke Rare Book and Manuscripts Library at Yale University, the Lilly Library at the University of Indiana, the Harry Ransom Humanities Research Centre at the University of Texas at Austin, and the Borthwick Institute at the University of York. Our particular thanks are due to Bernth Lindfors who generously transcribed a group of letters in the HRHRC in Austin.

Pat Tucker undertook the technical editing of the manuscript through its final stages of preparation. Her professional rigour and approach have added considerable value to our work.

Throughout the development of this book, we benefited from the unfailing support of the office of the Deputy Vice-Chancellor (Research) of the University of Pretoria, Professor Robin Crewe. Special thanks are due to Mrs Alta Scheepers, who ensured that administrative, financial and other research related matters were attended to.

As editors, we could not have wished for a better publisher than Wits University Press under the leadership of Veronica Klipp and her colleagues. We thank them most heartily.

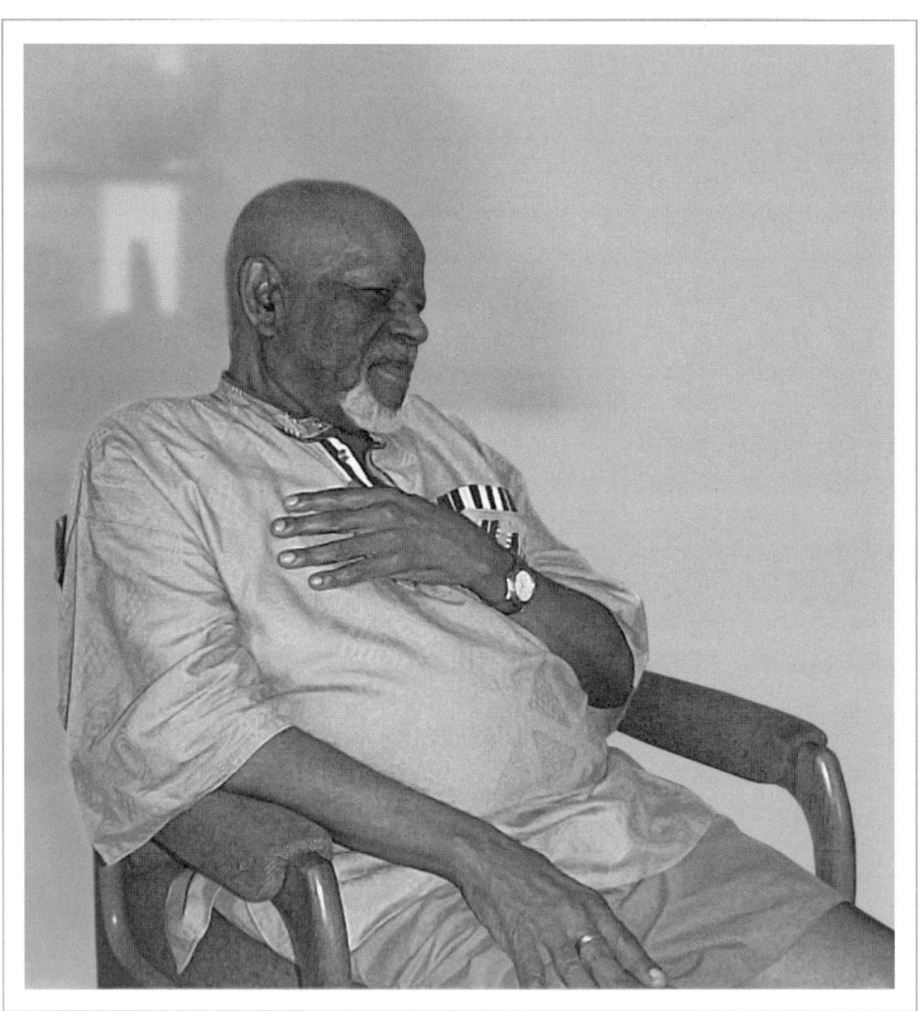

Ezekiel Mphahlele at home in 2005.
Photograph taken by N Chabani Manganyi

PREFACE

IN HIS OWN VOICE

The first edition of this book was a companion volume to my biography of Es'kia Mphahlele entitled *Exiles and Homecomings*.[1]

At the time the books were published there was a small group of enterprising and progressive alternative publishers in Johannesburg, among them, Ravan Press and Skotaville Publishers, who supported the anti-establishment voices of the day. In my introduction to the first edition of *Bury Me at the Marketplace* I wrote that from a biographer's point of view the letters were a worthy companion to *Exiles and Homecomings*, a standpoint I maintain today.[2]

I wrote, too, that Mphahlele's letters told the 'story of a life lived' to the fullest possible extent and were an invitation to enter into 'a privileged inner circle of intimacy, humour, compassion, love and pain'. Significantly, at that time, I raised the prospect of a future edition of letters from and to Es'kia Mphahlele, a hope that has been realised with the publication of this edition. Work on this book has been in progress for a number of years

---

1 N Chabani Manganyi. 1983. *Exiles and Homecomings: A Biography of Es'kia Mphahlele*. Johannesburg: Ravan Press.

2 N Chabani Manganyi (ed). 1984. *Bury Me at the Marketplace: Selected Letters of Es'kia Mphahlele 1943-1980*. Johannesburg: Skotaville Publishers.

and I have been privileged during that time to collaborate with David Attwell, an eminent scholar with a well-established understanding and knowledge of Mphahlele's literary oeuvre within the broader context of South African literature as a whole.[3]

While working on the manuscript of this collection I felt as challenged as I was in the early 1980s when I engaged with and responded to the many faces of Es'kia Mphahlele as he took centre stage in different situations, countries and in relationships with a cast of illustrious writers, academics, friends and family coupled with his emergence as a world figure – a literary and cultural critic and significant writer in his own right.

One of the most important lessons I learnt is that memorable moments in letter writing come to light whenever a letter or set of letters gives the reader as much pleasure as it did the writer at the time of its composition. I have come to the conclusion, following a close reading of Mphahlele's letters, that a well-written letter makes demands on the writer that are similar to those normally associated with short-story writing. Letters which are to command the reader's undivided attention must feel self-contained, reflect a moment of cognitive and affective concentration and confirm the importance of an ability to create an atmosphere similar to that found in good short stories.

One example that comes to mind, among several others, is the letter written on 11 November 1980 by Mphahlele to his daughter. In it he tells the story of the 'visitor' who turned out to be a closet alcoholic. The style is conversational and is coupled with Mphahlele's unobtrusive, yet potent and explosive sense of humour, used to good effect in dealing with the grotesque in everyday life. This 'mission' to be a storyteller is prophetically expressed in a letter dated 24 December 1943 to his lifelong friend and confidante, Norah Taylor, in which he writes of 'the passion of one who desires to tell a story'.

Author and academic James Olney, in a letter dated 12 March 1974, recognised Mphahlele's ability to engage his readers when he wrote:

> *I enjoyed very much and was deeply touched by your letter received yesterday. Thank you. All the qualities that have always distinguished your writing were there on that single sheet – intelligence, sensitivity, creative vitality and energy – and, in addition, what one could only guess at in the published work: personal courtesy and kindness. There are few men, – especially few of your literary and human achievements – from whom one could expect such a gesture of selfless generosity.*

---

3 See D Attwell. 2006. *Rewriting Modernity*. Pietermaritzburg: University of KwaZulu-Natal Press, p 111

What we find in Mphahlele's letters is the profile of an open-minded, fearless, intellectually engaging personality, writer and scholar in one compact bundle of unremitting energy and radiating humour.

Today I marvel at the fact that my earliest exposure to a collection of published letters was in the early 1970s when I was a post-doctoral fellow in Clinical Psychology at Yale University. The book in question was *Letters From Jenny* by the psychologist Gordon Allport.[4] I read it at a time when I was researching the interface between psychology and biography. I found the following statement of special interest:

> *Intimate letters, gushing forth from raw personal experience, have a unique fascination. Often better than fiction or biography, even than autobiography, they tell us what a particular concrete human life is like. The fascination is greater if the letters are written over a considerable period of time, presenting consecutively the inner narrative of a life as it unfolds.*

Granted Allport was writing during the late 1960s before the flourishing of more contemporary ideas about biography and autobiography. Today we are able to be more explicit and say that letters are first-person 'utterances' and that very fact makes them, according to one view, autobiographical narratives. In the two decades since the publication of the Mphahlele letters the chorus hailing letters as autobiography, as 'real and best biography', as 'giving first place to the writer's own words' has grown louder and more persistent.[5]

In this collection we amplify Mphahlele's epistolary voice with edited versions of two interviews I conducted and published some years ago. Like the letters in the earlier edition, the first interview, 'Looking In: In Search of Es'kia Mphahlele', is part of a larger series of biographical interviews I conducted with Mphahlele and several informants as a forerunner to the publication of *Exiles and Homecomings* in 1983.[6] 'Metaphors of Self' was part of a more recent large-scale South African study of auto/biography published as *Selves in Question: Interviews on Southern African Auto/Biography*.[7]

---

4 G W Allport (ed). 1965. *Letters from Jenny*. New York: Harcourt Brace Jovanovich.

5 See, eg, Philip Horne (ed). 1999. *Henry James: A Life in Letters*. London: Penguin Books, p xvi.

6 N Chabani Manganyi. 1981. *Looking Through the Keyhole: Dissenting Essays on the Black Experience*. Johannesburg: Ravan Press, pp 4-50.

7 N Chabani Manganyi. 2006. 'Metaphors of Self: Es'kia Mphahlele'. In Judith Lütge Coullie, Stephan Meyer, Thengani Ngwenya and Thomas Olver (eds). *Selves in Question: Interviews on Southern African Auto/Biography*. Honolulu: University of Hawaii Press, pp 243-253.

'Looking In' (conducted in 1979) covers a broad autobiographical sweep, confirming, in important respects, the life story that emerges through the letters. It is worth noting that the piece was published many years before the interview as 'autobiographical essay' or as 'book of conversations' became an established 'autobiographical' genre.[8] In the 1979 interview we meet Mphahlele, the child, in rural South Africa; the schoolboy and student in the black ghetto of Marabastad; the high-school teacher of the early 1950s; the *Drum* fiction editor and the writer and scholar of the exile years.

Today there is no need to search far and wide for published book-length interview volumes since there are numerous examples of such publications. In these texts, as in the case of composite collections of letters, the most vocal claims concern the authenticity of the 'voice' of the writer and subject of the interview. As one writer put it, an interview 'preserves the voice of the speaker', while Edward Said once said, 'In many ways, interviews are sustained acts of discovery'.[9]

'Metaphors of Self' is an autobiographical statement concerned with Mphahlele's ideas about the craft of writing autobiographies. The interview is loaded with his pithy, penetrating and thought-provoking observations, including the place of the imagination in autobiography, fiction, short fiction and expository writing. What we learn is made more remarkable by the ease and simplicity with which his wisdom and insights are laid bare. While Mphahlele's voice is paramount in this collection, the book is enormously enhanced by the addition of the voices of the famous and not so famous, of colleagues, fellow writers and lifelong friends.

Es'kia Mphahlele's sudden death in the late spring of 2008 was a poignant moment, not only for members of his family, but for his friends and his many admirers, both in South Africa and abroad. It was particularly poignant for the people of South Africa, his native land, for Mphahlele was a man who towered above so many of his national and international literary and academic peers. His spirited public rejection of the introduction of the infamous 'Bantu Education' system in the early 1950s earned him and two of his colleagues at the time the wrath of the apartheid regime and they were 'banned' from teaching in any school in South Africa.

Mphahlele had taken a moral and political stand against a perceived injustice. From then on, making difficult and painful choices while speaking his mind became the hallmark of Mphahlele the literary and cultural

---

8 See, eg, D O'Driscoll (ed). 2008. *Stepping Stones: Interviews with Seamus Heaney*. London: Faber and Faber.

9 G Viswanathan (ed). 2004. *Power, Politics and Culture: Interviews with Edward W. Said*. London: Bloomsbury, p xx.

crusader, the writer and academic. The range of his intellectual and literary pursuits throughout his long exile in Nigeria, Paris, Nairobi, Zambia and the United States of America was wide, deep and, in some cases, path-breaking. His literary, cultural and scholarly legacy is substantial. One is reminded, for example, of the fact that in the late 1950s and 1970s he, together with other prominent African and African-American writers and scholars, took a commanding lead in the lively, and at times acrimonious, debates about Negritude, the 'African Personality' and the Harlem Renaissance.

In the words of my co-editor, David Attwell, who has written eloquently about Mphahlele's legacy:

> *In Es'kia Mphahlele we have arguably the most sustained record in South African literature of the encounter between a South African writer and the cultures of the wider diaspora .... Between 1957 and 1977, he engaged with each of the major centres of intellectual ferment in the black world, in West and East Africa, with exiled Francophone Africa, the Caribbean, and the United States.*[10]

Need I say more?

N Chabani Manganyi

---

[10] Attwell. *Rewriting Modernity*, op cit.

INTRODUCTION

READING IN THE COMPANY OF ES'KIA MPHAHLELE

Es'kia Mphahlele died on 28 October 2008, in his eighty-ninth year. His passing gives to this collection – and its title – a special, if poignant, relevance. When Chabani Manganyi published the first edition of selected letters twenty-five years ago (1984) as a companion volume to *Exiles and Homecomings: A Biography of Es'kia Mphahlele* (1983), the idea of Mphahlele's death was remote and poetic. The title, *Bury Me at the Marketplace*, suggested that immortality of a kind awaited Mphahlele, in the very coming and going of those who remember him and whose lives he touched. It suggested, too, the energy and magnanimity of Mphahlele, the man, whose personality and intellect as a writer and educator would carve an indelible place for him in South Africa's public sphere.

That death has now come and we mourn it. Manganyi's words at the time have acquired a new significance: in the symbolic marketplace, he noted, 'the drama of life continues relentlessly and the silence of death is unmasked for all time'.[1] The silence of death is certainly unmasked in this volume, in its record of Mphahlele's rich and varied life: his private words,

[1] N Chabani Manganyi. 1984. ' Introduction', *Bury Me at the Marketplace: Selected Letters of Es'kia Mphahlele 1943-1980.* Johannesburg: Skotaville Publishers, p 1.

his passions and obsessions, his arguments, his loves, hopes, achievements, and yes, even some of his failures. Here the reader will find many facets of the private man translated back into the marketplace of public memory.

When the first edition was published Manganyi envisaged this expanded volume: 'a promising enterprise for future scholarship would be a collection of letters from and to Es'kia Mphahlele of which there is already an extensive collection', and 'a later edition of this work will probably include many more letters than are included in this collection. The gaps are now well known and it will be the task of future research to plug them.' In this second edition these hopes have largely been realised.

This selection of Mphahlele's own letters has indeed been greatly expanded; it has also been augmented by the addition of a large number of letters from Mphahlele's correspondents. The reasons for these decisions are, firstly, that the reader will be afforded a more complete record of the growth and development of Mphahlele's life and career; secondly, that the present volume seeks to illustrate the networks that shaped Mphahlele's personal and intellectual life, the circuits of intimacy and intellectual inquiry, of friendship, scholarship and solidarity that he created and nurtured over the years.

Despite the personal nature of the letters, the further horizons of this volume are also the contours of South Africa's literary and cultural history, the international affiliations out of which it has been formed, particularly in the diaspora that connects South Africa to the rest of the African continent and to the black presence in Europe and the United States.

The letters included in this volume cover the period from November 1943 to February 2006, sixty-three of Mphahlele's mature years and most of his active professional life. It is not our intention to recount his biography here. Readers are referred to the interviews published in this volume, to the many critical studies of Mphahlele's life and work, to the biography, *Exiles and Homecomings* (1983) and to the autobiographies, especially *Down Second Avenue* (1959) and *Afrika My Music* (1984). But for the benefit of readers who might not be familiar with the outlines of Mphahlele's life, let us take stock, albeit schematically, of the larger historical patterns that shaped him in the years covered by these letters. In the correspondence published in these pages readers will find these historical patterns felt on the bone.

In his early intellectual life Mphahlele lived through the 1940s when the political debates in the public sphere of the time, dominated by white politicians and planners, were about the consequences of urbanisation and the place of Africans at the centre of South Africa's modernity. This question was the elephant in the room of a myopic settler-colonial politics. The result was the hardening of segregation into apartheid by the end of the decade, following the electoral victory of the National Party in 1948.

It was in these years that Mphahlele's vocation was developing, when the aspirant teacher, writer and intellectual was beginning to find his place in the world. For an idealist, a young man with a generous spirit and wide sympathies – attributes that were hard won after a difficult childhood and upbringing in Marabastad and Maupaneng – this was an inauspicious time, to say the least. He was set on a life course that was bound to be conflicted. The teacher in Mphahlele, in particular, would rebel against the Verwoerdian principles inherent in Bantu Education, as an affront to personal liberty, social well-being and democratic citizenship, and the consequences involved his being banned from his chosen profession.

At the same time his artistic ambitions were beginning to develop and he published his first collection of stories, *Man Must Live*, with the African Bookman in Cape Town (1947). The correspondence with Norah Taylor, where matters turn frequently on Mphahlele's relationship with the theatre, is unusual for the time; at least, it is an especially personal instance of the non-racial activism that flowered in the 1950s. Mphahlele was more than conscious of its implications, remarking how important it was in 'this cauldron of suspicious, petty and often snobbish humanity'. Over time this friendship only deepened, the letters continuing well into the difficult years of Mphahlele's exile.

How different was the other major correspondence that began in the 1950s, this time with Langston Hughes. That Mphahlele was writing to Taylor and to Hughes almost simultaneously reveals something of his breadth and ability to give himself to different universes; a point that will be taken up at the end of this introduction. By now, Mphahlele had moved to the offices of *Drum* where he worked as fiction editor. Hughes was reaching out to Africans in a spirit of diasporic community; Mphahlele was reaching out to the Harlem Renaisssance and to the confident self-definition that was part and parcel of African-American cultural politics and artistic expression.

Mphahlele's worlds in the 1940s and early to mid-1950s both overlapped and collided: there was the vibrancy and edginess of the township as expressed in the ethos of *Drum*; the genteel liberalism of Norah Taylor (not to mention the anglocentric education of St Peters, Adams College and Unisa's English Department, where he did most of his literary studies); and the world represented by Hughes. Hughes had written to Mphahlele after a story of his appeared in a New York anthology. Of this encounter, Mphahlele would later remark: 'My systematic study of African American literature, thought and history actually began in 1955 – before my exile.' He added that it was an instinctive connection, a result of the mind 'reaching out across the frontiers of reference, seeking to know where it stands in relation to this or that. The act of knowing, the ways of consciousness, seem to me to be at the centre of human survival.'[2]

This instinctive reaching out, the crossing of boundaries as an investment in the self's survival, was to become a habit of mind and a lifelong moral and intellectual commitment. The letters reveal the extent to which these leaps of faith were a function of relationships with particular people in their specific circumstances.

Mphahlele left South Africa in September 1957 to take up a post teaching in a grammar school in Lagos. Although *Drum* was a literary and journalistic phenomenon and the camaraderie amongst its writers would prove legendary, it was a precarious base for a writer whose literary aspirations extended further than the commercial enterprise that Jim Bailey wanted his magazine to be. As its frustrated fiction editor, Mphahlele resolved to return to teaching, but he could not do so in South Africa. The horizon that presented itself was West Africa.

The resonance of this decision is striking: the great wave of decolonisation that began with Ghanaian independence in the same year (March 1957) was making its presence felt in South African political life even while the government of the day turned its back on it. In silky tones, Harold Macmillan would later warn against the consequences of its doing so when he addressed Parliament and spoke of the 'winds of change'. Mphahlele joined what was, at this stage, still a small group of South African émigrés who embraced the continent (by the 1960s the trickle would become a flood). None, however, would become as closely associated with the continent's cultural self-definition as Mphahlele.

Having edited the activist community newspaper, *The Voice*, in Orlando, and then worked at *Drum*, it is not surprising that over and above his teaching Mphahlele would quickly become involved in some of Nigeria's pioneering literary ventures, in particular the journal *Black Orpheus*, which he co-edited with Ulli Beier. Nigeria was exhilarating – 'there was the scintillating sense of freedom and daytime, after the South African nightmare'[3] – but inevitably Mphahlele found himself reflecting

2 'Your History Demands Your Heartbeat: Historical Survey of the Encounter Between Africans and African Americans'. In Es'kia Mphahlele, *Es'kia* (Johannesburg: Kwela Books, in association with Stainbank and Associates, 2002), p 173.

3 Mphahlele, E. 1984. *Afrika My Music: An Autobiography 1957-1983*. Johannesburg: Ravan, 1984, p 20.

on home: 'you seemed to hear, still, the distant proclamations of law and order across the Congo, the Zambezi and the Limpopo, down in the painful south of the south'.[4]

Lagos seems to have provided not so much a new home and a sense of place as a conjunction of places, a joining of the continent's south and west. It provided, firstly, the context in which he was able to bring to conclusion the book for which he is still best known, *Down Second Avenue*. Later, while working in Paris, through *Black Orpheus* and Mbari Publications – a project of the Mbari Club, with which he had become associated in Lagos and where he had rubbed shoulders with Wole Soyinka, Christopher Okigbo, John Pepper Clark, and Demas Nwoko – he facilitated a pan-African cultural traffic, notably bringing Alex La Guma (*A Walk in the Night* 1962) and Dennis Brutus (*Sirens, Knuckles and Boots* 1963) to an international readership.

While his creativity developed in Lagos as editor, autobiographer, poet, theatre practitioner and cultural organiser, he maintained a wide correspondence with South Africans at home and abroad: with Norah Taylor; Makhudu Rammopo (a lifelong friend who would join him in Nigeria, as did other teachers from South Africa); with Ursula Barnett, who had begun doctoral studies involving his writing; with Richard Rive and Jack Cope in Cape Town; with William Plomer in England. The reader will be struck by the generous energy and open-mindedness Mphahlele brings to each of these correspondences.

His life and work at this time were a conjunction of places and criss-crossing worlds. Mphahlele the teacher, however, was unhappy: having moved from CMS Grammar School to the Department of Extra-Mural Studies at the University of Ibadan, he had become 'an extra-mural donkey',[5] travelling extensively and teaching too many students with utilitarian motives. A cable arrived from Paris: Mercer Cook, retiring Director of African Programmes at the Congress for Cultural Freedom, asking if Mphahlele would be interested in succeeding him. If so, would he come for an interview with the executive director, John Hunt? The Mphahleles moved to Paris in August 1961 and would remain there for two years.

We now know that the congress was funded in part by the CIA through its front organisation, the Farfield Foundation. Guided by the sociologist Edward Shils, the American administration's Cold War reading of the situation was that the third world's intelligentsia, as it saw matters, should be supported despite its aggressive cultural nationalism because in that

---

[4] Ibid, pp 20-21.

[5] Ibid, p 30.

way it would develop a taste for a free public sphere and remain within the United States's orbit of influence. Whatever the motives behind this project, the outcomes would have been ambiguous for the American administration because the actors, Mphahlele included, made excellent use of the funding.

In addition to supporting *Black Orpheus*, *Transition*, and *Encounter* in Britain, the congress supported a number of South African periodicals, including *Contrast*, *The New African*, *Africa South* and *The Classic*.[6] When the truth emerged in 1966, after Mphahlele had left the congress, he was furious: 'the CIA stinks', he wrote in a letter to *Transition*, defending the activity of the African programme on the grounds that it was best judged in its national contexts and insisting that he took the position on the strict assumption that the intellectuals it supported would not be expected to 'develop with reference to the reflexes of the West'.[7]

Mphahlele certainly made hay as director: he co-organised some of the most seminal conferences in the development of African literary studies, including the famous conference of writers at Makerere University in Kampala in 1962, and he supported various publishing ventures and travelled extensively in Africa, Europe and the United States, facilitating projects and meetings of writers.

The Paris desk of the congress, but more directly, the Mphahlele apartment on the Boulevard du Montparnasse, became the median point for several diasporic cross-currents: South Africa's relationship with the continent of Africa, writers from inside South Africa and the exiles, anglophone and francophone intellectuals. Through all this, the link with Hughes remained intact. The surviving correspondence does not do justice to this range, but it reveals Mphahlele the organiser, cultural activist and friend.

In 1962 Mphahlele's stature as critic was established with the publication by Faber and Faber in London of the first edition of *The African Image*. The following year Mphahlele moved from Paris to Nairobi, initially to found Chemchemi, a cultural centre on the model of Mbari, later to teach at the University of Nairobi. The correspondence from the Nairobi years sees Mphahlele drawing some of his intimates, notably Makhudu Rammopo, closer to him. Surprisingly, since Mphahlele had worked for him many years earlier (between 1941 and 1945) at the Institute for the Blind at Ezenzeleni, Arthur Blaxall's letters appear only at this stage.

6 Peter McDonald. 2009. *The Literature Police: Apartheid Censorship and its Cultural Consequences*. Oxford: OUP, p 123.

7 Ibid, p 126.

The exchanges with William Plomer continue. Dennis Brutus writes from house arrest, hoping for support to leave the country, sharing his thoughts about poetry and protest, and bringing news of Arthur Nortje at Oxford and Bessie Head in Botswana. He sends Mphahlele a remarkable poem written while he was awaiting trial at the Fort in Johannesburg in 1963.

Kenya proved to be another cul-de-sac, however, and Mphahlele began to feel that he needed to refurbish his intellectual resources. He made arrangements to return to literary studies and teaching, this time at the University of Denver in Colorado, where Gerald Chapman, the chair of the English Department, would become a key interlocutor. In the two years he spent at Denver he completed a PhD in Creative Writing, submitting as his thesis *The Wanderers*, which, after some delay, was published by Macmillan in 1971. An autobiographical fiction dealing in some measure with his relationship with his son, Anthony, *The Wanderers* begins to develop the motif of restlessness as a personal mythology.

Mphahlele's wanderings were not entirely driven by the personal myth contained in his novel's title. More substantially, his restlessness was a function of being a go-getter, an idealist who was unable to resist an opportunity to realise the next vision. Some of his movements also involved a combination of idealism and pragmatism: on completing his doctoral degree he had to leave the United States to satisfy the requirements of the Immigration and Naturalisation Service. He decided to take a senior lectureship in English at the University of Zambia. It was a risky decision, given the judgements made in *The Wanderers* about exile on the African continent for the South African émigré, but Lusaka was as far south as he could get – the earth would have smelt right to him.

Whatever he was seeking in Lusaka proved to be a mirage, however: 'settling in has been harder in Zambia than anywhere where we've ever migrated', he confesses to Rammopo. Almost immediately after his arrival, despite financial and legal obstacles over his visa status, with the help of Robert Richardson in Denver he begins to explore the possibility of a return to the United States. Just as the Kenyan experience was to be reinterpreted in *The Wanderers*, so the Zambian experience was eventually to surface, transmuted, in his last extended fiction and major exploration of postcolonial Africa, *Chirundu* (1980). The letters from the Lusaka years speak of the contradictory and largely unfulfilled pulls of literary aspiration and a desire for home.

As he prepared for the return to Denver to join the faculty, anticipating that he would teach South African literature he wrote to Plomer and Cope to flesh out his resources. It is interesting that he was determined to reflect all the traditions of South African literature in his teaching, including white English and Afrikaans writing, but the Denver years would see his horizons expanding to embrace diasporic and world literatures. In these years he prepared his major work on African-American literature, *Voices in the Whirlwind and Other Essays* (1972). Its publication led to a clash with Addison Gayle over the relationships between Black Aesthetics and the Western tradition. The larger implications of this exchange will have to remain unexplored in this brief introduction, but literary historians will be interested in what it reveals about positionality within the diaspora. Mphahlele also prepared the second edition of *The African Image* (1974) in these years. Some of the emphasis on the cross-cultural tradition of his early South African period is muted in the revised edition in favour of a deeper rootedness in black political and intellectual life.

In 1973 he was offered a full professorship at the ivy-league University of Pennsylvania. While they had been developing for some time it is in the mid-seventies that the signature themes of his mature years – what he calls 'the tyranny of place' and African Humanism – began to settle into focus. The correspondence from this period reveals his stature as writer-scholar and public figure, but equally his key intimates share his longings and insecurities: among them are Khabi Mngoma, another lifelong friend and collaborator from the 1940s and by then Professor of Music at the University of Zululand; Makhudu Rammopo, and his eldest child and only daughter, Teresa, to whom he signs off as Ntate, father. In the letters to Teresa, in particular, we see perhaps the most vulnerable side of Mphahlele: his and Rebecca's worries about their children, especially the effects on them of their parents' exile.

One would expect Mphahlele to have settled at Penn with the American academy more or less at his feet, but by then the two-year cycle of restlessness seemed to have established itself. By 1975, despite the opprobrium of his fellow exiles, he was thinking of a return to South Africa, with mortality and the fear of dying in the United States gnawing away at him. Readers will find the classic statement of the effects of exile in this period in 'Portrait of a Man in a Glasshouse'.[8] Remarkably, he was granted a temporary visa to attend a conference of the Black Studies Institute in Roodepoort in July 1976. With the events and consequences of the Soweto uprising on 16 June vividly around him he returned home; in the prevailing excitement it would have felt as if the end was in sight for the regime in South Africa, and the scene was set for a more permanent return.

---

8 *Es'kia*, pp 233-236.

What a fraught return it proved to be. Cabinet-level interference forced the homeland authorities and the University of the North to buckle, blocking his appointment to a chair in the Department of English and he was forced to become a school inspector in the 'homeland' of Lebowa. His desire to reintegrate with an African community as a scholar and teacher would be ruled by the politics of the 'Bantustan'. Overtures from the liberal universities – Rhodes, Natal, Cape Town, and the Witwatersrand (Wits) – are attested to in the correspondence, but Mphahlele was not convinced that he should return to his country to teach in a predominantly white university.

In the end, Wits provided the most strategic option because from Johannesburg he was able to reach out to black constituencies close to his roots. One of his many achievements in this regard was to found the Council for Black Education, though he was unable to garner university support for his vision of the establishment of community colleges in or near Soweto. Especially telling in the letters' account of his return and settlement back in South Africa is the extent to which Mphahlele, having established himself as a world citizen of culture and a major international figure in the black diaspora, had to negotiate his return with white scholars, writers, and officials. Many of them were courteous and well disposed – notably Guy Butler, Nadine Gordimer, and Tim Couzens – but it was largely on the terms of the white establishment that Mphahlele would have to re-establish himself. The position he eventually settled on, as Professor of African Literature in the Division of Comparative and African Literature at Wits (later the Department of African Literature) was the most suitable niche available to him.

The exchanges with Guy Butler in the 1980s are particularly revealing. There is mutual respect, even friendship ('How are you?', writes Butler; 'retired, like me?') but there is also a sense that in presiding over the institutionality of English-language South African literature Butler held a position that in another dispensation might have belonged to Mphahlele himself. Mphahlele's resignation from the Council of the 1820 Foundation, which is the focus of attention in some of the late letters, expresses this tension. It reveals the extent to which, by the late 1980s and the end of his career, a properly national transformation in which Mphahlele could assume his rightful place as *the* academic figurehead of English-language literary studies in the country, had still failed to materialise. Meanwhile his interlocutors abroad would continue to position him at the centre of international diasporic literature. The contradiction between national compromise and international veneration is painful to witness.

What do we learn from Mphahlele's letters that we do not already know from his other writings? There are two questions here: the first is that, like the autobiographies, the letters give us first-person utterance in which we might expect to hear directly from the man; to have his soul bared, as it were. But is this the case? Is the soul so readily available to representation? The second question is that although letters are, like autobiographies, a form of first-person utterance, their distinguishing feature is the presence of another, the addressee. What is the significance of this person-oriented quality of letters and of Mphahlele's letters in particular? These questions would bear longer scrutiny than we can give them here, for they touch on the relationships between the self and language, between the one who speaks and the one who is spoken about, between autobiography and fiction, and between biography and autobiography.

Mphahlele's oeuvre is fertile soil for exploring these matters. Chabani Manganyi recognises this in *Exiles and Homecomings*, which, apart from documenting the life of its subject, explores the question of voice and its relation to selfhood. From his background in psychology (and a particular interest in psychobiography) Manganyi writes the life of Mphahlele in the first person, interspersing his narrative with passages of fictionalised dialogue. These experiments would merit comparison with J M Coetzee's where he does the opposite, writing autobiography in the third person (in *Boyhood* 1997 and *Youth* 2002). In a similar vein, in *The Wanderers* Mphahlele writes a largely autobiographical narrative through the third-person persona of Timi Tabane.

The common element in these experiments is their recognition that the 'I' is always to some degree a fiction: we use it to explain and to explore ourselves and to provide a point of focus for a narrative, the purpose of which is to search for the overarching meaning that lies buried in our experience.

What, then, is the 'I' of these letters and do we find here the real Mphahlele? The history of letters and their publication, and the scholarly debates about their relationship with biography, would caution us against this view. The publication of writers' letters, as part of an attempt to understand what was called their genius, goes back to Europe's eighteenth-century enlightenment. In that context, Samuel Johnson argued that letters were not the spontaneous expression of personality but a craft, as in any artistic form of expression in which the writer seeks to create a particular impression and adjusts to the expectations of the reader.[9] In his introduction to this volume Manganyi compares letter writing to the short story: this insight is in keeping with Dr Johnson's.

What, then, emerges as distinctive about Mphahlele from these pages? Firstly, he frequently wrote in order to reach someone whose presence to him was made especially difficult by circumstance: segregation, apartheid, cultural distance, political risk, family fragmentation, exile – these are the typical conditions which Mphahlele seeks to overcome in his correspondence. Under such conditions the act of letter writing is both a personal necessity and an ethical gesture, an expression of human solidarity.

The second distinctive feature of Mphahlele's letters is their extraordinary openness, the generosity with which he gives himself to his interlocutor. The ability to identify with another and to inhabit several personae simultaneously has long been recognised as a gift of any good writer, but what Mphahlele brings to these encounters is a distinctive quality of trust: the *person* matters deeply to him. A measure of Mphahlele's calibre in this regard is that he is seldom wrong-footed when it comes to tone, and the tone of Mphahlele's letters is a direct result of the relationship and therefore an expression of his emotional and intellectual integrity.

Collections of letters are rare in South African literature. As Manganyi observed of the first edition, it may well have been the first published collection of the correspondence of a black South African writer. Since then, two collections of Bessie Head's correspondence have been published.[10] In this volume, we have a rare thing: the record of a complex human being – writer, friend, teacher, critic, public intellectual, father – in dialogue with others during the most difficult years of modern South Africa's history, fashioning in these exchanges his unique testimony of an artist's relationship to his times. If there ever was, or is, a republic of letters, one might begin looking for it here.

David Attwell

---

9 James Biester. 1988. ' Samuel Johnson on Letters'. *Rhetorica* 6(2), Spring, p 146.

10 Randolph Vigne and Bessie Head. 1991. *A Gesture of Belonging: Letters from Bessie Head, 1965-1979*. London: Heinemann; Patrick Cullinan, ed. 2005. *Imaginative Trespasser: Letters between Bessie Head and Patrick and Wendy Cullinan, 1963-1977*. Johannesburg: University of the Witwatersrand Press.

CORRESPONDENTS

Please note that each correspondent in this volume does not appear in the list of correspondents. The editors have provided background information on correspondents that feature prominently. Some correspondents exchanged very few letters, and information about these people is provided briefly in a note after the letter concerned.

Lionel Abrahams (1928-2004), Johannesburg-based poet, novelist, essayist and mentor to countless young writers. He founded and edited the literary magazines *Purple Renoster, Quarry* and *Sesame,* publishing the work of Mphahlele among many other black writers. In 1971 he launched Renoster Books, which published the first works of Oswald Mtshali and Mongane Wally Serote. From 1975 he ran an influential writing workshop at the Johannesburg Art Foundation.

Chinua Achebe, Nigerian novelist, poet and essayist, best known for his first novel, *Things Fall Apart* (1958), which is the most widely read novel in modern African literature. He was the consulting editor for Heinemann for the African Writers Series. He is currently the Charles P Stevenson Professor of Languages and Literature at Bard College in Annandale-on-Hudson, in the USA.

Kofi Awoonor, Ghanaian poet, novelist, critic and commentator on African and global politics. He has held several ambassadorial positions, representing Ghana in Brazil, Cuba and at the UN, where he was Chairman of the Committee on Implementation of UN Resolutions Against Apartheid. In December 1975 he was arrested in Ghana on suspicion of being involved in a military coup, an experience he would later recount in two volumes of poems, *House by the Sea* and *Until the Morning After* (both published by the Greenfield Review 1978 and 1987).

Houston A Baker Jr, Professor of English and Director of the Afro-American Studies Programme at the University of Pennsylvania from 1974 to 1977. He and Mphahlele, who both joined the English department in the summer of 1974, maintained a long friendship (cf *Exiles and Homecomings*, pp 275-80). He is currently a distinguished professor in the English Department at Vanderbilt University.

Ursula A Barnett, independent scholar. Her critical biography of Mphahlele, *Ezekiel Mphahlele*, was published in 1976 and *A Vision of Order: A Study of Black South African Literature in English* appeared in 1983.

Arthur Blaxall (1891-1970), a clergyman who was born in Britain and came to South Africa in 1923, initially to work with the deaf. In 1939 he opened the first workshop for blind Africans in South Africa – *Ezenzeleni,* in Roodepoort – where he was superintendent until 1950. It is there that he met Mphahlele. A supporter of the struggle against apartheid, from the early 1960s he channelled funds to former political prisoners and their families who were in need. This led to his arrest in April 1963 and conviction under the Suppression of Communism Act. After spending a night and a day in prison he was paroled and the rest of his sentence suspended. He left soon afterwards for Britain. His autobiography, *Suspended Sentence*, was published in 1965.

Gunnar Boklund, former Professor of English at the University of Denver in Colorado. His close association with Mphahlele started during the latter's student days in the mid-1960s and continued after Mphahlele's return from Zambia in 1970 to join the English department as associate professor.

Edward Kamau Brathwaite, one of the major voices in the Caribbean literary canon, was co-founder of the Caribbean Artists Movement and is noted for his studies of black cultural life both in Africa and throughout the African diaspora.

Andre Brink, novelist, playwright and critic and Emeritus Professor of English at the University of Cape Town. He played a major role in the struggle against censorship after his *Kennis van die Aand* (1973) was the first Afrikaans novel to be banned. Many of his sixteen novels have been written in both English and Afrikaans. He has been honoured by the governments of France and post-apartheid South Africa.

Sonia Bronstein was, during the period covered by the correspondence, administrative secretary to the chair of the English department at the University of Denver. She became a family friend of the Mphahleles.

Dennis Brutus, teacher, political activist and poet, taught for fourteen years in South Africa, where he participated in many anti-apartheid campaigns, particularly those concerned with sport; activities which resulted in his being served with a banning order and subsequently to his being arrested for contravening the ban. After serving an eighteen month sentence on Robben Island he was permitted to leave South Africa on an exit permit. For a time he taught in London, then, in 1970, took a position as a visiting professor of English at the University of Denver, after which he moved to Northwestern University and later to the University of Pittsburgh.

Frederick Guy Butler (1918-2001), academic, poet and writer, lectured in English at the University of the Witwatersrand and later at Rhodes University in Grahamstown, where he was first senior lecturer then Professor and Head of English. He remained there until his retirement in 1987, when he was appointed emeritus professor and honorary research fellow. Butler was influential in achieving the recognition of South African English Literature as an accepted discipline.

Gwendolen Carter (1906-1991), one of the founders of African Studies in the United States and among the best-known scholars of African affairs in the twentieth century. She was born in Canada but moved to the United States, where she completed a master's degree and a doctorate in political science. She taught political science at Smith College and later African Affairs at Northwestern University, Indiana University and the University of Florida. After a trip to South Africa in the 1940s, she became interested in African affairs and specialised in the politics and economy of Southern Africa, making many research trips to South Africa and detailing the dynamics of political change in Africa in several books, including the four-volume *From Protest to Challenge: A Documentary History of African Politics in South Africa 1882-1964.*

Gerald Chapman was Professor of English at the University of Denver. In a letter dated 14 March 1966 Mphahlele was introduced to Chapman, then chairperson of the English department, by Herbert L Shore, then consultant in drama at University College (Dar es Salaam). Soon afterwards Mphahlele and Chapman started an exchange of letters relating to the former's admission into the United States and the PhD programme in creative writing at the University of Denver.

Syl Cheney-Coker, journalist, writer and poet, was born in Sierra Leone. He studied literature at the University of Oregon, later spent time at UCLA and Wisconsin, was visiting professor of English at the University of the Philippines and senior lecturer at the University of Maiduguri, Nigeria. On his return to Freetown he became head of cultural affairs for Radio Sierra Leone. In 1991 his novel, *The Last Harmattan of Alusine Dunbar*, won the Commonwealth Writers Prize for the Africa Region. In 1997 after a coup in Sierra Leone he returned to the USA and settled in Las Vegas.

Jack Cope (1913-1991), South African-born novelist, short-story writer, poet and editor, began his career on the *Natal Mercury* before going to London as political correspondent for South African newspapers. He returned to South Africa at the outbreak of the Second World War. Cope published eight novels, more than a hundred short stories and three collections of poetry, the last in association with C J Driver. From 1960 to 1980 he edited *Contrast*, a bilingual literary magazine. In 1980 he moved to England.

Timothy Couzens, literary and social historian and critic, is an honorary professor at the University of the Witwatersrand, where he originally taught English and later became a member of the African Studies Institute. His works include the study of the life and work of H I E Dhlomo referred to in his correspondence with Mphahlele. His most recent publication is the collaboration with former Robben Island prisoner Ahmed Kathrada on the story of Kathrada's life. Couzens met Mphahlele for the first time at an African Literature conference at the University of Texas (Austin) in 1975. From then on the two maintained a steady correspondence up to and including the time of Mphahlele's permanent return from exile in 1977.

Adriaan (Ad) Donker (1934-2002), born in The Netherlands and trained there and in the United States, was the founder of AD Donker (Johannesburg), a publishing company committed to nurturing and publishing South African literature in English. His anthology *Soweto Poetry: To Whom it May Concern* introduced South Africans to the work of some of the country's now iconic poets. Donker, who was awarded an honorary doctorate in literature by the University of Natal in 2000, was founding director of Durban's Centre for Creative Arts.

CJ (Jonty) Driver was President of the National Union of South African Students in 1963 and again in 1964. After spending time in solitary confinement in 1964 he left for England, where he had a long and successful teaching career, for 23 years of which he was a headmaster. For more than 20 years the South African authorities prohibited him from returning to the country. His biography, *Patrick Duncan, South African and Pan-African* (referred to in his letter written in July 1976) was published in 1980 and immediately banned in South Africa.

Dennis Duerden (died 2007) began his career as an education officer in the Nigerian colonial service. He then became assistant curator at the Jos Museum in Nigeria in 1956 moving on to become director of the Hausa service of the BBC World Service in London. In the early 1960s he established the transcription centre, where he built up a tape archive of interviews with African writers, some of which are featured in the 1972 book, *African Writers Talking*, which he edited with Cosmo Pieterse. The centre also published the influential Cultural Events in Africa and introduced the work of African writers, artists and musicians to the London scene.

Patrick Duncan (1918-1967) was the son of a Governor-General of South Africa, born in Johannesburg, educated at Winchester School and Balliol College, Oxford. He and Mphahlele met in what is now Lesotho where Duncan worked for the British colonial service, from which he was to resign in order to take part in the South African liberation struggle. Holding strong anti-communist views, he sought membership of the ANC but later joined the Liberal Party (editing the journal *Contact*). After a banning order he abandoned non-violent opposition and joined the Pan-Africanist Congress, for a short while representing the PAC in Algeria.

Ian Glenn, formerly Head of the English Department at the University of Cape Town, is Professor of Media Studies and Director of the Centre for Film and Media Studies at UCT. His research interests are media in the new South Africa, political communication, audience studies, media technologies, environmental media and the literature of exploration.

Stephen Gray, writer, academic and critic, was Professor of English at the Rand Afrikaans University in Johannesburg until 1992. He has published eight novels, is a prolific poet and has edited numerous anthologies. He edited the 2006 Penguin Modern Classics edition of Mphahlele's short fiction (*In Corner B*) and worked with Mphahlele on the PMC 2006 edition of Alfred Hutchinson's *Road to Ghana*.

Nadine Gordimer, recipient of the 1991 Nobel Prize for literature and *Chevalier de la Légion d'Honneur*. Author of fifteen novels, sixteen short story collections and numerous essays, she was a committed anti-apartheid activist and supporter of many black South African writers, Mphahlele among them. She has been vice-president of International PEN, is a Fellow of the Royal Society of Literature and was a founder of the Congress of South African Writers. Mphahlele was introduced to Gordimer by Norah Taylor in the late 1940s.

Andrew Gurr, born in Leicester, England, grew up in New Zealand and studied at the University of Auckland and Cambridge. He taught at the universities of Wellington, Leeds, Nairobi (at which he was head of department) and Reading. He has written two books on African literature but is best known for his work on Shakespeare and his contemporaries and Renaissance theatre.

Norman Hodge, editor of *To Kill a Man's Pride and Other Stories from Southern Africa*, was Professor of English at the University of Transkei. He has written literary criticism on Mphahlele, including an essay on the short story, 'Mrs Plum', published in *English in Africa* in 1981, soon after the ban on Mphahlele's work was lifted.

Langston Hughes (1902-1967), novelist, short-story writer, poet and playwright, specialised in insightful verbal portraits of black life in America from the 1920s to the 1960s, some of them influenced by his engagement with the world of jazz. His life and work had an important influence on the artistic contribution of the Harlem Renaissance of the 1920s. Mphahlele's essay on Hughes, which appeared in *Black Orpheus* in 1961, was probably the first literary appreciation of this great American poet by an African scholar or literary critic. Their mutual interest in Hughes also provided a literary link between Richard Rive and Mphahlele.

Stuart James, who was Professor of English at the University of Denver, Colorado, came to know Mphahlele first as a student and later as a colleague in the English Department. On 31 August 1976 James wrote a strong letter of recommendation to the University of the

North in Pietersburg (now Polokwane), South Africa, supporting Mphahlele's application for the chair of English at that university.

Martin Jarrett-Kerr CR (1912-1991), a monk of the Community of the Resurrection and an early opponent of apartheid, first encountered Mphahlele in the 1940s when Mphahlele was working as a typist-clerk and instructor at Ezenzeleni under the Rev Dr Arthur Blaxall. Jarrett-Kerr was, at that time, associated with St Peter's Priory in Rosettenville, Johannesburg. He later returned to England. A literary critic in his own right he published studies on D H Lawrence, among other writers.

Edward A Lindell, Dean of the College of Arts and Sciences at the University of Denver at the time negotiations were under way to secure Mphahlele's return to Denver from the University of Zambia in Lusaka in the course of 1969.

Bernth Lindfors, former professor at the University of Texas in Austin, and one of the founding members of the African Literature Association (ALA), founding editor of the *Journal of African Literature,* and editor of the bibliography *Black African Literature in English*. He amassed over forty years one of the largest private collections of African literature, comprising some 13 000 books, journals and rare tape and video material, now housed at the Centre for African Literary Studies (CALS) at the University of KwaZulu-Natal (Pietermaritzburg).

Teresa Mphahlele was born in South Africa in 1950, the second of the Mphahlele children and the only girl among four boys. After her parents' return from exile 1977 she, like her brothers, continued to live in the United States.

Khabi Mngoma (1922-1999), a lifelong friend of Mphahlele, was a leading figure in the world of South African music who facilitated the careers of many musicians both in South Africa and in the southern African region. He founded the Music Department of the University of Zululand, the Ionian Music Society and Youth Orchestra and the Khongisa Academy for the Performing Arts. Shortly before his death he was honoured by then President Nelson Mandela with a Presidential Award for merit.

Njabulo Ndebele, writer, teacher and researcher, was vice-chancellor and principal of the University of Cape Town from 2000 to 2008. During a distinguished academic career he was a successor to Mphahlele as the chair of African Literature at the University of the Witwatersrand. His collection of short fiction, *'Fools' and other*

Stories, received the Noma award for the best book published in Africa in 1983 and was joint winner of the Sanlam prize for outstanding fiction in 1986. His influential critical essays are published in *The Rediscovery of the Ordinary* and *Fine Lines from the Box*. His latest work of fiction is *The Cry of Winnie Mandela*.

Isidore Okpewho, State University of New York Distinguished Professor of Africana Studies, English and Comparative Literature at Binghamton University, was born in Nigeria. His areas of specialisation are African and comparative literatures, with an emphasis on comparative oral traditions. He has also published four novels, *The Last Duty* winning the African Arts Prize for Literature in 1976 and *Tides* winning the Commonwealth Writers Prize for Africa in 1993.

James Olney, the Voorhies Professor of English and Professor of French and Italian at Louisiana State University and a fellow of the American Academy of Arts and Sciences, is author, editor, or co-editor of eleven books and co-editor of *The Southern Review*, the premier literary journal of the American South. Olney is in the forefront of writers and theorists of autobiography.

Alan Paton (1903-1988), teacher and author, most notably of the iconic *Cry, The Beloved Country* (1948), published a further nineteen books between 1948 and 1989. He helped found the Liberal Party, of which he was elected leader in 1955, a position he retained until the party was dissolved in 1968 in the face of legislation banning multiracial political parties. He described his life as ‘a struggle between the writer and the activist’.

William Plomer (1903-1973) was born in Pietersburg (now Polokwane), South Africa, of English parents. His most famous (and controversial) work, *Turbott Wolfe*, which Mphahlele admired greatly, was written when he was 19 years old and offered a provocative insight into South Africa’s racial and political dilemmas. He published a further four novels and five volumes of short stories, as well as poetry, literary criticism, biography and his autobiography. He and Mphahlele first met over a ‘sandwich lunch’ when Plomer visited the *Drum* offices in Johannesburg, where Mphahlele was employed as fiction editor in 1956.

Robert D Richardson, a former Professor of English at the University of Denver and an award-winning biographer, who has written works on Thoreau, Emerson and William James, played a prominent role both at the university and in dealing with congressmen and other US officials during the negotiations for Mphahlele’s return to Denver in 1970. He also acted as literary broker in the United States for Mphahlele in the search for a publisher for the novel *The Wanderers*.

Makhudu Rammopo, who was, for a time associated with the Institute of Education (Advanced Teachers College, Ahmadu Bello University, Nigeria), was a childhood friend of Mphahlele (cf. *Exiles and Homecomings*, pp 151-61).

Richard Rive (1931-1989), who was born in Cape Town and grew up in District Six, became an English lecturer at Hewat College, at the University of Cape Town and then at Columbia University. He completed his doctorate on Olive Schreiner at Magdalen College, Oxford. Having turned to fiction, he was considered to be one of South Africa's most important short-story writers and an accomplished novelist. He and Mphahlele met during the latter's stint at *Drum* and again when Rive visited the Mphahleles in Paris in 1963. He and Mphahlele maintained contact through letters throughout Mphahlele's twenty-year exile.

Sonia Sanchez, one of the most prominent writers of America's Black Arts Movement, is acclaimed for her poetry, which depicts the struggles between black and white, men and women and between cultures. Mphahlele worked closely with Sanchez during his time at the University of Pennsylvania.

Sipho Sepamla (1932-2007), originally a teacher (in Sharpeville at the time of the Sharpeville massacre), was a leading member of the 'Soweto poets', a group that came to prominence in the 1970s, espousing a literary style overtly linked to Black Consciousness. Poet, novelist, journalist and teacher, Sepamla was also a cultural activist, who, in 1978 was instrumental in establishing the Federated Union of Black Artists (Fuba). He received the Pringle Award (for his poems) in 1977 and the *Ordre des Arts et des Lettres* for his contribution to literature.

Wole Soyinka, Africa's first Nobel Laureate in Literature in 1986. Soyinka is known primarily as a dramatist, working traditional Yoruba material into a wide-ranging encounter with contemporary Africa (in particular, postcolonial Nigeria) in genres ranging from tragedy to satire. His writing encompasses poetry, fiction, autobiography (including prison narrative), memoir and polemic. Mphahlele's friendship with Soyinka began during his exile in Nigeria in the late 1950s and his association with the Mbari club.

Jenny and *Sylvester Stein* were family friends from the early South African phase when Mphahlele was working for *Drum* magazine, which

Sylvester edited for three years before going into exile. During Mphahlele's first visit to London, in 1959, the Steins hosted him at their Regent's Park Road home (cf. *Exiles and Homecomings*, pp 122-30). Sylvester Stein is the author of *Second Class Taxi*, a satirical novel which was initially banned and later became a bestseller. His book, *Who Killed Mr Drum?*, was dramatised and performed at the Riverside Studios in London in 2005.

Norah Taylor (died 1999), founder of Norah Taylor Studios, a speech and drama school, made a significant contribution to the development of a theatre culture in Johannesburg, working, among other places, at Dorkay House with the African Music and Drama Association. Her meeting with Mphahlele, when she presented a charity performance at Ezenzeleni, was the start of an enduring relationship. She started off as his mentor, became his benefactor in the difficult years after he and two colleagues were banned from teaching at any school registered in South African (August 1952) and ended up a trusted friend – their relationship lasted throughout Mphahlele's life in exile. In *Exiles and Homecomings* Mphahlele wrote: 'Had there been three million Norah Taylors at that time the history of my beloved country could have been different.' Hers is the earliest Mphahlele correspondence available, illuminating various facets of the impact of apartheid on black-white relationships and, more specifically, the male-female dimension of such relationships.

Peter Thuynsma, currently manager of the Department of Institutional Advancement at the University of Pretoria and a prominent Mphahlele scholar, studied under Mphahlele at both the University of Zambia and the University of Denver, where he completed his doctoral studies. He and his wife, Dawn, became close family friends of the Mphahleles after their initial encounter in exile in Zambia.

Phillip Valentine Tobias is renowned worldwide for his work on genetics, fossils and early human origins. Tobias retired as Head of the Anatomy Department of the University of the Witwatersrand in 1990, but remains an honorary research fellow and is best known for his work on the evolutionary links between primates and early humans.

Charles van Onselen is a prize-winning author and arguably South Africa's leading social historian. He headed the African Studies Institute at the University of the Witwatersrand which gave Mphahlele his first academic home after he returned to South Africa. Van Onselen won the Alan Paton Award for Non-Fiction in 1997 for his book *The Seed is Mine: The Life of Kas Maine, a South African Sharecropper, 1849-1985* and has since published the widely-acclaimed *The Fox and the Flies: The World of Joseph Silver, Racketeer and Psychopath.* He is currently research professor in the Faculty of Humanities at the University of Pretoria.

Nick (Nicholas) Visser (1943-1998), born in America, spent most of his teaching career in South Africa, where he lectured at Rhodes University for well over a decade and for more than twelve years at the University of Cape Town. He also published, both in South Africa and internationally, on a wide variety of subjects relating to literary theory. As co-editor (with Tim Couzens) of the *Collected Works of H I E Dhlomo* (1985), he played an important role in establishing South African literary studies.

LETTERS 1943-2006

1943

Roodepoort

10 November 1943

Dear Madam,

For quite a number of years now I have taken keen interest in dramatic art.[1] I have acted in several plays at school including 'Merchant of Venice' (Shylock), besides writing and producing a few sketches and musical comedies. I am at present trying to recruit actors for a short musical comedy written by myself – a copy of which I should gladly send you if you were willing to give me some comments on it – such as only a person of your experience and training in this art can give.[2]

All these, of course, come to naught, considering how much there is to be done yet, and that they are but poor amateurish attempts.

It would certainly be extremely difficult, even if you would be willing to do so, to have me as one of your students, firstly, as an African, secondly as a worker, and so would be a part-time pupil.[3] As the latter I wonder if you would think it worth while having one pupil on, in the light of the fact that it would in the evenings, when you are undoubtedly too tired from the days work.

I could, however, get more interested people to attend, even if it be only a Saturday afternoon. If I am alone, I shall have to be content with the theoretical aspect of it; in this you would certainly be of much help, on the understanding that I shall pay for it.

Your suggestions and advice will be most welcome.

Thanking you in anticipation,

I am,

Yours faithfully,

Ezekiel Mphahlele

1 In the early 1940s Mphahlele made several attempts to begin a writing career. He tried writing verse plays and, when he was unsuccessful, turned to poetry. These manuscripts were subsequently destroyed. Later, he began writing short fiction. It was while he lived and worked at Ezenzeleni Blind Institute in Roodepoort that, with Norah Taylor's encouragement, Mphahlele wrote the short stories that were published by the African Bookman in Cape Town as *Man Must Live and Other Stories* (1947). His interest in drama remained latent – in later years (both in South Africa and in Kenya) he was to direct and act in various plays. His most mature attempt to write a play came when he lived in exile in Nigeria. There he completed *Shaka Zulu*, the manuscript of which was lost and has not yet been recovered.

2 Mphahlele sent a copy of the play to Norah Taylor, who offered to seek professional opinion about it. She considered that it needed development, but she recognised Mphahlele's talent and encouraged him to continue.

3 Circumspection was necessary during this period in the arrangements Norah Taylor and Mphahlele could make to meet for tuition, for fear of possible police action.

Roodepoort

20 December 1943

Dear Miss Taylor,

I thank you sincerely for your criticism of the musical comedy, which I read very carefully. When I read the play over again for reference the whole thing became clear to me – the faults which only your professional insight could bring into relief and thus help me to go carefully in my subsequent attempts. The criticism is very constructive because of its frankness, and, rather than be discouraged, I feel the long way I still have to go is intriguing and I thrill at the prospect of the adventure. Thanks for the encouragement.

I hope you will not wait long before you read my next attempt.

Allow me to wish you the very best this season and may the new year bring better and brighter days of good glowing health.

Sincerely yours,
Ezekiel Mphahlele

1944

Roodepoort
6 June 1944

Dear Miss Taylor,

Thanks very much for your very nice and encouraging letter.

I conveyed to Mr Sehloho your best wishes and we are both all anxiety to attend the rehearsal on the 22nd June and help during the performances – this will certainly earn us invaluable and thrilling experience.

I am glad that you appreciate my feeble effort at essay-writing and it gives me renewed courage to hear that I have good descriptive powers. I did once try short-story writing at college and won some first prizes, and I have been turning over in my mind the possibilities of success in this line.[1]

Two outstanding difficulties at once became evident: tuition – especially, who would undertake the task of teaching me, even if only the rudiments of the art; secondly, the commercial aspect of the art. The latter problem is made all the more acute because there is limited scope of short-story-writing (if any) in our weekly papers and what European magazines there are do not entertain publication of an African's efforts! There is undoubtedly quantities of material in African life for story-writing or play-writing, as you know, but, however much I crave to be able to put into writing, with all the passion of one who desires to tell a story, I feel my efforts crippled by the above factors – a grim situation, isn't it? I shall always welcome any advice from you.

I was reading the other day a dramatisation by Virginia Church of Tolstoi's story, which I found immensely interesting, but I shall not hesitate to read

Miles Malleson's play when you have found it. I shall also be trying (scour) the bookshelves for it.

I am glad to inform you that a collection of plays has arrived at our library from the Public Library and so we have much to keep us busy.

The verse will reach you under separate cover.

Again thanking you,

I am,

Yours sincerely

Ezekiel Mphahlele

1 The reference here is to a short-story competition held while Mphahlele was a student at Adams College in Natal (1939-1940).

1948

Orlando West

24 October 1948

Dear Miss Taylor,

The case of Mrs. Malele pains me greatly because it is one of those things one cannot do much about. You *have* done a great deal, I have reason to know, indeed more than she herself can estimate, to help her.

There is, unfortunately, no chronic sick home for Africans in this country. In fact the state hardly even mentions anything about the African chronic sick. I do not know of any mission home that accepts such cases. Admittedly, she needs change of climate and such a home would have to be where it suits her condition. The only mission institutions out in the country districts are hospitals or clinics or schools and not for such cases as Mrs. Malele's. Yes, it is very hard.

As far as external help is concerned I suggest you write to Mrs Henderson, Non-European Affairs Dept., His Majesty's Buildings, JHB, who is the senior welfare officer in that dept. She has, I know, a list of such cases which have no institution to care for them. She may not do something straightaway, but she will know about it.

I have known asthma to be incurable, but recently a man who had had it for over 30 years was cured completely by a Dr Mandelstam at the Benoni location. He has proven a wizard with a number of cases declared 'impossible'. This was the first time for me to see this ailment cured – I know the man personally who was cured. Have you ever tried him? If you have not and would like to try him, I shall let you know how to get to him.

As far as her own behaviour is concerned, I may say this: I know how asthma can beat one up and weaken the moral courage one may have. I was attacked by asthma in 1940 in Natal and such days and nights of agony I endured are almost unimaginable. I am perfectly alright at any place on the Reef, but I dare not go to Pretoria or the coast or any other place that is *lower* than the Reef. I gave up all hope for medical cure and it taught me to exercise, open air, good diet, constant movement on my legs help one to resist it.[1]

Medical science has it that one can almost always locate the thing that causes an attack – some are affected by the smell of a particular flower, or of dust of any type; then others by the smell of cat's fur; and then others by the eating of a particular protein. I found that the climate of a low country – dampish and hot, dust from a feather pillow, and from a coir mattress provoked the 'beast'. A European lady teacher then advised me to get rid of such a mattress and sleep on a pile of blankets on the spring and use a pillow stuffed with cloth – even before I had realised those were the things that made the asthma worse or started it off. I still do not use a feather pillow or a coir mattress and these, together with an ideal climate, make me forget I even had such a thing as asthma. One thing it hates is sitting down, especially indoors, which is what she does – she will not move about in the open, and I do know the husband's work does not bring in enough to help them afford vegetables and fruit. I have seldom seen them eating anything other than starchy foods.

She told us she had been to Warmbaths some time ago and there it was worse – which shows she needs a *higher* place – towards the Drakensburg in the Free State or Basutoland. But alas, there is no 'home' for her at these places. Do try that doctor and advise her to avoid the things mentioned above and move about more.

The latter of course, should be very difficult. The cruelest aspect of it, I think, is that it does not shorten one's life – it just becomes one long, dragging, miserable affair – I say this without any evil suggestion. I do hope you will have made appreciable progress before you leave.

When in England, if you by any chance meet Peter Abrahams please remember me to him. He will most probably recollect my first name and the fact that we were at St Peter's Secondary School together.[2]

Did you get your MS back of the play you entered for the competition? I have written to the Secretary of the F.A.T.S.S.A. [Federation of Amateur Theatrical Societies of South Africa] four times now and have not received a single reply.

I shall wait for a reply from you about Mrs Malele in due course.

Yours sincerely,
Ezekiel Mphahlele.

1 After Mphahlele's departure from Nigeria on 6 September 1957 he no longer suffered from asthma. He later concluded that the illness was psychosomatic, arising out of emotional difficulties.

2 Mphahlele was unaware that at this time Peter Abrahams, the Johannesburg-born author, was living in Paris. He had left South Africa in September 1939 with the outbreak of war and remained in London until 1 June 1948, when he moved to France, where, in July 1949 (while living in the village of Paley), he began writing *Tell Freedom*. He returned to London in early 1950. Abrahams spent only one year at St Peter's – 1937, which was Mphahlele's last year (he was there from 1935-1937) – when he completed the Junior Certificate. The matriculants of 1937 included Zeph Mothopeng and those of 1938, Oliver Tambo.

1952

Orlando West
22 July 1952

Dear Miss Taylor,

Would you allow me to keep your costumes until after Aug. 16 when we shall be performing? If you are using them before then, I shall bring them. I'm looking after them jealously.

I have just received a letter from the Tvl. Education Dept. dismissing me from the teaching profession. Two others of my colleagues[1] have also received like letters – as from July 31st. We are being paid for August also *in lieu* of a month's notice.[2]

This is the outcome of a commission of enquiry visiting our high school towards the end of the last term. They said they had come to enquire into 'staff relations'. There had been disturbing relations 'tween us and the headmaster owing to our radical views which we have openly expressed from time to time, – I as Secretary, another as president, and the third as Editor of the journal of the African Teachers' Association. The inquiry was evidently a pretext for a witch-hunt, and the authorities got every amount of help from the head. So – there it is. The last straw must have been when I condemned the Dept's syllabus for so-called 'native schools'. This letter of dismissal states *no* charge against any of us.

This afternoon we are meeting a solicitor as we want to contest the decision. There is, of course, a movement in governmental circles against a number of teachers who are considered too progressive to allow those that follow to accept such unprogressive measures as e.g. the recommendations of the Eiselen report.[3] Such an organised sweep is, of course, the first of its kind in the profession this side of the colour line.

If you happen to hear of anyone who might need the services of a graduate etc please let me know. I needn't mention how hard it will be for my wife & family – that's the 'the badge of our tribe'.

Regards.

Yours sincerely,

E. Mphahlele

1 The two colleagues referred to are Zeph Mothopeng and Isaac Matlhare.

2 By this time Mphahlele was teaching at Orlando High School. He was in charge of a community theatre group known as The Syndicate Players, under the auspices of the Syndicate of African Artists.

3 The Eiselen Commission Report formed the basis of the Bantu Education Act of 1953, which caused a great deal of consternation in African communities throughout the country in the early 1950s.

Orlando West

Saturday

Dear Miss Taylor,

Yes, my wife had a histerectomy; this is the history: Haemorrhage began last November, but then only slightly... May this year she went to hospital as bleeding was becoming serious. She went to the theatre for an op. Haemorrhage ceased and after a week she was discharged. No sooner was she out than bleeding started again, this time it was worse, and she was weak. July she went back to hospital. A biopsy and the medical research reported 'chronic cervicitis and erosion'. When she was thought to be convalescing, haemorrhage resumed, and for two nights it was pretty bad, and she fainted. Injections were given ... Bleeding ceased. She was discharged, but continued with this last treatment

... Haemorrhage started again on the 15th and this takes place in the mornings, stops during the day, and then again in bedtime. She is complaining of an aching in the bones and feels a pain just above the navel. She eats fairly well with the help of powdered malt extract with lime, iron and lecithin and with Vitrasan – imported German preparations. She looks quite anaemic.

After the birth of our last baby – March 1950,[1] she picked up very well and was well. But since this trouble started, she had always had attacks of chest colds and pelvic pains...

I wrote to Dr Gavron and asked about the doctor he said he would get if we should need him. I also asked him if it would be too much to ask him to treat her and wait till I work for me to pay him. I've not had a reply yet.

We should be glad of any help you kindly offer. I shall hear from you as soon as you have arranged with your friend. My wife finishes school at 1 p.m. daily, and can come in when required.

Yes, I'll go to the Reps[2] and also see the ladies.

Thanks, as always,

Yours sincerely,

E.M

[1] Teresa Kefilwe.

[2] Johannesburg Repertory Players.

Orlando West

23 August 1952

Dear Miss Taylor,

I wrote to the Mining House as you suggested, but I have only received a reply from Union Corporation Ltd., – to say they have no post I could fill. Just now I'm still at loose end.

Our advocate is still considering the facts of the case preparatory to instituting action against the Dept. for wrongful dismissal.

It is a great pity that Mrs Hoernlé[1] has deemed it fit to make the sort of statement she made, because if, as she says, we were dismissed as a result of an inquiry into *Conditions at the High School,* we should have been dismissed from the *school* itself, not from the profession. Then she omits to say what the findings of the commission were which warranted this action. In any case that commission had no specific charges against us, and the case is evidently one of witch-hunt. It is regrettable especially that she is considered a negrophilist and this is a political case because our professional work has several times been found to be beyond reproach.

There is no doubt that being out of High School suits the headmaster because it saves him the embarrassment of having to be reminded by the Dept. that he is harbouring political explosives in the persons of us three, and it suits the authorities to have us out of the profession for the same reason, looked at from a broader angle.

But somehow I don't feel bitter, because I tell myself that it was to be like this sooner or later. The government cannot reconcile itself to a situation where it has to pay people for speaking against it, like the progressive educationists in our ranks. And we shall do the same when and if we are reinstated!

My wife is getting better. She is at home until the end of this month. We wish, of course, she were in some paying job – teaching for married women is a miserable profession financially, moreso with us. But as you say, it never rains but pours. We both thank you for your untiring efforts to help us.

With sincere & best wishes.

Yours sincerely,

E. Mphahlele

1 Professor Alfred Hoernlé was Professor of Philosophy at the University of the Witwatersrand and was closely associated with the Institute of Race Relations. Mrs Hoernlé was a well-known liberal personality who, at the time, was chairperson of the Orlando High School Committee.

Orlando West

16 September 1952

Dear Miss Taylor,

I'm sorry I've not been able to reply earlier and thank you most sincerely on behalf of my wife and myself for all that you have done and are doing for us during this trying time. Yes, we did receive the money.

I'm convinced that if it were *The Voice*[1] that caused our dismissal and the Department thought that were a genuine cause, they would not be ashamed to state such cause for action. Nor would Mrs Hoernlé herself just stop at saying this was a result of the inquiry. However much prestige she has, one cannot help feeling that there has been a great deal of dishonesty in official and local circles, and a case based on dishonesty never stands long.

Our solicitor has issued summons against the Dept. and they ought to have received it by now. They have 30 days from the 9th inst. within which to decide what to do.

Mr Stoller, our advocate, told me how he was in constant contact with you during our imprisonment etc.

Again thanking you for your untiring efforts.

I am,

Yours sincerely,

Ezekiel Mphahlele

P.S My wife's old trouble is recurring. We are just at a loss what to do and think now. I had told Dr Gavron, Miss Gordimer's husband, what the diagnosis was at the hospital. He told me it needed great care to cure and asked me to contact him re: a specialist. But things being what they are, we cannot etc.

1 *The Voice* was run by Mphahlele and Khabi Mngoma from 1949. It was sold by schoolboys in the streets of Orlando for 3d. Mphahlele and Mngoma were once summoned to appear in court for publishing an unregistered newspaper. They were acquitted on a legal technicality.

Orlando West

Monday

Dear Miss Taylor,

We were shocked to hear that you have taken ill and had to undergo an operation.

How are you now? We sincerely hope you are better if not well. I'm sure you work too hard and it must tell on your health.

I've got a job as a filing and messenger clerk in a solicitor's office. As you know, routine work kills my spirit, but I must bear it until I find something more interesting, and with better pay. I get half what I used to get in teaching but I simply do not like to lean on others – it's not good for one's psychological make-up.

Do get well – with all good wishes from me and my wife.

Yours very sincerely,

Ezekiel.

P.S Should you want to ring me during the day, the no. is 34-2926. The gentleman is quite considerate.

Orlando West

3 November 1952

Dear Miss Taylor,

I went to the solicitor whom Miss Alexander introduced me to on Thursday last week, as he had proposed. When I got there he said he had unfortunately been very busy, and that I should call again this coming Thursday, when he will have discussed it with his clerk who is now away writing exams.

Of the half dozen or so applications I had made all but three have been replied to, all regretting that they have no vacancy, but that etc. etc. But I must just continue trying; some day I must land something.

You may have seen in *The Star* last Thursday that Mrs Hoernlé has been at it again – just being openly provocative by saying we started a 'rebel' school, when it was on the basis of this fallacy that we were arrested recently, and because it could not stand we were acquitted. Honestly, I think Mrs Hoernlé is putting what prestige she has to the wrong use: it is all very distressing. But it won't be long before the truth is out. My wife is showing marked signs of improvement, thank God. One is able to think a little more clearly.

I've been exploring for some time now what prospects one would have in starting a commercial school – for typing, shorthand etc, and I've discovered there is a great future for it if coupled with a duplicating service – all which the Blind Institute was a thorough training ground for me when I was there.

There are many African and Coloured pupils who leave high school and lose chances of getting a typing and shorthand job merely because there are no schools for this sort of thing. The plan is set, and I reckon I shall need £500 for equipping an office which I could try to find in town or establish in Orlando, although a town office would attract more people. This includes rent, furniture, typewriters, stationery and a little to live on for at least three months. Apart from anything else, this makes it even more urgent that I should get a job, during which I would be trying to borrow £500. Besides this business I am confident that I would provide lectures for private students in other than commercial subjects, so that I would not be deprived of the spiritual happiness I find in teaching. The other day when I phoned you and you were out, the woman who works for you mentioned that there was something there you wanted me to take to Mrs Malele. She was in hospital then, but is now out. I'm coming into town on Thursday morning, and if you'd like me to call for it I shall gladly do so.

Thanks, as always,

I am,

Yours sincerely,

Ezekiel Mphahlele.

P.S. Our Syndicate of African Artists[1] has been fortunate in wangling a chamber music concert from the Viva Musica Society. We wrote to them and they immediately replied that they would just be too happy to give such a concert at Orlando on Sunday afternoon 16th Nov. – free of charge. Isn't it just grand of them?

[1] Probably one of the most vibrant cultural organisations of the early 1950s in the Witwatersrand area promoting cultural life among blacks in respect of classical music, theatre and the visual arts.

Orlando West

11 November 1952

Dear Miss Taylor,

Do you know – your postcard dated 1st Nov. only came today? I found it in the evening when I came back from town! When you wrote last week and mentioned Miss Adams' recital I was puzzled. Had the postcard arrived before, I should certainly have come to the recital. As it is now, I missed that and the Reps' rehearsals. Isn't it shameful the way our post often crawls?

Today I also found *one* sheet of a letter in the envelope in which you say you enclose something which I would have collected that Thursday (unfortunately I did not get your reply, so that when I was in town I thought I would disturb you if I just gate-crashed on you). My feeling is that you forgot to put in the first sheet of your letter and the enclosure as well.

I'm really sorry and am kicking myself on the shin for missing Miss Adams' recital, because, as you say, it would have answered my questions. Thanks all the same for the information re: gestures and actions in recitation.

I have landed a temporary job at Doornfontein in a wholesale firm as typist clerk.[1] The pay is not good, but I'm glad to be doing *something* as the family coffer is about to dry up, and my wife has not been having the things to eat that the doctor prescribed. £5 a week is far from sufficient, but while I do this work I shall be looking for something better.

Now, I don't know when I can call for the syllabus etc because I finish work at 5 p.m. If you are in between 5 & 6 I can run up before catching my train.

This Sat. I'm addressing a teacher's meeting in Pretoria, so Sat. is impossible. I could try Monday if I would find you.

Yours sincerely

E.M.

1 It is notable that by this time Mphahlele was not only a well-known personality, he was also a short-story writer and a graduate of the University of South Africa, having been awarded a Bachelor of Arts degree in 1947.

1953

Orlando West

15 February 1953

Dear Miss Taylor,

Thank you for your card and address.

Since you went to the coast I have been trying to contact more commercial colleges. I approached Regis College and Damelin College. The principal of the latter felt employment and opportunities for such technically trained Africans did not warrant commercial training. The principal of Regis was interested, but wanted to make sure of the available pupils. I've since realized that academic subjects for definite certificates like J.C. and Matric are an 'honest bait' – for employment prospects. Then commercial subjects toward these certificates can be worked into the curriculum, so that later a commercial department can be gradually built up.[1]

In the meantime I have a few teachers on afternoons for Matric. Also, a friend approached me recently about a number of pupils in the township who have not been admitted to local high schools because of lack of space and those who have not gone back to boarding institutions because of higher school fees. Again there were many teachers who could not be employed owing to the fact that the government has not increased education facilities for a number of years, and, several teachers are without work. So I immediately got the teachers together and we started with 13 pupils in a church hall – Standards VII & VIII. The number is now 50 and they go up to Matric.[2]

Our problem, naturally, is finance and we are sending out circulars of appeal for money for blackboards, desks, etc and to pay the teachers, because the pupils pay £2 a year each. We should like this to remain a private school (not under the Education Dept.) where we can carry out educational experiments without fear of intimidation. A hard road but a necessary one in our set-up.[3]

Thanks for all you have done and are doing for me and my family. I do hope you are well now.

Yours with best wishes,

E. Mphahlele

1 Mphahlele was still pursuing the idea of establishing a private school. This project happened to be yet another he was considering at the time, the other being the study of law. Neither project was ever undertaken.

2 This school was one among several started by concerned parents following the introduction of Bantu Education in 1953.

3 The power to legitimate such schools as this remained in the hands of the new Department of Bantu Education. Students, parents and teachers alike soon discovered that students from unregistered schools could not enter as candidates for the national external examinations for the Junior Certificate and Matriculation.

Orlando West

19 March 1953

Dear Miss Gordimer,

Thanks for your letter which gives me courage. I am glad you have been able to get the story as far as that, and cannot thank you enough.

Thinking of it now, I appreciate your agent's remarks about the first page – i.e. as far as a publisher must avoid material that may prejudice a writer's audience. But as for the remarks are anti-semitic or smacking of racial prejudice I do not share his and your feelings, much as I understand all too clearly that it is possible for one to adopt the view that the remarks are insulting to one or other race.

Firstly, I write about the white race *in general*. But my Afrikaner characters are not as an African *should* view them, but as he does indeed look at them, and vice versa. Prejudice does not come in. (From my side as the one who writes.) Secondly, the Jew *could have been any other white man in South Africa*. Only, the greatest number of industrial employers are Jews in Johannesburg. Again, I often find, when I am in distress, long before I have been aware of it, that I tend to concentrate my attention on small unimportant and normally insignificant things – an ant, a fly, a flower petal a flickering candle light, human features, and [...] is I in the story. He observes the features of the white man because the state of his mind is what it is.

In view of this, I'm sorry you regard me as being prejudiced, because, as you say, I am a victim of racial prejudice. Because I am oppressed, my political honesty tells me if I want to shake off oppression, I must avoid any such accusation against me. So with prejudice.

Do tell me if the revised page is in place; if not I shall only be glad to do it over again. I shall use a pen-name this time, which I intend to keep. As soon as I get the opportunity, I shall ring you for an appointment. Thanks again.

Good wishes.

Yours sincerely,

E Mphahlele

Orlando West

6 April 1953

Dear Miss Taylor,

We have a new addition to the family – a baby boy – who came on Wednesday last week.[1] Mother and baby are well.

Two weeks ago I received a phone call from *The Star*. The reporter was asking about the letter you wrote. Did I know you? What more information could I give? Did I confirm the letter? etc. He said he was going to give a write-up. But we have looked in *The Star* every day since in vain.

One doesn't know quite what to think or feel. We are having a concert for funds in Springs, and we had a fairly well attended one on Sunday 5th at Orlando.

I met Mr Southern of the Reps. On talking over the job with him we realized that I would not be able to get my last train back home. Another thing, nine o'clock is usually the latest one can be about at night, especially because we have to walk from the station home. He said I could contact him this week to find out if the play is not too long to enable me to leave at 10 or so. The other workers there are from Wemmer Hostel – right in the city, which is comparatively safe. But I can risk 10 o'clock.

Best wishes.

Yours very sincerely,

E. Mphahlele

1 Birth of second son, Patrick Motswiri.

Orlando West
13 April 1953

Dear Miss Taylor,

I have received your letter enclosing that from *The Star*. I suppose as soon as their representative heard that I am connected with this school, and that I have been dismissed from Orlando High School, he dropped the matter. But what does surprise me is that he should try to fob us off with such a reply, which does not in the least reflect the true position. A normal high school, by Department standards, (i.e. among Africans) should hold 650 pupils at the most, which is a very high figure and unwieldy. But even then the local high school takes in more than this. Orlando alone had 15 hundred families, and the Departmental high school here caters for Moroka, Jabavu, Kliptown, Newclare and Sophiatown as well – very large townships. There are 20 primary schools in Orlando alone, producing an average of 50 pupils a year from Std. VI. This means 1,000 pupils. Supposing 200 of these end somewhere and do not enter high school (a high estimate in these days of greater enlightenment), it means already 800 from Orlando alone want to go to high school.

I do not suppose *The Star* would know that the City Council has given a site to the Department to build a second high school in Orlando West – a second high school: this I was told by the Circuit Inspector when I was still at Orlando High and we were discussing the impossible number we had to teach there. He said the Department had a plan for such a school, but money was tight.

It is a pity the *The Star* is being partisan, but of course these days I appreciate the fact that it is not easy to face up to the truth, because by so doing one will be hurting so-and-so and patronising so-and-so.

Thank you for all you are doing: it is most gratifying to know that somebody here and somebody there have some faith in one, outside this cauldron of suspicious, petty and often snobbish humanity. This is the kind of faith that is a driving force in one's life, and we are fighting hard to lay foundations for something great. I shall get in touch with Flora and arrange about a lorry.

Good wishes.

Yours sincerely,

E. Mphahlele

P.S. I try to write these days, but am hindered by the other aspect of the struggle to live and feed a family. I tell myself that things should shape up finally.

Orlando West

30 April 1953

Dear Miss Taylor,

Sometime ago last year, I remember, in the course of conversation I intimated that I was doing the B.A Honours in English, which was my major subject.[1] I am still doing it with the University of South Africa, which offers tuition by correspondence.

After I was dismissed from teaching it became hard to continue paying for the course, but I managed, from my savings, to pay on in January of this year. I owed £20, but alas, my savings were already depleted. Still, the University has continued to accept my MS for correction and criticism, merely because I never allowed myself to be in their bad books, even when I was doing the B.A., and paid well.

And now that they have sent me the full course of lectures, they naturally feel restless about my arrears of instalments – £12 at £3 per month from January. With the predicament in which I find myself, I feel if I could raise a loan of £20 which I owe in all, I should find myself free to the extent that even if I had nothing, I should be owing nothing as this is the one and only debt I have.

And now, I am reluctantly compelled to turn to you for help. I could ask the University to wait until I can pay my instalments, but then they may not consent, and again, I should not like to suspend my studies, because in the course I get tuition in poetics, practical criticism of poetry, prose etc and in thorough judgement of literature in general.[2] I still cherish the dream of one day going in for this aspect of journalism along with my creative activities.[3]

If I can pay even half, I should keep the creditor off the door until I am in better position to pay them the rest while I pay you back. I blush to impose myself upon you, but I know you appreciate my plight best.

Yours sincerely

E. M

P.S. My wife says she replied to your letter, which found me out. Please don't worry about not having offered me tea. I came at your busiest time, which was itself an embarrassment to me!

1 The BA (Hons) degree was awarded by the University of South Africa (Unisa), a distance learning institution, in 1955.

[2] As Mphahlele's terms suggest, the curriculum followed by Unisa at this time was canonical. (See also the letter to Norah Taylor, 13 April 1955, in which he lists the papers he wrote.) Practical Criticism was a rigorous form of close reading which had been formalised by IA Richards (and later refined by FR Leavis) at Cambridge. Although some departments of English in South Africa – notably that at Rhodes University under Guy Butler, with whom Mphahlele would later develop an interesting correspondence – were teaching South African literature, all remained predominantly Eurocentric until at least the 1970s.

[3] Mphahlele was thinking of a career as a literary reviewer while pursuing his writing. His later association with *Drum* would have partially fulfilled this aspiration but its lowbrow tastes are not what Mphahlele has in mind here.

Orlando West
5 May 1953

Dear Miss Taylor,

Thanks immensely for your cheque which came as a great relief. I shall yet be worthy of your magnanimity one day – it cannot be far. For the present I can only express very weakly how this kind loan lightens a load that has been on my mind – to think I can continue with my studies without that haunting fear.

I have told the University to direct the receipt to you.

With best wishes.
Yours ever
E. Mphahlele

1954

Johannesburg
3 July 1954

My dear Pat,

Sorry I couldn't send this earlier: as soon as I arrived home I was seized by almost incurable laziness. I feel triumphant about having got over it.

The deaf and dumb post isn't going so well because the Dept. insist on having someone with a social work diploma, my experience with the deaf and dumb notwithstanding. Still, I am looking around for something: as long as it will be something permanent, more or less. This shifting about I've been doing for the last 2 years must come to a stop. But I can't think of coming back to Basutoland without my family, which is out of the question at present.

I hope you will find this satisfactory (the translation). If I may say so, I find it a little on the 'intellectual' side, Still, perhaps it is as it should be, being an introductory number. My impulsive reaction tells me the man-in-the-street wouldn't care tuppence whether or not the Liberals won or lost in the provincial council elections: the Liberals couldn't be that important!

Best regards to you and the family, especially to Mrs Duncan

Yours sincerely,

Ezeke

Johannesburg

5 August 1954

Dear Pat

I received a long letter from Sir Allen[1], replying to mine. He accepts almost the whole scheme as I have explained. He thinks however that it would be best for me

(a) to trade on my own account in order to avoid the possible accusation that I am poaching on the preserves of other booksellers locally;

(b) to hire a van for a trial period of 6 months instead of expending capital at this stage – he is prepared to finance such hire provided it is not unduly high;

(c) to work on a return or sale basis to save me capital outlay, which means he would supply me with books and I would be responsible for the payment of only those I shall have sold. (I expect my gain would be from the sale per book, I don't know much about these things.)

I think myself it would be an admirable basis to work on. I have two worries: where to hire such a van and the procuring of a commercial licence, although I don't know if the latter is really indispensable – what do you think about these two points?

Incidentally Sir Allen says this scheme has worked successfully in Scandinavia and something like it is being mooted in England, and he writes very warmly.

I do miss you people tremendously, but I simply must do something about my future – at 34 one doesn't want to hop about without direction.

Kindest regards to you and yours,

Yours ever,

Ezeke

[1] Sir Allen Lane, founder of Penguin Books.

9 August 1954

My dear Ezeke,

Thank you for writing telling me about Sir Allen's letter. On the same day I heard from my friend Hans Schmoller of Penguins. He says that Lane is very keen on the idea and is willing to risk losing money in order to help you to succeed.

I'm afraid that at this distance I can't help with the van. May I urge one consideration: that you get the permission of the owner to paint it and that you get a qualified signwriter to make it look absolutely professional? I think this is most important, and what an advertisement in itself it would be. Then, get permission for a shopwindow to be put in the van, so that you can display a few books all the time, even when you are on the move. Lastly (my unasked-for advice) may I suggest that you make it clear that you want to sell to Africans? You may put me right over this, but I feel that if they can see that you are looking for them, they are more likely to buy than otherwise. I don't want to press this idea.

I'm afraid I don't know about the licence. I think that you could do it on a hawkers licence, but why not go and ask a receiver of revenue?

The sale-or-return arrangement is extraordinarily generous. I only wish we could do this! Incidentally if you wished to use our name as suggesting that you are selling books for Africans, I should be delighted.[1]

I do hope that all is well with you both. Incidentally did I write to you to tell you that I was out of the election? I have had a duodenal haemorrhage, and should be in bed for 5 weeks. Luckily the doctor was understanding and has met me. But I've had to chuck all the things that I possibly can.

Yrs Pat

[1] In 1952 Duncan had bought a book distribution business called Africa Books, specialising in Africana.

"And where autocracy lies broken – Our names shall yet be graven deep"

Johannesburg
7 September 1954

Dear Pat,

It was good of you to write so promptly. What a pity you had to withdraw from the elections because of illness: I do hope you are recovering: I know how annoying it must be to have to suspend all vital services and activities including means of livelihood, but I'm sure your doctor has everything in hand.

Thanks a lot for allowing me to use your trade name so as to impress on the minds of the people that I am selling to Africans. I agree fully with you about the underlining of Africans. Are you thinking of my using your name on the van or some other place? I went to the Receiver of Revenue to enquire about a licence and was told I shall have to get an application form. But I must get a letter from the firm whose books I shall be trading with, so I have written Sir Allen for this. I have also told him that I am still looking for a van. It seems to me that the best would be to buy a new one and re-sell it if things don't shape up as we have planned, rather than hire one.

I should so much like to use your name and shall be glad to hear from you exactly where you propose I can use it.

My best wishes to you and yours,
Yours very sincerely,
Ezeke

16 September 1954

Dear Ezeke,

Thank you for your letter of the 7th September and for your good wishes. About the name, I would have no objection to your using it anywhere, if you like the idea. It would not imply any trade connection, as we will be functioning in different fields. I only suggested it because it struck me as a name that might profit your business.

A new van would cost about £1200, and unless you could lay your hands on as much as that in cash, I would be in favour of doing what Sir Allen suggests. Of course, you might get favourable hire-purchase terms, which would come to much the same as renting it, and if you could, I think that would be the ideal way.

I hope all goes well, and look forward to hearing from you whether you are going to join our trade.

Yours very sincerely,
Patrick Duncan

New York
6 October 1954

Dear Mr Mphahlele

Please forgive me for being so long in answering your kind letter, but I have been absent from New York most of the summer and just recently returned to the city. It was certainly nice to hear from you, and I hope very much that if you have not already posted your stories to me, you will airmail them to me shortly, as I am almost ready now to begin assembling the anthology, and I would like very much to see more of your work for possible inclusion, since I have a belief you have a distinct talent for the written word.[1]

There has been a most generous response from the various English-speaking countries of Africa to my request for short stories, some 50 manuscripts having arrived during the summer. Not all of them, by any means, are good. And a number of persons sent animal tales or folk stories, which is not the kind of material we can use in this anthology, since it is to be a book purely of creative fiction in the shorter form. However, some of the material is excellent indeed, and I think that some of the best of the African non-white writers are represented. If you yourself know other writers of short stories, please ask them if they will present something to me. And if you see Miss Gordimer, please tell her that I have liked her work very much, as many other readers in our country do. I had the pleasure of meeting Alan Paton when he was here, and am just now reading his impressions of the American Negro running serially in *COLLIER*'s.

I am sending you some books and magazines by boat mail, although I understand that some of our Negro magazines may not reach you, *quoi faire*?[2] Anyhow, I am sure my books will reach you. Meanwhile, you have all my best wishes, and I hope to hear from you soon.

Sincerely yours,
Langston Hughes

1 The anthology to which Hughes refers is *An African Treasury*, eventually published by Crown in 1960.

2 What can one do?

Orlando
1 November 1954

Dear Mr Langston Hughes,

At last I am able to respond to your request – rather a belated reply I am afraid!! My problem arises from the fact that I am mentally unsettled – if anyone can speak of a settled mind at all in this God-forsaken country. And I have experienced this: that this state of mind, if it is acute, is not conducive to solid creative work.

You see, for the last 2 years I have been in one thing and out of another. Together with 2 colleagues I was banned by the Government from the teaching profession as a result of which we cannot teach anywhere in the Union of S.A. This came about because we dared to oppose the new educational system imposed on us Africans under what is called the Bantu Education Act, which is calculated to enslave the African child's mind.

Just now I am desperately trying to keep up a family of 3 children on what I can earn in one temporary job or another. Jobs for professional men among Africans are most frustratingly limited. If you are not a teacher you may, if you are lucky and not independent in your way of thinking, become a doctor (at a 'Bantu' medical school). If you are a woman you may also become a nurse: thus far, no further.

Writing under such conditions may produce astonishing results in one's art, but may also destroy one's art when it laps on the writer's rebellious self. To keep a delicate balance between the two is the problem.

I am sending you 5 stories for your consideration. I may point out that one of two stories: 'A Winter Story' and 'Moon And Fury' may be published by the periodical *PHYLON* in your country: a short while ago an acquaintance of mine sent them to the journal but I was asked to rework them and send them back to the U.S.A. for consideration of their publication value. I shall let you know in due course what their fate is.

I shall naturally be looking forward anxiously to a word from you on the ms., with the full knowledge that it will be a candid critique.

Another thing before I bring my letter to a close is this: my wife is most interested in beauty culture. Training for Africans here is out of the question. I promised that when next I write to you, I should ask you if you know some benevolent institution that can provide instruction on a scholarship basis – in the U.S.A. Any suggestion you may make will be most welcome.

Thanks immensely for the literature – it is still on the way. I am sure it will be fascinating, any interception or official censoring of the magazine notwithstanding. It is most generous of you.

I wish you success in this anthology.

With all sincere thanks and wishing you all the best.

Yours sincerely,
Ezekiel Mphahlele

P.S. An old story I re-worked – 'The Suitcase' – has just been bought for publication in the next anthology of *New World Writing*. Nadine Gordimer has seen it and she 'advertised' it when she was there recently.

A Winter Story

Moon and Fury

The Woman

The Woman Walks Out

Saturday Night.

P.S. Should you find any of them would be a good magazine contribution and you do not want to use it, I do not mind if you seek such publication on my behalf: I should be most grateful for such a service.

New York

6 November 1954

Dear Mr Mphahlele:

Your letter and manuscript to Langston Hughes has arrived during Mr. Hughes's absence from New York City. He is away on a trip to the Middle West, but I know he will be glad to know you have written him and appreciated your sending the manuscripts of your stories,

THE WOMAN

by Bruno Esekie

A VOICE IN THE DARK

THE WOMAN WALKS OUT

by Bruno Esekie

SATURDAY NIGHT

by Bruno Esekie

ACROSS DOWNSTREAM

MOON AND FURY

and

A WINTER STORY

by Bruno Esekie

These will all be brought to Mr Hughes attention upon his return to New York.

Sincerely,

H. Smyth

For Mr Hughes

Orlando

18 November 1954

Dear Mr Langston Hughes

Thanks very much for your nice letter which *Drum* sent on to me as I am on a visit, to Basutoland. It is indeed very flattering to me to have such warm complimentary comment from a great writer like you on my amateurish attempts (as I regard it) – for that matter, from a Negro to another. Believe me, we this end are starved for Negro literature, and I should like to grasp this opportunity of asking you if one can procure regularly some periodical Negro literature of a high standard in America. Then, of course, I should so much like to read more of your work which is so robust with down-to-earth humour and life.

As soon as I get back to Johannesburg (next week), I will look through some of my pieces and mail you four or so – I doubt if I could summon up enough courage to send you half-a-dozen – so many read such horrible stuff to me. Still, you'll have asked for it!

Nadine Gordimer is a great friend of mine as black-white friendships go today in South Africa, you know: in fact she has meant a lot to me in my writing. Peter Abrahams I was at high school with, and we are continuing a close association.

I'm a teacher by profession, but was kicked out 2 years ago by the Nationalist Government for vehement criticism of their corrupt educational policy for our people. I can't get back to teaching anywhere in the Union of S.A. Just now, after roughing it for 18 mths jobless, I am starting social work with the deaf & dumb; but I write because I have the tragic urge to.

Thanks tremendously for your good wishes.

Sincerely yours,

Ezekiel Mphahlele.

Note: BRUNO ESEKIE is my pen name, my real name being Ezekiel Mphahlele. Always use the above residential address please.

1955

Orlando

30 January 1955

Dear Langston Hughes,

As you will see from the letterhead I am now working for *DRUM* as fiction editor – have been since last December. It's no use staying on in teaching these days with everything in African education being subjected to party political policies. My wife has also left teaching altogether and is in a school of social work.[1]

I find this work fascinating and enjoy it thoroughly, as you may imagine.

I have not heard from you personally what you think of the stories I sent you, and am keen to have your expert opinion on them. 'Winter Story' and 'Moon and Fury' have after all been rejected by *PHYLON* a second time, so I must look elsewhere. But of course I leave the choice to you for your anthology. I am sending you two most recent and unpublished stories to make the choice wider for you. Do not hesitate to let me know if none of them is of anthology standard.

What sort of fiction do Negro journals in America go in for – is it worth trying them? if so, which? As I have said before, I should not mind if any of the stories you find unsuitable for anthology purposes find their way into an American magazine/s.

Thanks a lot for *WEARY BLUES* in which I have enjoyed some very moving poetry; and so for *THE WAYS OF WHITE FOLK* with a most entertaining style. I got a letter from Customs to say the magazines you sent me are being withheld as objectionable literature:- as you forecast. Thanks all the same for the trouble you went into.

Looking forward to a newsy letter from you soon, and with best wishes,

I am,

Yours sincerely,

EZEKIEL MPHAHLELE

ENCLOSED: 'Across Downstream'

'A Voice in the Dark'

1 Rebecca studied at the Jan Hofmeyr School of Social Work, which was located in Eloff Street. By the time she completed her studies, at the end of 1957, Mphahlele was already in exile in Nigeria.

Orlando West

9 February 1955

Dear Miss Taylor,

I have joined *Drum*, it seems I am going to like the position of fiction editor. We get stories from as far as West, Central and East Africa and it is a most interesting job reading them and criticising and corresponding with the authors. I have given him your address so that he sends you a copy in March or April.

There is an African who wants to take the Licentiate diploma in speech (Trinity). His problem is he doesn't make out in the handbook of syllabuses whether one *must* do the Associate diploma first or not. He is a graduate. What is the position?

My wife is now in social work training. With the teaching profession turning into a farce it is absolutely no use pretending that one can stay on with the convictions one has. Although it means living minus her income it is worth it, and I am just now trying to get up an evening school going or looking for a job in one. I have become so hardened, you know, that conditions have whipped up my energy and it is far from flagging.

Best wishes.

Yours very sincerely,

Ezekiel

Orlando West

10 February 1955

Dear Mr Langston Hughes,

I have been wondering whether there are any journals – Negro or white – in America that you know of that may be in need of a correspondent in South Africa on political affairs. There is so much happening here that such a journal may want to get first-hand information: if so I could do that sort of thing.

I believe most newspapers or periodicals there either have foreign correspondents attached to them or they get their stuff from press associations or syndicates. Still, as a matter of interest ...

Best wishes.

Yours sincerely,

EZEKIEL MPHAHLELE

(Fiction Editor)

Copies sent to:

Louis Martin, Carl Murphy, Claude Barnett, John P. Davis, John H. Johnson, P. L. Prattis

18 February 1955

Dear Mr Mphahlele:

Thank you very much for letting me know how *DRUM*'s third contest came out. I certainly agree that the first and second choices are the best stories. Ekwensi, I think, has written a number of stories that are much better than 'The Visitor'. Nwangoro's 'Message of the Drum' I am thinking of using in my Anthology. What is his native country? I shall probably be writing him a letter in care of *DRUM* in which case would you kindly forward it to him for me.

As to your request about writing for American papers, as you say most of them get their material from the syndicates and, of course, the big ones have correspondents on the spot. However, I am making copies of your letter and sending it to a half dozen of the larger Negro newspapers and magazines with the request that they correspond with you directly in case any should be interested. Certainly I should think with all the excitement going on in South Africa now, some of them might well wish a correspondent of color there. Luck to you! I am sorry the magazines which I sent to you did not get through, but

I rather expected that they would not. I am glad, however, that books arrive safely there.

My African Anthology – for which by now I have received well over a hundred manuscripts from all over English speaking Africa – is now being typed up to be submitted shortly to the publishers and I am including some forty stories. The stories of yours which I have selected are: 'Suburban Train', and 'Blind Alley', subject of course to the final approval of the publishers but I rather think that they will like them too. I like 'Saturday Night' too. It is very beautifully written but, from the American viewpoint, is more of a sketch than a short story. Here they go in more for dramatic incident, a single vivid happening. But I know that the English do a rather more sprawling spread out kind of short story than those most commonly appearing in American magazines. At any rate I am holding your 'Saturday Night' as a possibility for the ANTHOLOGY too. The other five stories of yours which I have, I am returning to you: 'The Woman Walks Out', 'Across Downstream', 'A Voice In The Dark', 'Moon and Fury', 'The Woman'. And I will send you carbons of the ones which are being typed shortly. Meanwhile would you kindly send me a brief biography.

Meanwhile all my good wishes to you, as ever.

Sincerely yours,
Langston Hughes

New York
2 March 1955

Dear Ezekiel,

I came across a picture of you the other day in a back issue of *DRUM* and you look so much like a friend of mine, Ralph Ellison (who wrote *INVISIBLE MAN*, winner a year or so ago of our big National Book Award, and who used to live at our house) that I sort of feel like I know you. Anyhow, you look like a very amiable guy. And I'm going to show Ralph your photo – and your stories, because you are certainly a good writer. I've just been doing a bit of 'styling' on your 'Blind Alley' – since English and American ways of paragraphing and punctuating differ – and so your characters are very vivid in my mind tonight. In answer to your recent note, of course I would be happy to serve as a judge for any of *DRUM's* future story contests, as I believe I wrote Mr Sampson.[1] And also, in case I haven't said so before, any stories used in my anthology that have first appeared in *DRUM* or *AFRICA* will be so credited, and gratitude duly acknowledged in a foreword. I suppose you got the information I sent for your wife regarding the Rose Morgan beauty shop. I attended the cocktail opening of a beautiful new one (that I sent you the invite) last Sunday and spoke to Miss Morgan about your wife. She says she will be happy to try to work out correspondence courses by mail for her, if desired. So I suggest Mrs Mphahlele write to her. Re your possibly writing for some of our papers, I've had two replies. Here's the main sentence from each: 'I certainly think we need to use such a reportorial resource as he is. However, we are not prepared to do so at this moment. I am filing his letter with the firm intention of utilizing him as soon as we have an opportunity.' Ex. Ed. of *PITTSBURGH COURIER*. And, 'Although we do not have anything in mind at the moment, we appreciate knowing that he is available.' *JOHNSON PUBLISHING COMPANY*. But maybe we'll have better luck from some of the others I wrote to. Send me a brief biography of yourself for the anthology, right now, please. Meanwhile, all good wishes,

Sincerely yours,

Langston Hughes

Note: To each of *DRUM's* Contest winners, I sent last year a book of mine. These all have addresses but L. O. I. Nwangoro. Please send me his address.

1 Anthony Sampson was an Oxford-educated journalist who came to South Africa in 1951 to edit *Drum* magazine. He later returned to the UK to a distinguished career with *The Observer* and wrote a number of books on British politics and corporate culture. His South African works include a book on the Treason Trial and an authorised biography of Nelson Mandela.

Orlando West

7 March 1955

Dear Langston,

I received both your letters which I have enjoyed immensely. I am so glad you are able to include two or three stories of mine in your anthology which I am sure will be of great interest to even readers in Africa where distances are so vast and writers do not have much in common.

I am also thrilled by your identifying me with Ralph Ellison even if it be merely on the point of looks. I have only just got his *INVISIBLE MAN*, and will soon read it. Thanks for your willingness to be judge, I shall also pass the great news that we may use any of the fine stories in your collection.

Yes, I gave my wife the printed matter about Miss Morgan's beauty shop, and she is delighted to know what the possibilities are. She will be writing to Miss Morgan shortly.

It is encouraging enough to hear about the journals, and I shall await a word from them. I have just received a letter from the Associated Negro Press Inc. offering me a space every other month at space rate and *EBONY* saying they are glad to know I am available and asking me to do some story about a white child who was taken away from her Negro mother because she is too white to lead a life among Negroes.

Herewith my biographical note:

BRUNO ESEKIE is the pen name of a 35-year-old African living in Johannesburg. He was born in the slum location of Marabastad, Pretoria. At three years of age his father took him out to the country 172 miles from Pretoria where he spent 10 years as herd-boy, attending school intermittently. He came back to the city of his birth and had to make tremendous headway in school. He read every type of old book or paper he could lay hands on. His mother was a domestic servant, and through difficulties she managed to pay for his high school. Bruno gained a scholarship for a first class pass for a teachers' course. Already he was feeling the urge to write. He took up a job at an institution for the blind as clerk-instructor-driver. At this time he wrote a small volume of short stories *MAN MUST LIVE* which was later published when he was teaching, which he took up after further private study. While a teacher he obtained a Bachelor of Arts degree by private study. Some of his short stories have appeared in *DRUM* magazine and a bilingual pamphlet edited in Holland, *STANDPUNTE*. His story 'The Suitcase' appears in No. 7 issue of *NEW WORLD WRITING* this year, and a number of educational articles have been published in some daylies and weeklies. Bruno Esekie is now fiction editor of a Johannesburg African magazine.

L. O. I NWANGORO's address is c/o AKINTOLA WILLIAMS & Co., II MARTINS STREET, LAGOS, NIGERIA.

Best wishes as always,

Ezekiel

Orlando
13 April 1955

Dear Norah Taylor,

This is just to let you know that I have passed the B.A. Honours in English with the University of South Africa – as an external student.[1]

There were 5 papers:

Poetics & Criticism

Practical Criticism

English Literature: Victorian Period

Shakespeare (all his plays, his contemporaries and the Elizabethan stage)

Middle English.

This has been a fascinating study to me, and I've enjoyed every moment of it – except dry linguistic saw-dust like Middle English!

I have a thesis to present – rather I've to present one – for the M.A. in English. This will be the last academic hurdle for me – I really want to get down to more writing.

The sum of money you lent me enabled me to have my work corrected and criticized during the year by the University tutors, and I can gladly say your magnificent help has not gone down the drain. When I'm more settled financially I'll certainly repay the loan.[2]

As always,

Yours very sincerely,

Ezekiel Mphahlele

[1] Mphahlele studied for both his BA (Hons) and Master of Arts degrees under Professor Edward Davis, whom he later considered the best professor of English to have taught him.

[2] Although Mphahlele may have been possessed of good intentions at this point, some of the money Norah Taylor lent him was never repaid.

[Written on the letterhead of Golden City Post]

Johannesburg

9 November 1955

Dear Pat

It was good of you to send the article and biographical note. Thanks for everything. I am sorry that it did not go in just as you had written it in certain parts. This paper, like DRUM, is treading softly on the political rope for fear of being closed down. But I have often thought that the editor is unnecessarily jittery at times, especially because when the "View Point" feature was conceived, it was to hide behind other people's independent views for lack of its own (I'm being a heretic!).

Your references to the Union's policy were removed, and I pointed out to the Editor when I read the proofs that the question of incorporation wouldn't be a thorny one if the Union were not as "unsociable". And so the whole point of the article was lost. After a good deal of more sub-editing, snatches from your original were inserted.

Well, that's the way of newspapers!

I met Arthur[1] last week when he was over here. He has hinted to me that there may be a vacancy in prevention of blindness work.

I am going to explore that. It seems I am growing more and more fastidious with jobs, but that's the way things are. Perhaps it is a bad sign because it may show utter incapability to adjust myself to things. But I also do know that I can only feel happy in a job where I have to deal with human beings – on an altogether different plane from that in journalism.

Dear old South Africa being what it is, you can't even be allowed to give of your best – not even to respect yourself.

Well, a rather gloomy letter, isn't it? I do hope you are keeping well, with Cynthia and the children, and that your book business is still keeping strong.

I see Old Basutoland is again advertising for the headmastership of the High School – what a ridiculous salary to offer any person!

Best regards to you & yours,

Yours as ever, Ezeke

[1] Arthur Blaxall

1957

Orlando West
24 Jan 1957

Dear Miss Taylor,

Would you please write me a testimonial and attach it to this letter and post it.[1] I am hoping that something comes of it.

My wife says thanks for what you sent her for Xmas. Thanks also for the book which is next on my list for reading.

You enquired about the late Henry Nxumalo:[2] There is a fund for him, to which you may contribute – addressed to the Editor, *Golden City Post*, 176 Main St, Johannesburg. Make out the cheque to *Golden City Post*, and explain the purpose in a covering note. It will be a magnanimous thing for his wife & children. I read with deep interest and appreciation what James Brown wrote in the *Sunday Times* about Nxumalo. Best wishes from Rebecca and I.

Yours very sincerely,
Ezekiel

[1] At this point, Mphahlele had had it up to the neck with working as a journalist for *Drum* magazine. He applied to the CMS Grammar School in Lagos and was later offered the job.

[2] Henry Nxumalo was a courageous and enterprising *Drum* journalist with a keen sense of investigative reporting – on farm labour practices and prison conditions in particular. He came to be popularly known as 'Mr Drum'. His murder remains shrouded in mystery and even though he was ostensibly on leave of absence to write his autobiography, it could well have been that he was murdered in the course of duty as a dedicated investigative journalist.

Sobantu
26 February 1957

Dear Jenny [Stein],

Still annoyed we didn't come to the party? But of course you wouldn't be – I'm never the soul of any party! I guess Sylvester told you Rebecca was impossibly ill. I think all continuous ailments in the Mphahlele family are mostly psychological, even when they affect the body – financial worry, bitterness and all that. But please don't ever think you and your family are at any time the focus for such bitterness. You are too humane for that, bless you.

The heat here is paralysing. But I like it that way. I can lap up handfuls of it anywhere. Tell Syl he must never again even suggest he is going to postpone a man's holiday for the sake of one whim like that of sending Can to Cape Town.[1] We all know what a holiday he will be having there, with a spot of work in-between times.

I know you will be interested to hear about the distinction I got in the M.A.[2] Many people keep asking me – aloud and tacitly: why all this study and collecting of academic honours? The reason is simply that I'm black and the determination seized me when, at the age of 14, I found myself only then in Std II and quite illiterate – had been looking after cattle and goats at the will of a brutal father. Behind all this – imagine such life, poverty crawling up to the roots of your hair etc. There you have the reason.

If I get proportionately frustrated it is at the least a respectable kind of frustration.

Well, let me not bore you with I – I, – I, etc. I hope you and the family are all well. It is a comforting thought to be able to say thank you to someone like you for the interest you have always taken in my thesis.[3]

Best regards to you all,

For ever,

Zeke

1 The reference is to the short-story writer and journalist Can Themba, who was, at the time, a senior member of staff under Sylvester Stein at the *Drum* offices.

2 The MA dissertation was on 'The Non-European Character in South African English Fiction'. It transpired later that Edward Davis and the second external examiner at Natal University had to stand firm on the question of awarding the degree with distinction because of strong opposition from some quarters within the university Senate.

3 Years later Mphahlele was to say that it was Jenny Stein, wife of Sylvester, who had first suggested the idea that led in 1957 (after the completion of the MA degree) to Mphahlele's autobiography, *Down Second Avenue*. It is possible that her suggestion was prompted by the autobiographical strain of this letter.

c/o DRUM

Dear Norah Taylor,

I passed on your letter to Mrs Blaxall. Yes, you are a country trotter, aren't you! I am sorry I could not contact you before you left for the coast. I have the receipt from the Native Commissioner, made out to Barclays Bank, stating that it is for a deposit on my behalf.[1] I was told that the deposit can be repaid to the payer when I surrender my passport or when I come back. As I want to settle there, I shall get myself a British passport, surrender the one I may be given.[2] And then of course the money will go to Barclays Bank, not to me. I hope that is sufficient guarantee for the Bank?

Thanks for everything. I haven't heard anything yet re passports. I am getting things in motion to enquire at Union Buildings.

Best wishes,

Love from us,

E. M.

P.S. Hope your husband is now well.

1 In order to secure a passport Mphahlele had to pay a deposit of £100 to the Native Commissioner. Here again, it was Norah Taylor who came to the rescue.

2 Once in Nigeria, the situation relating to the passport was no longer clearcut. He finally relinquished his claim to a South African passport during a visit to London late in 1959, mainly as a result of a failure to have the passport renewed as well as the travel restrictions imposed on him by the South African Government.

Orlando

5 June 1957

The Native Commissioner

Johannesburg

Sir,

APPLICATION FOR A PASSPORT TO TRAVEL TO LAGOS, NIGERIA

I hereby apply for a passport to travel to Lagos, Nigeria on July 25th, 1957. I have already sent an application form to the Secretary of the Interior, Pretoria, together with certified photographs and £1. I have also sent him a letter of appointment from the Headmaster, C.M.S. Grammar School, Lagos, Nigeria, where I hope to take up a teaching post this year in September. This is the letter which is referred to in the letter from the Institute of Christian Education (copy enclosed).

Enclosed please find the following documents:-

(a) 3 copies of a letter from the Institute controlling the school in Lagos.

(b) 3 copies of the Agreement between the Headmaster and me, filled, signed and despatched.

(c) Letter from my wife, confirmed and certified.

(d) Three letters of character.

(e) Cheque for £100 as deposit.

(f) Baptism certificate.

As planes must be booked for a month ahead, I should be most grateful and honoured, Sir, if I could be granted a passport and I hereby request your Department to assist me, for which I thank you in advance.

Yours faithfully.

Sgd E. Mphahlele

P.S. I hereby certify that although I commonly use Ezekiel Mphahlele, my full names as appear on my reference book and baptism certificate are Letobe Ezekiel Mphahlele.

Sgd E. Mphahlele

6 September 1957

Dear Norah Taylor,

I got the passport on the day before I left – whew – what four months of anxiety! Thanks to you for everything – not forgetting your husband's unobstrusive interest & sympathy. Here is the receipt. As soon as I get a British passport I shall surrender the present one and then the money will be released.

Warmest regards.

Yours ever,

E. M.

C. M. S. Grammar School
Lagos
28 September 1957

Dear Pat

It seems a long long age since we met in Jbg. And now here I am in Lagos. I arrived on 7 Sept. Just managed it because I fetched my passport from Pretoria on Thurs 5th when I was due to take a plane on Fri 6th. And that after 4 mths of waiting. My application was rejected on the strength of an unfavourable report from the Special Branch. My past record screamed against me. Then I got a Dutch Reformed Minister, an African I have known for a long time, to make representations on my behalf. After a long lecture from Col. Wessel, Special Branch Chief at Pretoria Headquarters, he decided to rescind his previous objection; the reason he gave was that he was saving me from Communism (quote). So I got it.

I have come to teach in the above school – something I was not allowed to do in the Union! It's a boys' school – 300 – writing Cambridge pre-university exams (no Verwoerd frustration either!) It's an exciting experience. The people; Lagos; Nigeria's 36 million on the shore of a great future; no harassing police raids etc etc. If ever I return to South Africa, the beloved country it wasn't easy to wrench myself from, it will be either as a better-equipped man or to return to a greater country. Maybe both.

I want to start repaying Mr Galbraith (from whom I bought a car) – incidentally I sold it, as my family should be joining me in December, Dongës willing. What I want to know is how I can transfer money to you as was arranged with Galbraith – from here. My bank is Barclays (D.C.O.). I am afraid I have betrayed his trust, defaulting as long as I have done. By god one keeps living on borrowed time, money, space etc in S.A. and one's obligations come to a dead standstill.

Please write and tell me how to get money over to you; tell me about doings in S.A. I read about Dongës' treatment of you in respect of the passport: to be expected!

Love to you and your wife.

Yours very sincerely

Zeke

8 October 1957

My dear Zeke,

I was simply delighted to have your letter of 28 Sept. which arrived this afternoon. I have always had a rather special feeling for you, and believe me I could not have a nicer surprise than your letter was.

About the cash. The simplest thing would be for you to ask your bank in Lagos to make a stop order payable monthly to my account in Maseru. If you made it payable to AFRICA BOOKS it would make payment to Galbraith very easy and cheap. They will arrange for an air mail transfer, which is really very cheap and convenient. We deal with Ibadan and Legon universities, and both pay us like this.

I was most interested in your passport difficulties. Perhaps I should start cultivating friendships among African DRC ministers. It was good of Col. Wessels to save you from communism. It was not clear from your letter whether he tried to save you from it by keeping you in the country, or whether he was going to save you from it by letting you out. Probably both at once.

It is difficult to say much about South Africa. Our party has found a backer which will make it possible to begin a newspaper in early December – it will be very hard-hitting indeed, popular, written for all races, basing itself on adult suffrage.[1] Its first number will coincide with the multi-racial conference which is the sequel to the IDAMF conference in Bloemfontein last year. In general I feel in my bones that the tide is turning against the Nats. They are in for increasing difficulties, which must lead to the ebbing of the colour-bar. It may be that the diabolic regime of Malan and Strijdom will be seen one day to have been a blessing. By bringing the whole issue to a head a generation earlier than it would otherwise have been they have shortened the rule of the white Baases by at least a generation.

This place is lovelier than it ever has been before. We had a wet winter, and are now having a wet spring and early summer. The result is blossom and roses and green grass on a scale I have seen only in England before. It is wonderful to be alive in it all.

I have succeeded in getting George Clay for our paper, snatching him from Jim Bailey (George got our two offers on the same day!) George was anxious to entice you to join us – we did not then know you were off to Nigeria. And now we have schemes for enticing Tony Scott to come over. I don't know why Jim Bailey still is on speaking terms with me. I remain extremely fond of him, though I would not like to work for him. As you will have heard Sylvester left DRUM, though not quite in the heroic manner which NEW AGE gave forth. He had resigned some months before; then Jim told him he could not print the picture of Althea Gibson kissing her opponent – a particularly lovely photograph I thought. So he just did not turn up to work again, and got the sack. That is a bit different from sacrificing one's job, and resigning, on grounds of principle, which is what NEW AGE gave out.

No more Zeke. I know this is a dull letter, but will try to do better next time. When you write to me do let me know your views on Nigeria. Am I right in thinking that Africa needs tough government and social advance in our generation and that the finer points of democracy can wait for the next? Is that behind Nkrumah's new line? How do you like Zik? Awolowo? Is the Moslem's North going to overwhelm the other regions after independence? My guess is that it is, but I would love to hear your views.

Yours

Pat

[1] In 1958 Duncan became the founding editor of the Liberal journal *Contact*.

Lagos

12 November 1957

My dear N. T.

You were one of the very first people I imagined I had written to after I got here. I was rather worried, thinking you were not well, when I did not receive a reply. Then Rebecca wrote to say you hadn't heard from me.[1] It is quite likely I made a mistake, or the post cheated me.

Since coming here, I have had startling experiences which made me feel as if I had just jumped out of a nightmare such as South Africa is. The freedom to move about without fear of the police, the civil treatment one gets in government offices, manned mostly by blacks, the freedom to be decent; the sudden feeling that one's hate has no object anymore, that there is a void and that one's bitterness has no point anymore. Still these give me oh, such a divine sense of release. I hope and pray that the one way, – the very least I can do – shall show my gratefulness to you for our friendship, your moral and material help, should be to make full use of this opportunity by contributing to the happiness of others, by affording my children the sort of education that will help them. So likewise, I hope also to make full use of my creative talents while I breathe this fresh air.

Lagos is a crowded town, but has an Oriental fascination about it. Our school is on the island portion of it, which is joined to the mainland portion by a beautiful bridge. The town is full of the smell of spices, an important item in Nigerian dishes. The national dress is gorgeous. I shall be sending you a photograph of me in it. This is a boys' secondary school – 350 boys, doing pre-university Cambridge exams, like all other West African schools. It's fascinating teaching Nigerians. They are so emotionally and intellectually stable. Often one feels they are too complacent, and then one comes here – so agonizingly – realizes that South Africans have reason to be restless and insecure. The school has provided me with a furnished house, with electricity and electric stove, but for the longing I have for Rebecca and the children, and the waves of home-sickness that often overwhelm me and paralyze me when I think of you & other friends, I have nothing to complain of. I consider myself a very lucky devil to have come out.

I have only 4 chapters to finish to complete my autobiography, half of which is in the hands of an English publisher who wants to publish it when it's complete.[2] I am looking forward to a busy time of writing activity – and that 'Greek tragedy' of ours is still churning in mind.[3]

Love to your husband and your dear self.

As ever,

Ezekiel

1 Rebecca and the children remained in South Africa until after her graduation. They left for Nigeria just before Christmas in 1957.

2 The second half of *Down Second Avenue* was written in Nigeria during this period.

3 The reference here is to the play *Shaka Zulu*.

Maseru

19 November 1957

My dear Zeke,

Just a rushed line to say that I have now heard from Prof. Galbraith, and that he has asked me to ask you to send the money to Africa Books, Standard Bank, MASERU, if you have not already sent it to him. He would like a credit balance with us, as he intends to get some books.

If you have already sent it to him, then of course, this falls away.

This part of the world is looking lovelier than it has ever looked since I reached it (1941), and our rains continue. I wish you could see it, but I do not wish you back, for the moment, in our madhouse. Enjoy it, you, Rebecca, and the children, while you may, and build up reserves of moral and spiritual strength for the time when you must come back and help to *ecraser l'infame.*[1]

Yours

Pat

[1] Destroy the wretch

1958

Lagos

13 January 1958

Dear Norah,

Thanks for your letter. Indeed we are a happy family. What we have been dreaming and wishing has at last come true. This is certainly a place where one can build up moral and mental reserves.

I don't know if I told you in my last letter that I wrote the 1st half of my autobiography when I was in S.A. and finished the 2nd half here. I sent Faber & Faber in Britain the 1st half and they were most interested. They will certainly publish it. I've dispatched this and I am breathlessly waiting.

Yes, I should tackle the tragedy. Unfortunately, I have not had the opportunity of reading Ritter although I was most impressed by the reviews it had.[1] If you sent it by ordinary book post, it will take about 3 weeks, but that doesn't matter. I've given myself 3 years within which to rework, expand & augment the thesis into something for publication.[2]

Rebecca joins me in my best wishes for abundant health.

Love,

Ezekiel

1 The reference is to E A Ritter's *Shaka Zulu*, published by Longman in 1955.

2 Mphahlele is referring to his collection of critical essays published by Faber and Faber in 1962 as *The African Image*, which, at the time, was unprecedented in South African scholarship.

Yaba, Nigeria

30 June 1958

Dear Norah,

Many, many apologies for not writing for such a long time. Reason was that Faber & Faber sent me back the last 2 chapters of my book to expand and then to bring the story as far as the Nigerian period. So I have been engrossed in this task and haven't been able to attend to my correspondence.

We're all doing very well here, barring torrential rains which have just begun. The rain comes down interminably, day and night, and the humidity often gets us down and we become chesty. Still, it is not unduly hard on us, and the children are wonderfully fit. Teresa, the middle one, is the cutest in the family at picking up Yoruba. In 6 months she has learnt a number of words, phrases and sentences.

Bantu Education hasn't done them any good. After 2 years of it we realize how much they have still to do to catch up with syllabuses here. So Rebecca and I share home lessons with them. Progress is good.

We've moved to a new site six miles out of town and we live on the school premises; but Rebecca and the children have to go out four miles to school and there's no bus transport. Still, the bus from our school helps, but one must really have one's own transport to do shopping in Lagos. To know that we are free to move anywhere we like, without curfew etc to bother us, – just the sense of freedom alone more than makes up for every handicap. We have electricity and water; the school has furnished the house and, as you know, there's nothing like coming from work to a nice comfortable home.

Thanks immensely for *Shaka* and *No Further Trek*. As soon as Rebecca is thro' with *Shaka*, I shall dig my teeth into it. I hope there won't be undue delay.

Yes, I read *2nd Class Taxi*. I even reviewed it for a local daily. A fresh deviation from the common run of S.A. novels, and a hilarious satire too. Doesn't it make you think of Joyce Carey's *Mr Johnson*. Staffnurse's silence and almost 'fanakalo' behaviour is an eloquent indictment. I received a stinging and indignant letter from Nadine.[1] She thinks I wasn't fair in my assessment of her works in my thesis – a copy of which I sent her. Of course I can't allow my academic pursuits to come between my friends and me – least of all a valuable friend like Nadine. I'm planning a long conciliatory letter in order to 'explain'. Perhaps it's the sort of crucible that fashions or tries friendship between a black man and a European, ghastly though it is for one even to talk in such terms.

I have been getting *Contact* from a friend of mine in Cape Town. Most stimulating, I think.

The Steins are helping me a lot – especially Jenny who can spare the time. They found me a valuable literary agent whom they revere. I think things will shape up beautifully in his hands.

Greetings to Flora. Also kindest regards to Sheila and Leslie Sachs. Lots of love.

Yours ever,

Ezekiel

P.S. Please use this address till further notice. Don't write *Lagos*, as Yaba has P.O. and such letters tend to end up in Box 394, Lagos.

1 Nadine Gordimer, who understood Mphahlele to be conflating her fictional characters' views with her own.

Yaba, Nigeria

1 July 1958

Dear Richard [Rive]

Thanks a hell of a lot, boy, for the journals. Gee, going through them, Rebecca and I felt a real breath of home, reminding us with a pang of the kind of nightmare we've left behind us. Most refreshing to read *Torch* once more and the *Educational Journal*. *New Age* and *Contact* had their own peculiar tang. Thanks again. Nigeria has it's own civilizing effect on a man; and the journals brought back to us another branch of civil civilization.

On this point of civilization; when I enter a shop manned by a bevy of dark- skinned girls and then look at a white man, something turns inside me. If it's the sort of white I have to talk to on a business matter, I bristle my hair, ready for the stink between us. And then, what do I see? An exasperatingly neutral character – just damned cheek for a man to be so neutral: makes you feel uncivilized.

I've received the book from Rollnick of African Bookman. Yours must be written off, I think. No harm done! Had a letter from Peter, sounding as urgent and jet-propelled and excrutiating as ever. Excrutiating, because there is about Peter's letters a divine pain – one large layer of it, throbbing all along its area, making you feel it is good most times to be, as he is, the medium through which life must be conceived and reborn on canvas. I don't think there's a richer life anywhere, Richard. If all the countries give him the kick in the back and impel him to produce, it's good.[1]

I was feeling that the kicks had diminished and that the mule was stamping on me, to crush me. I'm 37 now and I was thinking I'd never produce anything under that jackboot with its hobnails. In other words, I *am* an imaginative coward. Had a letter from Peter, too. Tells me he's writing. I notice that, after all, I was good riddance to *Drum*: no short story anymore and apparently no competition (£50). Damn pity, because with the absence of a literary or semi-literary journal, what will happen to African creative writing? Britain *doesn't want* to publish short stories. The biggest market is U.S.A., but there's an *American* idea of a short story and it is not African. How far are you with your writing?

Ek sé, hoe gaan dit met daardie Suid-Afrikaanse etes, man? – koorn en mieliemeel. Ons ly honger, man. Hier's te veel reis en peper en alle soorte vreemde kos.[2]

Best of luck – Yours ever

Zeke

P.S. You should have seen how Ribs got deflated by the assertion you're still far from marriage.

1 The artist Peter Clarke, who later provided illustrations for *The African Image*.

2 'Hey, how's it going with South African food, man? – corn and mielie meal. We're hungry, man. Here there's too much rice and pepper and all sorts of strange food.'

Yaba, Nigeria

30 September 1958

Dear Mrs. Barnett,

Your thesis ought to be most interesting: it should unearth a good deal that has been either forgotten or was never known.

My book will be coming out next spring – South African autumn – about March. About my other writings: There is a small collection of 5 short stories under the title: *Man Must Live*, the first attempt I ever made in short story writing. A mixture of protest and sentimental lyricism. It was published by African Bookman in 1947 (Cape Town). The publisher, Mr. J Rollnick, Box 2231 C.T., just dug up a remnant copy for me two months ago and said he still had a small supply. *Drum* has published quite a few of my short stories between 1952 and 1956. In the latter year there appeared a series of 6 with a running theme of township life. Your public library should have *Drum* files, or else you may try the Cape Town office of the magazine. That is the protest stage proper of my development.

In 1955 a story appeared under the pen name Bruno Esekie in *New World Writing Anthology* (Mentor Book, New York) No. 7. If you can't find a copy, let me know and I'll send you a spare copy I have. The story is 'The Suitcase'. *Drum* published it a little later. The present stage of my literary vapourings covers two published stories: 'The Master of Doornvlei', appearing under the pen name of 'Naledi' in *Fighting Talk* of some month last year. My stuff still lies unpacked since it arrived from SA., otherwise I would tell you the month. Second is 'The Living and Dead' in *Africa South*, Jan-March. The former is being reproduced in an Italian magazine *Africa* (Milan). *The Listener* of May 23 1955, or better still, an anthology of BBC talks just came out, contains a talk by me, among others, one by an Indian and a coloured. *Africa in Transition* is the title of the book.

A short story writer worth treating is Dyke Sentso of Fredefort, Orange Free State. If you write to Casey Motsisi, Box 3413, Johannesburg you may ask him to find you the address of Sentso. Mention my name; he also writes satirical bits which are really quaint and may interest you. Hope I've been helpful and do write and let me know what progress you make.

Yrs

EM

Yaba, Nigeria

13 October 1958

Dear Makhudu,

At last I have a breather, and am settling down to a shorter note than I intended to write. How I hate to say I am busy – sounds snobbish and executive posturing.

Life is still sweet here, with everything growing savagely around us: tall, tall palm trees – dwarfing your bluegums – thick bush, grass as long or tall as the longest mealie stalk, flying cockroaches, vicious mosquitoes etc. We are tucked in a corner just bordering on suburban Lagos, an area that's in the process of growing. Ribs has left off teaching in the secondary school – just fed up of teaching, she is, and is waiting to dive into a social work job. Social work here is restricted to things only the government can cope with at a time and on its own initiative.

You don't find voluntary agencies doing most of it on state subsidy as they do in your developed country (if one equates *development* with *industrialization*). But we aren't anxious about Ribs' not working because salaries are good.

I was amused by your analogy of surburban whites talking about the 'servant problem' with regard to Ribs' remarks about Nigerian workers. I'm sure she was acting, because, frankly, although it is necessary to have someone to help when a woman is working, we have always found it damned awkward to say to the person do this or that. It is just didn't click. Nigerians can treat one another in a way which can sometimes outdo the Boer slave-drivers and we have been accused of 'spoiling' the servants – in other words, *le re senyetsa batho barona ba itoketse.*[1] Now she's home all day, she has sacked the man. Domestic work here is done by men. Women keep in the market stalls. It's most awkward (understatement) to think of a man pawing and hanging and contemplating a woman's undies – ts – ts – ts!! A man big enough to be Danie's father.

How did you fare with your court cases? I hope the worst has been averted. I can imagine the agony of it all, Makhudu. I do know, also, that a legal acquittal doesn't automatically mean public exoneration or a clean bill of health. Do write and tell us.

Down Second Avenue is in the production department of the publishers and will definitely come out next March. Good enough as we hope to go to Britain then for our holidays (4 months).

Warmest greetings to Danie, Sam.

Love to you & yours

Zeke

[1] You are spoiling our people.

Lagos, Nigeria

[Postmark 8 April 1958]

Dear Mr Plomer

In 1956 when you visited the offices of *Drum* magazine in Johannesburg, I was on the staff as fiction editor of the journal. We had the opportunity of chatting with you over a sandwich lunch. Perhaps you will remember my saying how much I admire Forster's characterization of non-whites (*cf Passage to India*) – as the best in English literature. Maybe you will remember also my observation that in many respects *Turbott Wolfe* is a better novel than Paton's first.

I so sincerely hope that you conveyed my remarks about E. M.[1] to him as you promised you would. At the time you visited South Africa I was working on a thesis for the M A on 'The Non-European Character in South African English Fiction'. I was granted a pass with distinction for it, and now I am re-working certain parts and adding more material in the hope that one day a publisher will be interested in it.

A copy of the thesis is on its way to you in case you are interested in reading it. I warn you that the first chapter is nothing more than a catalogue. This is deliberate, as I intended to make the third chapter my *pièce de résistance* – an analysis of four novelists of the first rank: Olive Schreiner, Sarah Gertrude Millin, yourself and Paton. The first is the chapter that will need re-working.

I have left South Africa to teach in the above Secondary School as English master. I came over in September last, and hope to settle here or in Ghana. I decided that if I want to write I must leave S.A. Conditions are crushing there; what with all the economic, social and political barriers, one's bitterness becomes one's enemy; and both black and white writer are so deeply involved.

When you have had time to read the thesis I shall eagerly await your opinion.

Yours sincerely

E. Mphahlele

1 E M Forster, the English novelist, best known for *A Passage to India*.

Lagos

4 November 1958

Dear W Plomer,

How kind of you to write so promptly after your last letter. Thank you so much for your very warm reception of the thesis. I value your opinion most highly.

When I did the thesis I tried very hard to procure more of your work, but was unsuccessful. As it was, I found T.W.[1] in a dingy second hand bookshop in Jo'burg. Libraries can be ruthlessly exclusive in the South, as you may imagine. For this reason am I particularly happy to know that I can obtain your latest work. Should you come upon *Four Countries*, please let me know the price so that I may order it, together with *Double Lives*. As I am reworking the thesis and adding more material in the hope of finding a publisher one day – it doesn't matter when – I shall make good the deficiency in this particular quarter. It's most unlikely that I shall be persuaded to tone down my enthusiasm over T.W. any more than I have already done. I'm keener than ever before to meet *Ma Masondo.*

You make an interesting proposal re *Encounter*[2] which I shall certainly follow up. When this will be done I don't know, as I'm busy at the moment trying to collate a few published short stories of mine to hawk for publication in book form, though as I know Britain is in this direction. But may be America will bite.

I have just received a letter from Faber & Faber saying they are definitely publishing my autobiography *Down Second Avenue*, which I completed in Nigeria.

Incidentally, I used to read *London Magazine* when I was in South Africa. Since coming here I have lost touch. If you would kindly let me know the yearly subscription. I should be delighted! Sorry to heap so many things on you.

Best wishes,

Yours sincerely

E. Mphahlele

1 The reference is to *Turbott Wolfe* by William Plomer, published by Leonard and Virginia Woolf in 1925. *Four Countries* is a collection of Plomer's stories about Japan (Jonathan Cape 1949) and *Double Lives* is an autobiography (Jonathan Cape 1943).

2 *Encounter* was a leading, left-liberal English periodical started in 1953 under the editorship of Stephen Spender and Irving Kristol. It was an official organ of the Congress for Cultural Freedom (for whom Mphahlele himself was later to work as Director of its African Programme). In 1967 the Congress was exposed as a CIA front. In 1958 *Encounter*'s reputation was intact and it is not surprising that Plomer would have encouraged Mphahlele to publish in it.

1959

Ibadan

25 January 1959

Dear Mrs. Barnett,

Since replying to your letter of last September, I haven't heard from you. I wonder if you did receive my letter which I wrote almost immediately after yours arrived.

What I should be interested to know are the titles you have succeeded in procuring. The university, which I have just joined to lecture in English literature, is developing its researchers into African subjects, literature included. I should be glad to know what bibliography you are tackling on South African writers and if they are still in print, so that I get them. I have Dhlomo's 'Thousand Hills' poem.

Do write and let me know also how far you have gone in your research.

Regards

E. Mphahlele

Ibadan

16 Februrary 1959

Dear Norah,

Here we are again in a new place. I left secondary school and am lecturer in English to groups of workers who have not had the luck to enter university.[1] We are here for the next 3 months and then I set up a base in a town 90 miles north of us. I visit 3 towns each week and it is most interesting to meet the 'interior of Nigeria'. Also, it has a myriad suggestions for setting in my writing. Rebecca is still home. She left teaching as she said she was 'sick' of the profession after leaving it for 3 years. At the same time social services here are still very colonial and she hasn't struck a job in her line. In the meantime there is another baby on the way, and so it isn't so urgent for her to get work. I must say, Norah, that for the first time in our lives we find we don't have to split our hearts and heads trying to meet our monthly budget. Salaries here are 2½ times those for corresponding positions in S.A. But of course we have to try to cover long-standing commitments which with the passage of years in that miserable country have piled up. Still, we eat better and are spiritually prosperous. The children keep in excellent health.

At last I am able to report progress – some progress in the Greek tragedy: *Shaka*. Yes, what wonderful and awe-inspiring material! It's my current big job and I'm applying myself these days better than I could ever hope to before. I have a sudden spurt of themes for fiction, too. One novel has a synopsis already.[2]

From a few snippets I'm able to get from S.A. it is evident the gloom is gathering more and more, and it gives cause for even an exile to brood – impotently though it may be.

The university affords a U.K. vacation with 4 months' full pay free passages to and back. It was our intention to go to U.K. this coming June. But alas,

Pretoria has rejected application for Lagos to endorse our passports for U.K. So it looks as if our dreams, like so many others before, are to come to dust.

Love from all,

Yours sincerely,

Ezekiel

[1] Mphahlele was attached to the Department of Extramural Studies (English), University College, Ibadan.

[2] Mphahlele never wrote this novel during his stay in Nigeria. The closest he got to writing longer fiction was the story 'Mrs Plum', produced while he lived in Paris. He would only return to the novel much later during his doctoral studies in the United States.

Ibadan

12 May 1959

Dear Norah,

Thanks immensely for your congratulatory letter which moved me to tears for all the warmth it glows with. It is most inspiring to hear you say that, in gratitude for what you did for me you wish I do the same for someone else. I hope in my own small way I have anticipated your wish in certain directions, however only feebly significant I shall continue to treasure that faith you have had in me.

Reading your letter, with the poignant description you give of your physical disabilities and protracted ill health in the days when we had just got to know each other, I am overwhelmed with the feeling that I might have taxed your generosity overmuch. You did not complain, and as you indicate, the tragedy of our lives in the Deep South is the utter impossibility for people on both sides of the physical barrier to share one another's lives and travails and endeavours. But I do admire deeply your fortitude. My heart goes out to you in your aspirations towards that higher truth that both transcends and mends racial fissures. I trust that my book will remain a dedication to your good and loving self.[1]

I am sure I wrote you a letter from the above new address, saying that Rebecca and the children will be coming 'home' (with all the ironies that the term is loaded with!). By now she may have visited you. Please change the address accordingly as the Lagos people may just overlook to readdress whatever you send. I shall be most happy if you will send me any other reviews that you may see in S.A. Excellent ones have appeared in Britain.

Lots of love and keep in good health.
Ezekiel

[1] *Down Second Avenue*, the first autobiography, published by Faber and Faber in 1959.

Ibadan
4 June 1959

Dear Norah,

Yes, you may go ahead and see what can be done about the play: it will be fruitful to know what Gluckman thinks.[1] I agree about the opening chorus – that it can be confusing to the outside world. I shall wait till you have had the time to write.

After the 27 June, my address will be c/o 62 Regents Park Road, London N.W.1.

In the letter I wrote which didn't reach you, I said that Rebecca and the children would be coming to S.A. so that the baby is born there to avoid citizenship complications.[2] Also, her mother was ailing and she was being threatened with ejection from the house we left her in. There were the 2 stands waiting to be bulldozed. She being the only child of her mother, Rebecca was compelled to forgo a much-desired trip to the U.K. This will be our leave, and the college pays our transport expenses. I received a letter from her saying she had taken ill soon as she arrived – on 30 April and had to go to hospital. This must be the reason why she did not contact you. Orlando phones are hopeless, and she does not, in her advanced state of pregnancy, have better and ready transport than the train. She is in the old house – 8280 Orlando West.

In a hurry, best wishes,
Yours ever,
Ezekiel

[1] Leon Gluckman, a South African theatre director, directed the legendary musical *King Kong*.

[2] The reference is to the son, Robert Dichaba.

London

12 September 1959

Dear Norah,

I believe by now you have seen Rebecca and the new baby.

The summer here is glorious this year, the first in ten years, I'm told. I have been to North Wales, Birmingham, Manchester, Oxford and next week I go to Cambridge. A fascinating Old World atmosphere in a number of these places. I have met Dan Jacobson the young writer (S.A.), William Plomer, with whom I'm spending a day in Sussex next week. I'm going to try to see E.M. Forster at Cambridge.

I went to Stratford to see *King Lear*. A magnificent production. Charles Laughton carries some of the scenes creditably, and the mad scenes are particularly moving. Sir John Gielgud in a recital of the *Ages of Man* was a wonderful experience. What a range! The two musicals I have seen are superb – *My Fair Lady* and *West Side Story* – the latter is marvelous medium for a Romeo-&-Juliet theme (Puerto Ricans vs Yankees). The former is a lavish production. Yesterday I saw a moving Negro play – *A Raisin in the Sun*. The Proms have been an exciting experience – Haydn's *Creation* among them.

I have done two broadcasts already and am preparing a third for the Asian and Middle East service on the English novel in South Africa.

I have now at last taken out British passport – after a nerve-wrecking conflict. Either I should face the refusal to renew the South African one next September and come back for good, or else stay out – probably for good, because I can be declared a prohibited immigrant. Either way it is painful and so I chose the lesser evil. Rebecca will automatically get British citizenship; only I don't know if she could come out with a British one having got it while there.

I must say again and again thank you, Norah. You are such a wonderful person. When the S. African passport has been sent back to Pretoria by the authorities here, you can tender the receipt to have the £100 paid back into your bank. I should ask the bank to send the receipt to the Native Commissioner, Johannesburg and wait for the formalities to take their course.

Love always

Yours

Ezekiel

1960

As usual

5 January 1960

Dear N.T.,

Thank you for your letter. It came when I had intended putting a stop to my procrastination, since coming back, of writing to you. And now I've been caught up with this new book which Fabers have commissioned, my mind and mood sway between moments of exertion and loneliness. Believe it or not, Rebecca and the kids are not back yet! She has been going through a trying period, looking for a house to buy for the mother so that she leaves the house at 8280 and so get out of the position where the threat of ejection hung over her night and day. I've been anxious myself and only today I received a letter from her saying she has found the house and is trying to raise the money for it. I'm not surprised you had no letter from her as this is the first letter I get from her since the first week in December.

And then she says her passport is still at Union Buildings so that the name of the baby is included. It takes all that age to do a small thing like that. After having been separated for 8 months now, I feel poignantly why it is absurd for one to go back to that country – but for the fact that one has a mother to attend to.

She *is* a poor correspondent anyhow, Norah and she might at least have dropped you a postcard. It is an inspiring note, the one you sent me, out of *Race Relations News*. A novel is slowly taking shape in my mind now as I write the present book, which contains a hotch-potch of introspective essays, including part of that thesis in South African literature.[1] You once mentioned, after reading the thesis, the name of a South African lady who wrote a few things – who was it, and what titles can you think of of hers?

The visit to Britain was both enlightening, stimulating and depressing. I saw among 10 plays, *West Side Story* and *My Fair Lady*. I made it a point to see musicals as you suggested, but I'm afraid I still cannot embark on one myself – my impressions are still too muddled. If *Shaka Zulu* doesn't see the stage in its present form, it seems it will have to go into the waste-paper basket.

I know what a beaver you are, your mind being able to dart from one thing to another at the same time. But when you can find time, do write. Thank you on behalf of myself and Rebecca for your unchanging good heart.

Yours ever,

Ezekiel

1 *The African Image* was taking shape as a revised version of part of the MA thesis together with new essays.

Offa
10 February 1960

My dear Langston Hughes,

It was a pleasant surprise to receive your letter forwarded to me from our university college. Incidentally I've moved from IBADAN to the town in the above address, although I'm still under the college. I shall be here for the whole of 1960 – at any rate until the end of the academic year in June 1960.

I have been wondering to my South African friends Richard Rive & Peter Clarke (in Cape Town & Simon's Town) what had happened to your anthology. I came to Nigeria 2 years ago, to flee from oppression, and now I can do the job I was born for which I was forbidden to do in my own country – teaching – & of course writing. Last May my autobiography, *DOWN SECOND AVENUE*, was published by Faber & Faber in London, and had a terrific reception. I have just returned from leave in London and was on the point of sending you a copy at the AMSAC address which Prof Mercer Cook gave me. You see, it's so long we heard from each other – you & I – that I wasn't sure you're still at the address I have had all this time. It goes off to you – the book – today by ocean mail. An American agency has declined to hawk the book for a U. S. edition on the grounds that it requires a 'specialized audience' & there are already too many books in the USA about Africa. You will judge for yourself when & if you can spare the time to read it. Two weeks ago my publishers told me that a Checho-Slovakian publishing house is making a translation of it. Please accept my inscription which I make in the same spirit as you so kindly made yours in your book you sent me in S. Africa – *Ways of White Folk.*

Are you going to exclude the short stories by me you once thought you would put into the anthology: 'Blind Alley', 'Saturday Train' (can't remember the exact title offhand)?

Of course, you are at liberty to use 'Accra Conference Diary'. I don't know if the enclosed is what you call the credit you intend to give me. If not, you may indicate roughly what you require – in any case, you have my permission to use the piece.

I'm so looking forward to coming to USA one day and I'll remember to take your offer of hospitality – thanks.

Best wishes. Yours very sincerely

Ezekiel Mphahlele

CREDIT TO READ:

'By Ezekiel Mphahlele, who was a delegate for the African National Congress (South Africa) at the first All-African People's Congress in Accra in 1958. This piece was originally published in *Fighting Talk*, a South African journal.'

Offa

17 February 1960

Dear Norah,

I was most distressed to read of your nasty experience in the hands of hooligans. I know just how you must feel knowing with your sense of balance and justice that you ought not to blame your assailants and yet knowing that you cannot but feel deeply hurt when you are at the butt-end of such wanton violence. Alas, we are dealing with a huge, vast machine which is becoming more and more complex: we seem all so helpless, and yet we also know that the operator's job is a deliberate and purposeful one. My sincerest hope is that you have recovered fully from all the shock and that you will not allow the incidents to affect your outlook adversely. There's too much to be done such as you are no doubt sensible of. Yours is going to continue to follow the pattern of things until the sun goes over the land again.

Yes, it was Ethelreda Lewis you mentioned, *of course* I have the book and I had read 'Blind Justice'. What a story! I shall hunt for *Negresses*.[1] The book I'm doing is a collection of introspective essays with the common theme of the 'African Personality'. Part of the work will be a portion of my thesis on Southern African literature, extending into the Rhodesias [Zimbabwe and Zambia], East and West Africa plus the general sub-theme of European literary images of the African. I intend using one of Ethelreda's novels – of fascinating portrayal. How I wish I could seize upon other things she has written.

I think I can expect Rebecca etc on the 25th Feb. It will be an immense relief.

Best wishes as always,

Yours ever,

Ezekiel

1 Ethelreda Lewis, best known as the author of *Trader Horn*, published 'Blind Justice' in *The Best British Stories of 1928 with an Irish and*

Colonial Supplement, edited by Edward O'Brien. Norah Taylor had referred to Lewis's novel *Four Handsome Negresses* (Jonathan Cape 1931).

Offa

24 February 1960

Dear Makhudu

Congratulations! You certainly are a lucky bastard. I shall be most interested to hear in March how you worked the thing.

Well now, Ipetu-Ijesha! If it is on the road to Asaba, it's on the concourse of human beings and motor traffic. I shall fish out most information from people who come from that way. It is in the Mid-West, a region which has very interesting people of a different ethnic origin from Yorubas. Mid-Westerners are very easy to make friends with, the best, in fact, next to the Easterners. Westerners are the most difficult to draw out.

If you haven't yet signed a contract, put the people of Ijesha off, *until* you have arrived and seen whether the school is such as you can commit yourself to. A thirteen months' initial period is the usual thing. A contract must provide (apart from stating the salary scale) accommodation (*adequate*) with basic furniture for *all* members of family plus mosquito nets. Basic furniture includes all timber things, not crockery, curtains, bedding, lino carpet (which are yours). It must provide four months' leave with pay at home or in UK or elsewhere at end of 18 months, passages paid to and back as also passages now for coming here. Make sure of these provisions if no contract has been signed. You can manoeuvre when you are here and jump into another school which we'll have in a spare pocket. If it falls in the Anglican circuit of schools, you're safe.

Cheers.

Yours

Zeke

P.S. If the school is what's called a Proprietor's i.e. belonging to an individual, all more reason to be cautious. Such schools are a stinking racket.

Offa

27 March 1960

My dear William,

At last I am able to settle down to letter writing. Since coming back in the middle of November, I have been most restless.[1] I was to move to a new station as the above address will indicate. And then my family didn't join me until the first week of March.

We have to make new friends now, and it seems one must always have the feeling of a man sitting on one bum either because of overcrowded seating accommodation or because he doesn't know if he's being allowed to sit at all.

This is a nice little town. Geographically and administratively, Offa is in the Northern Region – still a very colonial region. Whites here are upstarts and live at peace with myself only because I don't have to meet them in or concerning my work. But ethnically, the town is Yoruba – the predominant group in the Western Region. I live in a Railway house – among the elect as it is in Senior railway office; and there is no African Senior man here. Offa is an explosive little town, the background for the continuous war between the autocratic Muslim North and the equally arrogant Yoruba West. In fact that is the reason why an expatriate like me must do this kind of work for the University College in the North: Northerners cannot tolerate Southerners – which includes Eastern and Western Regions. They prefer expatriates to fellow-Nigerians outside the North. It's damn ironic for an underdog like me to find himself in a privileged position: Good senior service quarters with electricity from the Station power plant not shared by the rest of the town. My whole being revolts against it. It continues to puzzle me and pain me how sensible people must be able to make the worst of class distinction acceptable. Although I don't accept the situation, I'm powerless to choose unless I quit. And quit Nigeria – indeed West Africa, I must soon. Where to?[2] I don't know. Once an exile; always one, no matter where. I'm sure – rather I know that you have been paralyzed by the thought of what has taken place in Vereeniging and Langa.[3] It is encouraging to hear as I did this morning from BBC that the African National Congress has asked everybody to burn their passes. No doubt, this *is* the beginning of things. The very nature of the pass laws makes this a continuous campaign, unlike a day's or month's boycott. And continuous, perennial if necessary, defiance must break down the structure; especially, as is bound to happen.

I see in the *New Statesman* that the Spring Books include your collected poems. I do remember your saying when we met in London, that you would like to leave things in a tidy order. Excellent, and Congratulations! My next big task, after this present one, is to prepare a long essay of your works. It is worth it and I feel I owe it to myself. Your collected poems will make my task 'venturable'. It is likely that I shall wangle a Scholarship for a 2 year study at Oxford to do the doctorate.[4] I intend, if I'm successful, to combine it with an essay on you for Fabers (if they'll bite). If it comes through, I should begin in October this year. The very best wishes to you and your friend in Sussex. I still cherish very happy memories of our day in your Sussex *khaya*.

Fondest greetings,

Zeke

1 From the visit to the United Kingdom and Paris.

2 A little over a year later Mphahlele accepted the offer to become Director of the African Programme of the Congress for Cultural Freedom in Paris.

3 The reference here is to resistance campaigns organised mainly by the Pan Africanist Congress, in particular the anti-pass demonstrations which led to the Sharpeville massacre on 21 March 1960.

4 This attempt to get into Oxford was part of the generalised restlessness referred to earlier. He wanted to move from the Extramural Department of English at Ibadan and another feverish effort of the kind alluded to was his abortive attempt to study for a doctorate through the University of London.

Offa

27 July 1960

Dear Langston,

It was indeed an immense delight for me to meet you personally. I had come to know you so well through our correspondence & through your works that it seemed we had met. So when we did see each other, it was like a reunion.

You have done an excellent job of this anthology of African writing: congratulations! It simply bristles with life & newness, unlike Peggy Rutherford's *African Voices* (seen it? It came out in Britain as *Darkness & Light*), which is cluttered with statuesque pieces. I notice you excised those juicy bits from my piece about personalities like Kenneth Kaunda (you may have heard he has become really big in Northern Rhodesian & Federation politics) and Harry Nkambula (who has been eclipsed). How gravely prophetic

I would have sounded. No, I don't really care: what delights me is that you have captured African writing which resounds through and through like the footsteps of a giant rubbing his eyes as he walks, just from a deep sleep.

Sam Allen hinted to you that I have taken up the co-editorship of *Black Orpheus* (together with Ulli Beier and a Nigerian playwright, *Wole Soyinka*).[1] I am going to put in a full-fledged essay about you and your poetry in *Black Orpheus* – the coming issue. I meant to ask that night (if we weren't so rushed) about your *Big Sea*. Is it still available?

I hope the filming of *A Raisin in the Sun* is going beautifully. I saw the play in London last year, and was thrilled. I haven't forgotten your proffered hospitality if and when I come to the U.S. Be sure I'll love to take it.

Cheerio for now, and much love

Yours ever Zeke

P.S. I loved your poem in *London Magazine*

1 The Ibadan literary journal *Black Orpheus* was named after Jean-Paul Sartre's influential essay on the negritude poets.

Offa

16 August 1960

My dear William,

I just thought to ask formal approval of quotations I am using from *Double Lives* and the story, 'Ma Masondo' which I have used in the book we spoke about last year. It's now with Faber – the MS i.e. Charles Monteich is impressed by it, although he thinks we need a reorganization of the material here and there.

After this bit of journalistic blah-blah I must really turn to fiction. I keep getting requests from editors for articles on this and that. The latest one is from Walter Allen, asking me to write on South African writing (black and white) for a supplement in the *N.S.*[1] which is an annual feature (on Commonwealth writing this time) I have done. No sooner do I think of settling down to my cup of tea than someone gets it into his head that I'm the 'right person' for one thing and another. I'm really sick of it and am putting my foot down.

On June 22-26 I attended a conference in Philadelphia called by the American Society of African Culture (a Negro body).[2] Then we were taken for a tour to

Washington, Chicago and New York, observing various aspects of Negro life. All so stimulating as a first visit to the United States and all the dollars of the Society. I ran full tilt into the argument on *negritude* at the conference.

It's a French-speaking African thing, as you might know, and I at least expected to find Negroes anxious to identify themselves with African roots (artists and intellectuals i.e.). In my Philistine way I told them that we who were born, brought up and educated in Africa take our Negritude for granted – no slogans about it are necessary. Besides, we are products of cultural cross-impacts in multi-racial societies etc etc. What worries the American Negro (the one who thinks about these things) is whether he can be integrated politically and economically without being assimilated culturally (which he doesn't want). All so puzzling.

I never thanked you for your excellently produced *Collected Poems*. I love it and of course will always treasure it for its contents. I hope you are in good health and so with Charles. Best wishes always and do write.

Yours ever,

Zeke

1 *New Statesman*.

2 Mphahlele continued to use the term 'Negro' before 'Afro-American', 'Black' and 'African-American' gained international currency.

Offa

19 September 1960

Dear Langston,

I have just finished a full-length essay on your poetry for *Black Orpheus* No. 9. A copy of this will be sent you when it is out. A copy will be sent also because it includes a review by me of *African Treasury*, which was a delight to do.

This is to ask you if you think the music shops still have these recordings by you:

Tambourines to Glory

The Glory of Negro History

The Story of Jazz

Simpu Speaks His Mind

The Dream Keeper

The Rhythms of the World

I should so very much like to procure them. Sorry for hassle.

Best wishes as always.

Yours ever,

Zeke

Offa

16 September 1960

Dear Makhudu

What a world of intrigue you have suddenly found yourself in! What *is* just wrong with the principal? Seems things are getting worse and worse. And that she should have bargained for a position where the big quisling from Ghana would come into the College, with all that she knows about him, is a mystery. But she is certainly playing a dangerous game by trying to keep clean in a pool of mire. It sounds so incredible that, knowing, as she should know, the kind of intrigue she comes from in the South, she should now adopt the dirty role of splitting the staff into two: doesn't she know a fragmented staff is a dangerous thing?

Maybe it's just as well that you have not signed a contract. With a car – *their* car – it's not likely you can be sacked at *any* time. I guess you must just stick on, do your work and no more, keep up a stolid, neutral look, and avoid getting emotionally involved in the mess-up. It wouldn't be difficult at all, if the worst came to the worst, to bale out into another school. Short of being held to ransom for having been adopted when you were in difficulty, you can, I think, bear a few things. Whatever happens, it seems you must keep on the most friendly terms with the Nigerians on the staff, without necessarily bending over backwards to do so.

Yes, when the time comes, just holler, and should be able to lend you the £45. Working at white heat as ever, so excuse a hurried note.

Yours

Zeke

Offa

28 October 1960

Dear Jack,

So sorry for not replying earlier. So many things were clamouring for attention when your letter arrived and am only now beginning to get a breather, for what it's worth.

Your letter, incidentally, was re-directed to me at my Extra-Mural station as the above shows. I'm in the Extra-Mural Department of the university college and teach English literature.

There are lots of stations scattered over the country, each with a resident tutor.

It was exciting to learn of your new venture. One literary journal after another has popped up and slumped in South Africa, partly because they were so exclusively white. It is most refreshing to look forward to something that promises to be representative.

As soon as I have cleared certain things, I shall see what I can send you.

Thanks for your kind remarks about my article in *New Statesman*. Yes, I did see your notice letter in the Journal. Thanks also for what you say about the story in *Following the Sun*.

I'll soon be biting into your *Road to Yesterday*, a copy of which I have.

Cheerio for now – and my best wishes.

Yours sincerely,

Zeke

New York

6 November 1960

Dear Ezekiel,

If I can get passport, visas, inoculation and everything in time ... since the invitation just came the other day ... it looks as if I might be in Lagos for Zik's inauguration on the 16th.[1] But have to turn around and come right back to New York as I have a TV show coming up at the end of the month, so don't think I'll have a chance to come up to the University. Would you by any chance be in Lagos? Drop me a note: c/o Nigerian Airways, P. O. Box 136, Lagos, and let me know, as I'd love to see you.

Cordially,

Langston

[1] Hughes is referring to Nnamdi Azikiwe's inauguration as Governor-General; in 1963 Azikiwe became the first President of Nigeria.

Offa

24 November 1960

Dear Langston,

A million times sorry, cowboy, for my abortive attempts to catch you in Lagos. Did you come? This was how: I received your note on the Saturday preceding the event. On Monday I tried to wire Nigerian Airways to say please wire me soon as you arrive to say you are there and I can motor down. We are 190 miles from Lagos & 102 from Ibadan but I was keen to meet you & wanted to be sure you'd be around. But the telephone lines were bad. That's how underdeveloped we are here, also! Until Tuesday I couldn't.

Yours ever,

Zeke

Offa

24 November 1960

My dear Langston,

It was good to hear from you, however briefly. Glad too to hear you found the *F.T.* piece interesting. *Black Orpheus* is bringing out 7 short stories of mine in a special number. Will send you copy as usual. Uneconomical venture (for me), but then it helps to put things together & when I've added to them, will confront my publishers with a volume. Otherwise, these folks won't bite short stories. A factual work – *The African Image* – has gone into production: maybe autumn or early spring will see it out.

You *are* a very busy guy, and I'm amazed at your agility to take in so much travel & lecturing. Bravo!

Have lined up M.I.T., Columbia New School & Northwestern for visiting lectureships in African contemporary writing from Oct. '61, & was arranging their sequence when I was invited to Paris last week as guest of the Congress of Cultural Freedom – the international body of artists, writers, scientists & scholars. Beier & some other folks had given them the idea I would be the best chap for director of their African Program which they have just opened. Mercer Cook was their first director for 9 months & now, as you know, he's going to be ambassador to Nigeria.

Yours ever

Zeke

New York

14 December 1960

Dear Zeke,

Certainly was sorry not to have seen you while I was in Nigeria, but I had only 5 days in Lagos and something happening every minute. I enjoyed it all immensely, and was delighted that I could come for even so short a time. I've got two TV shows here this month ... been filming one of them all this week ... after which I had to fly right back. But I did have a couple of days in London and Bloke Modisane gave a little party for me where I met Todd Matshikiza, Sonny Pillay, and a British friend of yours whose name I can't recall, but who calls you ZEEK. Anyhow, it was good to find your note on my return. It was something of a madhouse at Nigerian Airways in Lagos. They couldn't find any communications for me from other Nigerian residents to whom I had given that mailing address (on advice of BOAC in New York) and that they took plane and hotel reservations for my return trip that never got on the record in Kano or elsewhere. But I can understand with so many visitors and folks flying in and out those young clerks might get a bit confused. But they were so sweet and polite, I love them anyhow. And, being an old traveler, I did not mind too much arriving in a strange town and having nowhere to sleep, Kano for example where I stopped over for a couple of days. In Paris it happened I was with Richard Wright as he left for the hospital ... his last visitor at home. And he died while we were discussing him at Bloke's party in London, Koyinde Vaughn talking particularly about his BLACK POWER which nobody liked much.[1] And I was telling them how Wright told me he'd picked up an amoeba in Africa that sent him to the hospital every so often for treatments for which he was going when I saw him. Arna Bontemps is just back in N. Y. tonight from Uganda. I'll ask him about your maybe coming to Fisk University to lecture.

Langston

1 Richard Wright's *Black Power: A Record of Reactions in a Land of Pathos* (Harper 1954) was a personal narrative of a visit to Ghana in which Wright expresses numerous misgivings, particularly about African religion.

1961

Offa
14 January 1961

Dear Langston,

Thanks immensely for the records. These are superb recordings and are a worthy monument to your versatile capabilities. I shall treasure them, like your written work, till the end of my days. I keep thinking all the time what I've done to be placed at the receiving end of so much goodness, a thing my folk are so remote from.

I'm happy you have sounded out a friend about Fisk [University]. It has become an obsession with me and my wife now to come and work in the U.S. By June this year, I must be able to let my College know what my plans are. And then, as I'm thinking in terms of Oct. and Nov., immigration red-tape must be got over as early as possible. Then, there is a boat passage to book in good time.

Did I tell you what I'm offering? I forgot. Just in case: M. A. English Literature doing a doctorate thesis on Contemporary African Writing, Poetics, Practical Criticism, Victorian Literature, Contemporary African Writing, African Affairs are an extra interest for my junior degree.

So, whatever you can do for us by way for contacts, we shall be grateful.

The very best wishes for 1961.

Yours sincerely,
Zeke

Offa
22 January 1961

Dear Richard,

Your story about the woman and the rain is really good. Not so the fantasy. Ulli Beïer, my co-editor, thinks the same too. May I keep the fantasy – I'll tell you why later. The other will be published.

I notice you still tackle the story with the emphasis on atmosphere – a small incident with a slight plot built into something big-sounding through the echo of atmosphere. It's an interesting technique. One is almost inclined to think that if you tried the slow-moving big story, it wouldn't come off. But what the hell – you could try it – who am I to say this or that about a writer's capabilities!

I've been asked by Penguin to compile an anthology of contemporary African writing – fiction and sketches and essays.[1] For its price, it can sell like hell in Africa, and we have a sure market already. When I have collected the material, I shall let them know the form of the book and then on the strength of the number of contributions, they will be able to say what they can pay initially for royalties.

Can you send me three or four short stories to choose from? If you have sketches – satirical etc., shoot them across. Tell me, what other writers there are now – even if only promising – in the Cape apart from Alex la Guma? What is James Matthews' address?[2]

I'm writing to Peter Clarke to ask him to throw himself into the Fish or Kei River, if he can't write something for me. The Ocean – is it Indian or Atlantic where Simonstown is? – is too big for such as he.

Best wishes and do reply soon.

Yours ever,

Zeke

1 This book was subsequently published by Penguin Books in 1967 under the title *African Writing Today*.

2 Mphahlele arranged for the publication of an extract from Alex La Guma's *A Walk in the Night* in *Black Orpheus*. Later, Richard Rive would publish *Quartet* in the Heinemann African Writers Series, a collection of short fiction by the Cape Town-based writers Rive, La Guma, James Matthews and Alf Wannenburg.

Offa

22 January 1961

Dear Norah,

It is such a long time that I have not written. Even after the deluge had lifted. I found myself entangled in so much writing – much of it the stupid stuff one is asked by overseas journals to do on one political or cultural topic and another. I'm putting my foot down and refusing to have any more of it.

I was thrilled by your news of something more interesting that you are engaged in in theatre. I'm sure you will find it most rewarding. I am afraid I can't settle down to writing a play just now. I simply must finish my thesis this year for a doctorate (Ph.D) with London University. It's going to take up much of my time. And then I can only write a play when I'm inspired. It isn't like a short story that I find I must do, by some sense of compulsion which I cannot flout. I don't know when such a moment of inspiration will come on me. We'll see. I hope you'll be as patient as ever. When you can spare the time, do send me the Chaka verse play.[1]

It is most likely that I shall take up an offer for a visiting lectureship in the U.S.A. for 2 years – in September this year.[2] It will be an interesting experience, I'm sure. One thing that worries Rebecca and me: we've to learn to live with the painful fact of being exiles and remaining so, until one day we can come back. This means we shall have to make sure that we place our eldest children: Anthony (13) and Teresa (10) in secure hands for at least a period of 5 years – where they can stay in secondary school till university. Not a boarding school – we suspect this might not do for children with a ghetto background like theirs. If there were a family in England that could keep them (we would pay for them) we could move about knowing they won't suffer. We must always be in Africa anyhow except for brief excursions like this. If you know of a family or someone who could scout for us, please help us contact them. We could then fix it so that the children go over to begin the new school year in October 1961. They are useful in housework, and so they wouldn't sit around idle.

Our very best wishes and love as always,

Yours,
Ezekiel

1 *Shaka Zulu.*

2 This was a possibility Mphahlele entertained before he was offered the job in Paris.

Offa
14 June 1961

Dear Makhudu

Your wire and letter came. Struck me dumb, they did. How casually Tennyson can treat a serious promise like this. Actually, Mdudu deals with Scholarships in the UF but being near Makiwane, he might have been told we are so helplessly divided in Nigeria, one doesn't know where to begin. As a last desperate effort I wrote immediately to Tennyson. 'Desperate' because for all one knows he may be flying to and fro over Africa right now.

Only yesterday I had a letter from Kojo Cann in Accra – Manager of Kaneshie Technical College. This man came to me after my talk on South Africa at the University College of Ghana in December and said to me and Mdudu and 'Molotsi that he was so moved that he was prepared to pay £100 a year for a SA student to go to the University College – to the maximum of £400. He doesn't say in the letter whether the boys in Accra have found a student, but he says he has just given the first £100 to the University College and also that the student can live with him during the vacation. I have today written to him to use his influence to get his government to bring out the boys; gave him Gama's address in Salisbury. We shall see.

I am meeting a Reginald Green on Saturday 20, in Ibadan and will speak to him about this because in the letter which he wrote says he would like to meet me again (we met in Philadelphia and then in Accra). He says he has been hammering on the World University Service to give SA's Scholarships, and is succeeding. He may suggest something.

Good article you wrote for D E straight from the shoulder. Too kind to Ogon, though, I thought. To say as he does the Liberal Party is the best organization ... etc, is pure nonsense. He, Oloko and of course your victim, Omer Cooper (poor chap, he has been out of SA for 8 years and is out of touch) are all so woolly. Trouble is that although I believe ultimately it's the independent African States that will tackle SA they are at the moment blinkered by the old missionary dogmas etc in their view of SA, the view you want to haul down back to earth. 'Bringing SA down to her knees' as Thonrovia says can be given so many interpretations in terms of method. Of course one can't be more than mildly critical of one's hosts, which is what I know you were on your guard against.

Your wire about Muriel was exciting. Is she there? We hope this time it is *it* and no less. One years' enforced bachelordom is no plaything.

You have by now made your acquaintance, I'm sure, with PL of Blood Lane fame. The guy who believes in bashing his wife's nose – now and again, and whose moodiness freezes all conversation and makes it irrelevant. I hope things are all right now between him and his wife after the rough pulling up he got here from you-know-who who administered it like a virago of an aunt.

Let's know if Muriel and the gang have come.

Yours ever,

Zeke

New York

3 July 1961

Dear Zeke:

Delighted to hear about your new job in Paris – which means we might see each other sooner, as you'll get over here, or I'll get over there. It's only 4 or 5 hours flight. Putting off the U.S. lectures is O.K. as you can do them later or get others after you are settled in Paris you'll probably see Bloke Modisane and Todd Matshikiza in London. Bloke is becoming quite an actor, was in *THE BLACKS*, and now another play, he writes me. His address: 27 Parkhill Road, Hampstead, London N. W. 3. Also in London I think you'd like Rosey Pool, Dutch authority on Negro poetry, who has lectured in the U. S.: 23-a Highpoint, North Hill, London, N. 6. She does BBC shows on us, too. Nice jolly chubby lady who was Anne Frank's teacher in hiding during war. Peter Abrahams was here last week, on assignment for *HOLIDAY* magazine to do a piece on the African diplomats in Washington. Councilman Parker from Cape Town came through on his way around the world. And almost every week I have a visitor or two from some part of Africa. Today the contract came for the African poetry anthology. So if you've got new poetry, or know of anybody good in Nigeria who has, tell them to airmail it to me this month. Mabel Imoukhede I've written. If you know her, tell her *dépêches-vous, s'il vous plait,*[1] and send me some poetry, as I've heard of her but never read a word. Nicol in Sierre Leone sent some beautiful things. Okara, too. So it will be a good anthology. At AMSAG last week, they tell Isaacs caught hell from the other speakers for writing in the *NEW YORKER* that Africans and American Negroes didn't like each other. I never heard tell of such myself.

Drop me a card from Europe.

Best ever.

Sincerely,

Langston Hughes

[1] 'Hurry up, please'

23 October 1961

Dear Zeke,

It is a long time since I wrote to you and I trust that you remember our correspondence about my thesis on African Writing in English. I feel rather ashamed, after re-reading *Down Second Avenue* about the conditions under which you studied for your degrees, that I have so little time to work on my thesis, when all I have to do is to run a business and look after a couple of small children.

First of all I would like to take this opportunity of congratulating you on your appointment as director of the African programme of the Congress of Cultural Freedom. When will you be moving to Paris? How do you and your family feel about another move?

Since I wrote to you last I have been doing some reading, and once again have many questions to ask you. I can imagine how busy you are with your current work and preparing for your new work, but hope you will find me a little spare time.

Any chance of getting those Dickens dramatic adaptations which you once promised me?

I still haven't read your thesis. Up to now I have had little time to go to the libraries, but will concentrate on that next year when my children go to nursery school. Till now I have been buying, begging and borrowing all available books and magazines to read at home.

You once suggested that you would have preferred a discussion of African writing in English as part of a thesis including white writers. It sounds tempting but would be far too vast a subject to be accepted as a thesis. There is no reason, however – and I certainly intend doing so – not to draw comparisons where indicated. How could I avoid, for instance, comparing the characterization of whites by Africans and vice versa? 'One gets tired of reading about people as symbols of a group,' as you wrote in your article last year in the *New Statesman*, which I read with great interest. You apply it to the South African white writers, but in many cases I have come across it can apply to Africans writing about whites as well. I must tell you quite frankly that I do not entirely agree with your opinion of the popular *Drum* writers. I am rather impressed by some of Can Themba's writing. Perhaps my attitude towards magazine writing is coloured by my career as syndication agent – I still regard a newspaper and magazine as a commodity, the success of which is estimated in cash. I suppose I shall have to forget about that when it comes to writing my thesis. Incidentally, who are the writers you mention who left off working for *Drum* when it turned popular?

What is your opinion – off the record – of Noni Jabavu? Can you please give me any information about Richard Rive and Arthur Maimane?

I must thank you very much indeed for putting the publishers of *Black Orpheus* in touch with me. I'll be writing to them today, asking for their collection of your short stories. Apart from that they have sent me Nos. 4 & 7 and I shall be asking for No. 8. Do any other issues contain any of your writing?

The next question sounds rather silly, but seeing that the title of my thesis limits it to Africans I have to ask it. I know it sounds rather like, for instance, limiting a work to all English novelists born on a Thursday. I feel a little better about it after you admit in your *New Statesman* article that African writers have moved into a separate cultural stream. Well, after all that introduction, here is the question: Are Rive and James Matthews regarded as Africans or Coloured in as far as my thesis is concerned?

To come back once more to your *New Statesman* article: Your conclusion that African culture is a virile one becomes obvious when comparing your article with the rather watery ones of the other Commonwealth writers in the series? Incidentally, half the notes I have taken so far seem to be about Mphahlele!

I'm rather interested to know whether you wrote 'The Suitcase' while in Nigeria?

I am impressed with your poem 'The Immigrant' but am not as yet prepared to comment on it. In the *New Statesman* article you say which novelists influenced you. What about poets, apart from Herrick whom you mention in *Down Second Avenue*?

Have you perhaps a copy of your talk on the significance of the Accra conference in relation to Negro writers in Africa? I came across a reference to it in *Fighting Talk*.

Have you any information about a congress of Negro writers in Rome in April? Do you know whether the Society of African Culture of Alioun Diop would be of any use to me, or would it not deal with English writing?

In conclusion I would like to say that I hope I am not approaching my subject with either 'an exaggerated sense of mission or an excessive love of the exotic for its own sake'!

I look forward to hearing from you in due course.

With best regards,

Yours sincerely,

Ursula Barnett[1]

[1] Ursula Barnett was awarded her PhD in English Literature at the University of Cape Town in 1971. Her book, based on the thesis, titled *A Vision of Order: A Study of Black South African Writing in English 1914-1980*, was published by Sinclair Brown (Cambridge) and the University

of Massachusetts Press (Amherst) in 1984, and by Maskew Miller Longman (Cape Town) in 1985.

22 November 1961

Dear Jack,

The above Congress [Congress Pour La Liberté de la Culture], for whom I now work as director of the African Project, are thinking of publishing a journal to provide a medium of creative expression for non-white writers in South Africa. A friend of mine told them that there were a few African writers in S.A. who had nowhere to publish their stuff.

My first reaction to the suggestion was that we don't want to widen the split between white and non-white writers which tradition has forced on us. And as *CONTRAST* is a multi-racial organ, I wondered if they could give it sufficient financial backing, to enable it to give more space for non-white writing and perhaps to appear more frequently in the process.

The Executive Secretary of Congress has asked me to find out if in the first place *CONTRAST* does need money; in the second place would it accept such financial support if it could increase the chances of accommodating more good non-white writers and stimulate such writing by various devices: literary contests, writers club around *CONTRAST* etc, and third, if *CONTRAST* said 'no' to the above, do you think S.A. can carry another multi-racial literary journal? I strongly suspect it could not.

Incidentally, what happened to the writers group that was formed in Cape Town sometime ago? Peter Clarke, Alex la Guma, Jan Rabie etc were involved. Do you know whom I can write to for information?

Hoping to hear from you,

Yours sincerely,
Ezekiel Mphahlele

Cape Town
30 November 1961

Dear Zeke,

I was extremely interested in your letter and happy to hear that you are doing such a responsible and constructive job. Writing is a tender plant and no amount of cultivation can *make* a writer. But a great deal can be done to improve the climate in which a developing literature grows, especially in Africa. So I guess it must be regarded as a long-range task and the flowers, when they come, may look a little strange.

I think I can back up your opinion that a widening of any division between white and non-white writers would be regrettable. I personally don't know of any writer of any race who wants this division or who puts his race or colour before his ideals as a writer. This goes even for people on the far right in this Afrikaans camp who accept coloured writers like Philander, Small and Peterson with complete goodwill, publish and read their work and include it in their best anthologies. In addition, many liberal Afrikaans writers of talent are coming to the fore. Among the English-language writers of all races there is a broad and profound camaraderie and already such a lively movement that it needs only encouragement and critical guidance to develop into a significant literature.

Editing the first year of *Contrast* has given me considerable confidence in this view. There is talent everywhere, thought, vitality, passion, and optimism. What we need is to provide training and a platform, to build up all along the front rising critical and technical standards, to establish professional criteria and pride in the growth of our own local tradition.

Many people did not believe that *Contrast* would last a year. But it has done so, steadily improving, I think. It has been a difficult struggle and we have financed it largely out of our own resources together with a few small grants from cultural bodies. The editorial work has been considerable (and unpaid).

Replying to your questions, our magazine does need money and with financial support it is well placed to stimulate non-white writing and to publish the work of non-white writers on an increasing scale. At present we run to just on 100 pages an issue and aim at paying between £1 and £2 a page for contributions. This is comparatively low pay and I know from long experience that higher pay is a very real incentive to writers in the early stages. With more money we could increase the number of pages or enlarge the format and I am sure this could be done without lowering standards. This is very important, I think. Already we have established a feeling that it is a matter of pride to get into *Contrast*, and we want to keep that up. Most of our material we discuss with the writers in detail; stories, poems and articles are re-written and improved by the authors after careful criticism and analysis. Even with rejected MSS of promise we like to send criticism and suggestions. It is a very big job. Your idea of writers' clubs around the magazine is an excellent one and would mean that material would already have been discussed and improved before reaching us; it would also break down the isolation which is a bugbear of writers in a scattered community.

So the answer is: Yes, *Contrast* does need money and is well placed to forward the aims of the Congress, as you express them. We already have two English and two Afrikaans literary journals with a strong academic tendency and *Contrast* is the only one to cater predominantly for the creative writer. I don't think either the material available or the readership at this stage would warrant another literary magazine. Competition is always to the good, but I think the aim in the present circumstances should be to enlarge or bring out *Contrast* eventually as a bi-monthly, to increase the readership and bring down the price.

For your information, the magazine is owned and controlled by a registered non-profit guarantee company and its only object is to further the interests of literature in South Africa.

The S.A. Arts Union is still active and you could write for information to Jan Rabie or his wife Marjorie Wallace at 6 Cheviot Place, Green Point, CT.

By the way, when are you going to let us have a story for *Contrast*? I have received your book of stories from Nigeria and passed them on to Owen Williams for a review in the *Cape Times* and also for a crit in our magazine. I am looking forward to reading the book as soon as Owen is finished. Best of luck.

Please give my best wishes to François Bondy when you see him.

Yours sincerely

Jack Cope

Nigeria

11 December 1961

Dear Jack,

It was good of you to write at length on *Contrast*. Thanks.

The Executive Secretary is acting on your letter, and is of course very keen to be able to help. We shall keep you informed about things and hope you will be patient. *Hou moed* – not that you lack it of course.

Please tell Uys Krige I thank him warmly for his note. I shall write him as soon as I can. I'm working on four short stories, and will see what I can contribute for *Contrast*.

Kindest regards.

Yours sincerely,

Zeke

1962

Nigeria

4 January 1962

My dear Langston,

Bon ante! This is to ask you on behalf of Mbari in Ibadan to be one of the three judges of their literary contest which congress is sponsoring. I am one judge myself. The idea is to have the MSS elected by local persons in East and Central West and South Africa before we get them. Only English MSS.

Could you please help us, and can I have your reply in quick time so that we are able to put our notices in the African poems!

In haste.

Yours very sincerely,

Zeke

New York

Dear Zeke,

I'm just back from Nigeria to find your letter among a mountain of mail. Of course, I'll be happy to be a judge for the Mbari literary Contest.

With cordial regards,

Hastily but Sincerely,

Langston Hughes

Paris

25 January 1962

Dear Richard,

Thanks for your letter in which you indicate your project and future plans. We shall consider this and I shall let you know in due time whether we can undertake to sponsor you for a whole year or for part of a year.

We are having a writers' conference at Makerere, Uganda.[1] This is scheduled for the first week of August. Is it possible, in any case, for you to attend this conference? You will be the guest of Mbari Writers' and Artists' Club in Ibadan, who are calling the conference under our sponsorship. Have you ever received any literature or information about Mbari? In case you have not, I am asking Mr Ulli Beier to send you a few things. We plan to have 22 writers at this conference from different parts of Africa, for the main purpose of giving them an opportunity to meet and know one another. I am working out a programme and if you think you would like to go to Makerere, I shall let you know what exactly we plan to do for that week. It would be very good to have someone from South Africa direct as well as exiles. I am also inviting Alex la Guma.

Best wishes,

Yours sincerely,

Zeke

P.S. Whatever you decide to do, when you write to me, would you also at the same time write to Ulli Beier, P. O. Box 68, Oshogbo, Nigeria.

[1] The reference here is to the first international African writers' conference, held at Makerere University College, Kampala, Uganda, in June 1962. The conference was held under the auspices of Nigeria's Mbari Writers' and Artists' Club and was sponsored by the Congress for Cultural Freedom.

Paris

14 February 1962

Dear Richard,

I am sorry you will not be able to attend the Makerere meeting. I think it will be a wonderful experience for those who will be there.

We shall let you know as soon as possible what we have been able to arrange for your projected travel. Is it possible for you to send some of your short-stories, published and unpublished, to *Encounter*? The editor is Melvin Lasky, *Encounter*, 25 Haymarket, London. S.W.1. This would probably lead to a story being published by him. And, of course, *Encounter* wields tremendous influence. Please treat this as a serious suggestion.

Good-bye for now.

Yours sincerely,

E. Mphahlele

14 March 1962

Dear Langston,

It was very good of you to consent to be judge for the Mbari literary contest.

You will be receiving shortly my new book *The African Image* which is out March 23rd. I have tried as much as possible to make it controversial so as to stimulate and even provoke angry but useful discussion. You see, so many of these things I speak about do need to enter the dialogue of Africa, stripped of all the clichés.

But this is not what I wanted to write you about. Mbari is calling a conference of English-speaking African writers at Makerere College, Kampala, Uganda, June 8 to 17, 1962. After this Mbari will celebrate its anniversary. I am still waiting for Ulli to give me the date for this latter event. It would be very good if you could come to the conference to give a talk on the Negro literary scene in your country: something in the nature of a brief (approximately 45 minutes), sharp and explicit statement, to be followed by discussions. We are also inviting Ralph Ellison. I only have the London edition of his *Invisible Man*, and so cannot send his letter direct. Can you pass it on?

I have not received your latest poem: I think I heard you say last November that it was on its way.

Please let me know within a week or so if you will be available as a guest of Mbari on June 8 and soon after.

Best wishes,

E. MPHAHLELE

March 1962

Dear Zeke,

As far as I know now, I can come to Uganda in early June. My recent song play, *BLACK NATIVITY*, is going to Italy in late June for the Spoleto Festival of Two Worlds, and I intend to be in Europe then, so I could come to Africa first. Thanks so much for thinking of me in regards to the Mbari Conference.

Just last night I wrote Wole Soyinka, sending him J. Saunders Redding's article from the *AFRO-AFRICAN* mentioning his plays and Mbari, and comparing current Nigerian artistic activity to that of Harlem in the 20's. Redding is, as you no doubt know, in Africa now for some months of lecturing. Will he be in Uganda, too? He is a stimulating speaker and (contrary to myself) an intellectual. Ellison is, too.

Your letter I've forwarded on to Ralph. His address is:

Mr. Ralph Ellison,

New York 31, N.Y., USA.

(Phone: WATKINS 6-6804)

I don't know if he's in town or not, as I got no answer by phone today.

THE AFRICAN IMAGE sounds exciting. I'm looking forward to it. I loved *DOWN SECOND AVENUE*

Hastily, but with cordial regards,

Sincerely,

Langston Hughes

Paris

19 March 1962

My dear Richard

Of course I consider it a great honour to be invited by you to write a foreword to your *African Songs*. How could it be otherwise? I shall get down to it and send it to Seven Seas and a copy to you. You probably know that they are bringing out my *Down 2nd Avenue* in English.

Congratulations on your arrival – and in Sweden also![1]

We want to discuss actual African works at the Makerere get-together – now scheduled for June 8-17 – and I was going to write to you this morning anyhow to ask for 3 of your best short stories for this purpose. I can't lay my hands on the *Contact* story, so I should be glad if you could send me typescripts of all three. Can you do this soon? Please.

We shall let you know about the other thing in due time.

Best wishes,

Yours ever,

E. Mphahlele

1 Mphahlele is referring to Rive being published.

17 April 1962

Dear Richard,

I am enclosing a copy of a letter from Farfield Foundation to whom we usually apply for financial assistance for extensive projects such as yours.[1]

Would you please write to me and let me know what your reply is to the questions in the last 2 paragraphs. Please feel free to tell me everything.

Best wishes,

Yours ever,

Zeke

[1] Years later it was established that the Congress for Cultural Freedom received CIA funds channelled via the Farfield Foundation.

18 April 1962

Dear Jack,

It is not easy to remember when last I read a good love story by an African: it must be a very long time ago. As you say, the current ones are simply bad.

There are Bloke Modisane, c/o Transcription Center, 4-5 Norfolk Street, London W. O. 2; J. Arthur Maimane, (Reuters, 84 Fleet Street, London E.C.4). These are South Africans. Hutchinson is practically dormant. I have tried to stir him, kick him, insult him out of his depression and inertia, but all in vain.

For my part, I haven't attempted a love story since my first poor efforts such as in *Man Must Live*, and I can't bear to look at them again. I simply couldn't write one now if I tried, although I have a plot for one in a Nigerian setting. It would take too long for me to produce and so cannot even ask Paul Neff Verlag to wait.

Sorry I can't be more helpful.

Yours sincerely,

E. MPHAHLELE

Paris

23 April 1962

Dear Jack,

It was good of you to reply so promptly to my request. Thank you very much for the entries for the literary contest. My judgement coincides with yours.

As for the South African writers 'with strong political opinions', who refused to participate on the grounds of our classification based on colour, I can only remark as follows: until we can find a more suitable criterion for classifying competitors, in such a way that the less privileged candidate can enter without feeling that his linguistic equipment cannot stand against that of the privileged candidate (most often white), we must use this convenient criterion. I should hesitate to use this criterion in throwing a competition for the novel. One's formal education and linguistic equipment are not so severely on trial in the writing of a novel as in the short story. Would you not agree with this paradox? The canvas for the short story is so restricted that if one's language fails there is little else that can save it because here language is so much more tied up with theme. One can sprawl in a novel to such an extent that the weakness of one's language comes less and less jarring, and less of an obstacle as the reader takes in the pace, the measure and the impact of the people, the action and the setting as a whole. I shall be grateful for any suggestions you may care to throw across for our future contest meantime.

Thank you again for your co-operation in the immense task of handling so many hundreds of entries that reached you.

Yours with best wishes,

Ezekiel Mphahlele

Paris

3 May 1962

Dear Richard,

I am enclosing this from a man with a name he writes in a most irritating manner. I can't decipher it – will you? He remembers me and I don't; not while his name is in such outrageous handwriting. I pass him on to you as you are mentioned in despatches.

Haven't nailed John Hunt yet.[1] Will do so in due time. Ribs tells me you are installed at 106.

I just thought I should let you know that we are near financial Zero mark as a result of Peter's and Amos's stay, followed by P and yours and then a third. I have had to write a firm letter to another in London, who wanted to send his niece to us and another and he wants to come in July. I have told him we cannot house anybody now 'till we go back to Africa,[2] except a friend of Ribs' who is coming to stay with the children while we go for a weekend in Geneva. So, I am sorry to say so, but when you come back to Paris you will have to go to a bed-and-breakfast place. Please let us know in good time so that we can find one to be ready for your arrival. It is possible to find a cheap affair for about 25 Fr. bed and breakfast.

I never thought I would feel that my 'generosity' has cost me such a lot. I know normally I should not worry, but Paris is viciously abnormal.

Sorry again. Am reviewing your book in fat print in the *Bulletin* now in production.

You may find it obnoxious, who knows these days?

Best wishes,

Love

Zeke

[1] John Hunt was an administrative official for the Congress for Cultural Freedom, the organisation Mphahlele worked for in Paris, Nigeria and Kenya.

[2] At this stage Mphahlele was planning to move to Nairobi, Kenya, to establish the Chemchemi Creative Centre.

18 May 1962

Dear Zeke:

I have been trying to write you for weeks to tell you how much I was absorbed by your *AFRICAN IMAGE*, and especially by your discussion of negritude with which conclusions I agree and what you say about African-American relations of color. A fine and thought provoking book! I hope it is soon published here. *THE LIVING AND THE DEAD* I liked, too, with the Clarke drawings. And I would have written sooner, but I have been in California helping out my 86-year-old uncle with his affairs. And stopped a couple of other places on route back home. So traveling about, it is well nigh impossible to keep up with my mail. Then when I get home, 50-11 things of an URGENT nature have piled up to do. And I still have two most pressing deadlines to complete before I can take off for Uganda. How I will make it, I don't know. I hear tell Bloke will be going to Uganda. Good! He's a talented fellow. Did you ever hear from Ellison? I haven't seen or talked to him. He's probably still teaching out of town. First copy of my *FIGHT FOR FREEDOM, The Story of the NAACP*, came today, just one. But I'll probably have copies by the time I leave, so I'll bring you one to Africa. Of my other books, I sent copies to Uganda already, marked to HOLD pending my arrival. Nobody has ever told me what I am expected to do at the Conference except be there. But at least I'm prepared to give *a reading of my poems*, if desired, and to talk briefly about *fellow writers of color*. Or on the subject of the *Negro in the American theatre* or the use *of black folklore in writing*.

Right after Makerere, I'm invited by the USIS to the opening of the new American library in Accra, which means I cannot linger in Kampala or go to Kenya as I would like to do.

Langston Hughes

P.S. Finally got Ralph Ellison on the phone ... just now, midnight ... and he says he had to decline invite to Uganda, pressure of work, and having been away from home most of year at University of Chicago teaching.

Paris

22 May 1962

Dear Langston,

Thanks for your nice letter.

I am sure I wrote to you – evidently during your wanderings – to say please give a 45-minute statement on the American Negro literary scene: trends; the relevancy of protest; problem of roots and identity if and where they are relevant to the creative process (if the problem is not relevant, cut it out!). I'm going to insist that we do not spend useful time on sterile arguments about negritude. Only where and as it affects the writers' activity.

We have times for the reading of works by their writers, and you will please go into the box when the sessions come. Thanks for sending your books to Makerere.

Pity you can't attend Mbari's first anniversary immediately after Makerere – from what you say in your letter.

Good luck.

Yours ever,
Ezekiel Mphahlele

Paris

24 May 1962

Dear Friend [Langston Hughes],

This is to invite you to Mbari's first Anniversary to be held at Mbari Centre, Ibadan, June 23 or 24. 1962, which will be immediately after the Makerere Conference.

Please let us know at Makerere or earlier if you will be able to attend. If you do we shall look after your maintenance during this period. This includes your stay for a week if you would like to attend the writer's workshop we shall be conducting at Mbari on 25-29 June. Please send a reply to Mbari, Ibadan, or else let us know at Makerere.

Yours sincerely,

Ezekiel Mphahlele

Note: Accra 28th of June. July 4 to 8 Lagos ticket in Kampala. We will straighten up your BOAC trip. Françoise will get down to it on Monday 28th when she comes back.

Zeke.

New York

27 May 1962

Dear Zeke

WHERE and WHEN is MBARI'S first anniversary celebration to be held? Please let me know by return air post.

If in Makerere, perhaps I can stay a few days longer.

If in Ibadan, perhaps I can be there, as the USIS has invited me to Accra in late June for the opening of the new American Library there – however, the invite has not been finally confirmed. If I go, I could, of course, come on down to Ibadan.

But NOBODY'S told me when or where the Mbari party is. I'd love to be present, if I can.

And will you be in Kampala when I get there on June 7th?

My *BLACK NATIVITY* opens at Spoleto June 24 – 70 miles from Rome. Maybe on your way back to Europe, you could stop over and see it. Negro folksongs used to retell a traditional Christian story heretofore always presented as white. It's dark now! I expect to stop in Rome before or after (or both) I go to Ghana.

Let me know about Mbari. And Wole?

Sincerely,
Langston Hughes

New York
28 May 1962

Dear Zeke:

Our letters crossed, as I'd just posted one to you yesterday asking for time and place of the Mbari celebration. As I informed you, U. S. Information Service has asked me to go to Ghana for the opening of a new American Library there on June 28-29, and then wish me to go on down to Ibadan for a few days. I see no reason why I should not go to Ibadan first, in time for the Mbari Anniversary, and perhaps stay there until the 26th or 27th of June. Since the U.S.I.S. will be paying my fare Rome-Accra-Ibadan, there would be no expense to Mbari. Only thing is I would have to miss the opening of my *BLACK NATIVITY* at Spoleto on June 24th, but since it will be there a month, I can catch a performance on my Northward return from West Africa. I would say then, that I would leave Kampala on June 18th so as to stop in Cairo to see the Pyramids, thence on to Rome, and down to Ibadan. All of which would dove-tail o.k., I believe, as USIS is giving me an open ticket from Rome as to time. And I am glad to get the information from you today, so I can arrange the routing in New York before I leave. My BOAC ticket N. Y.-London-Entebbe is o.k. and I have it in hand, so I don't think you-all need to do anything more about it in Paris. But I've still to get Ghana and Nigeria visas, as the o.k. and information for that part of the trip just came today, both yours and the State Department. Samuel Allen, so perhaps you'd like to invite him to the Mbari Anniversary; address: Samuel Allen, Legal Department, USIS, Washington 25, D. C. He is, as you know, an interesting poet, and a negritude-ite. So can liven up arguments. I'll be seeing you in Kampala.

Sincerely,
Langston Hughes

New York

1 June 1962

Dear Zeke:

Since the latest announcements to reach me, dated Paris, May 24 which I received yesterday gives the dates of Kampala as June 11-17, I am leaving New York a couple of days later. I have SO MUCH to complete before taking off I can use the extra time to great advantage.

I am now ticketed to arrive in Entebbe on BOAC Flight No. 163 at 9:30 AM the morning of Saturday, June 9. Please be so kind as to advise the folks at Make College of this change in time, since I'd not know whom to write there myself.

I am looking forward to seeing you. It is all worked out with USIS for me to get to Ibadan in time for the Mbari celebration. They will fly me down from Rome to Lagos. And on the 27th I have to go to Accra for the opening of their new American Library there, for which Samuel Allen is flying over, too.

Cordial regards,

Sincerely yours,

Langston Hughes

Freetown, Sierra Leone

27 July 1962

Dear Richard,

Here is the piece for the foreword to your book. I have sent it to Seven Seas. If there are any comments to make, please feel free to do so. You can let me know and I can write to Seven Seas to effect the changes you suggest. I hope this is the general statement you required.

For purposes of a reply:

Aug. 4 – 16: Mbari Private Bag 5180 Ibadan, Nigeria

Aug. 17 – 24: c/o P. O. Box 30022 Nairobi

Aug. 25 – 30: c/o P. O. Box 2239 Dar-es-Salaam.

Best wishes

for ever,

Zeke

Cape Town

15 October 1962

Dear Zeke,

I received your cable and the South African entries are on the way to you by Second Class Airmail. They should reach you in a few days. I am sorry if my delay has held you up in any way. I allowed entrants to come in after the deadline and have been in touch with some of the more promising ones in the hope of getting better material – and this batch is the best available. You will probably be disappointed, as I was. There is a great deal of writing being done with strong and moving currents of thought in evidence. But most of the entries had not overcome the basic requirement of mastering the language. Quite a few of the more advanced writers, especially those with a strong political opinions, refused to participate on the grounds that their colour or absence of colour had nothing to do with them *as writers* and they objected to being classified on racial or any other grounds. This I could not argue away. It seems to be a point of view that will have to be reckoned with in future. At all events, it has meant that our South African entry probably has suffered by the omission of these writers.

The number of entries was very large, running into hundreds, but out of these I have judged it worthwhile to send you only eight stories and poems by nine entrants. In my opinion, the best entry sent to me consisted of two poems by Dennis Brutus, 'Kneeling Before You' and 'A Troubadour'. I also liked Leslie B Sehume's poem, 'My Pass'; K. A. Nortje's 'Nothing Unusual', and J. F. Sithole's 'My Slum'.

Of the stories I liked best 'The Grasshopper's Playmate' by S. L. Lesoene Rathebe, and to a lesser degree 'Hill of Fools' by R. L. Peteni.

Here is the list of the material I have sent you:

C.S. Jacobs (Cory) Box 182, Ermelo, Tvl. Vignette (story), 'We shall be men' (poem) E Walter-Girout, 42 McKenzie Rd. Durban.

R.L. Peteni, 31 Mtimka St. New Brighton. P.E. 'Hill of Fools' (story), 'Journey into Lunastan' (poem).

Leslie B Sehume, Box 3413, Johannesburg. 'Happy Holiday', and 'Joe's Last Journey' (stories), 'My Pass', 'I cry', 'South Africa', and 'Banned' (poems).

Benson J Masebenza, Orlando High School, Box 17, Orlando, Jhb. Poems.

Dennis Brutus, 22 Shell St. Port Elizabeth. 'Kneeling Before You', and 'A Troubadour' (poems).

S.L. Lesoene Rathebe, 71 B Zone 3, Meadowlands, Jhb, 'The Grasshopper's Playmate' (story).

K.A. Nortje, 2, 18th Avenue, Elsies River, Cape. Poems.

G Muthukrishna, Box 142, Port Shepstone, Natal. 'The Greater Bond' (story).

L Washington Chaparadza, Box 26, Darwendale, S Rhodesia. 'I'll make a ladder' (poem).

Miss Bhindoo Singh, 28 Salvia Rd, Asherville, Durban. 'The Awakening' (story) Aubrey C Mokoto, 98 (a) Vincent Rd, Meadowlands, Johannesburg. 'Across the Tracks' (story).

With best wishes,

Sincerely

Jack Cope

27 November 1962

Dear Zeke:

Fog delayed my jet plane for 18 hours in Los Angeles, so I am just back yesterday from California. But have carefully read all the material you sent me. I suppose you are aware that the manuscripts came to me by boat mail, arriving just before I left for the Coast a week ago, although your letter telling me they were coming (dated October 26th) came by air and was here two or three weeks before the stories and poems came. I think you must have meant to send the manuscripts by air, too, but someone in your office neglected to put the proper postage, or to stamp the envelope PAR AVION. At any rate here are my choices in order of preference:

SHORT STORIES

1st Prize: A KAFFER WOMAN J. Arthur Maimane

2nd Prize: THE SITUATION Bloke Modisane

3rd Prize: THE BED SITTER Gaston Bart Williams

POETRY

1st Prize: DEBUT M.J.C. Echeruo

2nd Prize: MY PASS. Leslie B. Sehume

3rd Prize: NOTHING UNUSUAL K.A. Nortje

Since you request the material returned by Registered Mail, I must wait until the Post Office opens tomorrow to register it, and will then send it to you by air.

I regret that most of the short stories seem to me not very good. I wish Christiana A. Aidoo's[1] tale were less of a sketch and more dramatically or poetically told, since it has most interesting local color in it. The three I have chosen are good narratives, I think, with Maimane's being much the best of all.

With cordial regards to you,

Sincerely yours,

Langston Hughes

[1] Later Ama Ata Aidoo, the Ghanaian novelist.

Paris

28 December 1962

Dear Langston,

The judgements of the three of us were pretty close. You had Maimane as first and Bloke as second, and Ulli had Bloke as first. I thought Bloke's story has greater breadth than Maimane's and rather found the latter's too hackneyed. I thought I should vote for Miss Aidoo for third because although hers is amateurish, it captures local colour quite well. We are all agreed on the first for poetry. But you differ with us on the second. I found rather more meat in Brutus' poetry than the slight one you thought worthy of second place. This communiqué will indicate how I have reconciled our results. It seemed fair to me that Maimane and Miss Aidoo should both take third place which does not mean sharing the prize but each receiving L30. Thank you very much for all you have done so promptly amidst all you travels, lecturings and creative writing.

I am rather excited by the production of *Beyond the Blues* by Rosy Pool. There is a real good stuff in it. I shall be sending you a copy of Gerald Moore's lovely book which has just come out – *Seven African Writers*. It makes history in the field of African writing and I am circulating it among all the Makerere participants as complimentary copies. I must again apologize for not having been able to get in your talk but I think you will like our little brochure.

Best wishes and compliments of the season.

Yours sincerely,

Ezekiel Mphahlele

1963

Paris

5 February 1963

Dear Dennis [Duerden],

It was good to be able to take part in your ICA programme. Dipoko[1] was particularly excellent and it was worth bringing him along. Maybe the problem was we tried to cover too wide a field such as the questions represented.

What I am writing about mainly is on a different matter altogether. I was very angry the day we talked about the bulletin – the three of us in the car. And I felt so depressed that I went to your house to collect my bags.

The thing that depressed me so much was the way you insisted that Lewis should not do the *Bulletin* even in his free time because not only did you 'control' his out-of-office hours but you think he will serve you better if he does creative writing during that time.[2] And this, after Lewis had offered to do it in his free time. Inasmuch as I am the last person ever to want Lewis to do a job like the *Bulletin* for peanuts, you are the last person I ever expected would have it in him to take on someone as a protégé. Frankly, it reminded me of the ghastly liberals of S.A. who love to protect their 'natives' and to think for them. An unfair image? Maybe; but there it is. And Lewis's silence made me wonder if you had thought it all out together before. But how could he then offer his services for £50? More important still, Lewis, on his own account, does articles for the press and this is what would have to be postponed if he did the *Bulletin*, *not creative writing*, although you say it would help you if he did this during his free time.

I should imagine Lewis is perfectly able to decide what is good for him. That's his own affair. I shall not represent his demand for £50 to John Hunt as I thought I would: not because I think he is worth *less*, but because you are both arguing on different premises and the spirit of the whole *Bulletin* has been muddied by this and I shall, without detracting in any way from Lewis's greater ability to do the *Bulletin*, take it back to edit it myself.

So much for my anger, Dennis, and I thought you should know how I felt. I should not take the trouble to parade it if I didn't have a high regard for you.

Best regards. Yours sincerely,

Zeke

1 Mbelle Sonne Dipoko, a Cameroonian writer.

[2] The *Bulletin* was *South Africa: Information and Analysis*, edited in Paris initially by Mphahlele, then by Lewis Nkosi, and later again by Mphahlele.

Nairobi
31 October 1963

My dear Dennis,

I have been intending to write to you, and Frances' letter jolted me out of my reverie.[1] 'Reverie' is hardly the word, though, as I have been busy establishing a physical presence here – neo-colonizing the place. We now have premises: 2 offices, an art gallery, two rooms for a reference library and a writers' workshop respectively – all for a rental of £546 a year. Can you come across that anywhere in London? Shows you how civilized Africa is – as you know. How long it will remain civilized depends on how prosperous people become, alas.

Elimu Njau the Tanganyikan painter who is in charge of our visual arts section, is exhibiting for our official opening on November 16. We are set to put into effect the suggestions you made in the art section of my *Africa Report*, staying clear of the Fine Arts departments of the university colleges except when we want to exhibit the students and in our relations with them as individuals. I am setting up a permanent writers' workshop, and have written the enclosed letter to the Kenya Broadcasting Corporation. I should like the co-operation of TBS and UBS, but if KBC bites and sends a man, we shall not have anything to ask of the other two beyond offering to send them scripts that are produced, from time to time under our sponsorship. What do you suggest – in the matter of writing and in your line of things?

This brings me to what John Nagenda said to me yesterday. He said you asked him to organize some programmes for you from time to time and asked if we had a tape recorder here. We are buying one, and I shall be only too glad to help him with recording facilities, if he can find the personnel to speak. You know what a willing native I am! Perhaps you can suggest what we can do to pad off street noises – not bad but audible, and our rooms are big or small enough. By the way he is in the same building as we: we are on the 6th floor.

How did the Dore-Lewis project go?[2] I'm keen to know. Someone wrote to me from the States to say H.D. succeeded in insulting everyone in West Africa and the river vomited him out on the banks, as we say in Bantu: meaning he did not get what he wanted and had to leave in a hurry. Is this true? Somehow it sounds like a rumour in an Orlando suburban train (ask Lewis about that).

Please send your transcripts direct this way: 2 copies each.

Before I fling another foreign metaphor at you – perhaps Swahili – Arabic – I should stop. But not before I tell you that the family is settling down very well, the whole tribe of 5 have been placed in schools and Rebecca is happier than I have seen for years. She says you must come and stay with us whenever the Vasco da Gama winds blow you this way.

Love to Rhoda, the kids and yourself.

Yours ever,
Ezekiel Mphahlele

1 Frances Ademola, who worked at the Transcription Centre office.

2 H Dore and Lewis Nkosi were involved in filming interviews with African writers that were later broadcast on National Educational Television in the US.

Director General
Kenya Broadcasting Corporation
(enclosed in letter to Duerden)

Dear Mr. Cahan,

This is to introduce Chemchemi Cultural Centre which we have just established in Nairobi.

Before I plunge into the matter that prompts me to write to you, may I briefly give you background information about ourselves. This is one of a family of creative centres now in existence in Africa, established under the sponsorship of the Congress for Cultural Freedom in Paris, which publishes *Encounter* and several other magazines of social, political and cultural comment. The other three centres which I had the privilege of founding together with Nigerian writers and artists, are in Ibadan, Oshogbo, and Enugu. These are called Mbari writers' and artists' Clubs. I shall send you in a week's time a pamphlet which is being printed to mark the occasion of our official opening on November 16.

Our programme, like that of our sister-centres, lays the accent on creative activities, and includes the promotion of the visual arts like music and theatre, and creative writing. This is the main point of my letter. In January 1964 I shall launch a writers' workshop which I shall run for a period of 3 months in the field of fiction. The aim here will be to give talks once or twice a week (depending on the stamina of the participants) on the short story and the novel, their techniques etc.; I then read models of African writing in English (although I want to encourage those writing fiction in Swahili to attend). We shall turn out scripts as homework which will be discussed at meetings, and they will either be redone or replaced by new ones. I shall keep track of the participants after the workshop in order to encourage them to keep trying. We shall publish in modest form any writing turned out here that deserves it. We intend then to follow up this workshop with another lasting perhaps 2 months or even 3 months, in radio writing – the short story and drama. The participants of the first workshop who are particularly interested in writing for radio will be allowed to continue, as well as the new ones.

My Executive Committee thought your Corporation might be interested in helping us by sending a member of your staff to conduct the second workshop, again with a view to stimulating this form of writing and turning out scripts where possible. We assume that you would in turn like to use more and more home-grown material and that you would be willing to do this. We could not offer a fee, unfortunately, because we are a non-profit-making centre. But we have the premises and we shall do the organizational work. We also hope that you will be able to cover the official opening for your programmes, and you will receive an invitation card etc.

If you find the project interesting, I shall be glad to come and see you so that we may talk about it. You may appoint the day and time for such an interview in your office.

I should finally mention that Mr. Elimo Njau who is in your General Advisory Council is in charge of the visual arts of this centre and he indicated that you might like to give us your support and co-operation.

Hoping to hear from you.

Yours truly,
Ezekiel Mphahlele

Nairobi
1 November 1963

Dear Richard

So you have gone back to roost! Fine. I'm glad things turned out well for you – for your return. I say, when have you developed a vicious pen for vicious epigrams – no, not that but just plain precise sledgehammer epithets?

The men you mention you met are so aptly drawn. But of course, after *Emergency*, *Quartet* and Heinemann's anthology, why? You've become very sophisticated – and even cosmopolitan. Boy, boy, travel doth make a man. I am really happy for you: in a matter of a year or so, you've made a name for yourself. Nairobi, Kampala and Addi, still echo your name. Why is it that what used to be a group of letters on paper has taken on importance and significance in the world of letters? You can't complain, still less can S.A. – our land – sorry Cain that you have returned as a prodigal son. You have brought it laurels.

Thanks again for *Quartet* – it arrived, a neatly-produced article – and of course for the dedication I'll insist that it be put in my coffin, the day I pack up.

Leonard Dixon has written at your instigation and I have replied promptly to say I shall keep him in mind when our theatre workshop project comes off, which I hope it will.

Well, well – so *African Songs* has joined the gallery of infamy![1] Good for it – these guys still don't realise the honour they do their own prophets, eh? I'll write a love letter to Interior (or does it come under coloured affairs?) to praise him for this recognition.

Ethiopia has invited me to the inaugural writers' work-shop at their new creative centre in November. I've threatened to accept.

The family are settling down, all – the whole tribe placed in schools. Tony, the only one in boarding school – to save him from the girls; we want him to marry in the aristocracy! Ribs sends you her warmest regards. Patrick no less.

Cheerio for now.

Zeke

[1] The banning of Richard Rive's *African Songs*, published by Seven Seas Publishers, Berlin (1963).

Johannesburg

22 November 1963

My dear Zeke

I'll wager this comes as a surprise to you – and so indirectly! Unfortunately, I do not have your new address, so must make do with your old one. Hope you've settled down to your new job: what a pity! I'd hope we could settle down to a real chinwag. Well, we'll simply have to take a rain check on it – for a long time I fear; but will only know after I've faced my five charges on the 9-11 December (incidentally I'm allowed social letters till then, so try to drop me a line). Try to find out from Jenny what happened to her tape and give her my regards.

Are you doing any new writing? What about 'the great African novel'? Unfortunately I have, among other things, a creative block, but at least I've bags of time for solitary thought! Warm regards to all friends and yourself.

Sincerely

Dennis Brutus[1]

PS Case adjourned to 23 December, Prospects unbright. Yrs. D Fort. Managed to go through Law Exams, however.

1 Dennis Brutus was arrested in May 1963 for contravening a banning order. In August he attempted to escape to Mozambique but was arrested by the Portuguese police and returned to the Fort in Johannesburg. Later he was shot in the back during another escape attempt and imprisoned on Robben Island. He was released and banned again in 1965 and left for London on an exit permit the following year. His first collection of poems, *Sirens, Knuckles and Boots*, was published by Mbari Publications while he was in prison.

Nairobi

25 November 1963

Dear Richard,

I was not aware that one could invade a library and photograph material there and then. Your project sounds very interesting. The following points will have to be clarified before I proceed to ask the Congress for support and they would have to be confronted with them:

1. Where is the library to be housed?
2. In the absence of an organisation, which you say is out of the question, would the library be accessible to a number of people?
3. If these copies can be photographed, can you say why you think it is necessary for people to come to your library instead of the one that houses the originals?
4. Can you fully convince would-be sponsors that this is not a mere private venture in return for which you would give out a copy of what you produce?

I ask these questions as some bureaucrat might do; because I want to help you present the motives in the best light. In fact I wonder if you would not present the project as coming from some sort of group who would be regarded as a nucleus for other activities – which may seem to go back to what you declare out of the question.

You certainly have tons of hay on your fork at the moment and so more strength to your elbow.

Best wishes,

Yours sincerely,

Ezekiel Mphahlele

12 December 1963

My dear Zeke

Thanks for your welcome note – though sorry to hear you've put that novel out of your head. But I agree with you: there is just as much satisfaction in helping the new breed to develop. I used to tell students like Nortje[1] that first rate writers stood on the shoulders of generations of third-raters. I should be pleased if I thought I was pioneering for others: I hope your centre will serve a similar purpose – there is such a splendid ferment these days that one can do a great deal of promotional work.

Personally, I have entered my sterility/senility creatively, I think. Jenny's tape should go to Neville, but you might well find some use for it first: please handle with great care – some of it may yet turn out to be irreplaceable!

Let me know more, if you can soon, about the work of your centre: I am very interested and convey my greetings to the 'Centrists' and to all friends. Warm regards to yourself and your wife.

Sincerely

Dennis Brutus

1 The poet, Arthur Nortje.

1964

25 July 1964

Dear Langston,

It's a long time since we heard from each other. How's life these days?

What I am writing to you about is theatre. I have established a theatre group attached to this Centre – the African Theatre Company. We are doing a play – *The Prodigal Son* by Bob Leshoia (South African) in which I want to incorporate gospel singing. I am asking you to send us gospel music – preferably in tonic solfa, but if impossible, send it to us in staff notation – as many pieces as possible. Your *Black Nativity* I saw in Paris inspired me to this sort of theatre. If you can send it by air, so much the better. Also if you can send us a book of Negro spirituals also preferably in tonic solfa etc. we shall regard this as a most treasured gift from you.

Best wishes as always,

Yours ever,

Zeke

10 August 1964

Dear Zeke:

I am purchasing some gospels and spirituals for you and airmailing them tomorrow... some, at any rate, if all are too heavy for air, as I'm rather broke right now. *BLACK NATIVITY* closed owing me £10, 000 on the American tours. So I am suing, case in court now. And the management has the gall to announce now a European and Australian tour this fall. 2 companies! Anyhow, *SPONONO*,[1] beautifully done here, did not have a run, but almost everyone is in the African Pavilion's show at the World's Fair. Unfortunately, Barney Qhobosheane was in a bad auto accident and all smashed up, but I spoke to him on the phone in the hospital today and he is getting along. I am going to see him this week. Is Bob Leshoia there with you? If so, tell him HELLO and ask him when he is coming back to go to the University.

I am head-over-heels busy trying to get ready to leave for the Berlin Festival of the Arts in September. Are you going to be there since the accent is on things African and Afro-American? If you are coming, it will be good to see you again. On the way back, I hope to stop by Paris, then London where I am helping BBC edit a series on American Negro culture for which I just taped 12 poets here in the States. My own interview has to be done all over again, since the Harlem riots upset the apple cart. You should've heard the shots around the corner from my house! And I was in the middle of the first firing!

Let me know if you get the music.

O. K.

Regards

Langston

[1] *Sponono: A Play in Three Acts*, based on three stories about Diepkloof Reformatory in Alan Paton's *Tales of a Troubled Land* (Scribner's 1961), co-written and directed by Krishna Sha, opened at the Cort Theatre on Broadway on 2 April 1964.

9 August 1964

Dear Langston,

Thank you very much for the music you are sending us, some of which has arrived.

No, I have not yet received *New Negro Poets: U.S.A.*, and I am looking forward to seeing it. I do have *Poems From Black Africa*. Maybe your publishers may want to send us your 5 plays? I am told that there is a booklet called *Literary Market Place*. I would very much like to get from it titles by and about American publishers to send us such literature as part of their advertisement. Do you think they would be impressed? – I mean gratis?

I am sorry to hear about the misfortunes of *Black Nativity*. I hope sincerely you will recover some or all of the money you claim.

Thank you again for everything and warmest regards,

Yours ever,

Ezekiel Mphahlele.

Nairobi

26 August 1964

Dear Richard

The publishers of Penguin books have asked me to compile an anthology of modern African prose and poetry. They have in mind a volume that will contain short stories, extracts from novels and plays and poetry by Africans; one that will provide a selection of writing, which will enable members of the reading public who cannot easily keep up with literary trends all over to get an idea of the literary culture of Africa and its flavour. The volume will be one of several that are being compiled in other parts of the world.

I am writing to you to ask you to contribute a poem or *short story* or sketch, that you are happiest about, or allow me to use an extract from any of your plays or from any *one of your novels*. The underlined literary form will indicate what I would prefer from you, but you are at liberty to offer whatever you feel best represents your talents.

This anthology should not be confused with the one Ellis Komey and I co-edited for Faber & Faber which is already in the press and should appear in a month's time.[1]

I should like to set December 31 as my deadline. So, I shall be most grateful for your co-operation. The normal anthology fees will be paid to contributors.

Yours very sincerely,
Ezekiel Mphahlele

Again begging, please oblige. When is the novel out? Am all eagerness. And your other routine chores like the Heinemann anthology? Good luck.

[1] See, Ellis Ayitey Komey and Ezekiel Mphahlele. 1964. *Modern Short Stories*. London: Faber and Faber.

Nairobi
11 November 1964

Dear Makhudu,

Hell, man, life has been upside down the last two months. But actually when your letter arrived for Ribs in which you wanted information about a visa, I was back. Only, there was a heap of work waiting for me. I am in a clearing now. Immigration here insist on a visa obtainable from the UK Commissioner in Lagos. Then your letter came saying you had to send your passport to Pretoria. Let's hope the bastards realize the urgency *and* importance of your visit. After all they still have representative settlers here – quite a community 180 miles from here – a place called Eldoret where they trekked to from SA. How single-trek minded can you get! It would be real fun if you came here. You wouldn't find plantations but milk galore – fresh, i.e.

Received a letter today from Basie: he is improving and thinks of finding a job except for the fact that he has to keep reporting at the hospital for a check-up. His letter pulled at my heart-strings with news of those who have died at home. Paul Mogale (which I knew already), another Paul Mogale, a blood cousin. Some others whom you couldn't know. And of course Moloi, whom Muriel mentioned. How long is it going to last – this disappearance in the ground at a young age? We just don't live long, and when one thinks of Moloi who was so close to you and me in Marabastad just turning his back on us and his family – the pain numbs one and one waits only for the shaft to be pulled out and for the ache to begin again.

Dennis Brutus? You're right: his poetry palpitates with pain. Seldom does protest poetry make literature at the same time like his.

By the way, while I'm on a sentimental journey like this, Basie says he has just been to Molsgat (what a name!) – the postal name for Maupaneng and the environs – with Isaac Mphahlele to go and see Isaac's mother. He says they went to see grandmother – my father's mother – who used to sit under a mimosa tree and frightened us so much. He says she could hardly believe her eyes when she saw him. She even remembered me! How nostalgic one can become for even those things, those people, those places which inflicted such savage pain on one.

Life is still good here. We've been having hell with Tony since June. Will tell you when (and if) you come.

I travelled with Bob when I was going to Berlin, and we parted in Paris, for him to proceed to the University of Illinois. He is doing theatre arts there for 10 months. Then he doesn't know if he will go back to teaching in Zambia or come to East Africa. His family is still in Ndola. As they have not written to us yet, we must presume that all is well. He has written twice already. He lectures (or rather teaches) oral English part-time, which enables him with the money he earns by it, to pay his way through.

Love to Muriel and the brood from us.

Yours ever

Zeke

1965

London

28 June 1965

My dear Zeke

Our friendship is too firm, and too precious for any beating around the bush – it is naturally a disappointment to me that you were not able to write the sort of foreword the publishers hoped for, but I am not altogether surprised – however, I do hope you will share your misgivings with me because your thoughts are always helpful.

R.D. sorry this morning to say they can wait no longer. Having decided on October 18 for publication they apparently worked out deadline for every stage, that involved sending the page proofs back to the printers last week.

I wonder whether Ruth First's *117 Days* has reached Nairobi, and what do you think about such publication.[1] *The Times* surprised us by giving it a sub-leader which ended by saying that if the book is not stark truth, it is up to the South African Government to tell the world what are the facts! Of course besides such writing my effort is kindergarten!

I did not go to the Freedom Day rally in Trafalgar Square yesterday because I was star preacher in the evening at a Salonika 1915 landing reunion service. Solomon Ngakane, who lives near here, told me the turn out was less than usual which is surprising because Ruth was one of the speakers – actually I think it only goes to show how that the mind of the public can be over nauseated. The only member of any of the delegations to the Commonwealth meeting I met was Herbert Chitepo who came over with the Tanzanian team, he took the trouble to come and see me so we had an all too short chat.

My grapevine tells me the Zambian University project is still undecided, have you heard from them?

I must not keep you longer from your mountain of work!

Nomsa has gone down to the launderette but if she were here I know she would add her usual affectionate greeting to Rebecca and with love to all the family, including Locksley.

As ever yours

Arthur Blaxall

1 Ruth First's prison memoir *117 Days* is an account of her confinement in terms of the General Law Amendment Act of 1963, known as 'the Ninety Day Detention Law'.

London

5 July 1965

My dear Zeke

As you remarked yourself in your first book, I am far from being a conventional or orthodox person, but here is one thing to which I cling – belief in the fact that behind us all is some Being (or Power) who pulls strings! In that spirit I take it my book was destined to go to the world without a foreword, and thus my desire has been proved stronger than that of R.D. (for whom I have profound respect). Frankly, I am glad it has worked out in this way, indeed I disliked the idea of being introduced by anyone from the beginning, as you will see when the time comes for you to read the bundle of stuff I will leave behind when I take the long road. By that time I imagine you will be occupied with far better things than writing about me, but just in case the true facts in connection with my arrest and trial have some significance in the total picture of these days, it will be better that you write what you then feel moved you to write without having committed yourself in any way at this stage.

R.D. told me last week that the page proofs have gone back to the printers with some sort of publishers' note so I see no point in asking whether a foreword can be rushed in even at this late hour: I prefer to be finished with it all, the agony has been drawn out long enough.

Clive phoned yesterday morning from London airport as his plane was delayed by some trouble. He told me that you have been so occupied since your return that you have not had time to see anyone, and he also was thrown off centre by the tension of his home news. He is going to try to break the return journey for a night so we can have a good chat. Shall I discuss with him points arising from *Suspended Sentence*,[1] and the wisdom of further analysis now, rather than when my body is being used by medical students, or would you prefer that I say nothing and wait for a day when you and I can get down to this subject and make our decision? Let me not keep you longer. Hope Locksley is shaping well.

Arthur Blaxall

1 Arthur Blaxall's autobiography (Hodder and Stoughton 1965).

Nairobi

30 July 1965

Dear Makhudu,

At last, at last, I can take a breather, and do what I have been wanting to for ages. I went to Israel for 3 months ending June 10 and returned to find a mountain of work. One simply cannot cope with this life without ulcers, and am considering – but of that later.

Israel was fascinating, as you will see from my accounts of it. If we had a 100th of the energy the Israelis have we should move mountains here (in Africa). But of course we do nothing but deport, debate blackness and sit back and bask in the glory of our black colour.

What a thing to have happened to Palmer – and his family – to die like that! Two South Africans claimed by the roads so far! I was so shattered by news of Moloi's death that for long spells these days I make a mental inventory of those whose names have to be struck off.[1] I find myself too often these days bogged down, in my thoughts, in musing about death. I say to myself each time I hear someone's gone beyond the hills: why was it not me? It could easily have been. Then I literally brood and find I am stricken with despair and fear. Two things that always occur to me are: small children who must be left fatherless, and the amount of work I still want to do on this earth. I find myself also contemplating old age, and look at the mannerisms and gestures of old people.

Again I despair. But why infect you with this gloom in me? The terror is really mixed up with that for Basie, still laid down with intermittent spells of relief. He now weighs 87 lbs he says! I never open a telegram without trembling these days. Enough!

When I came here I made it understood to my employers (who paid Bob [Leshoia]'s fare to the States) that I should only stay here for about 2 years – running this centre – and that I should hand over to a Kenyan. Already one can notice the restlessness among some of the denser and dimmer members of the elite. Budge! myself says to me. So I applied for the post of Director of Extra-Mural Studies or of Correspondence Studies at the University of Zambia, Lusaka. I was called for an interview last week and it seems I made an impression on them – the provisional council so, who knows, we may be on the move again. If I fail to land the Zambian thing, there is a place open here at the University College in the Department of English. So in any case I'll budge from the local position, I should do some voluntary work at the centre. South Africans are irrepressible – that's why we upset the natives so: we create a state of discontent in them, and people don't like [...

We were sorry to hear that Zambia fell through as notification arrived too late. I was to get a post for Duma Petso here, although these MP's have such loud mouths when they promise posts, *ga batjoe selo*.

Met Nat Masemola in Lusaka. He's grown plumpy and struts like a cockerel displaying its self-awareness among hens. He is still noisy, and was sworn into the Zambian Bar. Ntloedibe is there, I was told, but I missed him.

A South African born fellow (white) was deported two days ago. He is now a British subject and was recruited here for teaching. Started to raise hell for the formerly exclusive European schools: slow and reluctant integration, race discrimination etc, were his charges. Schoolboard advised advisor (white) for secondary schools in the Ministry of Education, to have Jaffe deported for subversion, says Minister of Defence and Security. Actually, he's being used as a bugbear to frighten off African 'trouble-makers' – Kenyans, who want the government to move faster in land and education etc, than they're doing. That's the irony of things in East Africa. White advisors shall hold and sway their African bosses, most of them unfitted for the positions they hold anyhow.

Will let you know what the trend of events is when plans sort themselves out.

Cheers for now and love to Muriel and the gang.

Ever

Zeke

[1] The news of the death of Moloi, a childhood friend, greatly distressed Mphahlele.

London

31 July 1965

My dear Zeke

It's good to hear from you and have your generous letter. Charles is so pleased at your remembrance of him and sends his warmest wishes to you.

You speak of my energy, but I think you have ten times as much as me. And today I feel so depressed, having had news from two different sources, of two South Africans' suicides. One is Nat Nakasa, who started that little magazine *Classic* in Johannesburg and went to Harvard with a scholarship on an 'exit permit'.[1] The Nats wouldn't give him a passport and it is believed that the thought of not being able to go home preyed on his mind. The other, at Cape Town, is the young Afrikaans poet Ingrid Jonker.[2] I met her in London last year, I thought her childlike, easily vulnerable by this mad world, and certainly very gifted as a poet (though I know Afrikaans very sketchily).

I wonder if your university work will be in Kenya. I do hope it won't keep you too busy to do your own work. It's only really busy people who ever get anything done, so they say. I find I get busier and busier as I get older, and enjoy it.

I look forward to your Penguin anthology – and Nadine Gordimer's.

By the way, *Turbott Wolfe* comes out with Norrow in America in August. I see they advertise it as a 'classic'(!). I call that sales talk and hope to sell the book.

All best regards to you

William Plomer

1 As fiction editor of *Drum* Mphahlele had worked closely with Nakasa, who also worked for the *Rand Daily Mail*. He founded *The Classic* (named after a shebeen in Sophiatown) with Barney Simon in 1963. Nakasa left the country on a one-way exit permit to take up a Nieman Fellowship in journalism at Harvard in 1964. He committed suicide by jumping from an apartment building in New York in 1965.

2 Ingrid Jonker was an Afrikaans poet, the daughter of a prominent Afrikaans intellectual and parliamentarian, Abraham Jonker. The failure of her parents' marriage, subsequently the unhappiness and deprivation of her childhood, her own divorce and troubled relationships with prominent writers, contributed to her suicide by drowning in 1965. She received posthumous national honours for her poetry, most famously 'Die kind wat dood geskiet is deur soldate by Nyanga' ('The Child Shot Dead by Soldiers at Nyanga'), which was read by Nelson Mandela in his inaugural address to the first democratic Parliament in 1994.

Hertfordshire
22 September 1965

My dear Zeke

This must be a short note because once again we are moving! Five months on Teneriffe should give me time to catch up with worthwhile correspondence, unless I get launched on another writing effort (which is unlikely after the sweat of the small thing coming out next month – by the way thanks for kindly comment, of which more in the letter-of-the future!)

I realize you must have been disappointed about that Zambia job but take it in your stride – whenever I cannot do something I wanted to do I always say to myself that doubtless another job will prove to be round the corner, and it is invariably so!

I do not know why but somehow when I first heard that you were taking up the Congress job and going to Paris, I was uncertain about it, but when you returned to Africa as your base I felt satisfied and said to myself that now Zeke and Rebecca are settled until retiring age. Perhaps I had the wrong idea of it all, I did not so much think you would build up one centre in one country, I rather imagined you would use Nairobi only as a base and move around considerably, in which case I was happy to think that Rebecca would be building up her home in a congenial city, and so on, etc. However, one cannot write about these things, they are matters for talking, and that must wait. I do assure you I hold up thumbs for you all – including Locksley: when it comes to planning out my small finances in connection with the move I will try to squeeze out a couple of pounds so he can buy himself something for Christmas.

Have you seen Peter Abraham's new novel *A day of their own*? I bought a copy the other day but have decided to keep it for reading on the boat – I do not know what to make of political fantasy stories. When are you going to cough up a novel?

As ever yours

Arthur Blaxall

Nairobi

24 September 1965

Dear Makhudu

Thanks indeed for your letter. First, I return the PO's [postal orders]. *The Classic* ceased to come out after Nat Nakasa left SA. It was his intention to let it come out from Swaziland when he would have returned from the States. But alas, as you must already know, he threw himself down from the 7th floor of a building in New York. The Executive Director of the Foundation that sponsors Chemchemi and helped finance part of Nat's programme at Harvard School of Journalism, was told by another South African in New York that Nat had been talking suicide and he was worried. So the Director fetched Nat in order to let him stay in the house before deciding on his return to Africa. The night of the same day it happened – from this man's apartment.

Bob passes thro here on his way back to Zambia. He said a few months before Nat's death he had met him and was sure the man was cracking up. Politics, exile, prospects of return to Africa, alleged disappointed with the Negro in America?? Ribs says when Nat stayed at our house before she joined me in 1957 he revealed to her his disturbed home background – mother in mental asylum, father a blackguard etc. This would have aggravated the situation.

So *The Classic* will certainly be left in suspension, and I'm urging the sponsors (same foundation) to take it to Cape Town where now all the writers who matter are. When it does surface again, I'll let you know. As you have not stated the PO that has to pay on the PO's it will be easy for you to sign any name and cash them.

About the plagiarism, I have meant to reply especially to John Pepper Clark but time has slipped by and it is too late for *Transition* to receive the dialogue. The bile has been up to my throat over Clark's smugness and irrelevancies. Somehow Rubadiri's 'theft' did not spark off any indignation in me when I first read his piece. It did when he replied in the insensible manner he did.[1] But again, I'm a bit tired, and too old maybe to follow up these lunacies. I do however appreciate all you say; thing is that my energies have been absorbed elsewhere.

Zambia fell through – they offer me an English lectureship – which I can get locally anyhow. If they don't consider a darkie fit to head a department like that, how do they expect me to earn my pride and settle for something lower? So I shall be stuck in Nairobi till I can find elsewhere to go. Pan African talk is shit in these African countries and a foreign African has no refuge except in his own land.

Lots of love to you all.

Zeke

1 Writing from Makerere University, a correspondent, R L Wigglesworth, pointed out the similarities between an article by David Rubadiri in *Transition* 15 and Mphahlele's *The African Image*. In his reply to Wigglesworth Rubadiri seems unaware of the implications of being accused of plagiarism (*Transition* 19, 1965, p 8).

1966

2 January 1966

My dear Zeke

Very pleased to get yours – obliquely – today: hope you will have got mine by now. I wrote, quite without knowing that you were also trying to contact me. And I hope you have had a chat with a friend from Farfield who might be interested in me.

So you will be leaving Chemchemi to lecture at varsity. Very nice, but I hope that this will only mean an extension of your work in fostering creative interests. It may have one advantage; that the students will be bound to certain specific tasks, whatever their own interests may be: one needs this direction, I think, especially since there are many who peter out as artists because they do not come to terms with the fact that creative work is HARD WORK.

I liked your own bit of verse very much: do you do much verse now? Some think that verse is for the young, but – after having shared this idea to some extent, I begin to think that it can, as well, be a very satisfying pursuit for the mature! But perhaps I'm just biased in favour of myself as I begin to age. But I should be glad to see more of your work – my range of contacts is severely circumscribed, as I am sure you are aware.[1]

You will also know – if my letter got through to you, that I am now thinking very seriously of pulling up roots, and am beginning to look around at pastures. It is for this reason that I wrote for some advice from you, and that I hope you spoke to the man from Farfield.

I know you will be glad to know that despite the grinding mechanicalness of my present existence – apart from the hours I am confined to my home, I spend my time in an engineering factory. I have managed to do a bit of writing. The thing I include is one of the very newest, and one that pleases me quite a lot, at present, at any rate. I like its procession – a kind of organic growth, which is, fortunately, quite natural, even if it seems to be carefully calculated. At a very early stage in it I wanted to give up, it seems so trite, but I kept going on – literally 'just to see how it would turn out'. I hope you like it, and would be pleased to have your opinion. I know there are lots of writers who prefer not to examine criticisms of their work, but I find it really helps me to re-examine my work in the light of the criticisms of others: even a casual comment by someone working alongside me in the factory can provoke me to some careful thought of the nature of my verse, or of poetry in general.

I am, of course, pleased to know that my work is studied and grateful to those who think it sufficiently rewarding for this: but I am sorry to say my experiences with Mbari have been quite disappointing. I am simply unable to secure any kind of response from either Ulli Beier or Dennis Williams, in spite of all my efforts. I can't help feeling that they have done little to keep in touch with me.

What library publications are you able to send me? Either student or public? I should like to keep in touch with writing. *Transition* has been good enough to give me a gift subscription, for which I am very grateful. I should like to see *Black Orpheus* – even back numbers if available. Do you know Butler's *New Coin* here?[2] It seems to have some good things too. Perhaps like *New Writing in South Africa*, it may be taking the line that only white South Africans can write English.

I am glad to say that Arthur Nortje, who is now doing an English honours at Oxford, continues to write fine verse: perhaps you would like to keep in touch with him – he is at Jesus College.[3] And Bessie Head is doing some fine work in Bechuanaland.[4] And there are one or two others of promise beginning to emerge: unfortunately, one of my bans also prevents me from helping others to be published, so it is unwise for me to assist or become involved with any publication.

I have to find room for my verse, so had better stop now. Thank you for your kind good wishes. Our very warm regard to you and to all friends.

Sincerely yours

Dennis

Red brick in a quadrangle
surrounding me
and the much-scrubbed concrete yard
and the clear highveld blue
across it –
what were they?
swans? spectral presences?
masses of tissue in flight? –
clouds
sweeping, sailing, simply moving
With nothing else to see
Except the high red walls
And some small black barred squares
– windows, but not for use –
the sky grew interesting;
one discovered the clouds

So one watched their flight
discovered, breath-takingly, their grace
their deceptive appearance of stillness
watched them form and re-form
alliances,
fragment,
merge into seamless garments

Discovered too the rivers of air
flowing far above the earth
when the wind around was still
and the higher strata of cloud

higher currents of air
moving contrariwise
in an obscure logic of their own
a secret aesthetic –
another, foreign world.

But it was, chiefly, motion one discovered
its grace and ease
the unheard melodies of motion
and a sense of inner propulsion
which is rhythm, drive
freedom.

So one discovered freedom
as an exquisite lyrical impulse
indefinable
poignant
and heart-aching.

And then one discovered
in the interstices of the clouds
in all that intricate interplay,
fabric, filigree, varied planes
the birds.

1 Brutus is writing under a banning order, before his departure from South Africa later the same year.

2 *Transition* was founded in Kampala, Uganda, in 1961 by Rajat Neogy and *Black Orpheus* by Ulli Beier in Ibadan in 1957 (see Peter Benson. 1986. *Black Orpheus, Transition and Modern Cultural Awakening in Africa*. University of California Press). Mphahlele worked with Beier on *Black Orpheus*, ensuring a South African presence in the activities of the journal and Mbari. *New Coin* was founded by Guy Butler in Grahamstown in 1965.

3 Brutus had been Arthur Nortje's English teacher at South End High

School in Port Elizabeth. After a period in Canada Nortje returned to Oxford, where he died in 1970.

4 Bessie Head, having worked in South Africa as a journalist, left for what would become Botswana in 1964. In 1968 she published her first novel, *When Rain Clouds Gather*.

2 January 1966

(A re-creation: awaiting trial at the Fort. 1963)

Copy for Zeke,

Regards, Dennis

Nairobi

[Post marked] 14 January 1966

Dear Makhudu,

I'm sending under separate cover some things: (a) a play I wrote based on a short story by a Kenyan – something I had had published in an anthology of short stories I co-edited. I don't know if you have seen the volume: *Modern African Stories* (Faber & Faber). The story has no dramatic tension, but was originally written really as a lyrical piece. So I treated it as a poem and just decided to be lyrical, damn the orthodox European (Western) ideas about dramatic form and content. It had been commissioned by a girls' high school here, and they performed it with remarkable success that I felt was most flattering. See what you make of it. (b) Some material I prepared for Writers' Workshop: the idea of the pieces of dialogue is to encourage writers to listen to the speech idioms of their own people and, if they are writing in English put them across in a way that will capture the African imagery and therefore mood without straining after idiomatic English which always falsifies African character when people don't speak English everyday. The two pieces of composition I did in order to encourage teachers to insist on more subjective writing – usually called 'intensive writing' for essays instead of the dry and uninspiring writing one gets on topics that don't even encourage imagination. This will also stimulate the intending writer. It means one has to know what to present for exams – full sentences etc, and what to do to capture the rhythm of one's thoughts and moods.

Best regards.

Zeke

15 February 1966

Dear Zeke:

I hope I shall be seeing you at the Dakar Festival in early April. And where will you be later? The State Department has asked me to read my poems in Ethiopia, Kenya and Uganda in late April and May. Where will you be then? Certainly, I hope our paths will cross somewhere. So let me know. Besides, how can I send you my new books, if I do not know where to address you or where you are? Long time no hear, so drop me a line soon.

Cordial regards, as ever,

Hastily (so BUSY!), but

Sincerely,

Langston Hughes

26 February 1966

Hi Langston!

It was good to hear a snatch from you after such an age. I know I have been guilty party and the last 2 years have been hectic – organizing culture. Now I have joined the English Dept of University College, Nairobi as lecturer. It's an easier place. So I can surface and write to friends like you.

It's exciting to hear you are coming this way in April-May. *Please make a note of this.* I am helping a literary club at the College and would like to ask you to keep a special day free to talk to them as the guest speaker for the inauguration. Please tell your programme makers to give us a day, preferably at *5:30 pm on a Thursday*. Please, please, please. Don't let the State Dept tie you up too much – I'm in your hands – that sort of thing! Best wishes,

Zeke

P.S. Can't go to Dakar. Could if I wanted to. I'm getting too old to find fun in art festivals, even at 45!

Zeke

Please send me your latest books.

18 April 1966

Dear Makhudu

It was good to hear from you. Your detailed account of the events of these dark days throws much light on the happenings for us which is impossible to appreciate from bare news reports. And to think you were at the doorstep of the cave that swallowed up the bigger guns!

This is going to be a very brief note as I'm rushed. First, received a telegram this morning from Isaac Mphahlele to say Basie died on Friday 15 April, to be buried the 20th. It stunned me, even though I have been breathlessly opening every cable and telegram in frantic expectation of the worst. With 7 children, Christina will be lost. Still we have to steel ourselves somehow.

I have been invited by the University of Colorado to spend a week on their campus as visiting lecturer – African Literature. All travel expenses paid and living expenses and a stipend of all the things! Those Americans! Haul a fellow across the Atlantic for one week at such cost! Nay, fly him across. I leave April 27 and return May 14. But I'm not in a state of mind to feel elated after the telegram from home.

Best wishes and love galore to you and all.

Zeke

Nairobi

18 May 1966

Dear Professor Chapman,

This is to let you know how glad I was to have the opportunity of meeting you and Dr John Williams and to be able to talk about my project.[1] Thanks again so much for your generosity in granting me a fellowship at Denver and all the other things that go with it.

I have written to Farfield Foundation to let them know what the new situation is, and to ask them to make good the balance to bring the total to $1,000 difference for maintenance. They would like a letter from you saying that your university is offering me a Fellowship that carries $4,450 with a waiver of tuition fees etc. I am asking you kindly to write such a letter to me which I can then forward to them *as soon as convenient*, as we are pressed for time. You need only state what Denver is offering me and how much I need to raise to make up $9,000 a year for 2 years plus a certain amount for fares.

Then I will juggle with figures in tapping the sources.

I am looking very much forward to coming to Denver, which looks physically attractive apart from other things. I shall be sending you a break-down of my courses for the B.A. Honours degree I took in English.

Best wishes.

Yours sincerely,
Ezekiel Mphahlele

1 During his short visiting lectureship at the University of Colorado Mphahlele managed a visit to the University of Denver, which led to his returning to Denver later to undertake a PhD in creative writing.

Nairobi
23 May 1966

Dear Prof. Chapman,

I have now received assurance from the Congress for Cultural Freedom in Paris that they will take care of our transport to Denver. I have asked Mr. John Hunt, their Executive Director, to communicate this assurance to you.

I also asked Farfield Foundation, 145 E 52nd St., New York 22, if they could increase their existing grant by $1,000 a year (which should bring it to a total of $4,750 a year from them). Their Executive Director thought it should be possible to manage this. I also asked him to communicate the assurance to you. Technically it is now only this $1,000 outstanding, which is also why I contacted the Institute of International Education. I shall tell them that I have transport funds, and they can give what they can – at least $1,000 a year.

I am anxious that as little delay as possible should be risked before you 'assail' Immigration and Naturalization Services in Denver for our visas. We have now decided to leave here on August 1st, all going well.

I am a persistent letter writer – an addict at that – so please do not be impatient when you receive a continuous wave of words, words, words.

Best wishes,
Yours sincerely,
E. Mphahlele

Nairobi
23 May 1966

Dear Prof. Chapman,

Rather than send this break-down to Dr. Williams, I shall send it to you. South African universities tend to steer a course between the British and American systems. The B.A. degree has a minimum of 11 courses. These are indicated on the certificate. Of these, two subjects have to be majors, which means the maximum number of courses have to be taken in each and *both* have to be passed at the same examination. My majors were first English (three courses) and Psychology. I passed English and failed Psychology, but rather than repeat English, I took Psychology and Native administration (African Affairs) as majors the following year. Now an Honours in B.A. is an intensive study of one of the majors, and it is a one year programme. As I had done very well in English III, I was permitted to take this for Honours, even though it did not feature as a major the second time.

The course for English I, II, and III (each being a year's study): Old English; Middle English; Shakespeare; Poetry: 1350-1780: 1780 to present day: Prose: 1600 to present day: the development of drama to the present day. I specialized in Victorian literature; and in year III I took Poetics and Criticism and Practical Criticism among other courses.

The courses for B.A. Honours in English: (five papers for examination)

1. *Poetics and Criticism*: Aristotle's *Poetics*; Longinus; Horace Reference works covered: Scott-James *The Making of Literature*; F.R. Leavis' New Bearings; F.L. Lucas: *Tragedy in English Poetry*; Saintsbury's *History of English Criticism*, I.A. Richards' *Principles of Lit. Criticism*; Cleanth Brooks', *Literary Criticism: A Short History*.

2. *Middle English: Language & Literature*: Chaucer: *Canterbury Tales; Troilus etc*; Sisam: Sir Gawayne etc; *Piers Plowman; Fourteenth Century Verse and Prose.*

3. *Special Periods*: 1784-1832; 1832-1900 (Poetry, Prose & Drama).

4. *Shakespeare*: Prescribed texts and reference texts by his predecessors and contemporaries: *The Spanish Tragedy*; *Tamburlaine; Doctor Faustus*; *The Jew of Malta*; *The White Devil*; *The Duchess of Malfi*; Reference works: Nicol Smith: *Shakespeare Criticism*; Bradley: *Shakespeare Criticism*: Quincey Adams: *Life of Shakespeare*; Dover Wilson: *The Essential Shakespeare*; E.E. Halliday: *Shakespeare & his Critics.*

5. *Practical Criticism*: Passages for practical criticism based on I.A. Richards'

scheme basically, but also drawing from: Empson's *Seven Types of Ambiguity;* Thompson's: *Reading & Discrimination*; Q.D. Leavis's *Fiction & the Reading Public*; F.R. Leavis's *Revaluation & The Great Tradition*; T.S. Eliot's *The Use of Poetry and the Use of Criticism*; *Selected Essays*; Lionel Trillings' *The Liberal Imagination*; Arnold's *Essays in Criticism*. (also I.A. Richards' *Principles of Literary Criticism*.)

I thought to give you this information so that you have an idea of my orientation. Having been exposed to the British school and subsequently to the French school of literary criticism, I am keen to be exposed to other schools, as well as to American literature. I have written several papers on African literature for conferences, and am sending you two in which I comment on French literary criticism. I thought you might like to see these, if it is not overburdening you with reading material of which I am sure you are ready cluttered.[1]

Best wishes,

Yours sincerely,

E. Mphahlele

[1] This letter reveals the extent to which Mphahlele's undergraduate degree at the University of South Africa was based on what came to be known as 'Cambridge English', with a strong emphasis on practical criticism and close reading and, through F R Leavis in particular, a sense of social mission. It is also apparent, however, that Mphahlele was becoming aware of wider literary-critical horizons, through his experience in Paris and his impending move to the United States.

Nairobi

10 June 1966

Dear Professor Chapman,

I have not heard from you, and am rather worried that time is moving fast.

Farfield Foundation has agreed to grant me the extra 1,000 dollars a year for 2 years, which means 4,750 dollars will be coming from them a year. I asked Mr. Frank Platt, Executive Director of Farfield, to write to you to confirm this.

You will by now, I am sure, have received the guarantee of transport from the Congress for Cultural Freedom in Paris, who has sent me a copy of the letter they wrote you. If Mr. Platt has not yet written, a telephone call to New York from your office will do something. Farfield is at 145 & 52nd St.

As these are the two matters that were outstanding when I left Denver, I am hopeful that you will admit me for the Ph.D. programme. In anticipation, and in order to save time, we have sent off our personal effects and my library – or rather part of it – by sea. They will arrive about the same time as we if we leave on the 1st August as envisaged.

The matter of a visa should be tackled soon if not *now*, with your office of I.N.S.[1]

A friend of ours teaching at the University of Illinois, Carbondale, has already offered to take our 13-year-old to attend high school there, so he will be leaving sooner. We shall be coming with 4 children consequently.

Best wishes,

Yours sincerely,

E. Mphahlele

1 The United States Immigration and Naturalisation Service.

Nairobi

10 June 1966

Dear Dennis,

Thanks for your letter. I have been cooped up in university teaching, and didn't much care for what goes on culturally in Kenya. Since Chemchemi closed down, I have got so thoroughly fed up with my human & physical environment that we just want to get out. What irks me so much is the futility of fragmented efforts by such rival units like Njau's Paa ya Paa Gallery, which was expressly set up to crush Chemchemi, purporting as it did to do exactly the same things we were doing but holding only exhibitions eventually. In fact what scared off Farfield was just this cultural chauvinism which they felt would tend to make Chemchemi irrelevant once I had pulled out, because the leadership that might have taken over had become disgruntled over their failure to turn Ch. into an elite window exhibition affair. So, I'm afraid I've not even the least atom of drive for & interest in cultural work here.

I've been granted a fellowship at the University of Denver, Colorado, to teach & do my Ph.D. It's the only other (the one being Iowa) that grants a Ph.D. on the strength of a publishable novel or volume of poetry or essays. After the 2 years, I'll teach in the States for 3 years more, & when the children are in university – at least the first 3, we'll come back to Africa, to any university that is not, like that in East Africa, bedeviled by 'Africanization', of which even foreign Africans fall foul. So we decided to obtain a base from which our children can acquire uninterrupted schooling. We leave Aug. 1st via Stockholm.

As from Aug., would you please send me 2 copies of *Transcription* material & *Cultural Events* each at the Department of English, University of Denver, Denver, Colo, USA. I shall still need them and there is every possibility of an African Studies dept being set up at Denver. There is already an International Studies programme & I'm going to teach a course or two for it.

How are Rhoda & the children? Hope fine. Rebecca joins me in wishing for the best.

Yours ever,

Zeke

Nairobi

21 June 1966

Dear Dean Lindell,

Since writing to you, the American Embassy here has asked me to fill in immigrant application forms so that in case the INS there decides that this is possible, time will have been saved. Among other things, the form requires the applicant to state when last he was in the US and with what kind of visa. It then occurred to the Embassy that if I went to the University of Colorado April 29-May 13 this year on an Exchange visa, then by US immigration law I cannot apply to be an immigrant until 2 years have elapsed from the date of my return to Kenya. This should mean that I should have to wait until May 1968.

Now, the form which would have enabled me to obtain a visa was for Exchange status, but it arrived late and I cabled CU to tell New York immigration that I was coming without a visa, and that they should allow me in; otherwise I would have sat waiting for the form and failed to make the trip in time. So it is just possible that INS in Denver let me in, or rather confirmed my entry, on a different status altogether. In this case, I would still be entitled to apply for immigration. If on an Exchange basis, the Embassy here say that the only two alternatives will be as a student or as an Exchange lecturer. In either case, I cannot, after two years at D.U., apply for immigration. I shall have to leave and reapply two years after my departure from the US.

It seems ridiculous that a week's stay in Colorado last April-May should prevent me from applying for immigration. I am determined to come to Denver anyhow: my books and personal effects are already en route to the US, and I have resigned from my post here. If the worst comes to the worst, an Exchange lectureship or student status will have to do, but I accept Prof. Chapman's offer without any reservations, as I felt it will give me a reasonable chance to do the Ph.D. in the two years. I shall be quite happy to contribute what I can in the field of African literature.

As it happens, either an Exchange or student visa requires a much shorter time to obtain – less than half the bother and time it takes to obtain an immigrant's visa. A case is known of a South African exile who entered the U.S. on an Exchange visa, and without leaving the country for 2 years, managed to wangle powerful support to switch over to an immigrant's status. If I failed to do this at the end of the 2 years at D.U., I should ask for consideration at least for my older children to remain in college while I, my wife and the youngest two cross into Canada or go to Brazil where there is a reasonable chance of obtaining a lectureship for 2 years before immigrating to the US in proper fashion. I would not consider coming back to Africa where foreign academics like myself have a tough time of it owing to 'localization' of jobs.[1]

Would you, therefore, in the light of this, ascertain with the INS in Denver just on what visa I was let in, and also let them tell you honestly which the best course is for me. Whatever it may be that might require forms from them, please ask them to make it possible for us to leave here on August 1.

Best wishes,

Yours sincerely,

E. Mphahlele

[1] As it turned out, Mphahlele went neither to Canada nor to Brazil. The two-years requirement forced him back to Africa after the completion of his doctoral studies in 1968. This time, the host country was Zambia.

Denver

12 October 1966

Dear Bob [Robert McDowell, English Dept, Univ of Texas],

I'm able to write soon, after all. My library has arrived, but I must confess I must be a little behind with the S.A. (white) scene, as I'm hearing about *The Pact* for the first time. One thing I find difficult is even keeping *au courant* with African news sufficiently to feel one is psychologically moving. I receive *Africa Digest* now, so that's a help. I'll be receiving *Manchester Guardian* – weekly edition – soon, so that may help. One used to keep up with book reviews in *The Observer* very well in Africa, & I miss that: their reviews have an excellent coverage. So I'm wondering how [I] can do this short of ordering an airmail edition. Do you keep contact direct with publishers, or do you depend on reviews to give you a sign when something has popped up? Heinemann send me their series, so that side is covered.

I know James Brown very well. I worked for *Drum* in the same building in which he worked for *Sunday Times*. His first novel, *Bright Sunday*, was published in 1956 or '55 – a typically raw novel – in the sense of the raw experience in African township living recounted by an amateur. His children's play about a circus cat is quite entertaining: I saw a performance of it in Tel Aviv last year. Quite an experience as Israelis are developing a children's theatre by getting *adults* rather than children, to perform children's plays.

Damn it – I'm rambling! So don't be upset by this hopping from one theme to another like this.

Nkosi is a common Zulu name: there must be as many of the breed as there are Jones's. Probably even more, because once you belong to a clan in Bantu-speaking societies, you are saddled with a second name (surname) of the whole community. Mphahlele's are several, although fewer than Nkosi's as we are just a section of the Bapedi *tribe* – a section much smaller than the Zulu tribe. A mythical attachment to such a name is the novelist's fancy, particularly one like Abrahams who knows little or nothing about S.A. ethnic groups. To a non-Bantu-speaking person, Nkosi might come most easily & readily to a man's mind searching for a name. (Incidentally, it means 'Master' or 'Lord'.) So don't strain your intellect about it! I use Sotho names for characters more than Zulu or Xhosa ones because they come most readily to me. Not to sound tribalistic (I flatter myself that I'm not, as Lewis Nkosi still is to an extent he would not admit to – see his *Home & Exile*), non-Bantu speaking Africans like Abrahams & the whites give most if not all of their characters Zulu names. This is because of the Zulus' past glory as a militaristic people. In fact there are many non-Africans who will ask you: Are you Zulu? – never any other tribe – not even Xhosa. Even whites in S. Africa. There is also a kind of romance about the Zulus operating.

Just in passing: *Bantu* refers to a *language* group and not a 'race'. It covers the whole area from Southern Cameroons to S. Africa & east to west below the Equator. So we don't speak of 'a Bantu character' or 'a Bantu'. Bantu will include languages like Zulu, Xhosa, Sotho, Swahili, Kikuyu, Luba, Shona, Ndebele etc, & we talk of Bantu-speaking people/s. If we want to be liberal, we speak of 'white or black Africans' (in a S.A. context) or *negro* when we refer to blacks; less liberal would simply be: 'African' as against 'white'.

Why am I lecturing to you like this? I think I'm just being garrulous & pedantic. So forgive me if I'm being tedious and telling you something you know already (I wouldn't be able to live that down!) I just happen to be in a talkative mood, so I've buttonholed *you*.

I am going to help George Shepherd of International Relations here in editing *Africa Today* – a journal that has been a product of American Committee on Africa in N.Y. & which they have now decided to relinquish publishing. A Board of people has taken it in hand (A.C.A. will, I believe, continue subsidizing it for a start).

I shall take care of the literary side of it – what there will be of it – eg reviews & features on African Lit. I'll be doing it pro deo, as George will also be. Would you be a contributor for it? I'm sure there should be a lot you could tell the Americans about African Lit. (The journal is really gunning at the American audience to enlighten them about Africa.) If you have a feature or book review, I should be grateful to have it. I'm not sure what fee they pay – it can't be more than peanuts, I'm sure. The idea is to build up the journal to a point where it can boast a distinctive style (at present undefined) & support itself & pay its contributors well. Is this attractive-sounding? Please let me know.

Best wishes,

Yours sincerely,

Zeke

P.S. I teach one section of Freshman Eng: & attend courses for the Ph.D. Why a man in a creative writing programme should do Anglo-Saxon (maybe Spring Quarter) & History of English Language is beyond me – but I believe they want one to feel he is still an academic! So I can't even begin on my novel until, perhaps in the Spring Quarter (I do 10 hrs a qrtr). Otherwise my family (4 children) & I are settling in well. Z.

P.P.S. I notice the library does not have a card for your thesis yet, which they will tell me usually indicates that the work is either being bound or already in the library. So this shows that it is not even in for binding yet. Coloradans strike me as timeless as we Africans are – in correspondence etc. Am I right?

Denver

16 December 1966

Dear Bob,

You are on a useful as well as interesting trail with regards to a further examination of Greene's, Joyce Cary's & Conrad's Africa. I believe you will come out with that kind of conclusion.

Yes I missed the Houston meet – was invited too late to be able to go. An Achebe monograph – why not? I haven't seen a sustained essay on all of him. So I'm sure he could bear one. Incidentally I'm off commentating now: I promised myself that if I have to do even a review, it must be very rarely.

Thomas Molmar: a magazine called *Diplomat* in N.Y. had a piece by him – 'Clichés on Safari', a commissioned thing which turned out to be so reactionary that they simply could not let it go in by itself. They asked me to write a counter, which I did. They haven't yet sent me a copy which was due out in June or so. Perhaps it is doing the rounds via Kenya, if they were published. He's an objectionable fellow, that.

Paton? No, I'm not aware of any criticism of him outside my very short thing in '*A.I.*' I'm sure he is an idol here & the myth needs to be exploded. Americans are strange that way: *God's Stepchildren, Cry* – , *Uncle Tom's C* are a strange mixture for acclaim, and yet perhaps not so strange, considering the guilt complexes they should set up in people who have a morbid liking for being maligned.

I'm intending to translate *Chaka* afresh, & as soon as I have cleared a number of things I want to start. I don't want to worry about a publisher yet until I'm half-way through. Your elevating remarks about the 'Guide' warm me inside: thanks for them. I had great fun writing the 'Grieg' story – everything concerning my uncle's life is authentic biography, except for the beauty queen episode. I had meant to send a copy to him, but it might land him in trouble as my books are banned.

I have now read your thesis. As a survey it succeeds, both in organization and execution remarkably in what you set out to do. It also meant you had to include some very poor material like Aluko's *One Man One Wife*. But you also have the best selections. It can be an exhausting business to keep pace with what keeps coming out, good & bad, which you can only determine after reading the texts. With more consultation, perhaps, you would have been able to fill in some gaps with philosophical material, some discussion of the relative lack of humour in so much of our writing; what Soyinka calls 'Narcissism' in African literature – the eagerness to explain ourselves etc. But as I say, you have done a commendable job of it as a mapping out of themes & the social conditions that give rise to them. You say some flattering things about *Second Ave* &, coming as it does in juxtaposition with Abrahams' *Tell Freedom*, your remarks are even more gratifying.

It seems that in a survey like this, even at the risk of getting in too much, a chapter comparing say Jacobson, Paton, Gordimer, Cope (even the old gargoyle Sarah Gertrude Millin), Joyce Cary, Elspeth Huxley with the Negro Africans, would not be amiss & would give it another dimension. This is just an afterthought & the omission is not serious. It would mean jettisoning chaps like Conton whose book is pretty poor. So much for what it could have done but succeeded within its scope all the same.

I meant to send you an article that appeared in a Columbia magazine by Wilfred Cartey in which he discusses me, Baldwin & another Negro writer, against a protest motif. But I can't lay my hands on it just now. A larger thing like that, as you once suggested, is overdue.

Best wishes,

Yours sincerely,

Zeke.

1967

9 February 1967

Dear Makhudu

Am here to preside at a conference of Scandinavian and African writers for this week. One of these affairs Sweden does to project itself into cultural areas it knows little about as an act, as I see it, of shaking itself out of a deadening complacency.

Incidentally, there are a number of African students (including South African refugees) at universities. They go through a course of Swedish first. Depending on what Naledi would like to do, this is a place that can be tried for a scholarship. I have friends here of long standing who could *at least* make enquiries on my behalf. I've ceased to be discriminating as to the country in which my children study – short of going to Spain or Portugal etc. if you think the same thing, I can, after I'm back in Denver, write back here. It is certainly education of a high standard. There is also the African-American Institute in Lagos for other directions. The thing is for her not to mark time after Form V and become frustrated.

Man, we feel with you on the visa palaver. There's plenty of shit all over in Africa. And as I said, we've long ceased to be sentimental about working in Africa, although I'm sure you suspected this fraud all along in East and Central Africa. To have come full tilt against it is a bitter experience. You have no recourse to higher authority at all once the small *white* expatriate or Indian or African (in East Africa) *a nyaka go rotela kaganong gagago*.[1] Ribs always says 'we'll meet in exile' and then she'll tell a native *gore a eo nyela koa thoteng*.[2]

I'm always tickled blue when I imagine '*thoteng*' – just a vast bare field *motho a kotame*[3] because he gets no hospitality from Ribs. Indeed they try to look familiar on meeting us outside their countries. And the threat 'we'll meet in exile' is a real one, with the coups running on as they are. Lust for revenge sits down there inside me. It will be interesting to know what the high Commissioner in Lagos has to say.

You're dead right about my having delayed the Ph.D., I think. The problem was I was most disinclined to do research into some academic thing simply for the thing, and the difficulty was, furthermore, that I could not do it with London University as an external student as I was not in a constituency College. What I shall always regret in my life, though, although you feel my writing has continued usefully, is the utterly wasted 3 years in Kenya. It turned out that I was among a community of petty, sticky, finicky, pseudo-intellectuals who don't want to be helped by a foreign darkie, but accept white help with tongues hanging out and saliva oozing from their goddamned glands. And I waged a war against the white colonial institutions running the theatre and music to the Kenyans, and tried to instil a sense of dignity that can only realize itself when the Englishman has stopped looking over the Black man's shoulder to surprise or direct him. And when the white fought back, I had *no* protection from the blacks. Looking back to that period I see only a waste land with cactus growing, signifying a negative capability – that's independence on a waste land. I never forget the smell of the pollen in the flower that grows on a cactus blade that I experienced when I was in Pietersburg. Cruel, spelling futility.

Funny thing has happened. In July 65 I went to Lusaka for an interview for the directorship of extra-mural studies at the university. I left with the mistaken impression that I might be appointed. I wasn't. A woman was specially asked from Ibadan University extra-mural (then deputy head) to come down to direct things. They wrote me a most apologetic letter, in effect (between the lines) suggesting they could not entrust the leadership of such a department to a darkie. They indicated if I was interested in an English lectureship, I could be considered. I told them not at the time.

Now, while here in Stockholm, I received a cable from the Vice-Chancellor asking if I could indicate whether I would be interested in a lectureship in African Literature after my Nairobi contract expires (they think I'm still there). Denver wants to keep me after the Ph.D. And I must extract from these African bastards (through their white masters) a promise that they will not Africanize my post and even throw me over to the immigration dogs. The Ministry of the Interior (or Home Affairs) *and* the Ministry of Education would also have to give an undertaking in writing (if I can get them to do that) that I'll be given an indefinite contract, depending on my merit, which I must make them appreciate is unquestionable.

Ek moet nou stop.[4] Love to all at home. (*Ba kana ba eo nyela thoteng MaNigeria.*)[5]

Ever

Zeke

P.S. I appreciate what you say about your verse. Constant writing is necessary in the matter of techniques – as with every other genre. And of course it's natural just to feel a void when 'nothing come o't'. If you write out of an inner compulsion it's fine and keep going when you boil over.

[1] 'wanting to urinate in your mouth.'

[2] 'that he/she should go shit in the field'

[3] 'someone is squatting'

[4] 'I must stop.'

[5] 'The Nigerians can go shit in the forest.'

General note on translations:

Please note that the phrases written in Northern Sotho in this letter and others translate poorly into English. The English translation does not adequately communicate the meaning or the tone and nuances are often lost.

Denver

27 February 1967

Jerry

Mrs Davis of the Centre for Students from abroad has drawn my attention to the fact that the extension of my programme for another year – ending 1968 – is something that should be applied for locally through another DSP form from her office. She advises it's none too soon to submit the form to Immigration now.

She is asking for a letter from you stating the terms of my employment for the extra year being applied for – stating stipend etc. Farfield Foundation's subsidy, as you will remember, is a two-year arrangement, and the amount will be the same – being the difference between DU's stipend and $9 000 in a year. This news to be stipulated on the DSP form. Although my stipend for

1966-67 was calculated for 9 months – 1st Sep1966-June 1967, I am actually being paid over a period of 12 months, the same p.a. figure. This is to cover me for the summer quarter, which is an excellent arrangement. Naturally, I want to take courses in the summer, and hope this is all right with you. Also, if you would like me to teach a course for the period – i.e. the summer quarter, I shall be only too happy to do so.

As soon as Mrs Davis can receive your letter, she will send in the DSP form for an extension.

Thanks.

Yours,

Zeke

Paris

1 August 1967

My dear Ezekiel Mphahlele,

You'll never guess how happy I felt reading the three poems you have published in Joe Okapu's *Journal Of The New African Literature And the Arts.* I always thought that poetry was your intimate concern: I heard you too often blazing up at approximate poets and their pretentious stuff to be convinced of the contrary. So, for:

What If I go as the unknown soldier
or attend by a buzzing fly?
what if my carcass were soaked in organ music,
or my ancestors had borne me home?

and for the rest, I say: Bravo! A new poet has come to light, and a real one. This is what I have already said and written in one of my broadcasts for French-speaking Africa. For I have translated your poems in French (I apologize for not having asked for your permission first, but I know you'll understand!) and taped them. One thing more they will be published together with three poems of LeRoi Jones translated in French and three poems of Tchicaya translated in English, in the blue pages of the next issue of *Présence Africaine.* I am responsible for those pages. My aim is to establish a real link between Negro poets writing in English and French in giving them the opportunity to read each other's poems in the language they know. I suppose you agree with me. Moreover, if you have a sufficient collection of your poems, I'll feel proud to translate them and publish a bilingual edition at *Présence Africaine.* Alioune

Diop to whom I have read your poems is willing to have such a book in our poetry collection. By the way, how is your leg since Stockholm? All right, I hope!

You will find enclosed, a series of nine poems directly written in English: *The Wasted Concerto*. I'm sending them to Okpaku for his next issue: he came home and I have great sympathy for him. He is doing fine work. Did you receive copies of my books I mailed at your address in America? ... Read these poems and send me more of yours : I am sensible to your voice.

Yours sincerely

[Identity of sender not established]

Denver

5 December 1967

Dear Makhudu

Ek glo die son brand dat die gat sweet eh, of hoe?[1] Snow here galore, and the real winter, we're told, is still coming – January-March. Otherwise life is good and kind to us all round, except that we are in distress waiting for the worst about Ribs' mother. Maybe I'm getting old, but death may be has been long with us – so much – that one has come to expect it, endure and let time wrap one up with its healing balm: Life towards death and vice-versa, so operates the tug.

We've began another quarter after 3 weeks break. Some of the work is a preparation of BA Hons., some not, some fills in gaps. Each course takes a quarter – 10 weeks. One has to fill in a period of literature by private study, provision for which is made, because you discuss things with your adviser. After autumn this year, I begin my novel in earnest and don't do course work. It's a good refresher period and I don't feel sorry. The American MA also has coursework together with the dissertation. I should think there are more people teaching and doing course-work and dissertation than full-time post-graduate students. This is the charm of the system against British rigidity.

I was the only one of 15 students to pass the French translation exam – Ph.D requires possession of two modern languages outside English without which a degree cannot be granted even if all the other requirements are fulfilled. Thanks for my Paris stay. I would have done Dutch/Afrikaans, but they have waived a second one for me. (*so bleddie geleerd kan 'n mens wees*!)[2]

So you failed to go to Zambia and Muriel to SA? Pan African shit at the one end of the spectrum and boer shit at the other – that's where we're wedged. I find some morbid satisfaction in being able to say *masepa' mmabona! Le megwete ya tatago bona*![3] December 17th I completed 47 years, and yet I keep feeling the next decade will be the most crucial, the highest fulfilment of my life – either direction. Success or failure as Baldwin says one must *earn* one's death: that makes me feel it can be a worthwhile decade. But that's on the personal level. On the Librarian level – a sigh's the answer.

Love from us.

Ever

Zeke

1 'I imagine the sun is so hot there that the arse sweats, not so?'

2 'A person can be so bloody learned!'

3 'their mother's shit! And their father's arse'

1968

6 January 1968[1]

Dear Makhudu

Been talking to Martin Kaunda about you. When he learned you were available, he contacted St Marks Sec. School in Mapanza South of here. He's on the school committee. At the same time Humphrey Langa (Todd's brother) was leaving after his 3 years' contract to Lusaka to lecture in an adult education college here. So they want a principal in his place. They asked for information from me. I gave them as good an account of your capabilities as I could. They say they'll cable you. I presume they will follow up with a letter spelling out the rest. Just thought I should fill you in on my interpretation of the situation to help you decide. It's a boy's boarding school; 400 strong, 19 on staff. You'd also teach 'a little'. It's 40 miles from the biggest town – Choma where shopping's done. There's a school truck; you'd need to finance whole cost of a car yourself (no advance). Electricity is generated locally – works till 10 pm. Water good. There's a craft school that needs a woman teacher and administrator attached to the school. The nearest girls' secondary school at Choma – reputed to be good. Primary schools exist at Mapanza. You'd need to work in collaboration with the existing chaplain.

I don't know the state or condition of your religious beliefs. I told them so. I know I couldn't work in a missionary school or religiously oriented one. But it might be the stepping stone if you can last the 3 years to a larger town and state school. Lusaka is not by any means an exciting town. It's dead-dead culturally. It is only nominally a town. I gather the Copperbelt is much livelier. The house provided (before I forget) is 3 bed-roomed. I'm told some part of a veranda can be converted into an extra bedroom. There is a boarding master so you wouldn't need to muck around with greasy dining room table and garbage for the piggery.

Haven't seen Victor or rather I have but he is silent about his side of the enquiries about a school.

I have just received word that my novel (*The Wanderers*) won the 1st prize in an African novel contest run by *African Arts* Magazine in Los Angeles. No publication news yet.[2]

So long

Zeke

[1] Written from Lusaka where on the completion of his PhD in Denver, Mphahlele later accepted a position as Senior Lecturer in English at the University of Zambia.

[2] Mphahlele is referring to a pre-publication version of the novel, which was entered in the *African Arts* competition.

From letter to Prof. Robert McDowell
Denver

Dear Professor McDowell,

We intend to bring out an issue of *AFRICA TODAY* (August/September) devoted entirely to a literary theme. For the sake of convenience we want to call the theme REALISM AND ROMANTICISM IN AFRICAN LITERATURE. In all the literatures of the world these two factors merge or overlap: sometimes to a fine degree, sometimes only generally; sometimes the lines of overlap or departure are vague and defy identification. There is in each region of Africa a body of literature that leans more to one side than the other. One can also find in any one novel or body of poetry a portrayal of situation, or character or mood which indicates a romantic projection on the part of the writer into an ethnic or tribal past or present, a nostalgia for traditional values that are being challenged; one can also find a mood of realism which implies social criticism: criticism of the past or the present. Even a romantic flight into an idyllic past or living tradition can be a form of social criticism.

We should like to explore these factors in modern African literature of English and French expression and hope to come out with a group of essays that will demonstrate the relative merits or place of Utopian ideals and the awareness of socio-political realities in Africa.

Our theme is divided into the following heads:

1. Realism and romanticism in South African Bantu literature
2. Realism in South African English fiction
3. Realism and romanticism in East African literature
4. Traditional values in West African English poetry: the search for traditional roots.
5. The theme of the 'new African' in West African English fiction
6. Social criticism in African drama
7. Diplomacy and compromise in French literature (Dipoko)
8. Realism in African French fiction

We are asking you to contribute an article on No. 6 of about 1500-2000 words, which we would like to have by the 15th of June 1968. As *AFRICA TODAY* does not have any funds for paying for contributions, this will be a labour of love, and we sincerely hope you can be kind enough to make your service available so that we may bring out a worthwhile feature. We shall value your ideas immensely.

Perhaps a discussion in depth of the more important works will be better than a survey of a large miscellany of works. But please use your own discretion. Any suggestions on the contents of the projected issue will be most welcome.

Thanking you in anticipation,

Sincerely yours,

Ezekiel Mphahlele

Editor

[Postmarked] Denver

2 April 1968

Dear Makhudu

Hell, it's been a long age since we heard from each other. But Muriel's letter explained the sound barrier. How ridiculous exiles can be among themselves. But South African tribalism is something one knew existed but rationalized it almost out of existence. Also creatures one never suspected come out in their true colours – e.g. S! We've had pretty nasty experiences with X's and Z's in exile which we never or only seldom experienced at home. We've now decided to be aggressive too and refuse to be taken in. Something we never dreamt we'd one day entertain. We're going to be tough to get, shut the gates and only let in those who deserve attention.

We hope things will work up for you in your present setting. On the other hand, there's always a chance for a change of setting.

How did Naledi fare in the exams? We hope well. I haven't heard from Sweden since I wrote the second time. I can't understand the workings of the UN at all. We'll be leaving Motswiri in boarding school here, and hope Teresa will succeed in finding a college. She's finishing high school in August but children of 16-19 can be so erratic in ambition, self-appreciation it can be heartbreaking.

I met Juta and Cynthia at Pittsburgh when I was lecturing there, they are very happy. Don't know what he plans after his MA. Heard Bob's now at University College in Dar? He writes to say he hopes it will be well. Heard of Todd Matshikiza's death? and Can Themba's in Swaziland earlier?[1]

Have finished the novel. Took me 2 months to write. But then I had it all in my head for five years. It turns out to be even more than the average 70 000 words. It's 90 000! Am finishing typing it in 2 days. I hope to publish it in the US before England as there's more money here. Title is *The Wanderers*.

It's in 4 books, 1st – set in SA, 2nd in Nigeria, 3rd and 4th in Kenya. All countries have fictitious names but are recognizable – like their cities. The central theme is the agony of exile and I try to orchestrate it with bits of lives of several exiles. I'm happy with it, but then one never knows.

Have you hung fire with poetry?

Do we understand that S is married to Mrs P? It's not clear in Muriel's letter if 'his wife' means C or – ?

What a pity we can't come thro' Nigeria; we've to stop two days in London and the West African flight would be gruelling for Chabi and Puso.

Love to you and tribe.

Yours ever

Zeke

1 Todd Matshikiza and Can Themba were fellow journalists with Mphahlele on *Drum* magazine. After emigrating with his family to London, where, following the success of the musical *King Kong*, for which he wrote the score, Matshikiza had struggled to re-establish his career, he returned

to Zambia where he worked as a broadcaster and archivist for the Zambian broadcasting services. Can Themba emigrated to Swaziland to take up his first profession of English teacher. He was declared a 'statutory communist' by the South African authorities and his work was banned. His death was linked to alcohol poisoning.

Denver

10 April 1968

Dear Bob,

Thanks for agreeing to write a piece for us. Do you have Alfred Hutchinson's *The Rain Killers?* (you know – writer of *Road to Ghana*). Quite an interesting play. If you don't have it I can lend you mine.

Say congratulations to Judy on her translation – am looking forward to seeing it.

We shall certainly leave for Zambia on Aug 8. Everything's fixed now. I shall teach a course in the summer while you have a lovely time in the Caribbean. How I envy you!

We have a friend at the University of the West Indies, Kingston – Arthur Drayton, so do look him up. You may even hit upon Peter Abrahams who lives just outside Kingston, he told us. Jamaica Radio should tell you exactly where – he works for them off & on.

I finished classwork & comps in December & in Jan. launched upon the novel. I finished it on March 8 – 2 months in all! But then I had been walking about with it in my head for 5 years! It's come to 385 pp now in typed form, although I hardly added anything when I typed the MS. This week I'm beginning to make the necessary corrections. It's set in S. Africa (first 2 books), Nigeria and Kenya (1 book each). It's partly autobiographical but much is fictional of course. Deals with the comedy & agony of exile & I call it *The Wanderers*. John Williams is going to introduce me to his agent so if it is publishable here, it should first appear in the U.S. I feel somehow if the subject does not interest American publishers, it should interest a British publisher.

Am again teaching African lit. this quarter, & it's fun – with 42 students in the class. Will be teaching the African novel in the Summer.

Warmest regards to you both from us,

Zeke

[Postmarked] Denver

16 April 1968

Dear Makhudu

We continue to hear some nice juicy gossip from Muriel when she writes to Ribs. Good to be able to enjoy laughing on the sidelines!

We have been informed there is a Scholarship body here catering for foreign students without placing them under any obligation afterwards. While I write to Sweden, it would be good if you wrote to them being in a father's position. Don't hesitate to mention you are an exile. Write to Secretary,

The Wien Scholarship Office

Brandeis University, (proper name is

Wien International Scholarship Program,)

Walthan 54, Mass. USA.

sending a curriculum vitae of Naledi. I am writing to Sweden, lumping together Naledi and Teresa, who wants to do dentistry, so that we cast our nets wide. I'm not writing to the Brandeis office for Teresa, because I want to see how Tony acquits himself, on the strength of which I'll write to Brandeis at the end of the year. He should, like Teresa, complete High School in June '68. Fortunately, in the States, age does not matter. But Tony knows we can only help him if he merits it. He'll be 20 in July. When I remember I passed Matric at 22, I grieve to think how youngsters can fritter away their time and fail to do better than their fathers in conditions which make it possible for this to happen. Let me know, what 'Wien' says.

Just received *Black Orpheus* 20. Seeing your verse again I feel its impact all the more. It rips, slashes and stabs and its effect is not that of a blunt instrument. You have a sense of words and their effect in various combinations. With poems that cover other experiences of life, here and others like them can still write, you should be able to collect an impressive volume. There is no money in poetry publishing, but anthologies are still being brought out. How much poorer I feel my anthology is without this groups of poems you have in *B.O.* Still, another time ... The publishers who brought out a paperback edition of *2nd Avenue* – Seven Seas Publishers, Glinkastrasse 13-15, 108 Berlin, Germany – publish protest literature. They've done Richard Rive's *African Songs* (short stories), Harry Bloom, Jack Cope, etc. When you think you want to try them (I've not seen any poetry from them, but they might consider yours), send them a bunch and await their reaction – say 10 pieces – before you proceed. A magazine here that publishes specifically Negro verse, particularly good protest poetry, is *Freedomways*, 799 Broadway, New York. N Y 10003, USA, is a good one to send a group about 3-4 at a time. I'm doing a book review for them just now and I know the editor well. Send them something anyhow.

Love to you and the tribe.

Ever

Zeke

Denver

11 July 1968

Dear Makhudu

Haven't written for a long age because I was trying to round off things before we leave in August 8. We are just as disappointed as you are that we can't come via Lagos. We were so looking forward to seeing you. The stamina problem with regard to Puso and Chabi is not so big as the fact that I have to see the publishers in London about the novel. With distances as they are between Africa and England, it pays to see people personally when one can, especially that by the time we arrive in London they will be ready to talk about the MS. I'm hoping the American publishers will bite! Still waiting for them to talk.

On the 30 July I go in for oral defence of my dissertation and will be capped in absentia. That will have capped a hectic two years. Somehow being away from dear old Africa has helped us look at her differently and understand her differently. I can see how necessary it is for you to keep there for the sake of the children's education, and to see Naledi into University. Teresa will be entering university, Motswiri will stay in a boarding high school. Tony is still in East Africa, still in a state of revolt without any thing positive to show for it. We left him behind to finish his GCE after fouling up every stage of his high school career. So we wanted him to be on his own and earn our respect rather than bring him to such a society as this, where he might not survive. Now he has finished his GCE ('0') but only did well in English Literature – not well enough to admit him into university.

He will have to decide *on his own* (he's 21) what to do next and we've told him we can't keep a person his age unless he goes to school or works and earns his keep.

We still read about the plight of the b's and the ravages of kwashiorkor among them. What a disturbing situation! *Dan moet sommige ouens nog praat van* 'Africa is not violent' *en al daardie kak. En die verraad van die Britse en die Russe! Verskriklik.*[1]

Love to your tribe.

Ever

Zeke

[1] 'And some people still say "Africa is not violent" and all that crap. And the treachery of the British and the Russians! Frightful.'

31 October 1968

Dear Bob [Robert Richardson],

Hi over there! I can imagine how you people are beginning to suffer with the snow and every other winter malady, while here we're weltering in the heat. We sleep without blankets on and half naked. But this is the sun for me. I must find a sculptor who can create a wooden image in dedication to the sun god, and I can stroke it every morning and evening and mumble soft words to it. Zambia is flat country, hardly any mountains, and so the solid shimmering heat stays down, unbroken. In November we expect the rains to begin.

I didn't intend to write an idyll on the weather, it came spontaneously. I sent you the manuscript of *The Wanderers* early in October by surface mail. It takes about 4-6 weeks, and you should receive it shortly. Grove Press say with things African their emphasis is on non-fiction. So I must trouble you to be my fiction pusher. Please use your discretion as to what publisher you try, excluding as we agreed Henry Regnery. By the way, their man has written again to ask for the MS. The irony may just turn out that *they* are the only ones who might want to take it!

Did you see in your newspaper the ridiculous report that I was among the candidates being considered for the Nobel Prize in Literature? *Le Monde* carried an item to this effect. As it happens, the Japanese (I forget the name) – an old man and certainly 100 times a greater man – got it. Some of these sponsors are clowns, and I think each time they are determined to suggest a negro African just so we shouldn't think we're forgotten – however frivolous the suggestion may be.

We think of you and Elizabeth much. Love to you both and the brood.

Yours ever,

Zeke

10 December 1968

Dear Makhudu

At last we're able to write. Settling in has been harder in Zambia than anywhere where we've ever migrated. But there's not anything like the tough inaccessibility of the Kikuyu here. The political attitude towards aliens is the same. Nigeria would still be the best, I think or comparatively easy in this respect. Maybe it's only in a very local context, as small as a school and one's working conditions, that one could be reminded constantly he's an alien. I didn't experience it in a natural context over there.

Then we were burgled and my car is still waiting for red-tape to act itself out before repairs begin. I fetched it from Malawi where the thieves drove it to, with most of the clothing they'd stolen.

University work has its excitements, initial shocks and one's reflexes find themselves back in action and alertness again. Again, this becomes a normal existence once you've been reminded that white retreads in African universities are always going to set the pace unless an African government, a black intelligentsia calls their bluff, then you learn to adjust without acceptance.

We're sad to hear about your ... trauma. Let's hope Tai will keep you till we can settle you here. Ribs will tell you what enquiries we've made, as well as Martin Kaunda's concern and active interest. I don't know if Ribs has sounded you about extra-mural teaching. But I never really want to recommend something to someone I wouldn't care to do. Extra-mural teaching is a waste of time and energy for a lively, restless mind such as yours and mine. I would suggest the whole damn structure of the thing in all of Africa should be scrapped. It's a farce, an utter wastage of material and human resources. I'm keener on Livingstone teaching and I hope Martin can pull it off. We'll press hard and fast in any useful direction. Good news about Naledi – we're happy for her and you.

Much love.

Yours ever

Zeke

Lusaka

27 December 1968

Dear Bob,

Thanks very much for your letter. I'm glad the Ms arrived, and thanks again for the trouble you're taking over it. Yes, if John thinks as he does about his agent, let her take it in hand if Viking turns it down.

In the same mail your letter arrived, came one from the magazine *African arts/arts d'afrique*, a fine glossy journal published by African Studies Centre, UCLA to say *The Wanderers* had been awarded 1st prize in their annual literature and arts competition.[1] The 1967-8 one, which closed in June this year, was for the African novel. The prize isn't very large, but one can't sniff at it and what's more is the recognition by the panel that there is something of value in the novel after all. I feel elated over this. The editor refers to it in his letter as 'your interesting and most painfully perceptive novel'. They will publish a self-contained abstract in the journal but this does not prejudice our efforts for the work (the prize is $1 000). Maybe will yet crack a bottle over that one day!

Someone in Indiana University writes to say he couldn't get my *Down Second Avenue* for his line-up of Colliers paperback editions of African writing because he's told by Faber that it's been taken by another American publisher. I'm still to hear who they are. But that's gratifying as the Americans have sniffed at it much too long since Faber brought out the hardcover in 1959!

Thanks for being willing to send me books I may need – it's so generous of you as usual. Please tell John I haven't yet received the *Denver Quarterly* that contained my address or lecture 'African Literature: What Tradition?' which I asked for in the dim distant past. Dover has brought out George H. Knight's *The Evolution of the English Language from Chaucer to the 20th Century*. Is Lewis Mumford's *The Golden Day* (Dover) any good? If so, can I have both books?

The rains are here and the Zambezi is rising and the hippos are jumping!

Love to Elizabeth and Bob's dear self.

Ever

Zeke

P.S. The University now insists its recruited staff must sign up for at least 3 years otherwise they have to refund transport fares for a member, family and goods. So we have to do 3 years, alas. We shall have to hang fire with the waiver and simply come back in as immigrants who can stay in the US. This is probably in our best interests, but how can exiles ever tell with these things? In our second year we shall set things in motion to apply for immigrant status. That's how erratic the Mphahleles are!

[1] *The Wanderers* was ultimately published by Macmillan in 1971 after protracted negotiations.

1969

Lusaka
30 January 1969

Dear Bob

Just thought to drop you a line to spell out my P.S. in my last letter, as it might have been cryptic – yes?

We are tied up for 3 years and wouldn't settle for less as the school wants to be sure it can keep expatriates for more than the usual 2 years to get the best out of them. I can of course break my contract after the 2 years required by American Immigration on condition I pay the university back the money on fares to Lusaka and £400 ($1,100) for freight of our goods. They would then not pay our fares back to the U.S. We wouldn't have that kind of money. And yet *we are* disillusioned by Zambia and the life of a black exile here is one of perpetual fear of deportation, government suspicion and general emotional dampness. The university is not a particularly stimulating place, is full of British retreads of the worst narrow-minded sort. And we do feel 'homesick' for Denver.

In any case, during 1970 we must set things going to apply for immigrant status. I have received a letter from a Human Sheveloo who was a teaching fellow at the GSIS of D.U. and has been battling against the authorities to obtain a waiver of the 2 years' absence requirement. He tells me that he has it – through the help of U.C. at Davis where he's teaching, local Congressmen, Senators, the Davis faculty and students. So it is possible – more possible than our man, Marcum ever dreamed of. There is another friend who's here on research, a South African from UCLA. He also obtained a waiver through the efforts of the L.A. campus.

Rebecca feels bad the experiment isn't promising of returning to Africa. As I never got up any enthusiasm about it, I felt the pain less.[1]

Love to Elizabeth & yourself from us.

Ever

Zeke

P.S. Tell John still haven't received Denver Q. with my piece in – the D.U. address

1 Zambia was the closest to home the Mphahleles ever reached in two decades of life in exile. Initially, they had entertained the hope of settling in Lusaka.

11 February 1969

Dear Zeke,

Thanks for your recent letter and I am terribly sorry to hear that the Zambia venture is not turning out very well. I have approached the Dean and we are going to try to work out some sort of agreement. It is too early yet to be certain of anything of course and I would not want to raise any false hopes, but I do want you to know what we are doing and what we are hoping to do. First, we will try to get the ear of one of our United State senators to get a bill through the Congress which would get you into the country presumably during the summer of 1970. Secondly, I am going to try to earmark a position in the English Department for you to begin in September of 1970. Third, we are going to try to find the money to pay back the University of Zambia the $1100 freight advance plus air fare they paid. At the same time, I would hope very much to find the money to fly you and your fine family back to this country. All this will take some doing, but I will keep you informed of our progress. I don't recall the exact amount forwarded to you by the University of Zambia, so if you could itemize for me the full extent of your debt to them, this will help me raise the money necessary to spring you.

The chance of your return here is a very exciting and much-to-be-desired possibility, and I have high hopes for it. Much love to Rebecca and the kids.

Yours,

Robert Richardson

Chairman

18 February 1969

Dear Bob,

It strikes me that if, as Lusaka's Consul says 'the law places responsibility for granting exceptions in the office of the Attorney General rather than in the Dept of State', D.U. lawyers could work on the Attorney General. Maybe even with the help of one Colorado senator.

Ed Kahn, our friend who looks after Pat & Terry, has often used some of his legal acumen effectively and you might not do worse if you ask him what he thinks of all this. He is also in with Dominic – no, that's not the right way to put it – he has, I think won him to his side once or twice over some points of law in state matters etc. He could be helpful as long as somewhere along the line D.U. lawyers and him could co-ordinate things.

Again, it strikes me that if it eventually turns out that I have to stay out till August 7 Rebecca and the 2 boys could enter the country as visitors on tourist visas. And then when I have immigrated their status could be converted accordingly. I could then wait out the period in Ghana, on a tourist visa, Ribs and the kids could enter *any* time. Maybe again Ed Kahn can explore this discreetly with Immigration in Denver – in order not to scare them off!

Cheerio for now,

As ever

Zeke

Zambia

24 February 1969

Dear Mr. Lindfors (we really must scrap the Mr mumbo j.)

I should be quite happy to act on your board of your advisory editors.[1] It sounds a most interesting project. It somehow never occurred to me that the U. of Texas goes out for African lit. I shall be glad also to do an article for you on the proposed subject.

I've conveyed your message to Dan.[2] He's pushing things to make ready for his return early April.

I'm afraid Zambia is most unpleasant these days, and I think we'll pack it in much much sooner than we had hoped for. As a matter of fact we had thought to settle here, but anti-South African (black not white) feeling is taking on absurd dimensions. Deportations of S. African refugees working as nurses, doctors, teachers are frequent. I end *The Wanderers* on a note of pessimism & it's unresolved where the protagonist will go from East Africa. But he feels he must go, keep moving. I seem to be acting that part right now, and the irony presses like an injection needle that seems to strike bone.

Best wishes.

Yours ever

Zeke

[1] He had been invited to serve as an advisory editor for *Research in African Literatures*.

[2] Daniel P Kunene, then also teaching at the University of Zambia. He was about to return to the University of California at Los Angeles.

Lusaka

2 March 1969

Dear Bob,

Thanks immensely for your letter which, although it warns against false hopes, gives us the confidence that you will do all in your power for our next move.

I have reread the contract. For some reason or other, I had read into it provisions that obtain in West African universities, which, paradoxically, are more advanced & generous in other respects than our institutions here. If one breaks a contract, it is only necessary to give *six month's notice,* which period must terminate on the date prior to the commencement of a new term. In my case I would need to give such notice to terminate on either June 6 or Sept. 4, 1970. I should prefer the former, as it will enable me to teach summer school in the U.S. – anywhere I can: there are a few open invitations I can pursue. The advantage of going up to Sept 4 is that I shall have completed the prerequisite 2 years outside the U.S. by then. Two years expires Aug. 6. Application for immigrant status may be easier. On the other hand, it may be possible for you to enlist the Senators support to allow me to immigrate two months earlier i.e. June 6 – anything to help me avoid an exchange visa. If I immigrate on June 6 or 7, I must give notice here Dec. 6, 1969 (six months to June 6).

Secondly, there is *no* provision that I pay back the university the money it spent on air fares and transport of goods this way. All the contract says is that I must return on my own steam as it were – pay our own fares and transport our goods ourselves.

This is the money that would be needed to free us from here:

Air fares – one way Lusaka/Denver – myself + Rebecca + Anthony – K259.10 / 3 adults: 777.30

2 children K129.05 / 2 children = 258.10

K1035.40

Transport of goods – about 3500 lbs = $2150 apx.

(1 Kwacha (K) = 10 shillings sterling = $1.90

So we are thinking of a total of $2150 + $1966.5 = $4116

We would naturally try to keep the weight of personal effects down to a minimum.

Best wishes.

For ever

Zeke

Lusaka

10 March 1969

Dear Bob,

Yes, thanks very much for *Denver Quarterly* reprints or rather off-prints and the two books I asked for. I shall take advantage of your kind offer and generosity from time to time and ask for books as I need them. We've reopened, and things are jumping once again.

In between our letters I have been hearing from Al Stephens at Santa Barbara. He first wrote briefly in January to ask if I was interested in coming to S.B. I explained my problems at length just as I spelled them out to you. He promised he was going to plug a number of lines to get the Dept. and the administration interested. Now this morning I've heard from him again.

Al says the Dept has voted unanimously in favour of requesting the Administration to make me an offer. What they contemplate is an associate professorship with tenure. He says preliminary signs are that the Administration is 'very much impressed' with me, and a formal offer will follow. There's a good chance, he says the chairman reports, that the money to pull me out would be forthcoming.

I thought to mention this, Bob, since I don't know at all what the ethics of academic exchange and faculty mobility are in the US. In Africa one would be inclined, purely as an instinctive hunch, to stay with those who first offered assistance – in this case D.U. And in addition I like D.U. which I know, and can only love the idea of Santa Barbara and the heat as I don't know it. We want to be guided by what is customary in a case like this and match it against what we think we want to do. In either case we know only the possibilities beyond the definite offer you've made and the potential Al holds out. I'll be glad to hear from you.

Yours ever

Zeke

Lusaka

29 April 1969

Dear Bob,

I am so sorry to hear the news of your father's death. One never knows when to 'accept' death and when one doesn't want to, and yet always it gives one a jolt which one never gets used to. But I hope – well, what does one ever hope for at times like this? The word 'sorry' sounds so futile, inadequate for the bereaved. I always find it's an utterly poor derivation from 'sorrow'. Maybe what one hopes really is that we can carry our sorrow with dignity, and chastened love.

I was going to write but waited until I should have received definite word about my US visit. It's now certain I shall do some lecturing to earn some money between May 11 and 23 before proceeding to Paris.

Cheerio till then,

Best

Zeke

Lusaka

27 May 1969

Dear Bob,

In Paris once more, and am just preparing to fall apart after the exhausting hell run I had in the US.

This is just a brief note to say that I need not even wait for the official letter from Santa Barbara: my mind is settled for the University of Denver, and needless to say, I shall be delighted to be back and working in your department. I have written to Dean Lindell accordingly, giving him a formal word of acceptance.

I shall be chewing over the possible course/s on the literary side and relevant texts for 1970 – summer and autumn.

Warmest regards,

Yours very sincerely

Zeke

Lusaka

12 June 1969

Dear Bob,

Just a brief note to confirm my acceptance of the position in the English Dept at D.U. I shall be thinking seriously and purposefully about possibly 2 courses I would like to teach next summer and 2 in the fall. I'll make a proposition, together with texts required. About this, then, anon.

Larson at Indiana tells me Colliers will want to publish the novel. He speaks ravingly about it, and thinks it is a huge step ahead in African literature. Says it's fascinating to see an African novel deal with ideas.

Now he says Malcolm McPherson of Colliers feels as Viking knows Colliers are reading the MS, it will be perfectly ethical for me to take the better offer, if Viking does go so far. I am telling Larson that I'm writing you to suggest that if Viking doesn't respond before June 30 (about a week from the time you'll receive this letter allowing for the underdeveloped American postal system) then Colliers should go ahead. This is an additional concession to Viking.

We've started the new term June-Aug. and I feel the fitter and the more relaxed after the trip to be able to look forward to D.U. next year. Just had a letter from Gunnar.[1] He seems to feel as restless as we. Rebecca is all excitement over the prospect of Denver next year.

Warmest regards to you and Eliz.

Ever

Zeke

1 Gunnar Boklund was, at the time, attempting to settle in his home country – Sweden. He subsequently returned to the University of Denver.

Lusaka

30 June 1969

Dear Bob [Robert McDowell],

I feel thoroughly guilty for being so negligent in my correspondence. I've [not] written a line to you for ages.

First, this dramatic move back to Africa not only claimed all my energy and attention, but, when it had been made, proved such a disaster that I've been angry every week since our arrival here last Aug. So has Rebecca been.

Second, as a result of all this, I've not written to friends – just sheer lack of gusto or zip etc.

The Zambians simply reject S African & Rhodesian blacks & their government expresses this by refusing to renew work permits, demanding travel documents that allow one to return to SA or Rhodesia [sic]. So exiles & refugees in the professions are on their toes all the time. Deportations are the order of the day. The university itself is in the hands of a clique of British retreads who want to keep the place the last citadel of British traditions & thus render the Englishman indispensable indefinitely.

The irony is simply this one – that whites can come & go & stay on but *black refugees & exiles* can't.

So I've decided to break my contract (3 yrs) this year 1969 & leave the country next March or June. We shall then be qualified for immigrant status & will return to D.U. – associate professorship in English dept.

That's the fiasco our Zambia venture has become, as the Kenya 'expedition' (3 yrs) became. How can I ever live down this utterly wasted 5 years of my life?!

Colliers will publish *The Wanderers*, so *that's* some comfort. How are things with you and J[udy][1]. Hope splendid. How was the Jamaican excursion? Sorry the Austin visit never materialized. Fisk was off & my itinerary became crazier & crazier but stimulating. Love to you from us.

Ever

Zeke

1 Robert McDowell's wife.

15 July 1969

Dear Bob [Richardson],

What a pity this university never took advantage of you and Lindell's proposal to establish an exchange programme! Now the Vice Chancellor has left before he ever did anything about it. He had the effrontery to say to me he never worked on it and left it at that. His 3 years – the first in the institution's life – were a dead loss to Zambia. His departure was most welcomed. As I shall be coming over, I don't think there's any purpose in bringing up the matter with the new Zambian V.C.[1]

I'm writing about a student here who is taking African Lit. under me and is completing the B.A. in Dec. He wants to do the M.A. in African Lit. Peter Thuynsma (pronounced Taynesmah) is a refugee from South Africa, more exactly an exile. Although he can't return to South Africa he can return to Africa to teach.

I have suggested he write you and find out the prospects of a scholarship at D.U. He will be married by Sept 1970, (his target) and his wife can work. She's a qualified nurse.

Thuynsma is a most keen, hardworking, able student. Serious but most pleasantly so.

What are the chances?

I did receive a letter from Larson – he says Colliers are definitely set to publish *The Wanderers*. So that's fine. It's good to have you around for these contacts – thanks very much.

We are fine here and send you warmest greetings.

Ever

Zeke

P.S. Did I tell you I received a letter from Kelling at Boulder who is offering me full professorship with tenure and rise in pay more than D.U. or S.B. can pay?

1 After Mphahlele had handed in his resignation at the University of Zambia machinery was set in motion to promote him from senior lecturer to Professor of English!

Zambia

21 July 1969

Dear Bernth and Bob [McDowell],

Thanks for your sheet asking for use of 'He & the Cat' in your proposed *Black Literature in English.*[1] I should gladly give the permission BUT for the fact that the story has been anthologized to death. It appeared in *The Living & Dead*, then in *Kenyon Review*, then in Nadine Gordimer's *South African Short Stories* (Penguin), & also in my *In Corner B* collection. I don't think it can make that good reading with its tongue hanging out as it were. What do you think? Why not take something from *In Corner B*? Then there's some story or two in *Living & Dead* not in *In corner B.* (Certainly not 'The Suitcase', also done to death.)

There would be no problem in taking it as appearance in a journal does not mean (as I take it) one loses rights over a piece. In the case of *In Corner B*, the rights are mine but reference has to be made to East African Publishing House in Nairobi. Didn't you receive my letter, Bob, saying I'm returning to the U.S. next academic year? Will be at D.U., where I've an Associate Professorship with permanence. Will be in Denver in time to teach summer school in 1970.

Colliers will be publishing *The Wanderers.* Sorry [I] couldn't get an invitation to come to Austin when I was over there.

Best regards,

Ever,

Zeke

[1] An anthology Lindfors and McDowell were planning but for which they did not find a publisher.

Sierra Leone

16 August 1969

My dear dear Ezek,

What a small world this is and how quickly time flies. The last time I wrote to you, you were holding fort in East Africa, while I was trying to convince Oxford – or the institute of social Anthropology, who have always championed African culture cause – that a genuine and rapidly growing West African literature in

English and French existed and was worth studying. Your short note was a great encouragement.

I see you are now in the States, still managing to spread the importance of a modified form of negritude/African personality. This is very good. I enclose a few papers which I know will be of much interest to you. Do what you can with them. Publish them in African forum, if you choose to or think they are worth all the fuss I'm making. But you must, please, let me have your comments on them as soon as you possibly can.

Kind regards

Sillaty Dabo

Lusaka

1 October 1969

Dear Bob,

I know at this time you must be up to your eyes in work for the beginning of a new year, so I shall not expect you to reply soon. Let it be just as you find the time – *ça ne fait rien.*[1]

The courses I should like to teach for Summer 1970 are two:

1. *An introduction to African Literature* (300 level)
2. *Beyond the Blues: Readings in Contemporary Black American Poetry.* (200 level)

I append my bibliographies on separate sheets.

The courses I should like to teach for Autumn 1970 are three:

1. *Thought, Ideology and Literature in Africa* (300 level)
2. *African, Black American and Caribbean Fiction: Aesthetics and Black Experience* (300 level)
3. *The Literature of Self-Definition in Black Africa: Autobiography* (200 level)

I append bibliographies. The texts headed References, I would strongly suggest, need to be requisitioned for the Library (i.e. Main). Is this possible? The African and Black American sections were pretty thin when I was there.

Here is tentative list of courses I am capable of handling for future quarters as we go along:

200 level: — Early Romantic Period (1780-1815): Blake, Wordsworth and their contemporaries.

200 level: — The Victorians: Tennyson, Browning, Arnold & their contemporaries

— Readings in later 19th century Victorian Prose.

300 level: — African, Black American and Caribbean Poetry: aesthetics and the Black experience

— Understanding Literature

Seminars — Poetry and Revolution

— The Novel and Revolution

— Conrad

— Hardy

— White South African writers and White American writers of the South: Fiction and Drama.

I think it would be a good thing to offer *two courses* – one African, the other Afro-American or one of these and a comparative one including Africa and the diaspora – black American and Caribbean.

i.e. Two per quarter. The quarter I teach 3 courses I can take any of the others I have listed overleaf. I am sure there will be a quarter after two cycles or so when I shall not feel like teaching more than one 'black' course. While I teach two a quarter, we shall also be strengthening the black section of the library.

Let me know your views on these matters, and if you give me the green light, I shall collect my material against my arrival. I give you lists of texts so that they can be ordered in good time and the necessary adjustments can be made where texts are not available. The Humanities Press now supplies African titles that Heinemann of London publish. And now Collier are redoing African and Caribbean titles as well as Black American.

I shall also be sending you material for mimeographing which I shall need to use as background stuff not easily available that side of the Atlantic, i.e. for both Summer and Autumn courses.

Karen will have passed on the message that I have signed the Agreement with Colliers for *The Wanderers*. I am at the moment touching up the last book again so as to tighten it, and also excising some of the dreary patches in the light of what Lee Chambers and Gunnar suggested during the oral defence.[2] It's always exciting to do this to a MS when I know it's going to be published. During the long vacation December-March I mean to break the back of the new novel – a political satire about clowns in Africa.[2] Wish me luck.

Much love to Elizabeth, you and kids from this tribe.

Ever,

Zeke

1 It doesn't matter.

2 Mphahlele is referring to the oral defence of his doctoral thesis. *The Wanderers* (an earlier version) was written in partial fulfilment of the requirements for the PhD degree at the University of Denver.

3 Mphahlele refers to his novel, *Chirundu*, first published in 1980. For almost a decade British and American publishing houses would not bite, as he put it.

Zambia

21 November 1969

Mon cher Jerry & *ma chère* Karen [Powlowski],[1]

Thanks a lot for your letter, and of course our warmest kissingest congratulations to you Karen on your Ph.D. Isn't it a mighty relief! Look, don't work yourself into a state of anxiety about a job. I've seen Ribs do it and it didn't do her any good. You *end* up by feeling sour. It poisons your system. Just take time and meantime do your translations.

First, of course I am excited about the idea of your teaching a course on African-French literature. You're way ahead of me in this, you've read much much more than *I* ever hope to do, so why shouldn't we take advantage of it? Would you like us to split the class so that the students can branch out and do two separate streams of fiction and poetry – English and French? Or would it be better for them all to cover both E & Fr., so that *we* can split the time? – 5 weeks each? Or should we enrol students for a specific course that you alone can handle on African-French fiction and poetry? There may be a little overlap, but it shouldn't matter. Maybe by 'special course' you mean not full course – yes, no? I should like you to do this, Karen why not work out the mechanics of it with Bob, even if you think the Summer or Fall course should be restructured to fit you in. I'll be happy to comply. Second, I wanted to include *Climbié* of course, but didn't know when it'll come out. Ask Bob to include it in the autobiography section, will you? I'm glad there's hope for publication.

I'm not sure when *The Wanderers* will be out. In mid-December I will be sending Colliers a re-worked version of Book IV. They've already paid me, so I'm keen to get it out of the way and start another this long vacation. I still have you in mind as *la belle dame sans merci* in the novel – *cela me fait rire sans cesse*: *Formidable*![2] *Certainement*, we may yet have a joint party on *Climbié* and *The W. que pense tu?*[3]

Tell Terry when you see her I'm shocked she doesn't think of dropping us even a lousy greedy p.c. on her safari between here and Denver. Ask her if she had Lusaka up to her gullet to such an extent. Tell Terry an intellect that can cope with Pope leaves me no hope for redemption.

Much love.

Ever

Zeke

[1] Colleagues of Mphahlele at Denver.

[2] That makes me laugh endlessly: Tremendous!

[3] What do you think?

Lusaka

28 November 1969

Dear Bob,

Thanks very much for your letter. Let me ask two things of you:

1. I need a letter from you to the American Embassy, P. O. Box 1617, Lusaka, (addressed to the *Consular Officer*), to say the Univ. of Denver is appointing me as of Sept, 1970, *and wants* me to teach Summer School June, 1970, that you hope that I and my family can get a 2 months reprieve from the requisite 24 months' stay outside the US for purposes of applying for an immigrant status. Say you understand that my resignation takes effect on May 16, 1970, which I have already submitted as it requires 6 months' notice as of Dec. 1, 1969. As May16 is close of term, the University of Zambia will allow me to leave then in order to be in time for the summer school at D.U., that you understand from me that it would be advisable for my wife to precede me and be in the US to look for accommodation – say May 9 at the latest. Could he, the Consul, use his good offices to obtain Immigration visas and to obtain the necessary 2 month or 3 month (in the case of Rebecca) reprieve?
2. It seems we may have to stay at the Married Students' quarters while we are looking for a house – *preferably* to buy. Or are they only for *students?* If we can be allowed a 3-bedroom apartment there, it would help. Can you investigate?

3. We have asked Mrs. Millie Steiner at 121 So-cherry Street to help us look around for a house to buy. We would prefer University Park, the area where the Chambers live *or* where you are, where Gladyce Lyman lives, the area bounded by So-cherry, Valley Highway and Mississipi i.e. around Cory School – in that order. We need a liveable basement and 3 bedrooms. Have told Karen her idea of teaching African-French Lit. is excellent.

Regards as always.

Ever

Zeke

Lusaka

5 December 1969

Dear Bob,

Just a hurried note to say this University wants to give me a professorship. The Dean of Humanities says although I have sent in my resignation, they want to make a gesture in acknowledgement of my worth (sic) and this won't mean I'm obligated to stay. He is asking for 3 references and I have cited you as one of them. I hope this is all right, and when they write to ask for a testimonial please give them what they ask for. As I say my resignation is now in the hands of the administration and they know it is to D.U. I'm coming.

They may, of course, go against the dean and decide as I'm leaving it's not the thing to do. In that case you won't hear from them. I'm too bored to care.

If the State Dept. does not send me the numbers that authorizes Lusaka to issue us immigrant visas (the Consul here says as we started as early as last March to apply this should not happen) then I'll ask you to plug it on your side with Washington – we'll write and ask you to give Dean Lindell the green light to send the cheque to the shippers.

Love to the family.

Ever

Zeke

Lusaka

24 December 1969

Dear Bob,

Thanks for your letter giving me the details about the Summer School and my part in it. Everything you say suits me fine.

I asked you to write a letter to the American Consul here regarding the need for us to arrive in Denver in time for the Summer School etc. If you have already done this, fine. If not yet, don't write it, but let it accompany something else addressed to whomever the Naturalization & Immigration Services recommend.

This something else, I have now been told by someone who knows the ropes. Owing to the fact that there is a certain preference category for immigration meant for general applicants which is dealt with by a monthly quota system, my friend stresses *the importance of the institution employing me itself filling forms* which state unequivocally that it wants me as of Summer school time etc. These forms are available from the *Immigration and Naturalization Services in Denver*. They will serve as an application from D.U. to bring me in as an immigrant, returnable, as I say, wherever INS recommends. This procedure is for another kind of preference that goes quicker. If, as may very well be the case, my application of March 1969, falls under this preference, as I indeed stated then that I was being employed by D.U., then your application will reinforce it, and this makes for better preparedness against bureaucratic 'sense'. Together with this application can go the letter I asked to be written to the American Consul here, whether or not you have done it already. May is not very far off, and if this is done speedily – by the Dean or yourself – whichever you judge will look more ostentatious – results should be quick.

Meantime the university here has accepted my resignation and as I would be due for 3 months' 'home leave' (Britain is regarded as my home because of the passport) in mid May, they'll pay our fares from here to Britain. Air fares from London-Denver will therefore be our responsibility. As Dean Lindell didn't close the door for further consideration of our application for air fares, I wonder if he'd be willing to consider this part of the trip. Am writing to him about this one point.

Will write a little later about courses for Winter and Spring.

Cheerio for now.

Ever with best wishes,

Zeke

1970

Lusaka

3 January 1970

Dear Sonia,

I am sending you the material for mimeographing – *all* for the Summer School & the Fall course. So, could you have a big number of copies made?

I am sending you at the same time, in one of the two packets of the stuff, a handwritten Contents sheet as a guide. This should not be typed. It merely shows that I have arranged the stuff in 'volumes': 1–7.

There is an *Introductory Note* which goes separately – marked 'To be done separately: no volume one.' Then follows vol. 1 – *The Wisdom of Africa ...* etc. Some volumes have a single essay, others have a number of essays. The Contents sheet indicates e.g for Vol. 2. *three essays.* Two are extracts from a book *Race & Colour* etc which I'm trying to Photostat or the whole book with the extracts indicated, plus Essay 3.

Where a volume has more than one essay, these should be pinned or stapled together to look like a single volume. The vol. no. indicated , and the pages should be numbered progressively, so that each essay does not have pages 1 – n.

The titles of the volume are all indicated on the *Contents* guide i.e the general title for the volume *plus* the titles of the individual essays.

Apart from the *Race & Colour* book that I have (for vol. 2), the paperback edition of Senghor: Prose & Poetry is the only *book* I am sending. All the other material comes from the journal *Africa Today* (orange cover), typescripts and off prints. All indicated in the Contents guide.

Footnotes: Footnotes in Senghor should appear

Footnotes in *Africa Today* should appear

Footnotes in typescripts should appear

Footnotes in *Race & Colour* should appear

and therefore index nos. *not*.

I do hope sincerely there will be good enough time for all this to be done by the Summer. We are of course needless to say all anxious to be back in Denver. Are you laying on a big party? All we are waiting with trepidation for are an order from Washington for visas to be given us, so keep your fingers crossed.

From Zambia with love.

Ever

Zeke

Lusaka

5 January 1970

Dear Sonia,

Am writing briefly to say I'm sending off *three* 2nd class airmail packets numbered (1) (2) (3) just so that you're sure they are all in. I shall be grateful if you will send a brief note of acknowledgement soon as they arrive, just to settle my mind as it's such a long trip they'll have made!

This is stuff for mimeographing for *both* the *Spring & Autumn* courses. So a number of copies of each will be required. I've in one of the packets a Contents sheet as a guide. It shows that there are 7 volumes (vol. 4 is still to follow). A volume may have 1 essay, or a few essays. The volumes are numbered, so are the essays in each volume. The Contents sheets show the headings for the volume and for the essays individually. Essays of a volume should be bound together and page-numbered progressively 1 – to whatever number in each volume. A volume will always begin at page 1.

I've said the essays from *Africa Today* come from an orange-covered journal, but in fact I've torn out the pages to make the parcel lighter.

From Zambia with love.

Zeke

Lusaka

22 January 1970

My dear Sonia

Thanks for the forms. Here they are:

ESI – 575 – in duplicate. See page 2 where marked.* I believe this space is only for an agent if I have not signed it myself (?)

See p.1 marked *. I have to attach my Ph.D certificate which presupposes the lower degrees. But I have only yesterday packed my diploma off with my goods for dispatching to Denver. I am sure a statement from the Chancellor or his Vice or the Dean certifying that I have a Ph.D. should suffice. Goods take about 3 months by sea. (See note of Instructions in # 1-140).

I don't know if p.1 at the bottom they want Rebecca's married surname or maiden surname. If maiden surname, it is Mochelibane. Fill in whatever appropriate.

Please call Cyndi Kahn, Teresa's and Pat's guardian – 2345 Leyden St and ask her to give you a cheque for $25.

Last week I sent Vol II material, so it will have reached you by now. Keep looking for a house. Thanks ever so much, as always, for your efficiency – always right on your toes!

Love

Zeke

22 January 1970

Dear Sonia,

Just sent off the forms and forgot to ask you in the letter therein to keep all book parcels sent to you for me or addressed to me – until I arrive. I've packed off everything and if books come to me I shall have trouble of remailing them. Letters can still be sent to me here. Journals should also stay there till I come.

Ever

Zeke

P.S. I just hit 50 on Dec. 17 last year and tell Bob I'm trying to feel what I'm supposed to feel like at 50. I can't. Seems all the same as I was 10 years ago. No wiser, more garrulous. Rebecca says more choosy.

30 January 1970

My dear William

What an age since I last wrote to you. This is to re-establish contact and also to impose upon you with a request. In mid-May I shall be returning to the University of Denver, Colorado, as Associate Professor in English on a permanent basis. The same old story – hostility in Zambia against Black aliens.[1] I felt wanted in Denver when I was there 1966-1968, and that's the measure of a man's vanity to return there.

I shall be teaching a course next autumn which is intended to be a comparative study of white American writers. I shall of course use *Turbott Wolfe* as jumping-off ground, together with your poetry of the South African phase. What I should like to know is what of Nadine Gordimer, Dan Jacobson, Lawrence van der Post is still in print. I have Paton's latest book about his late wife, but I don't know if *Cry*[2] is still in print, also *Debbie Come Home*. I am thinking of Gordimer: *A World of Strangers; Occasion for Loving*; Jacobson's *Price of Diamonds*; *Evidence of Love; Dance in the Sun;* Paton as above. I lost van der Post altogether and would like to know what of his is in print, even his non-fiction work. It would be particularly helpful if the things in print are paperbacks, as it makes it easier to 'sell' a course to the department of English. I shall also be teaching *Poetry and Political Conflict*. I want to include poetry for and against fascism, war etc. I have never really done Roy Campbell in depth, and our library is still very poor.[3] You may have some of his poetry and tell me which are, as has often been the accusation against him, pro-fascism.

I know this is a tall request, but any information in this direction will be greatly appreciated.

My novel, which I finished last year – *The Wanderers* – will be published by New York's Macmillans. Faber rejected it – for Faberish reasons. It will come out in November this year and I'll certainly send you a copy. London's Macmillans are interested in a proposition I put to them – to bring out a collection of articles by me that have appeared in various journals – stuff of literary and cultural comment on the African and Afro-American scene. They are now looking at the material. If they refuse to bite, I'll try elsewhere.

How are things at Cape? Hope you are still flourishing. Working on any literary piece?

Give my best greetings to Charles, and my fondest regards to yourself.

Ever

Zeke

P.S. I'm reminded of Jack Cope. What of *his* stuff is in print?

1 In addition to feeling unwelcome, Mphahlele was acutely concerned about the plight of South African refugees in Zambia. He was also disappointed with the failure of the promise of independence, partly due to the undue interference in Zambian affairs of white expatriates from Rhodesia and South Africa.

2 Alan Paton's elegy for his late wife, Dorrie, was published as *Kontakion for You Departed* (London: Jonathan Cape 1969). Mphahlele also refers

to *Cry the Beloved Country* (New York: Scribners 1948) and the collection of short fiction, *Debbie Go Home* (Jonathan Cape 1960). Plomer was a reader and editor for Jonathan Cape.

3 Plomer had worked closely with Roy Campbell and Laurens van der Post as co-editors of the journal *Voorslag* ('Whiplash') in 1926. By the time of his death in a car accident in 1957 Campbell had published seven collections of verse, two volumes of autobiography and several critical studies, notably on Wyndham Lewis and Federico García Lorca. He lived in England and Spain before settling in Portugal.

13 February 1970

Dear Jack,

I read with sadness the news about the banning of your new novel.[1] One has come to 'accept' such news with a sense of apathy, though, which is *the* sad thing about it, rather than the news itself. It used to be a joke that the banning of one's books lends a stamp of merit and increases circulation elsewhere. It's not a joke anymore – not to me, and one does not have to display such heroics to prove the worth of one's writings. And anyhow there is so much obtuseness about the banning procedure that it can't be a signal for anything more or less than pettiness, meanness.

I am returning to the U.S. in mid-May for good this time. Will be Assoc. Professor in the English Dept., University of Denver, Denver, Colorado 80210. We've had enough of the chauvinism and exclusiveness of African States directed specifically against S. Africans and even Rhodesians in the case of Zambia.

I shall be teaching a seminar class when I'm back there and want to conduct a course in *Poetry and Political Conflict*, and an ordinary course in the comparative study of S. African and American fiction in relation to race. I want for the latter to include what fiction of yours is available and in print in hard-cover, which in pb.? If I know this, I shall know what to select. Are there any in print in American editions?

For the first-mentioned seminar course, I want to include Afrikaans poetry – much more than you have in the Penguin book – around the conflict between Boer and Briton by the Totius, Cilliers and generation and later poetry that treats of political conflict – whatever kind. What anthologies of this kind of poetry or in during it – coming right down to the Sestigers? Even single-author volumes will help as long as they have this kind of poetry wholly or in part. I can then order them – if you guide me as to what bookshops in C.T. I can write to (address etc). I shall then translate as many as possible for a cyclostyled volume. I shall be more grateful for your assistance.

Meantime, *hou koers*[2] and good luck,

Yours sincerely,

Zeke

[1] Jack Cope's *The Dawn Comes Twice* (Heinemann, London) was declared 'undesirable' in October 1969.

[2] 'stay on course'

18 February 1970

Dear Bob,

I know the bureaucratic tangles you are in with regard to this immigration business. The Consul here, as Washington is, is going by the book. The man I have in mind who got a reprieve is Human Sheveloo, now in Pol. Science at the University of California, Davis. He was at Santa B. previous to this, and the Univ. of Cal. used its guns to have him stay. Maybe an advantage here was that he was still in the country and so used the possibility of embarrassment on the part of Washington against him if they tried to send the police to lift him and the family out! But there it is, he succeeded. Perhaps you can call him for more details about strategy. Another thing of course is, as you suggest to plead hardship on the part of our children. Third, there is the fact I am technically stateless. I have a British passport, but it is by *registration*, and I am subject to the Immigration Law (Commonwealth) which forbids immigration except on the quota system. So that I can't immigrate automatically. Only my wife and I have British passports. Our children, as they were born in S.A. are not eligible for British passports. Pat and Terry over there travel on Kenyan documents issued under the Geneva Convention for refugees. They are all, like us, stateless, for all practical purposes. This all means that we can only work in Africa on employment permits renewable every year or two. African countries do not grant any refugee or any kind of alien citizenship or immigrant status. The state Department can verify this if it wants. I'm talking in *literal* terms. I have to work in an African university that offers the best contract and work permit facilities. Zambia had a better contract than Kenya (where we were previous to the US). (I'm declared a prohibited immigrant in S.A. and therefore banned). The regulation says 'or in another foreign country'. Surely it must depend on the conditions prevailing in that country, which must be expected to enforce its own immigration rules, like the US!

What about trying to plug the Sheveloo issue, that of the children and that of my statelessness.

If the worst comes to the worst, we shall go and wait the 2½ months (24 months expires Aug. 7) in Ghana. The pity would be that I couldn't work at any university there as we don't have Summer school in Africa. I couldn't stay the period in Zambia as my work permit ends when I resign – May 16 and I'd need to leave the country and reapply for a visitor's visa – without employment. *Voilá, mon ami! Vraimeni ridicule*![1]

Love to Liz etc

Ever

Zeke

1 'That's it, my friend! Truly ridiculous!'

Cape Town

23 February 1970

Dear Zeke,

It was nice hearing from you again. I guess I understand pretty well your feelings about chauvinism etc. It will be a great relief to get back into the freer mental climate of the States. There is such vast leeway to be made up in Africa that one gradually builds up a feeling of endlessly getting nowhere. But then I guess that wherever we are we are all in one way or another bound to the wheel and efforts to free ourselves are an illusion. Is that African humanism or Oriental mysticism?

Your planned course at Denver seems to raise fascinating issues, but documentation is going to be a problem. On the Afrikaner-Briton conflict in poetry, I don't think you'll find any anthology or other concentrated source. The poets who dealt with this mainly were the old generation: Eugene Marais, Jan Celliers, Totius, C Louis Leipoldt. Others like A.G. Visser and even C.M. van den Heever (who was born in a concentration camp) also used the theme. And Langenhoven if you can call him a poet. Of course as poetry it is all very poor stuff, drenched with sentimentality and self-pity. These poets are frequently being reprinted and so I reckon you need only ask for *Versamelde Gedigte* of each of them. The best bookshop for searching out this kind of book is C Struik (Pty) Ltd Box 1144 Cape Town. I take it you have the *Groot Verseboek* which gives something of a cross-section of the older poets but is very poor on anyone since about 1950. By the time Van Wyk Louw came along Afrikaans nationalist poetry had got well infected with Nazi ideology, *blut und bodem* nonsense, Watermeyer with his Duisend-jaar Republiek etc. The first Afrikaner poet to identify artistically and emotionally (not merely for picturesque effects) with Africa, the African and coloured peoples was Ingrid Jonker. I could send you a translation of Leipoldt's *Oom Gert Vertel* which is on the Boer-Brit theme. Pure x corn, of course. My own books are all out of print and available only in libraries, except *The Dawn Comes Twice* (banned in S.A.). You might get a very few copies of *The Man Who Doubted* (stories) in London through Foyles. Ingrid Jonker's books are available in Afrikaans and there is a translation of a selection of her poetry done by William Plomer and myself, Jonathan Cape, London. This is the only book of translations by an Afrikaans poet although there are a few selections of translations from other poets, nearly all bad. I am afraid, Zeke, you are here on rather barren ground, but if there's any way I can help I shall dig around and see what I can unearth.

Incidentally, I haven't yet had a book published in the U.S. and that makes things a bit difficult. Had dozens of stories in *New Yorker*, *Harpers* etc now all buried in dust laden files!

All the best and *voorspoed*[1] in your new job. Write again if there's any point on which I can help.

Jack Cope

[1] 'good luck'

3 March 1970

Dear Jack,

Thanks very much indeed for your informative letter. I will write to Struik for the *Groot Verseboek* – I don't have it. Actually I merely want to give a cross-section of this anti-Briton stuff from the Totius generation. Then I want to present Ingrid Jonker to point up the contrast. I shall also write to William Plomer for your joint translation of her. If there is any part of Uys Krige – anti-war, anti-repression – (I'm not aware of the existence of the latter) it might be good to include him. I lost touch with his poetry years ago when Afrikaans poetry was beginning to stick in my gullet. Please do send me your translation of Leipoldt's, *Oom Gert Vertel*. I remember the Afrikaans version vaguely from my teaching days in the 1940's and 50's.

I plan to translate a cross-section from the *Verseboek* and collate the lot into a small verse anthology. I'll try to get your volume of short stories.

Thanks again, I may worry you once more.

Ever,

Zeke

Cape Town

11 March 1970

Dear Zeke

I'm sending you a couple of translations which may help in your teaching course. One is the extract from Leipoldt's *Oom Gert*; then there's Cellier's *Kampsuster*, a bit of Boer War stuff, both of these being saccharine with sentimentality. I've added a translation of SV Petersen's *Bede*. This also does not stand too high as poetry but you may find it useful as an illustration of a certain phase of the Coloured writer's reaction against colour bar. Petersen uses irony in suggesting that even God is unjust and in accepting his punishment he condemns the injustice of it. I guess you know this poem. The translation is not entirely successful but gives some idea of the poem.

About Uys, he is never really outspoken in his poems though he sometimes issues a panic-stricken appeal to the *volk* to be more large minded. You will find this in *Verre Blik*, and more personalized in *Plaashek*. Both of these appear in translation in the *Penguin Book of SA Verse*.

Adam Small is the most interesting Coloured Afrikaans poet. In the Penguin we included his *There's Somethin'*. He also has some excellent pieces of protest and irony in his inimitable and untranslatable Cape Afrikaans. His books are *Kruis my Kitaar* en *Sê Sjibbolet* which you might get from Struik. Adam's poem *From here to Eternity* is first rate and was once read in Parliament and caused quite a sensation in one of the debates on the deprivation of the Coloured voters of their franchise.

If I think of anything else that might help you I'll send it along. Please send me a copy of your renewed collection when you eventually get it together.

All the best

Ever

Jack Cope

12 March 1970

Dear Bob,

The first round has been won, so three cheers! Thanks for the ammunition you put into the tray. What did you do? Senators, the lot? Whatever you did must have been a devastating salvo. The Consul here received a cable last Friday (the 17th) from Washington to say the 2 years' requirement has been waived and we can now apply for visas.[1]

I say the *first round* because the Consul seemed baffled. He showed me a cable he had received earlier from a Rogers – presumably the Secretary of State's name (?) which instructs him NOT to exercise any sense of priority with regard to 6th Preference visas. This means we must wait in the queue and no priority status can be accorded us. According to him (the Consul) we entered the queue in Feb 1970, after, I guess, some other people – that is only when you wrote him the letter. (I can't for the life of me figure out why he now thinks we are on a 6th Preference application as he does not seem to have heard this from Washington.) *In Feb 1969*, I registered for an immigrant visa and, although I didn't know it, he put me on a *non-preference list*, and why he did not put me on a 6th preference list the devil alone knows. So I have only entered the 6th preference queue in Feb. 70! We have to wait our turn, he says. He has no hope it can be out before May, which is when Ribs and the boys want to leave. You see then that the earlier cable threatens to defeat the purpose of the waiver. Maybe you can put through a call to Washington and ask for an explanation of this apparent contradiction between the two cables.

Sorry to harass you once more, I do however appreciate that the harvest rock has been blasted – it's now just the mechanics of the visa that remain. I would like to have the green light to go ahead preparing for the courses I suggested for Winter and Spring '71. (Matter of the goods fixed.)

Warmest regards.

Ever

Zeke

[1] This success was due to Richardson's relentless energy. To appeal on Mphahlele's behalf he wrote to several congressmen, including the then Attorney General of the United States, John Mitchell (25 February 1970). The negotiations had been so difficult and protracted that the University of Denver's Vice-Chancellor, Wilbur Miller, wrote in a memo to Richardson dated 5 March: 'I have never seen anything so complicated and have decided to retain an immigration lawyer until we get this straightened out.'

17 March 1970

Dear Sonia,

Thanks very much for your letter explaining the further complications, which I also spelled out in a letter to Bob R that must have crossed with yours and his.

This is now the latest. The waiting list for Sixth Preference applications is entrenched by law and no priority can be claimed, so says the Consul here. As you say, the cut-off was Oct. 1969.

Now the Consul has 3 numbers for three South Africans who have evidently fallen out because they have not replied to his letters to them. As we applied in Feb. 1969 on the non-preference list, and these S. Africans are on the same list, we can have them as the March quota. So Rebecca and the two boys will have their *visas* in a day's time. For me he will apply for a non-preference number for the April quota. His application is due to go out on March 23. So now I suggest we plug the non-preference category as I *am* eligible, having put in so early in 1969. Maybe Bob can call Washington only if the Consul here has failed to get an April number in the non-preference category, although he thinks the chances are great I'll get it. I'll cable Bob in April if I'm stuck. But if on the other hand he would like to insinuate a priority request to synchronize with the Consul's application from here, he may call Washington.

Can you, Sonia to save me a full-length letter, call Edwin Kahn at Holland & Hart or at home to explain this new move so he's *au fait?*

By the time you're done with me you'll have lost weight.

Bye now, & love.

Zeke

Surrey

21 May 1970

My dear Zeke

Your note from Lusaka caught up with me here this morning – I am sorry Rebecca had such a harassing time before leaving, but by now I am sure she takes everything in stride! It is good that there is someone of your stature who has the ability and the courage to 'call a spade a spade' because historians of the future will be greatly helped when it comes to building up a pattern of these days. During our recent move from those hired rooms into a tiny flat –

but our own – I did some more sorting out and was strongly disposed to burn a pile of papers, but in the end I bundled them up and sent them to join all my 'trial papers' in the archives of my college library. I know it is passing the buck and when they do open them (I believe the rule is 25 years after the death of the sender) there will be students objective enough to know whether any odd document has value. Now there remains only one more bundle which I work on steadily whenever the mood descends on me that is all my notes built round the Treason Trial with potted biographies of individuals which I bring up to date from time to time. Thus by and large I like to feel I am not wasting these less glamorous years, in which my main preoccupation is to ensure as much happiness as possible for Florence (by the way she is 81 to-day but I told her not to come up here until the end of the week, too much travelling fatigues her and we have the phone!). Thinking of personalities, there is an interesting group here in London, some of whom visit us from time to time, but the majority look upon me as an 'has been!': the grape vine brought me an interesting whisper from America about Mangaliso – have you heard anything?

Concerning this operation which was performed on the 8th in a research hospital for that group of trouble (urinary tract), the doctors appear quite amazed at my physical reaction declaring they find it hard to accept that I will be 79 next week. My programme was simple – May 6 admitted for preparatory dosing etc May 8 operation May 10 lifted into chair after a blanket bath May 11 went to toilet alone. Carried on with the wretched programme (and it is a miserable affair!) until May 18th stitches removed, and self transferred to this comfortable place to convalesce! When the surgeon congratulated me and talked a lot of rubbish about 'must have lived a careful life etc' I kept quiet and said nothing.

Then just as I was leaving to come over here a younger surgeon who had handled me under direction of the top-surgeon who operated, came and sat down, looked at me and smiled, then said 'You know you are an interesting case – a colleague and I would like to do some research but it will involve taking blood specimens, do you mind?' Of course I replied, 'Why should I mind? Anything that helps you is OK with me.'

Then I told him that I belong to the Anatomical Society – a group of people who bequeath their bodies for research if needed. As a result of that this morning I was 'blooded' pretty freely and warned that it is quite possible I will be asked to visit them from time to time. Rotten fun, don't you think, to be a bit of use somehow!

Sorry I am rambling on which is largely selfishness on my part – no visitors turned up this afternoon and I got a bit bored of reading so I thought I would chat with you. I hope you are not yawning! One of the days it will be fun to set some tribal history, in the meantime say – Love to Rebecca, and all the line, hoping that something will bring you over to this island one of the days, but I guess it will not be this year which you will need to dig yourselves in. One final gossip – I do not know how far you have been in touch with Mary Louisa Hooper thro the years. She came over to London at the end of last year intending to 'settle' in order to help! What subsequently happened I know only vaguely – she changed flats frequently because she said certain individuals molested her: she had to make arrangements with the postal people to check in-coming calls, before putting them through ... and several other nonsensical things! In the end she returned to her daughter's farm in Oregon, declaring to me in overflowing language 'I shall come back – my African friends need me etc'.

As I see it a classical example of a good person not knowing when to stop, but I may be naïve! I trust you, Zeke, to be careful and not use this sketchy information: the end of the story is that she has at last accepted the inevitable and will live out her days in the States.

As ever, yours

Arthur

Liege

27 May 1970

Dear Professor Mphahlele,

We were in touch a few years ago, when I had barely embarked on my research about modern African literature. I am now working on a concise history of creative writing in sub-Saharan Africa which is to be printed by Crowell's in New York in 1972, and because you had such remarkable influence on the growth and orientation of literature wherever you went, I should like to have some more details about your activities since.

At the time, you had started working with the Chemchemi Cultural Center in Nairobi, which, in fact, I assume had been founded by you. Most of the biographical information I have concerning you comes from an article entitled 'Always an Exile' which appeared in *West Africa* in 1963. It was, I presume, the outcome of a personal interview, and so must be reliable. Nevertheless, there are a few questions that bother me:

You joined the editorial committee of *Black Orpheus* when Jahn left it, or the other way round. Was that pure coincidence?

You taught at Ibadan as a lecturer in the English Department for quite a while. When did you leave there, and where did you go? I should also be glad to know why you left Nigeria unless this be a personal matter.

When did you set up the Chemchemi Center? And when did you leave Kenya? What is the connexion between Chemchemi and the movements that arose in the following years: Nexus, the East African Publishing House, etc? Have any of the writers in Chemchemi made a name for themselves since?

When did you join the University of Zambia? Am I wrong on assuming that you are responsible for the launching of Jewel of Africa? Did you set up a Chemchemi-type centre there as well?

Since you arrived in Zambia, you may have become interested in the vernacular writing that has been done there since the fifties. I have been vainly trying to get information about this. While it has been possible to gather a lot of biographical data about vernacular writers in Rhodesia and in Malawi, I have not been able to find someone capable or willing to enlighten me in Zambia. Miss Dorothea Lehman advised me to contact Mr Stephen Mpashi, which I did, but my letter must have gone astray. You can perhaps tell me if he is still director of the Publications Bureau, so that I may try again.

I hope you are enjoying your stay in Lusaka, which I visited in 1959. I am looking forward to hearing from you, and I thank you in advance for your welcome cooperation.

Yours sincerely

Albert Gérard

London

6 June 1970

My dear Zeke

Thank you very much for letting me know that you arrived back in Denver safely and for giving me your first impressions of the world after two years of zambianization. I hope by the time you receive this letter you will have solved your accommodation problems, and you were lucky to have a bit of money handy, so that you can negotiate 'from a position of strength'. The *ngongos* would be sore at heart to learn that their sadistic pound-of-flesh taxation piracy has been rendered ineffectual.

I was expecting Nzim and the girls last Sunday. But they did not come. On the 21st of May I went back to the Home Office to find out what was happening. I was told the Department of Employment and Productivity had not replied yet. I then decided to use more pressure. I went to the Head Office of the N>U>T> to discuss the matter with them. They got in touch with the Home Office and we subsequently learnt that somewhere along the bureaucratic pipeline someone had mucked up my application. We were then told that Lusaka would be contacted the same afternoon and authorised to issue the visas. I communicated the information to Nzim who subsequently wrote to say they would be arriving on the 31st. But as I have said they did not come. She wrote to say that the Office of the British High Commission in Lusaka said they had not received any word from here!

Another complication had also cropped up. As you will know, the Rev. Finlay who was instrumental in getting me a loan from the World Council of Churches to enable me to travel to Britain and with whom I had made firm arrangements regarding similar loans for Nzim and the girls fell foul of Kaunda's benevolent fascism and was declared a prohibited immigrant to Zambia. When Nzim went to collect the tickets from the man now in charge, she was told that the matter would have to be referred to Geneva! Well, well, they say it never rains but pours.

In regard to the first problem, I have since checked with both the Home Office and the Foreign Office here, and have been assured that Foreign Office has since repeated the authority. The problem now must be that U.N. crowd. It's a problem I'd not anticipated at all. I shall keep you informed of developments.

The more I think of your departure from Zambia and all it signified, the more appalled I am at the behaviour of our people there. Such betrayal baffles all description. Even Ryan who had been treated like a piece of dirt, and who came trotting up to you to thank you for vindicating him, does not scruple to sell you down the drain. *Sies!*

Of course, the price of integrity is very great, but the thought that one has refused to sell one's principles and has lived up to one's convictions, is truly satisfying. I personally think that nothing could be nobler than a man who is capable of taking his stand consistently upon his principles and be prepared even to stand alone if needs be.

Please give my regards to Ribs and the children. We shall always remember you. Your coming to Zambia made a world of difference to us. We had been very much alone until you came. Cheerio.

P.S. For Ribs's transcontinental gossip: 01-859-0595. That's of course when all the contraband stuff – timber, loin cloth and all – has been securely tucked away at No.7, Tudor Court

[Writer unidentified]

New York

30 June 1970

Bra Zeke

If you call me all kinds of bastards and don't know what else by now, you are perfectly justified. The past two years or so were, I think, the worst years of my life; so that if I had written you I would only have burdened you with extra load of frustration and anguish you could do without. I think it would have been very selfish on my part.

I am a broken man now. I know my death, our impotence, very intimately. I know the resulting stench of cynicism. You see, I was very romantic. A great deal of it is in my writing, affirming shit that does not even exist past words. But that's a long story I'll tell you some day when I'm not in a hurry like this.

Doubleday is going to publish a book of mine later this year: *MY NAME IS AFRIKA*. It is also a book of poems. Send me your telephone number. If you can, why don't you get me invited there for a poetry reading this summer so that we can get together very soon?

We have a daughter, Ipeleng, six months and 2½ teeth. *Sedutla se se kae*![1] I will probably not be able to pick her up in another month or so and since Melba is bigger than I am they will have to have it out together.

I am trying to write a bit of fiction. It is very poor work, I think, and my present attitude towards writing makes chances of inspiration practically nil. But I will plod along like the old ox I feel like.

Bra Zeke, I am very lonely. Give the family my love. If there are any books, or whatever, you would like me to get for you this way, let me know.

Love

Willie Kgositsile[2]

1 'Such a heavy-set girl!'

2 Keorapetse 'Willie' Kgositsile is a South African poet who spent many years in exile in East Africa and the United States. He has several anthologies to his name and, in 2006, was named South Africa's Poet Laureate.

London

27 July 1970

Dear Zeke

Hope you're well and settled in by now and not finding I left too much of a shambles in my rush at the end – know I've left much undone and hope still to make amends.

Just back from Paris, planning SA Week for October there: be nice if you could take part in the 3 day symposium!

I wrote you tentatively about a seminar in Denver and a number of folks are interested: London – Nkosi, LaGuma, Pieterse, Okai, Brutus, Jegede, Mustapha: Paris: Diop, Dipoko, Ngango and others. So the potential is there, if you care to take it up. May or October seem best months from here – it's International Year Against Racism and some will be travelling to the States. We might also get dates at UCLA, Wisconsin, Chicago, Austin and Boston, so Denver could fit. A theme? My own choice would be around the 'Black Writer and Communication' with two aspects – how he communicates i.e. questions relating to his craft and how he manages to communicate – i.e. the material aspect with a survey of the publications field, publisher's policy, finances and his difficulties.

But there will be other themes you would want to suggest. Karen C was willing to help, Bob R, was sympathetic and Geo Shepherd was interested. S ... Do let me know what you think.

Busy, poetry wise, including a Reading with [WH] Auden, Thom Gunn and others. Saw [Wole] Soyinka briefly in London.[1] Write something soon.

Yours

Dennis Brutus

1 At this time Soyinka was based in the Department of Theatre Arts at the University of Ibadan. He had worked at the Royal Court Theatre in London in the late 1950s.

London

11 August 1970

Dear Zeke

Yes I understand how you feel and sympathise with it. However: (a) you might feel differently by next year (May? October?) and (b) you might consent to simply CHAIR the thing – and act warderly! And (c) Karen C might be willing to take the admin load off you. As a number of African writers will be in the US anyway, you might as well use them. Don't please, wholly dismiss the ideas.

More concerned about your mood which seems very depressed. But things change and don't let your Nedean address give you a robe or flame! You would of course, be entitled to a rest – you've done so much, but there is so much more you can still give to the writers who have come after you and will come.

I, too, have my sadnesses, but for that another time perhaps. Trying to get our 'SA Week' in Paris going. Do you know of the Yaounde October Seminar? Spent a pleasant time with James Ngugi, who goes to NWU and Taban Lo Liyong, Lindfors' *RIAL* is out and looks splendid.[1] He does a great deal and is working on some of my verse as you know, not very good stuff. I like the *Denverse* better, though you've not commented, not out of consideration for my feelings, I hope.

Yours

Dennis Brutus

[1] Brutus refers to the inaugural issue of *Research in African Literatures*, of which Bernth Lindfors was the founding editor.

1 November 1970

Dear Zeke

A line to say that I've been reading your *Voices in the Whirlwind* again, and with considerable pleasure, preparatory to prescribing it for classes in the winter. It is kind of sustained and pioneering inquiry into poetics and black esthetics, which we greatly need, even if it doesn't answer all the questions. The range of your survey is truly impressive, taking in just about all the areas and writers we need to help us to make up our minds and it has added special advantage of helping black studies people to see the interconnections with black writing in Africa.

On a personal note; I am sorry you find *Poems from Algiers* fragmentary and lacking in statement: from what I remember, *Driftwood* seems to me one of my few attempts at a sustained statement. If *No Banyan* is about the world and passion, and *Seething Earth* is about the world and power, then *Driftwood* is my comment on the world and exile – an issue on which you have yourself said many important things from *2nd Ave* to *Wanderers* and including *Voices*.

Generally, as you know, I am content to make my statements by fragments, hoping that they can add up to a kind mosaic – e.g. in *Letters* and even in *Thoughts Abroad*, though there the final statement is shaped by the editor of the compilation, it is rare for me to try to say it all in a single breath (e.g. even in the Luthuli sequence. I found I have to rely on bits and pieces) but when I attempt a rounded-off statement, I expect it to be given more weight than individual fragments.[1]

This is not, of course, a defence, though like you I welcome a good argument, it is more by way of drawing your attention to something that may have been an oversight!

Glad to learn you're at another novel; hope it goes well. I was sorry to hear that Mtshali will publish no more; my classes greatly enjoy reading and discussing his work.[2] Hopefully he will continue to write, even if not at this stage to publish.

I despair of ever writing anything sustained myself. Perhaps I should get that mess of autobiographical material out of my system first! It comes out in dribbles in taped interviews etc anyway. But you have correctly diagnosed my ambivalence, so I do not need to spell it out to you.

Are you likely to get to the Canadian conference after all? What about the one next month in Yaounde? On the critic, I was invited, but cannot get off from my Department about coming here next May?

The family is almost all here now, and we settle in slowly and awkwardly and now the winter settles in! Greetings to the family and friends. I have a lasting affection for Denver, and my last visit strengthened it.

Yours ever

Dennis Brutus

1 This is a rare exchange, with Brutus appealing for a sympathetic reading from Mphahlele in his search for coherence between his politics and his elusive, modernist leanings.

2 Oswald Mbuyiseni Mtshali was, in fact, about to publish his collection of thoughtful lyric poems, *Sounds of a Cowhide Drum* (Johannesburg: Renoster Books 1971), which was an unprecedented success in South Africa. Later he would publish the more militant *Fireflames* (Pietermarizburg: Shuter and Shooter 1980), which was banned.

3 November 1970

Dear Makhudu,

Your letter was distressing about Naledi. I know what you feel. Indeed A level is utterly useless. I'm told the educational authorities in Britain are considering abolishing it. In the A level they're merely doing what a student should be doing in the first year of a 4-year degree programme.

If you can get her a scholarship to come to US to do her degree, it will pay off in the short and long runs. I want to make enquiries about such a possibility. In my experience over the years thrashing about for money for students to come to the US I know (a) foundations are no use for individual academic sponsorship; (b) African-American Institute goes for post-graduate and graduate sponsorship in consultation with an African government; (c) individual universities take on graduates to teach, whereby they earn a stipend and a tuition waiver while they are attending courses for the Ph.D. The enquiry I want to make, which you also can do among Americans you meet out there, is into the possibilities of a bunch of students in a particular university sponsoring jointly as an organization a student for their university. I know a fellow from Sophiatown who is at the University of Massachusetts Amherst, Massachusetts who is sponsored by its students. Why don't you write to the Secretary, Students Union, same university and say you understand a body of students there may like to sponsor someone like Naledi for under-graduate studies etc. Can he put you in touch with such a body? Also write to the fellow – Eugene Job, College of Arts & Sciences, same university and ask who sponsored him in particular. Write also to the Dean, College of Arts & Sciences; who knows me and say I suggested you do and ask if the university gives scholarships for this etc. This way you'll be striking with a multi-armed weapon.

About your personal position. Would you like to do a degree in International Relations – M.A. to begin with at our famous Graduate School of International Studies? You can of course major in Polit. Sc. or International Law if you like. *If so, let me know quick* so I can approach them for scholarship. They budget now for the next academic year, so we can move in now. If it comes through, you can then worry about fares and a further grant from another source to transport and maintain your family here. It's usually a year for an M.A. So, unless you immigrate like us, you could consider leaving the family behind for that year. In order to increase your marketability, as I myself had to, you need to consider a Ph.D. here. Which means you can come under (c) in the 2nd paragraph and wangle a supplementary grant for maintenance of yourself and family. So write soon, and I can see the administration.

Zeke

Denver

[Postmarked] 3 November 1970

Dear Makhudu

Life's hectic for me this term. Teaching 3 courses and working my ass off. We're halfway the quarter and that's a comforting thought.

The Wanderers will be out this month, and a copy will be sent to you. Am finishing a long essay on American Negro and African poetry in political conflict for a work of essays to be published next year. The other essays will be things of mine that have appeared in Journals – mostly Literary Criticism and Cultural essays. Who knows? I may yet be notorious after my views come out on poetry. But then controversy is my natural habitat.

I'm rushed and must stop, although I've so much, one cuts one's losses, etc, so often, it becomes a way of life. I don't care anymore, and we dig for a little warmth where we can find it as I hear turtles will do. They travel with the sea currents from shore to shore and make a home where they can. Love to Muriel and kids and say hello to Phillip.

Ever

Zeke

P.S. You should make several copies of your Curriculum Vitae and let me have 4 or so to send round to sources we can tap in addition to Denver.

Denver

21 November 1970

Dear Bob,

Hi there! Yes, here we are. After teaching summer school, I'm writing with my tongue hanging out. Am looking forward to 2 weeks from now.

The Wanderers will be out in March & I have asked Macmillan to send you a copy. Bernth has sent me Brutus's Algiers poems for reviewing in *Africa Today*. I'll see what I can't cook up for *WLWE* [World Literature Written in English] by way of a review.

Since we communicated, lots of things have happened. Doubleday, on their own initiative, got the American rights for *Down Second Avenue*, so they're bringing [it] out next April. As Macmillan were hesitant about their African & Caribbean series, & Doubleday hadn't yet approached me, Hill & Wang were considering a volume of essays made up of my published articles plus a long unpublished essay [25,000 words] on Poetry & Political Conflict in the Black World. They will now be doing it next year. London's Macmillan are doing *The Wanderers* next year too, *and* the essays.

What have you and Judy been doing?

Quite frankly, if Dennis doesn't watch it, his poetry is simply going to deteriorate into airport verse. There's a kind of soullessness & spaceless [sic] about his Algiers stuff. But let me not pre-empt things. It isn't going to be easy for me to review it.

Love to you & J from me & R.,

Ever

Zeke

Cape Town

31 December 1970

Dear Mr. Mphahlele,

I was very pleased indeed to receive a letter from you – I did not realize that you were back in Denver. Everybody here seemed to think you were still in Zambia. The reason for the delay is that I was trying to track down a book on Afrikaans poetry for you. I consulted with various people and they all said that Opperman's *Groot Verseboek* was the only one. But it wasn't available anywhere, as it is in the process of being reprinted. Eventually the publishers said that they had dug out one with a rather dirty cover and would let me have it for nothing. They promised to put it in the post to me, and I will then send it on to you. It goes back to the *Eerste Taalbeweging* and has a good selection of modern poetry – Krige, etc. but it was published in '67 or 68 and the new print will bring it more up to date.

You are quite correct; you were very helpful to me when I first started working on my thesis on African Literature in English in Southern Africa, in 1958. Eventually you wrote me a long letter – I asked a friend in England to find out – which never reached me, so there seemed no point in writing again. I did not know then that the work would stretch out like this. Twelve years and three children later I am still at it (babies and research work just weren't a good combination but I hope to finish in April. I do hope that I will still be able to read *The Wanderers* before then. I have a thick wad of correspondence with the Censor Board and the Ministry of Justice and have latter's assurance that there is nothing in the Act to prevent my acquiring or reading the books, only in distributing anything I quote. Since I will not distribute my thesis – just hand it in to my professor – U.C.T. will have to worry about that. I just thought this may interest you.

By coincidence, I was just writing the sixth foolscap page about your short stories, when your letter arrived. Have you never thought of doing anything with the old *Lesane* stories in *Drum*? I think that is a terrific series, and can't understand why it has never been in any anthology.

It's still a small world in South Africa, and you may be interested to know that my step-daughter met your cousin Victor Mphahlele a few weeks ago in Johannesburg. Also about 10 years ago they worked together in the library of the Institute of Race Relations, and I believe he is still there. She has gone into the theatre, and was touring the townships with a British play – they were very surprised to see each other.

The reason why Struik did not reply to you is probably that Mr. Struik died recently. He must have been ill for some time and the place is quite impossible now. I'll be glad to help with any books at any time, but if ever you want to write to a bookshop you will find Frank Thorold in Fox Street, Jo'burg much more helpful.

Seeing that I am writing on Old Year's Eve, I would like to take the opportunity of wishing you a very happy 1971. I am about to go on a short holiday near Hermanus. I shall probably see Richard Rive there as he always spends part of the holidays with Jan Rabie. He will be very interested to know that I had a letter from you.

With kind regards,
Yours sincerely,
Ursula Barnett

1971

10 June 1971

Dear Makhudu,

Re lla le uena mois'a gešo.[1] The death of a parent far away from you tears you up inside in a way it doesn't in more 'favorable' circumstances. Was Muriel at home then? That's the agony, or part of the agony of exile.

Things are fine with us here. Ribs is working. Social research, with the hope of going into more stable and less strenuous work in the state govt. or private agency.

I believe Leballo must be panicking in Dar at the news Sobukwe's likely to come out![2] He's been in the news with the Tanzanian treason trial and it is evident *dithuri tja ga Leballo di mo shireleditje.*[3]

The Wanderers is on the way by surface mail, the publishers report.

London's Macmillan will bring it out later in the year. They'll also bring out my essays *Voices in the Whirlwind.*

It's good to hear about your poetry and publishing prospects. Haven't seen *The New African* for months. I wondered if it's still appearing.

I need Nigerian shirts. Since I got me some Ghanaian made ones and East African, I don't wear a tie anymore – that's now since 1966. My suits are Nyerere style. I wonder if you know a woman who makes them – you know the style with embroidery in front instead of buttons, round the neck, at the sleeves. Good cloth – not the ordinary cotton. Can you enquire how much 4 shirts would be – different colours – cloth and labour? I can then send you money and measurements. For colours, any shade between olive green, deep brown, bright khaki colour, variations of these. Broad sleeves.

Let's hope the wound heals soon. But then I realize all too well statements like this at the time of grief are empty, dry as cork.

Love

Ever

Zeke

1 'Our hearts are with you our dear brother.'

2 P K Leballo was acting president of the Pan Africanist Congress (PAC) of South Africa in exile, its headquarters in Dar es Salaam, Tanzania. Robert Mangaliso Sobukwe, president of the PAC, had been jailed for three years, initially for incitement following the Sharpeville massacre of 21 March 1960. The apartheid regime used what came to be known as the 'Sobukwe clause' to keep him in solitary confinement on Robben Island after his sentence expired. After his release he was banished to Kimberley, where he died in February 1978.

3 'the spirits of the Laballos are protecting him'.

Denver

31 July 1971

My dear Mike [Josselson],[1]

I know you were always unhappy to be confronted with a letter in longhand. But I will write in script to placate you. Fact is that I'm too darn lazy to think on a typewriter. When I compose a book too, I do it in long hand first because I can think better – far better – without the woodpecker's rattle.

I have wanted to write in a long time but last year was hectic. We arrived back in Denver in May 1970. Zambia didn't work. A year and 10 months were enough – the government was sending out South African and Rhodesian refugees and exiles and if you did not have work because you were retrenched, you couldn't stay – without a work permit.

Incidentally our common acquaintance Bentsi-Enchill preceded our leaving by a few months and is back in Legon, Accra. Did a fine job – highly commendable – as Dean of the Law School in Lusaka.

We came back here as *immigrants* and bought a house and are happily settled. Funny, but not so funny, that Americans can give us the asylum Africa cannot offer, even at the most basic mechanical level. We will live here indefinitely and Denver is an excellent place for teaching and writing. I am on a new novel now and will be publishing a book of essays in the Fall. Do you still take an interest in reading large books? I mean so many are being turned out in the various languages and if you are multi-lingual as you are, you must find it all tedious. For this reason I did not send you my latest novel – *THE WANDERERS*, published here last March – until I should hear from you that you would want to be bothered with all this pulp. If you say so, I will shoot over to you a copy.

Our children are all here (4) except the eldest, still in East Africa, is still trying to find himself.

And you, Mike, and your family. How goes it with you all? We hope you keep in good health, that life is still good to you generally. I got your 'new' address from Soas [Jones-Quartey] in Accra when we met a year ago out there.

Do drop us a line if you can, when you can spare the time. Rebecca joins me in sending you warmest regards.

Take care.

Ever

Zeke

[1] Josselson was director of the Congress for Cultural Freedom when Mphahlele worked for that organisation.

New York

1 October 1971

Dear Prof Mphahlele

Many thanks for the complimentary copy of *The Wanderers* which you had publishers send me. I have found it absorbing, and hope to include an excerpt from it (together with some other pieces by you) in an anthology described herein under the tentative title: *ARK – An Anthology of the New African Literature*. I am about to start looking for a publisher for it. I would push for a hard cover trade book and a paperback mainly for textbook adoptions. The purpose of this letter is to ask whether you would care to associate yourself with this project as co-editor.

Let me hasten to say that considering your teaching responsibilities and other work which you probably have in hand, I fully realize that I could hardly expect you to do a great deal of the actual editorial chores of getting out this book. On the other hand, I am an unaffiliated free lance and do have the time to carry through these chores. Accordingly, I would be very pleased if your situation and inclinations permitted to offer you a 50% share of royalties (and of advance, if any), if you would agree to come in as co-editor, with the understanding that basically you would function as advisor and offer such further help as you found possible.

The outline table of contents on the accompanying sheet should indicate pretty well the general shape of the book. I believe this particular presentation can make a contribution as a well-rounded, readable and high quality introduction both for the interested general reader and for undergraduates in various courses in African culture, comparative literature and humanities. How does this prospectus look to you?

Actually, I have done most of the selecting and some of the introductory notes, so that the work is fairly well along. However, I feel that your advice, suggestions, corrections and criticisms would help immensely in making this book a leading book in its field. I hope you will agree and that I may set about approaching publishers using your name as a co-editor.

I assume that you are familiar with my first anthology, *AFRICAN HERITAGE*, and so I am pleased to send you herewith with my best wishes a copy of my second book, *THE MANY WORLDS OF POETRY* which was done under an arrangement similar to the one I am now proposing to you. Incidentally, both books are now in the third or fourth printings.

I look forward to hearing from you.

Sincerely

Jacob Drawler

24 October 1971

Dear Mr Wolf

I am sorry that this reply is late but it has just been forwarded to me in Europe where I am temporarily on an assignment. I regret also that I am unable to accept your invitation to the conference owing to other commitments.

I regret even more that you have listed Osier Davis' film *Kongi's Harvest* for screening. If you do please ensure that you give publicity to the fact that this work is neither a film of my plan nor of my script. The abysmal affair of his film is in fact in the hands of my lawyers in New York at the moment. I would not like your public to be deceived that the mangled product on celluloid right now is what a number of us worked on in Nigeria.

Thank you once again for the invitation.

Wole Soyinka

Zeke I wanted you to have a copy of this which is self explanatory regarding *Kongi's Harvest*. Most sorry I am unable to come to the States at present in spite of so many temptations and the pleasure seeing you and Dennis. Hope you and Rebecca are well. Say Hello to Brutus

Iowa

18 November 1971

Dear Ezekiel Mphahlele

I was very pleased to receive a letter from you and appreciate your kind remarks about my essays. I wish that I could be of more assistance in supplying you with information about critical histories of Afro-American literature. Unfortunately, the best have not yet been written. For a list of titles, I would refer you to my bibliography, *Afro-American Writers*, which was published by Appleton-Century Crofts. In case you have not seen a copy, I am sending one in a separate package.

The Logging's book is fairly good for older materials. I like Saunders Redding's book very much, but it is too out of date. The only book on poetry is Don L. Lee's recent publication, *Dynamic Voices*, published by Broadside Press in Detroit. That book, however, treats only some of the poets of the '60's. The Abramson book on drama in the supplement is the only one in the field, but it has errors in fact and in interpretation. I understand that a man named Huggins has just brought out a good book on the Harlem Renaissance. I have not read it. The Margolis book is relatively recent. I don't like most of it, but it has one or two useful essays on Ellison and Demby.

I hope this helps. Needless to say I have read and admired your work. I hope that we have a chance to meet. I will be at the Modern Language Association meeting in Chicago at Christmas.

Sincerely

Darwin T. Turner

Visiting Professor

Department of English

1972

Denver

31 January 1972

Dear Martin [Jarrett-Kerr],

I have not written in a long time. Time contracts so. One tumbles from one block of time to another so and yet there's little to show for it. The novel I began last time has been nagging me and I could scream to take time off to continue; but one must earn one's keep. Must wait for the next summer.

I enjoyed the Faulkner monograph. I find it so stimulating, so balanced, so sane, so economically done, yet with so much intellectual toughness. I always wondered what to make of Faulkner's religious beliefs and moral stand. Now I think I see. Thanks for the illumination. I am sending you an article by a colleague of mine here on WF. He is working on a book about Faulkner. A very warm person.

Whatever happened about Roger? You mentioned some time ago that he was very ill. It was sad of course to hear of Arthur Blaxall.

Life is still good to us here, such as it is. So many things make one angry, and that is ironically elevating: Pakistan and Bangladesh, Rhodesia (Zimbabwe), the lot.

Macmillan in London has sent me a copy of the edition of their *The Wanderers*. Their publication date is February 24th. A neat little product. Lots of things changed regarding 'Cecil Sprite' etc, which verge on libel, their lawyer said. Also, it is much freer of errors. As soon as the essays come out this Spring, I'll send you a copy.[1] Macmillan will bring out that too. Fontana Books bought the paperback rights of *The Wanderers*. Give my very best to Arthur Ravenscroft.[2] Had a letter from a friend in Cape Town (incidentally) who has finished her Ph.D. thesis and graduated, but cannot let any library keep a copy because she has quoted and discussed banned writers, like me!! *Ca c'est le comble!* [3]

Love from me and Ribs.

Zeke

1 Mphahlele is referring to his collection of critical essays entitled *Voices in the Whirlwind and Other Essays*, published in 1972.

2 A founding editor of the *Journal of Commonwealth Literature*, Arthur Ravenscroft was a leading figure in the study of postcolonial literatures at the University of Leeds. He published a critical monograph on Chinua Achebe in 1969.

3 'This is the limit!' Mphahlele refers to Ursula Barnett's correspondence with the Ministry of Justice over her use of banned publications.

Denver

24 February 1972

Dear Martin,

I am concluding a seminar on Blake, Wordsworth and Coleridge and the 18th Century Background. I try whenever I teach these guys to emphasize that they are a product of the 18th Century philosophy and poetic practice and 17th and 18th Century science, even while they use their heritage to explore further the psychology of perception, both in writer and reader and the imagination as the writer's equipment.

It has been an exciting seminar and I learned a lot myself. I shall be ranging around the later half of 18th Century and 19th Century themes for a long time, side by side with my interest in Africa, Black American and Caribbean literature.

Some time next year I want to teach as a straight lecture course fiction and poetry connected with, arising from, reflecting, the imperial theme of 19th

Century England. The Kiplings etc. But, I want to read up more on this. I need to read a book specifically on 19th Century imperialism in England and then look for the fiction and poetry I can prescribe for reading. Have you any ideas? Preferably a text that is up to date (on imperialism itself). I must say I have not, curiously enough, read more Kipling than the *Jungle Book*, *Kim*. Would *Disraeli* fit in? When you have time, I shall be most grateful if you could jot down texts one can look into.

The course will not be till Winter 1973, so I have time to construct it.

Does my voice reach you amidst all that din out there, all those drums and whistles and cannons and voting and speechifying and coal power?

Zeke

29 February 1972

Dear Zeke

Now I'm really in your debt – 2 letters. Forgive me. But I'm not sorry I waited, as I can get more in now. For only a few days back I was talking about you. Richard Rive was here, talking about Olive Schreiner, on whom he's working (at Magdalen Coll, Oxford, trying to do a critical biography – which to judge by what he told us will be vg indeed). I didn't hear him give a 2nd talk, next am, on the predicament of the African writer; apparently he was good on that too. I'd not met him before; but he's great fun, v. shrewd. I also met Mr Nkondo (GM, is it – can't remember his Xtian name):[1] & I've lent him the Amer. ed of *Wanderers*, as he only has the UK edition and wants to compare them. I find he not only knows you, but is 'working on you'. I'm very impressed by him: he's extremely intelligent, and he talked very well about FR Leavis. Poor man, what is he doing, his wife, teaching in a 'Bantu University' – Turfloop, isn't it? Anyway, I hope to keep in touch with him. In fact, he wants to come round again and discuss African writing. I shall see Arthur Ravenscroft this coming Thursday again, as he will be introducing a discussion with the W. Indian novelist, Wilson Harris, whom I'm hoping to read soon; Arthur thinks very highly of him. I shall then remind Arthur that's he's promised me the Engl.ed of *Wanderers*, which I'm reviewing for *Journ.Commonw.Lit*. So it's a small world. Meanwhile Ursula Laredo is not far away, working for her doctorate on South African writing. Unfortunately she was not confirmed in her temporary post in the Univ. here, which was a shame as the man who's got it isn't half as good as her. But she's got a job at a Teachers Training Coll. not far from here. I shall look fwd to seeing your collection of essays, too.

About your next lecture project: I'm not really a social historian so I'm afraid my knowledge of this field is a bit limited. I've glanced at, seen vg reviews of, *Christine Bolt, Victorian Attitudes to Race* (Routledge & Kegan Paul, 1971). Anthony Nutting has written a book on *The Scramble for Africa*, which I guess is a popular book though no doubt based on expert studies. If you don't know it, you certainly ought to read KM Pannikar's devastating *Asia & Western Dominance* (Lond, 1953), tho it's not always quite fair. I see John Hatch has written a book (just out) on *Gt. Britain & Africa*, which looks a useful summary of imperial attitudes and practice. I think, too, someone is writing a life & study of Henry Labouchere, the radical MP who was involved in colonial debates, and was a great stalwart on the anti-imperial side. (Fr. Roland Langdon Davies, at Mirfield, has used him quite a bit for the 19th cent. discussion of Rhodesia.) Look out for Douglas V. Steere's forthcoming book (should be out from SPCK, London in June) on Arthur Shearley Cripps, (probably to be called *God's Irregular* (to be distributed in the USA by Pendle Hill Bookstore, nr Philadelphia, Pa). The point about it is the colonial policy towards the Mashona, & the fights in Parliament by the 'Aborigne Protection Society' to respect their land-ownership: Arthur Cripps, who lived as a black among blacks, kept the leftwing in London informed, and this resulted in blocking of a number of reactionary moves by the RSA Co etc. Roland L-D at Mirfield might be able to add to this list. But that's something to keep you going. There is another book on Victorian Attitudes to Africa, but I can't remember whom it's by, at the moment can't track it down. *Sir Harry Johnston & The Scramble for Africa* (R. Olivier) is a classic, & so is Prof Oliver's the *Missionary Factor in E. Africa.* Oh I suppose you know Phillip Mason's Patterns of Dominance (OUP, 1970)? The sections on colonial policy are masterly. By the way, my own massive and over-ambitious tome came out last Friday, 24th (the same day as your Eng. Ed of *Wanderers*!) I wanted to call it *Xtians in the Third World*, but OUP (its publishers) didn't like the title, so instead it has the dull title, *Patterns of Xtian Acceptance*. It's about what it was like to be missionized, studied through the biographies of some 30 individuals, Catholic and Protestant, Anglican, etc Chinese, Jap, Afr, Ind, Melanesian, Amerindian, etc ... Mostly 'good boys', but not all. I must send you a note on it, for curiosity's sake. Did I tell you I'm hoping to go (but it's only a faint hope) to Nigeria (Nsukka) in Sept, if a Conference Arthur Ravenscroft and Donatus Nwoga (who says he's met you) & I have been cooking up, comes off. A faint hope, as at the moment there's only money for one to go from England, & that must be Arthur. But if it comes off, it should be fascinating. It's about Literature and post-independent Africa – values and goals, philosophy, culture and religion. Largely sponsored by a Xtian ... Chinua Achebe, of course; and John Pepper

Clark; and all the other African and Ghanaian, etc writers. But it's still in the air. Anyway, it's making me read more African writers (including some French, Muslim novelists, some of whom are vg.)

Yes, we survived our Coal strike. Alas, Harold Wilson and the Lab. Party have sunk almost lower than the Tories, though Heath is about as wooden and inflexible and dumb as they come.

Love to you and Ribs.

Martin Jarrett-Kerr

1 At the time of this meeting G M (Gessler) Nkondo was a lecturer at the then University of the North (now Limpopo). He was on study leave reading for a Master's degree in English at Leeds University.

Cape Town

8 March 1972

Dear Zeke,

Thank you very much for your letter of February and for your congratulations. I must also thank you very much indeed for *The Wanderers* which arrived safely yesterday and which I know I shall very much enjoy reading. Nadine Gordimer, whom I met for the first time when she was here recently to give a series of lectures on African writing, liked the 'generation-gap' part best. I wish I could return the compliment by sending you a copy of my thesis, which I would do if I had a spare copy. But if I get it published which I sincerely hope I will, the first copy will go to you. I am still waiting for the University's permission. This is supposed to be a formality, but the Chairman of the Ph.D. Board, who happens to be an old friend in his less formidable days, was worried that I could get into trouble even for overseas publication. He made me get an advocate's opinion which arrived today, to the effect that I would be quite safe. So once I have that formal permission I shall go ahead and offer it to publishers. Once it is published overseas I shall try to get the quotations cleared with the Ministry, both for publication and for placing the thesis itself in the library. The U.C.T. librarian said it was all a lot of nonsense and she was putting it in the library, but administration thinks otherwise and I think they are having a sort of tug of war over it at the moment. Well, the way things are going, maybe by the time I apply to the Ministry of Justice there will be a different Minister there ....

I have written to Columbia about lecturing and shall see what they say. I was a student of Journalism there in 1948 and one of the professors is actually still there and remembers me, so he might put in a good word. It would be nice to make a side-trip to Denver etc. I also wrote to someone at the African Studies Association.

I enjoyed meeting Nadine Gordimer – had always heard she was rather aloof but did not find her so at all. Her lectures were excellent; she is less a lecturer than a speaker, with something to say, which appealed to me.

The principal of Langa High School in Cape Town has promised to let me have a batch of examination papers as soon as he gets round to it. He apologized for the delay but they do have their hands full.

All the best,
Ursula Barnett

Denver
30 October 1972

Dear Martin,

It was exciting to read your letter of last September, about your visit to Nsukka.[1] All those intellectual guns out there. Yes Nigeria is a formidable stronghold of intellectual life. How often I have wished we could go back there to live. But for exiles we are reasonably 'secure' here, right on top – a dump that is continually being threatened by a landslide. I hope the papers will be published.

Finished the revised edition of *The African Image* and Faber are highly impressed.[2] Still waiting to hear from Praeger. The novel has come on well so far and I am making a desperate bid to have broken the back of it before December – at any rate winter quarter when I start to teach. Had a really good review in *New York Times Book Review – Voices.*

I'm fishing for a grant to allow me to take the year off 1973-4 to work on a book Indiana University Press has agreed to publish – *A Critical Anthology of African Writing* – to be something like 1000 pp. – Poetry, short fiction and expository writing.[3] I want this to be a *pièce de resistance* in the field. If I succeed, I'll spend 2 months in the British Museum and a Paris library, digging up old expository writing. The rest I will do here. This should be September and October '73, if the grant materialises.

Autumn in Colorado is superb. The mauve and brown and yellow colours give me a feeling that I have lived many many years and I'm wiser than I have ever been in these years. Wise about nothing in particular – only vaguely, but damnably so. But of course the illusion won't last. I'll have to wait for next Autumn to enjoy the feeling and so on.

Love from me and Ribs.

Zeke

[1] The University of Nigeria at Nsukka.

[2] The second edition appeared in 1974.

[3] This ambitious project was never completed. After his permanent return to South Africa Mphahlele's research interests seem to have shifted temporarily to oral culture. He began immediately to research oral poetry in Tshivenda and Northern Sotho.

1973

9 January 1973

Dear Professor Mphahlele

I have recently been reading your new collection of essays entitled *Voices in the Whirlwind* and found them to be more than exciting for me. I was also pleased to discover that your approach to literary analysis appears to be quite close to my own method of analysis. I have also had a good response from those of my students who are using your book for their own end of term critical essays about Afro-American literature.

I am a published Afro-American poet whose work has appeared in a number of small magazines including *Freedomways, American Dialog*, (where I am also a contributing editor), *Roots*, *The Fiddlehead* (University of New Brunswick, Can), *Black Collegian*, and other quarterlies. My work has also appeared in several anthologies including *Night Comes Softly* edited by the poet Nikkie Giovanni; *People in Poetry* and *Poetry by Blacks*, Volumes 1 and 2. My poem 'Glow Child' is both the title and lead poem of a new anthology edited by Sister Ruby Dee called *Glow Child*. I have taught Afro-American drama at the Lincoln Center campus of Fordham University during the fall semester of 1971-72, and am currently teaching under a year appointment of Vassar College. I have recently completed my Masters at Columbia University and am now working toward my doctorate in Comparative Literature at New York University where I project that I will work in the area of Afro-Asian literatures through the medium of the Arabic language which I am presently studying. In my spare time I am still writing and working on several dramas.

During the past five years since my return to college I have never lost sight of the fact that I am first and foremost a poet whose thought is concerned with the common humanity of all the world's people. So that during my years of school I have also been very active in oral poetry readings and lecture discussion sessions throughout the New York area. During my academic study I always considered it my duty as a poet to combine routine scholarship with both creativity and penetrating beyond the normal requirements for students. As a result of this method of work I have written a few essays which I consider valuable enough for publication. Since my concentration in literature has been drama all of the pieces are concerned with a critical analysis of the works utilized in the papers and theoretical postulations of how the social milieu within which the poet-dramatist lived forced his work to assume a particular literary format. In addition I believe my papers reflect an awareness of and utilization of the concept of all men's continuing interactions, over and beyond national barriers, in a single continuing cultural history of Constance E. Berkley.

I too believe that drama presents the most viable artistic form for the presentation of and analysis of any particular society. My Master's essay dealt with how the staged *dramatic image* itself worked within the mind of the audience to help fashion a *living image* (human being) whose social behaviour actually derived partially from the staged dramatic image created by the poet. For my analysis of this concept I chose four works from the European renaissance concentrating upon Shakespeare's *Othello* and *Titus Andronicus* which I compared with Calderon's *Love After Death*. Another essay deals with dramatic structure and *The Stranger* as exemplified in one drama each of JM Synge and W Soyinka. Another piece discusses European drama since 1890 and the political basis of those works whose form I believe to have been dictated by the specific political climate of that age. The last essay examines how the daily social and political American ritual has caused black American playwrights to create a particular type of dramatic hero whose stage life could not transcend the socio-political reality of the historical period in which the work was written. When I wrote this last piece I had not read *Our Land* by Theodore Ward so that I will append four or five pages of analysis of that drama to illustrate how it fits my analysis of the creation of a new type of Afro-American hero.

I have written to you in such detail because I admire your work and wish to ask you for assistance and collaboration. So far I have had no success in having any of the articles published either because of their expository length or their content. I have also not been able to have my collected volume of over hundred poems published by a major publisher and have shunned self publication which is the traditional method for most American poets who have later become well known. I wonder whether you would be interested, have the time, or wish to read some of the pieces I have described for possible inclusion in another collection of your own essays or for possible submission to your publisher with an introduction by yourself. The combined four pieces without editing would comprise a little over two hundred pages; if however just the last three essays and the preface to my Master's essay were used they would comprise approximately 110 pages.

I hope that my letter to you will prompt your curiosity thereby compelling you to answer my request positively. May you have a successful New Year.

Yours in the struggle,
Constance E. Berkley

Mississippi
5 April 1973

Dear Dr. Mphahlele:

First, I wish to commend you on your book, *Voices in the Whirlwind.* I had the pleasure of reviewing it for the *Houston Post*, (Houston, Texas), and I found it to be a landmark work in the area of minority literature. Next, I wish to enlist your assistance for a magazine article I am preparing concerning Langston Hughes. Please write to me, and inform me if you had the privilege of meeting Langston, if so, your reaction at having met him, and any interesting stories you remember about him. Also, please inform me of other individuals who might be of assistance in this venture, and how these individuals may be contacted.

Your immediate response will be appreciated.

Sincerely,
Michael Leonard King

Howard University
6 June 1973

Dear Brother Mphahlele

Thank you so much for your very kind letter. I am indeed pleased and honoured that someone of your caliber has read my essay and found it helpful. I am aquainted with your first book but have not read *Voices in the Whirlwind.* I would appreciate it, then, if you could ask the publishers to send me a copy. In turn, if you haven't seen my piece, 'Survival Motion' which accompanies an essay by Prof Mercer Cook, in the *Militant Black Writer*, I'll have a copy sent to you.

Yes, the business of judging and defining seems to go all too often to the Europeans and Euro-Americans, who are so sure of their 'university'. We need to develop the habits of mind to set our views down in systematic useable form. We waste so much good stuff hoping. Don L Lee's *Black Books Bulletin* is an attempt to keep tabs on black books but frankly leaves out useful information. The Howard University Press and the *Journal of Black Education*, also here, are both interested in the kind of review you speak of. I will keep you posted on their progress.

The idea of 'saturation' has annoyed some of the white reviewers, one of whom finds it 'misty', but blacks generally who have read the essay understand it. I would like to explore it further with some help from other black people, like yourself. I need examples from history, biography, autobiography, fiction etc. A friend of mine – a linguist has provided help also. So I would appreciate any further thoughts that you might have on the subject.

Finally, I have been asked to direct an institute for the arts and the humanities here at Howard and thought that you would be interested to know what we're up to.

Again, thanks for your encouragement.

Sincerely

Stephen E Henderson

29 June 1973

Bro Mphahlele

Thank you so much for your beautiful and vigorous thought. You raise important questions and suggest fruitful approaches. Your immersion in several traditions helps to bring things into focus. When I get the time, I'll write at greater length. But I wanted to thank you for your kindness and to send you this small imperfect token of my esteem.

Sincerely

Steve Henderson

Denver

12 July 1973

Dear Makhudu,

Monna Makhudu re botje gorileng go ile tu ko Katsina? Bophelo bo joang batho ba gešo?[1] This silence is getting on my nerves. Did Muriel go home, did you go to East Africa? How is teacher training teaching? We never get to know how things are with you professionally. Come to think of it, you are most uncommunicative about that.

Ribs went to Madison, Wisconsin last month to visit Martin Kaunda and family and met Saka there. Reports that *hy's vol draadwerk*[2] – fussy, querulous, cantankerous etc. Says it was his place you took when he left K? Life's still ok here, Watergate, fuel shortages, high food prices notwithstanding. *Dis noustrop trek, feela re tla re botshabelo bokae?*[3]

I have waited to hear from you your reactions to *The Wanderers* and *Voices in the Whirlwind.* Did the letter ever reach you? I did send it, I'm sure.

I have been invited to take up a visiting Professorship at University of Pennsylvania, English Department 1974-75. I will go, and if its livable etc, Ribs and the two boys will join me and that will be our abode.

How's the baby getting on? We hope Muriel has completely recovered. *Monna ipofe u tiishe, lefase leankga.*[4] Did your daughter go to England? Did the other one get into university there?

Much love

Ever

Zeke

1 'Hey Makhudu, tell us why Katsina is so silent? How is life, my fellow people?'

2 'he's full of barbed wire'

3 'It's a struggle. Yet where will we find our refuge?'

4 'Man, be strong, the world stinks'.

Cape Town

26 July 1973

Dear Zeke,

I trust that you received the second part of my thesis safely.

I recently returned from a business trip to Europe and was thrilled to find that a letter awaited me from Professor Jones, asking me to do a critical biography of you for the Twayne World Authors series. Of course I accepted with great pleasure and have already started work on it.[1]

I am afraid I shall have to pester you from time to time and already have some questions and requests: Have you perhaps a spare copy of the new introduction to the new edition of *DOWN SECOND AVENUE*? I should be very pleased to receive this. Has the new edition of *IMAGE* been published yet? Is it very different from the original version? In your last letter you said you were working on a new novel. Can you tell me anything about it yet? Is it likely to be finished before next April, the deadline for my book? I understand it has a Zambian setting; have you ever considered an American setting?[2]

Have you kept the letter from the authorities informing you that your writing is prescribed etc? If so, could I possibly have a xerox copy?

That's all for the moment; hope you will not mind if I trouble you again. Thank goodness the University of Cape Town library has become a little more liberal regarding banned books, since I last did research there.

I met Lewis Nkosi in London, had asked Sydney Clouts to introduce me and we had a most interesting evening at Sydney's house.[3] Lewis has a reputation for being very embittered but we didn't find him like that at all.

With best regards,

Yours sincerely,

Ursula Barnett

1 Ursula Barnett's critical biography of Mphahlele in the Twayne World Authors Series was published in 1976.

2 Barnett is referring to *Chirundu*.

3 Sydney Clouts, poet, born and educated in Cape Town. In 1961 he moved to London at the age of 35, carrying with him a strong sense of his South African origins. His volume of poetry, *One Life*, won the Oliver Schreiner and Ingrid Jonker prizes after publication in 1966. *Collected Poems* (Cape Town: David Philip 1984) appeared after his early death in 1982.

Washington

17 August 1973

Dear Teresa

Good to hear from you. The prospects look bright indeed for you in a job like that – with all the fringe benefits. The salary is not bad considering these fringe benefits. Are you going to hold on to it? We sincerely hope so. Sit tight on it and don't let go of it, because it holds great promise for your education and livelihood. It is quite evident that you have been through a rough time, but what would it all be worth if it didn't give you a glimpse of the truth about yourself, your capacity, your shortcomings, etc. etc. And it seems to have done that for you.

Good to hear you have met the Andersons. They are really good friends. Laurentia and Yvonne are here. Came Wed. by bus from N.Y. Enjoying themselves. We are taking them to the mountains – the Kahn cabin – next week. Summer school is over and we are unwinding.

Have a good offer of a full professorship in the Eng. Dept., University of Pennsylvania for 1974-5. They want me on a permanent basis, but we'll resettle there, for keeps. We'll sell this house, because even if we return to Denver, we'll want a house with bigger rooms, although not more than we have here. But before we decide to sell or not, I must know if Mangoaela can come here and take my place for '74-75, or for all time. And I am not hearing from him at all. Can you find out, and if you can reach him, tell him its *urgent* for him to send me what I asked for. But don't tell him what I plan to do.

Love, your

Ntate

Denver

21 August 1973

Dear Ursula

Good to learn you'll be doing the Twayne on me. I know you'll do a thorough job. I am sending some things to you. But how can I be sure they'll reach you? It will be a package, including the American edition of *2nd Ave*, with intro; some papers I've written lately. Did I understand you've read *VOICES IN THE WHIRLWIND*? Macmillan in London is publishing it this month.

New edition of *IMAGE*: Faber is going to send me galleys in September, so it should be with me in Spring (English). You might ask them to send you a set of galleys and you may say I've referred you to them. Write to Frank Pike (sorry for this untidy writing – am in a great rush). Yes, it is very different especially for Part 1 – political images, where I've revised my views a lot. I have added more books to Part 2. I would like to be judged by this revised edition, as on *VOICES*, where it concerns my social criticism.

The new novel. I should finish it this autumn (ours) because I'm off teaching altogether for the quarter to work on it. At least the first draft will be. Set in Zambia, although I don't ever mention the country. Provisional title: *KWACHA – A BRIGHT NEW DAY!* About a bigamy case involving a cabinet minister. Am exploring the dynamics of political power in relation to domestic life, marital relations, bringing in the African's attitude towards polygamy & the modern woman's rejection of it. It certainly won't be published until perhaps autumn of 74 or spring of 75. Can't think of writing in the American setting except when I do journalistic and critical writing. Can't get the smell of it yet. It's still a great big blob in my mind. And I am very much a 'victim' to the tyranny of place, as my paper will show (University of Missouri one). When I do write, I shall certainly use ethnic material. I am learning Spanish – have been for the last 8 months – so that I can explore the Mexican American setting. I'm making great progress ... Look up, also, a comment I make in the big volume of prose – *Contemporary English Prose*, published by St James' Press, London – re the S. African setting. If *The Wanderers* says anything at all, it should, I think be a personal record of this search for place. People keep wanting to judge by 'purely' novelistic standards which are orthodox, forgetting that the novel form is most receptive of all kinds of materials. What you want to say defines its form.

The banning of my works was gazetted together with (that blanket banning order, remember, about 1960/1) several other writers outside. Incidentally my friend never did receive my book. And I know what happened just as I told you would happen. So I asked Macmillan to send another copy through a friend in JHB. So much for the liberal conscience, Ursula! It makes me very sad although I understand it. What can the University of Cape Town library do now that they couldn't for banned books? Did I hear *Second Ave* can now circulate in S. A.? I'm keen to know. Good luck with the book. Don't hesitate to ask any questions.

Best

Sincerely

Zeke

Denver

28 August 1973

Dear Stuart,

This is just a formal note to confirm my arrangements for 1974-5, about which we have talked at length. I wish to take leave of absence for 1974-5 in order to teach at the University of Pennsylvania as Visiting Professor. I understand that will be done without prejudice to the Sabbatical I shall be entitled to three years from now.

I shall do everything I can to obtain a suitable substitute for my position here for that year.

Very sincerely

Zeke (E. Mphahlele)

7 September 1973

Dear Teresa

The last letter you wrote was the most pleasingly adult we had ever received from you. We are so glad you are fixing to make a go of things and keep together. That you are prepared to kick the ass of anyone who has bright ideas about quitting school, that you have reassessed Tony and have seen him for what he is, indicates your own maturity.

Of course you know the circumstances under which I said for you not to stay with us here. The fact that when you returned from D.C. the first time I tried (even after I had written to say our house could not hold you any longer until you were grown up enough for us to have a healthy relationship) – I tried to get you to visit us and talk things over (Remember I said you need people more than you think, that you may not have the capacity to take shocks alone that you imagine) – the fact that I did should have indicated to you that I hoped we could work towards a healthier relationship, that my restrictions were not absolute, but grew out of your attitude. I cannot now recount the things I have written about in previous letters all over again. You cannot drift away from us, create a wall, and then complain that we are not on your side! I have said before that we are fixtures – parents are fixtures, they don't orbit. It is the one who orbits who must return to the fixture. If parents orbited and children were fixtures, there would be no growth in the latter.

I wanted to see how far you would drift, and I still want *you* to take the initiative to resolve the kind of relationship that will work for all of us. We are fixtures, but we cannot accommodate change and phases in the growth of our children, as long as they are in a forward motion and are learning to take control over their lives. You know yourself you would not be happy in our house as our life styles are simply different. Our rhythms of life are different. Having flown from the nest, and this is what I told Motswiri, a *new* relationship must be arrived at. It can't be any more based on the idea of custody and responsibility a parent shows children under 20. There is still parental love, but both sides must make adjustments that are not a strain to themselves.

So, then although you would not feel happy living with us as a 'base', you are welcome to visit. We have told Motswiri exactly the same thing. And we are on the happiest terms with him. He comes to us to talk about some problems and there is mutual appreciation of each other's independence. It is for *you* to work towards a psychological return. But understand – *work*. You have changed radically, and you can't simply fit back into the household mould. You must not be surprised when now and again things don't click in this process of return. You have to deal with the paradox of the fixture (parent) that also changes in attitude towards its offspring as the latter's attitude changes also.

Take care now, and love.

Ever,

Ntate

Cape Town

10 September 1973

Dear Zeke,

Very many thanks for your letter. I shall enjoy doing the Twayne book more and more. I have been re-reading some of your critical work and find that it has not dated, unlike a great deal of other African criticism. It's sad to think what has happened to so many of the writers since. I see you referred once to James Matthews's 'angry prose'. He is now turning out very much angrier poetry, but his volume had a very short life-time: one week before it was banned. James swore a year ago that he wasn't going to publish any more, but I suppose he just couldn't help himself.[1]

Thank you very much indeed for all the things you have sent. So far everything has reached me and if by any chance it does not, I'll see if UCT library won't order it for me. You ask what they can do now for banned books that they couldn't before? Apparently various libraries interpret the

Censorship law differently. They all keep the banned stuff in locked cupboards but many libraries hand out the books to so-called 'genuine students' (apparently as opposed to people seeking some sort of illicit satisfaction). Until a new librarian took over they wouldn't take out the books for anybody, but now they do. I don't think *Down Second Avenue* is supposed to circulate in S.A. but I have heard that one can get it. I'll investigate on one of my next trips to the bookshops.

Thanks very much for all the information. I shall ask for the galleys of the new edition of *IMAGE* as you suggest, and I'll consider it instead of the first edition; also *Voices*. Yes, I did receive the copy and did write and thank you. Sorry about your friend not getting it. If I had known it would take all this time and then not succeed it could have waited till my next visit to Joburg. I just didn't fancy the mail here. When I do go to the Transvaal, probably next January, may I get in touch with your brother? I have his address at the school.

Your new novel sounds most interesting and I wish you the best of luck for it. I am not surprised that the American setting takes some time to absorb. I have just read a book called *The Drama of Nommo* by Paul Harrison Carter which staggered me. Do you know it? I shall be looking up the various references you mention.

Would you mind, when you have time, having a look at the short story chapter in my thesis and checking whether the biographical notes about you are completely correct. They were gathered together from many bits and pieces.

Do you know whether Eugene McDowell's thesis on the African-English novel ever appeared in book-form? If not, would Denver University lend it to me? It was accepted at the university.

Regards,

With best,

Ursula Barnett

1 Barnett is referring to James Matthews's *Cry Rage* (Johannesburg: Spro-Cas 1972). Matthews would become a prolific writer, producing six further volumes of poetry, a collection of short fiction (*The Park and Other Stories*, Johannesburg: Ravan 1983) and a novel, *The Party is Over* (Cape Town: Kwela 1997). Well known as a cultural activist, Matthews spent September to December 1976 in solitary confinement. He founded BLAC publishing house and was a founder member and patron of the Congress of South African Writers.

Athlone

3 October 1973

Hello Zeke,

It's been a long time since I've written. I lost track of your whereabouts. Hope you've received the copy of *Cry Rage*. It was my first attempt at writing after a long, bleak period brought about by several factors which I shan't bore you with. Am busy compiling an anthology of poetry *Black Voices Shout* containing the works of eight poets scattered from the Cape to Rhodesia. On the poetry side, things are coming along very well. We've discarded the formal structure of poetry, most of us. Poetry is more protest in content and is not chained by poetical nuances which confuse the man in the township and ghetto. We are writing poetry for ourselves and not for an elitist group. As you can imagine, the majority of poetry produced is one of protest; social and political. Literature has taken a back seat. Nothing seems to be happening in that direction. Or maybe it is that the avenues do not exist. *Drum* ran a short story competition. I entered a story and am very disappointed. I was a runner-up. I'm not disappointed because I did not win the major prize but because of the poor quality of writing. The winning story was novelistic and one published after mine had no right in a short story competition. I was on the point of writing to *Drum* to get my story back after reading the winning entry when mine was published. *Drum* is doing a dis-service to black writing by encouraging such crap. I'm slowly turning back to writing. I'm compiling my scattered stories in one bundle and am also working on a novella. Could you make use of three poems I've included? I tried to get through to Joseph Okpaku of The Third Press in New York but was unable to reach him. *Cry Rage*, apart from being published in South Africa where it was subsequently banned, is being published in Holland and it's hoped to bring out a German and French edition by the end of the year. I'd appreciate it if you, in any manner, could get an American publisher interested in it. Also, at the same time, try for the anthology *Black Voices Shout*. Have you come across the writings of Bessie Head?[1] She's stuck in Botswana. Her third book should be coming out by the end of the year. She is in trouble. Her problem is that she might be sent out of Botswana with her 11-year-old son. She has travel documents from United Nations for the pair of them but no money. She is desperate. Because of her anxiety, she ended up in a mental hospital. She's out, now. Her address is Box 15, Serowe. Could anything be done financially your side? Could we keep in touch?

Regards

James Matthews

1 Matthews is referring to the semi-autobiographical *A Question of Power* (London: Davis-Poynter, 1973, later published in the African Writers Series). Bessie Head trained as a primary school teacher and worked as a journalist on *The Golden City Post* before moving to Botswana, where she lived as a stateless refugee in Serowe, in a situation of dire poverty. Her childhood was unusually difficult: born in a mental hospital in Pietermaritzburg, she was placed in foster care and, later, in an orphanage. Her writings include such celebrated works as *When Rain Clouds Gather* (London: Heinemann 1968), *Maru* (London: Gollancz 1971) and *The Collector of Treasures* (London: Heinemann 1977).

18 November 1973

Dear Teresa

Hi! A brief note so we speed up things. I did file a petition for you and Motswiri, his came though, yours drew a blank – 1970. So we must treat this as a *new* petition – I'll pay the $10 just as I paid M's. You need only worry about the 25.00 that end. The form says I must state where you are and where you will be given status. So I've put Washington DC, which means the dudes that side will be informed. *But*, I can only send in the forms together with your *birth certificate*. Please send this to me or else an affidavit for it if you don't have it. Then I'll submit the forms which are waiting here. Hope you can resolve the dilemma re the research group you want, esp. the *African* one, with both sides agreeing. I'd hate to see you lose both!!!

Love,

Ntate

Cape Town,

19 November 1973

Dear Zeke,

I recently came back from the Transvaal and while in Pretoria I visited Mr. Dickson Mphahlele at the Mamelodi High School. I can't begin to tell you how very kind and helpful he was. I hope you do not mind my having gone there to ask him for a little background information. He knew I was coming and had asked various members of the family for information. I now know quite a lot about the Mphahlele clan, the old chief and so forth. I shall still need quite a bit of biographical detail, but since mine is to be a critical biography there is no need to pry into private affairs! I do not have the maiden-name of your mother and where she came from. Do you think you could give me this information. Also the birth years and places, and full names of your children, please.

I think you would be very happy to know in what high esteem you are still held in South Africa in spite of the fact that no one may read what you have written. I come across this again and again. Not only is your family so very proud of you – Mr. Mphahlele spoke with such warmth not just of your achievements but of you as a person – but your name comes up whenever Black writers are mentioned. If and when the time comes when one may read again what one wishes, you will not come back as a stranger to the readers of this country.

Mr. Mphahlele seems to be in touch with many members of your family and says that your sister and her family are well. He is also very pleased to have your late brother's daughter at his school.

Going to a Black township in Pretoria is still a sad pilgrimage; if there were a transitive verb for humiliating it would describe the experience, entailing as it does a long and dusty drive, innumerable people to see before finding the right one to fill in the form for permission.

I am at the moment making a very close study of the new *African Image* and finding it most interesting to follow the development of ideas since the early version. Would you say that Soyinka's address at the Scandinavian Congress, which Povey finds such a crucial speech, had any influence on you or did you arrive at similar conclusions simultaneously?

If I may say so, the facts on education in South Africa are no longer quite correct (p.22). I remember you did ask me to send you any cuttings from newspapers about education but I did not know what sort of facts you are after. At the moment I am particularly involved with teaching through English in African schools because of the new regulations and the difficulties connected with them. African languages will no longer be the medium of instruction after standard 3. It will be either English or Afrikaans, depending on the dominant language of the district, and the Government decides what that is. In Cape Town, for instance, they have decided it is Afrikaans and our teachers have told me that they intend ignoring this and using English. However, the new regulations have not yet come into force.

I am sending you a copy of the Report of a Symposium about the Sestigers which took place at U.C.T. last year, as I think it will interest you. One cannot talk about Afrikaans literature to-day without taking this movement into account. As the South African English have tried to be more English than the English, so the Sestigers have tried to be more European than the Europeans, with the result that they are living in a world of their own. It is interesting to see how Adam Small, to-day the rallying-point of intellectual Black consciousness, at least in the Cape, fits into the movement.[1]

Just a few more random questions: The more I read of your work, the more I feel the emphasis on education, on the imparting and sharing of knowledge, so I would very much like to have an impression of you as a teacher. Would you mind if I approached the students at one or the other of the Colleges at which you have taught?

Could you please tell me which of the Afro-American writers you have met personally. I know you have met Langston Hughes. What about Baldwin, Ellison? Did you ever meet Dan Jacobson and was the *Encounter* argument ever resolved? Who was the lady who encouraged you in the production of drama (*Down Second Avenue* p.166)?

I think I have pestered you enough now. Bernth Lindfors mentioned in a letter that you are going to another University next year. If this is correct I would like to wish you all the best.

With kind regards,

Ursula Barnett

[1] Born in Wellington in 1936, Adam Small grew up in Goree, a mission station near Robertson. He studied at Oxford, London and Cape Town universities, was a lecturer in Philosophy and later Professor of Social Work at the University of the Western Cape. A celebrated poet and playwright, he worked predominantly in Afrikaans. See *Kitaar my kruis* (Pretoria: HAUM 1961), *Kanna hy kô hystoe* (Cape Town: Tafelberg 1965), *Black bronze beautiful: quatrains* (Johannesburg: Donker 1975).

5 December 1973

Dear Teresa

Just a note to let you know that I've received a shocker from United Bank day before yesterday to tell us that they are closing our checking account on 14 Dec, after which we must not make out checks. Because they had to return 36 checks to us unpaid, so huge our overdraft was. Part of this was of course due to the fact that your Mother is not earning *and* I am having to pay $300 a quarter for her tuition.[1] I thought to tell you this because you said I should not panic, but I *am* panicking. Just one month in arrears on your part will break me.

Another thing, you will now have to fill in the money order – payable to (my name) – with your *signature* and make it out exactly for the amount - $76.00 – whether you split it in two of $38.00 or one monthly amount, it's got to be $76.00. Reason is that I have $254.00 balance from the last couple of checks, and you must send the difference between $76.00 and $24. It's already the 5th today, and things like this kind of delay put me in the most embarrassing position with banks.

Love,

Ntate

1 Rebecca was then a postgraduate student in Social Work at the University of Denver.

1974

22 January 1974

Dear Teresa

It is good to see your checks come in regularly. The two came in, so January month is in the bag, so to speak. It is a tremendous relief in these hard days. How are the courses coming along? Hope good. If I recall you said you'd gone back to Journalism as a major – right? What other courses do you do? How were the grades?

The boys were very grateful for the dollar bills. They told me Chabi had written to acknowledge – did he? They are not hot on the Philly idea. So we told them if they want to remain they must be in boarding school. Their brother told them all about it, and you know he has an elephant's memory for hurt! They're looking forward to coming to D.C. by bus one day – from Philly.

I don't know if you ever heard us talk of an Anthony Sampson?[1] He was my first boss on *Drum* in Jo'burg, then he left for England, succeeded by Sylvester Stein.[2] He has been working for the London *Observer* since and is one of the crack reporters (not cracked!). He is American correspondent for his paper in D.C. Said he'd like to meet you some time. Information should have him listed – I have misplaced his number.

When you have the time, I should like a few copies of *Afro-American* – the black-run newspaper there. I want to see if it would be worth subscribing for from Philly. We are starved for news about the black world in this Rocky Mountain hole-in-the-wall. And my colleagues still hope I should return!! Some people say *Baltimore Afro-American* is better, richer in news – maybe you can steadily enquire from some of those black dudes out there who *do* read newspapers. No hurry, just when you have the leisure.

We should be packing up our goods in the Spring and putting the house up for sale then. We'll keep you informed when in June we shoot off.

Love, Your

Ntate

1 Anthony Sampson (1926-2004), an Englishman with a life-long involvement in South Africa, was invited by Jim Bailey, a fellow Oxford student, to Johannesburg to edit *Drum* magazine in 1951. He later had a stellar career with *The Observer* (including, as Mphahlele writes, a period as Washington correspondent in 1973-1974). He was the author of more than twenty books, most of them analysing the political and financial establishment in Britain. His authorised biography of Nelson Mandela is widely admired (London: Harper Collins 1999).

2 See the conversation between Stein and Mphahlele recorded in Chabani Manganyi, *Exiles and Homecomings: A Biography of Es'kia Mphahlele* (Johannesburg: Ravan 1983), pp 122-30.

University of Southern California

11 February 1974

Dear Ezekiel

Many thanks for your kind letter, and for your complimentary remarks on my CNL paper. I know how you have been feeling about the *Black World* school of self-conscious *enfants terribles*. When I wrote that *Black Aesthetic* paper I was very much in a 'plague-on-both-your-houses' frame of mind, as far as the *Black Aesthetic* demagogues and the Western reactionaries were concerned. It puzzles me a great deal that Gayle says some of the things that he does in *Black Aesthetic* since his academic background bespeaks, perhaps misleadingly, some familiarity with the facts of the Western aesthetics. I expected that sort of thing from the enthusiastic, but informed, graduate students and poets who populate the pages of *Black World*. The latter's crass simplicities I can understand; but in someone of Gayle's background it smacks of intellectual dishonesty, or of an inexcusable failure to do one's homework. Indeed I rather admire your temperament, in that you chose to enter the debate at a time when I have rigorously declined to do so. You may have noticed that my paper rather explicitly questions the ultimate usefulness of debate as such, instead of research and informed analysis. For this reason I declined an invitation from a new European-African group that wished to publish my paper as part of a debate format. And even now, I am a bit uneasy that Anne Paolucci – the director/editor of CNL – is sometimes more interested in the forensic headlines of debate for its own sake than she is in substantive discoveries.

I had the great pleasure of reviewing your *Voices in the Whirlwind*, and your contribution to African 'Writers Talking' (together with other titles) for the *Conch Review of Books* recently. I think that the CRB and its parent publication, *The Conch*, holds a great deal of promise for substantive research in our area. So, in a sense, you have been pre-occupying me, pleasantly, in recent months. I, too, would like to meet for a dialogue or two: there is a sense of isolation, a growing one, which is the inevitable lot of those of us who cannot accommodate the facile old hypocrisies and the easy new dogmas. And for us, some kind of fellowship is an indispensable renewal of things. Would you care to visit us for a lecture-visit? I'm sure that my African Literature (in translation) class, and our Ethnic Studies students, not to mention some of our Comparative Literature students, would like to hear you on a topic of your choice. If you are interested, please let me know. I'm afraid that the remuneration is very thin for that sort of thing here, though. We could come up with airfare and an honorarium of $100 or so. But may be we could arrange something simultaneously with UCLA, Long Beach, or Cal State Los Angeles to supplement your U.S.C. fees, if you have not visited one of those places already.

It was very welcome, hearing from you.

Best regards

Lloyd

Durham

12 March 1974

Dear Ezekiel Mphahlele

I enjoyed very much and was deeply touched by your letter received yesterday. Thank you. All the qualities that have always distinguished your writing were there on that single sheet – intelligence, sensitivity, creative vitality and energy – and, in addition, what one could only guess at in the published work: personal courtesy and kindness. There are few men – especially few of your literary and human achievements – from whom one could expect such a gesture of selfless generosity.

Because of the thesis and plan of my book there were many things in your work that, much as I admire them and would like to have expressed my admiration, I simply could not comment on. *The Wanderers* is a case in point. I was aware that there was much more to say about *The Wanderers* than I could allow myself to say, and I worried about that, yet, given what I was doing, could see no way out of the dilemma. Of course, this only makes me more grateful for the really extraordinary generosity and understanding of your letter. Had I simply been reviewing *The Wanderers* then I would have given attention to some of its many virtues which, as it was, I felt I had to disregard: e.g. The depth and intensity of thought and rightness of thought – in the last dozen or so pages; and the tremendousness of your experience, which you so convey that no reader of the book can doubt it and which makes the experience of so many of us who are never forced from our homes to seem narrow, thin, colorless. These are but two of the novel's strengths and I recognized them though it might not be apparent in what I wrote. 'The Tyranny of Place', by the way, exhibits again all these virtues and all the autobiographical virtues (and creative ones) of *Down Second Avenue* – which, as you know, I admire greatly and without reservation. Thank you for the essay. I am sending under separate cover a copy of *Metaphors of Self* (I have taken the liberty of inscribing it; I hope you won't mind). It takes quite a different tack from *Tell Me Africa* but I know the subject of autobiography is of interest to you – I only hope my treatment will be also.

If you come out to Pennsylvania we might get together some time – I should be honored and would like it very much. At least, Pennsylvania is much nearer than the Rockies. I was to have met Dennis Brutus in Chicago last December (lunching with people in the English Department at North Western) but he had to be out of town.

Your remark about Black American autobiography is intriguing: I have been doing something with the subject in a seminar here (at N.C. Central University). I have been very interested in the courses you have done in African and Black American literature as reported in *Research in African Literatures*.

Thank you for your good letter. I am much looking forward to the review in *Africa Today*.

All best wishes

Yours

James Olney

2 April 1974

Dear Dr. Mphahlele,

I hope you haven't been expecting a letter from me as I wasn't sure whether you wanted to read *THE GRAVEYARD* in ms or in book form. I was torn between sending you the ms and waiting until I heard from you, knowing how busy you are.

I have been giving the idea of having Heinemann do it, some serious thoughts, because of the problem of distribution in Africa. If you ask me, I would much rather have an African publishing H. do my publications but for the age old problem of distribution. The same is true of most US. Houses who would do a good job in the States but would be unable to cover Africa.

I already sent the ms to Heinemann and they are going to do it early next year, citing the paper shortage for the delay.

I don't know whether I wrote to tell you I had been invited to the USSR this summer, to attend the Pushkin Poetry Festival? I feel honoured to be invited there and to have *CONCERTO* translated into Russian.

Why I wanted you to read the ms was because I was hoping that should you like the poems for their literary content, you might consider writing an intro to the book. I leave the consideration entirely to you and I would understand, if, for one reason or another, you are unable to write an intro.

On the home front, things are really bad. After turning down the offer to come to Iowa last year because of pressure from family and government, and because they wanted me to go to Germany as Cultural Attaché, I was stabbed in the back by the bureaucracy of this country.

My Government hasn't yet caught up with the idea that an artist has to be ruthlessly true to himself in order that he might fulfil that monumental responsibility he carries for his people.

Because I cannot show that degree of compromise they want from me, and because of my belief that it is not for the writer to be part of a system that buries truth and humanism, I have been forced into a position where I have had to resign my job as a senior Producer Critic on the government radio and being unemployed for three months.

Fourah Bay College is such an anachronism that the idea of teaching there is anathema to me and the only alternative is exile.

Can I ask how things stand vis-à-vis the market now? I'll accept anything for the time being, just to get out of here, as I would end up (in your words) shrivelling up in my bitterness and doing something.

I am keeping my fingers crossed in the hope that you or someone else would know of a position to which I could come, after my Moscow engagement.

My deepest regards

Syl Cheney-Coker

23 April 1974

Dear Teresa

Here is the cancelled cheque.

Days are drawing closer and we can hardly wait to be on the road.[1]

It seems women have an irrepressible urge to pour hot pepper on old wounds. Your mother showed me your letter and it made me think that if it were between *men*, we would not mention by-gones, we would recognize in each other's silence an acknowledgement that life must go on, and if there is a basis on which to construct a new relationship, that would be enough. Yes, your mother felt offended, but I have tried to keep the lid on. I think myself that she is offended more by your frankness than what you say. 'Frankness' is perhaps a weak word. I think it is your decision to justify yourself and the manner in which you do it. This, I *think*, (how can one be sure? – there remain enigmas in a long-married couple that can never be reached in either of them) makes her feel the desire to reprimand or gently caution or, as you bluntly call it, 'preach', as a *mother* – that this desire is frustrated by your kind of justification of yourself. You have ably characterized yourself as a daughter of Aries. But *language* is vital in human relations. When you say someone preaches, preaches, preaches, you immediately sow the seed of antagonism, justified or not. Then when you load your terminology with words like *domineering*, things get worse, *no matter how true*. My habit – and sometimes I react sooner than I should have – is to wait until I can find the right vocabulary to phrase my indignation to someone I *care about*, or else keep quiet. I mean when, as I deduce happened, your mother pointed out why she thought things went wrong, your keeping quiet would have suggested that you acknowledge her mother's concern and some of the things she implied or otherwise you were to blame for. And yet it would also have kept her guessing as to what we ourselves may have overlooked. That way you would have made it possible for a closer approach, for the distance to narrow, even while you each maintained your beliefs. *That* is the beginning of wisdom often. Your letter, on the contrary, has in it a number of things about which it would take generations to explicate and argue. Simply because you have the compulsion (and succumbed to it) to justify yourself.

Let me ask you *not* to breathe a word to her about what I have said, as she may not expect me to talk to you about it, and I must try to maintain peace and try to make possible a closer understanding. You said in your letter that you need a mother, so you should realize that your mother needs a daughter.

Do me a favor, will you? Don't write a letter with *red* ink!! It makes me nervous and has a harsh character about it.

Love,

Ntate

1 This is a reference to the move from Denver to the University of Pennsylvania, where Mphahlele had been offered a position as full Professor of English. He was to remain there until his permanent return home in August 1977.

Denver

6 May 1974

Dear Teresa

Thanks for this. As I do receive journals dealing *exclusively* with Africa, I think I should pass this one up. Also it's as antiseptic as the Swiss themselves!

Thanks for your newsy letter. Yes, that manager needs tons of ID pumped into him, doesn't he? Must be a survival of the fossils that got blown into this country from SA by some natural catastrophe. Good luck with him, I know you'll stick to your guns. That way you always remind me of Aunt Dora in her young womanhood – no, never a dull moment for that one.[1] You and her must come from a strain somewhere in the Mogale-Mphahlele past. Somewhere along the line the breed stopped coming! I wonder if you know our line or tree? Something tells me you might be interested, and I put it in.

Manager or no manager, we hope you will be able to receive us in your pad. Motswiri *now* says he'll be able to get permission to come with us (in the car). He may change his mind. I'm happy the way he's standing up – for himself. It will be a happy reunion.

Love,

Ntate

Congrats on your transfer to Africa! Sounds an interesting bunch of weird and straights and cranks and cloister types you'll be working with. Hei, you should certainly make it your specialty.

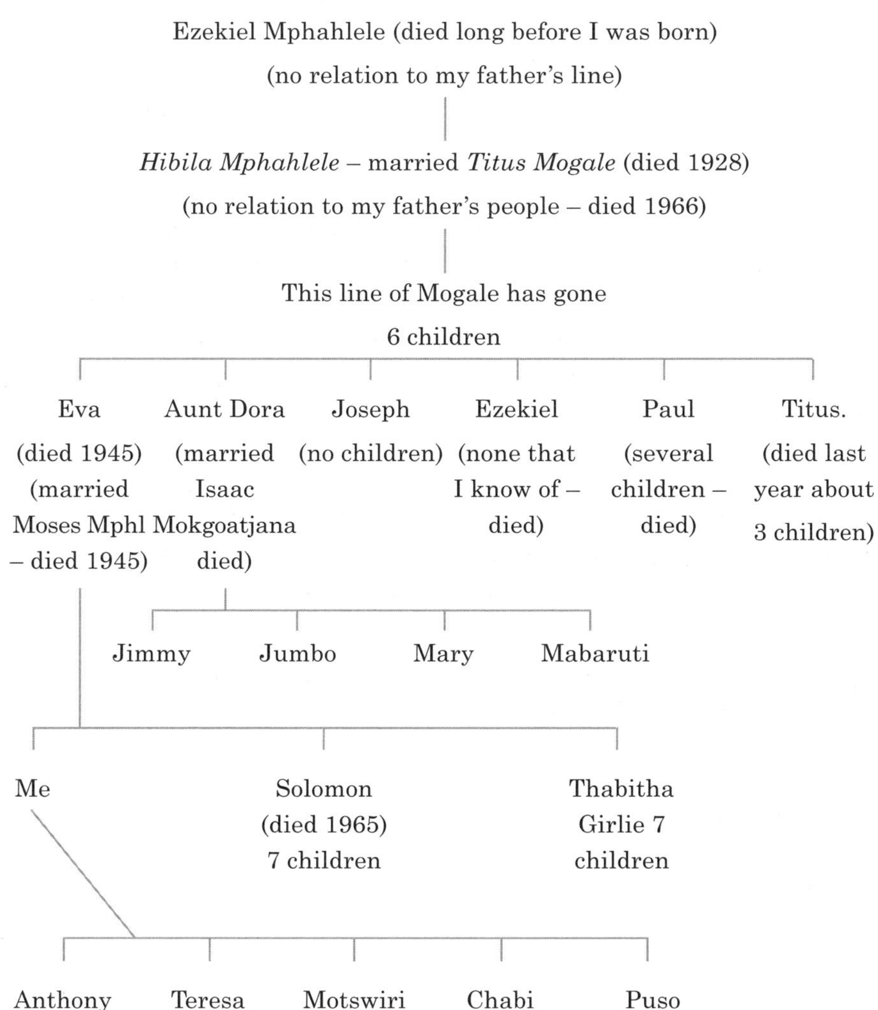

[1] Aunt Dora was Mphahlele's maternal aunt. See *Down Second Avenue* (London: Faber and Faber 1959) for a full characterisation.

Philadelphia
12 July 1974

My dear Sonia,

Hi there! You thought you were never going to hear from this guy again, I bet you! I have met the assistant to the Chairman at Penn. and I've wondered who between the two of you is more charming and obliging. Well, I still have to find out. For initial approachability, you get all the points. Further than that, I still have to judge! Are you disappointed?

The enclosed needs attention of the Bookstore. They keep the book downstairs. Could you please drop Emenyonu a note to say in future he should write to the *bookstore?* That's a good girl!

We're settled now, or should I say we're beginning to settle in? We had a foretaste of the dog days notorious for July and Aug. here. 95 for 3 days running this week. It's cooler now. But of course this fellow here can keep it at bay.

We have a lovely area in Wayne here – trees, trees, birdsong, and yet we're only a mile from midtown Wayne. A chain of towns on the Mainline stretching further west of Wayne and leading to downtown Philadelphia. An impressive city – more character than that synthetic Denver. You disappoint me as a big city broad – Chicago of all places – to choose small-town life!! But of course you love to ski, I know. Do you know, I don't miss the Rockies at all. I keep feeling we may be destined to keep moving east till we are in the Orient. Who knows? No, the West still has its enchantment for us, even if it's only the Rocky Mt West.

The Dept. has given me an office *twice* the size of the Pioneer H. one – literally so. Shelving space galore and air conditioned.

We miss you and Bob and let's hang on to a hope ...

Love to him & to you,

Ever

Zeke

Philadelphia

22 August 1974

Dear Ursula,

I am so sorry I have not been able to write to you. Your letter reached me when everything was topsy-turvy, on the eve of my departure. I couldn't find it among the papers waiting for attention after my arrival. Got lost somewhere – that's my speed!

I remember one question concerned *New World Writing* in which 'The Suitcase' first appeared: N.W.W. – 7th Mentor Selection, New York: The New American Library, 1955. It was a two-yearly anthology, containing writers from several parts of the world. I appear among greater luminaries like Böll, Elizabeth Jennings, Thom Gunn, A. Alvarez, Dylan Thomas (his letters),

Donald Hall etc. I used my *Drum* pen-name – Bruno Esekie, then I often tend to demean the steps by which I climbed, but 'The Suitcase' takes me back to days of creative vitality and hunger – when I was desperate to say things right. Right, i.e. by the thing I was aching to express. I call it 'vitality' for lack of a better word for a state of mind in confusion, full of bitterness (I had just been sacked) in August 1952 and I hated *Drum* work, hated myself each morning I woke up to prepare for the train journey to *Drum*. I had been showing Nadine some (now I remember) 'heavy stories', and one day after she had read 'The Suitcase' she just shouted, 'This is it Zeke!' etc. and herself sent it to the *New World Writing*. I've since learned that the more spontaneously a story writes itself out of one, the better the chances that it will be the thing. 'The Suitcase' came out like that, the rewrites, polishing etc, follow later as a matter of course. First the *whole* thing has to explode.

Please write and restate your other questions. Oh, the new novel: Macmillan here, Double Day, Hill and Wang say no – not saleable. Panther says yes and a third reader says no. Now it's with Howard University. Heinemann in London are most enthusiastic and have sent it for confirmation to their East and West African correspondents. So it's still in the air.

Warmest regards

Zeke

Liverpool

3 September 1974

Dear Professor Mphahlele,

Please pardon me this intrusion on your valuable time, but I feel that I must tell you how much I enjoyed your book about your life in South Africa and in Nigeria.

I have no personal experience of South Africa, but two years ago I returned from eight years spent in Western Nigeria seven exceedingly happy years in Ijibu Province and the last year was most unhappy – spent in Oyo. I didn't want to leave Ijibu-Ode, but yielded to pleadings that I should be doing something for the Church – R. L. It would be unwise and undiplomatic of me to expatiate further on the terrible troubles of that last year during which but for the grace of God I should have been left a physical and mental wreck.

I know Tai Solarin well and have visited his place and have been well entertained there. The Reverend is still there a most charming calmly gentleman.

I did not have the pleasure of meeting Ulli Beier nor Suzanne Wenger but I have a beautiful book by Ulli Beier.

I met many people of importance during my stay there – more people than other people from here who have gone out to work there. I enjoyed their hospitality which is like our own fresh hospitality. I was invited here, there and everywhere. There is no doubt but that there were some who were most jealous of the way in which I enjoyed myself.

I should explain that like you I was engaged in teaching. I taught French the whole time. I encountered the dark side of life as you did too.

Your book revived many happy memories for me. I have sent it to a great friend in Freetown who was with me in Ijubu-Ode. I hope she will find great enjoyment in it too.

To my everlasting grief, a small wooden box containing fourteen snap albums disappeared mysteriously two years ago. There were many snaps of my stay over there. There has been no satisfaction from the film. The albums are of no interest to anyone else. You will understand how the loss can be felt.

I believe we have relatives in Denver, but I do not have their address. My brother has been out there to visit them.

I hope that you are very happy in your work and in your home life over there.

If this letter gives you as much pleasure to read as it has given me to write then I am very happy.

I should like to hear from you when you have some spare time. Thank you again for giving me so much pleasure through your most interesting and delightful book. A very good wish.

Yours sincerely,

Noelle Brawley (Miss)

P.S. With all due respect I should love to have a little autographed picture of you if you have one to spare. I was born on Christmas hence the name – nickname really – the proper one Mary Christina is used for official papers.

13 September 1974

Dear Teresa

We see your point about fulltime studies. You'll have to do what you think is best. Your mother and I do think you need to go full blast at the thing instead of doing this kind of patchwork. It will drag on until you hit 30 and then you'll quit, because unless circumstances forced you to do the BA in your 30s and therefore you must get up steam and keep it on for the duration of your degree, it's hard for things to stay in your head. I graduated BA at 30 (Dec. '49) but I would have liked to have done it earlier. But immediately after marriage in 1945, I plunged into private studies (correspondence) – at 26, and had to stay on. Even so, I'm glad I got it at 30 – I was more mature and knew my direction. If I had dragged on into the thirties, it would have been painful. Your sense of adventure peters out too in your thirties.

Your budget sounds reasonable, not too fancy, not too modest. The problem is going to be the loan. You still have 1975 and half of 1976. It's a 42-month project and you started at least theoretically in Jan. 1973.

I have made enquiries at the Admissions office of U.P. and they must have sent you forms by now. I have to fill in a form myself and have it certified by my dept., and your tuition will be paid in full. But, you have to pay $350 a year General Fee – which the Registrar tells me covers campus facilities, library facilities, etc. Health you will still need to take care of outside of the $350 with their scheme.

You need to send transcripts by mid-October for admission in Jan.'75. You need to solve the loan problem so that you give yourself time to get a job and digs (maybe 3 months advance payment). Maybe the University can give you a loan of the General Fee (it's payable by the semester – half the amount) and maybe even for books. It seems next year would be right for you to be admitted (I mean calendar year). If you can jump the loan hurdle the other items should not be impossible. Let us know your intentions just so you know how much you'd be credited with course wise and how many units are still required and estimate the length of your project. You would do well to submit your application by mid-October and I'll wait with my form till I hear you've sent yours in.

We were distressed about the break-in and hope you've gotten over the initial shock etc.

Love

Ntate

P.S. Interesting thing is happening. All those years at DU my African and Black American Lit. classes were 88% white (never more than 3 out of 25) students. Here both classes have *one white* in each, out of 15. I'd rather have it this way. There is an Afro-American Studies Program which invites outsiders to lecture in any semester course and students who go in there are encouraged to come to my classes. One can do a Masters in Afro-American Studies.

1 October 1974

Dear Ursula,

That is perhaps the essence of it: that the novel is more involved than the short story, and I feel only generally satisfied or not. I also know that I wouldn't do a novel better if I tried to rewrite it completely, whereas, with a poem, the story is more likely to get better as you (I) rewrite it after that first explosion and effusion.

A pity I can't send you the reviews of *The Wanderers* as they are all pasted in my scrapbook. I tried this morning to Xerox them off the book and as they themselves are Xerox copies, the result was a disappointing haze, just illegible. Those I have original copies of, are pasted in such a way that certain columns overlap – you know when you want to conserve space! The enclosed comes off an original.

Reviews are in:

The New Heaven Register, New Haven, Conn. 9 May '71

Best Sellers (Semi-monthly), Scranton, Pa. 15 May '71

The Boston Herald Traveler, 25 April '71

The Virginian – Pilot, Norfolk, Va. 21 March 1971

Chicago Sun – Times; 5 May 1971

Seattle Post – Intelligence, 4 April '71

The Detroit News – 5 Apr '71

Saturday Review – 19 June '71

New York Review of Books, 23 Sept 70

New Yorker (undated but must be '70)

The Times Lit. Supplementary to March 72

Anti-apartheid News 1972 (by Caroline de Gapingly)

There is also a good review of *Voices* in *New York Times Book Rev* 22 Oct '72 – by Julius Lester, a scholar. I give you all those names in case you are able to con the U.S. info. S into procuring the papers or copies through its library facilities if not, I might hire a typist to do three or four major ones off my scrapbook. Let me know.

I had a lovely letter from William Plomer after he had read the novel dated 11 Oct 71. We had been corresponding steadily since 1959 after I had stayed with him in his house during my vacation in Eng. He said of Naledi (in his letter) 'Naledi in her grace and dignity, I found as touching as a portrait of someone known to me.' He regrets he lost sight of her (his acquaintance). 'It is, don't you think, a crowded book. It gives one a feeling of a lot of different people being about, and have the busy-ness and indifference and strangeness of crowds.' I've kept wondering also if Naledi didn't echo for him the girl Turbott Wolfe is stunned by. Still most exhilarating discovery for me – that novel by P. I had a profound admiration for him and his writing – also *awe* because of his craftsmanship. Especially in his poetry – I mean a craftsmanship that does not stand in the way of emotional response and which exasperates me.

'Mrs Plum' still stands top of my list as the best thing I ever pulled off and the same thing happened after I had written it that 'The Suitcase' did to me. Alongside 'Suitcase' I've been happiest with 'Mrs Plum' and 'The Living and the Dead'.

No, I did not 'discover' any one as fiction editor. It was evident that Rive, Clarke, Matthews had already been writing by then and they simply continued to publish. *Drum* was always apologetic about publishing fiction. Only the editors kept it alive against the wishes of their superior, even then fiction had to be phased out.

Its good to hear Rive did his PhD. If you can find his address I'd like to write and congratulate him even although he said some nasty things about *Them* to someone who quoted him in a review.

My sister will be back in J'burg on the 16 Nov. She lives at 36 Mapetla, P. O. Moroka.

Best wishes,

Zeke

P. S. Good news about your forth-coming book. Looking forward to seeing it. I wonder if you could enquire from a bookshop what book they have – something standard – on the history of Afrikaans literature. I don't know if the ones I used in my Afrikaans-Nederland courses for the BA are still around. I would like the kind of thing in current use at University. They can let me know how much it costs and I'll send them a draft.

Thanks

Cape Town

15 October 1974

Dear Zeke

Very many thanks for your two letters and all the useful information. I think I shall be able to get hold of most of the reviews you have listed, either through the libraries here or by asking the newspapers themselves, who are usually quite willing to send a Xerox. Many thanks.

I must explain about Peter Grose. I run a literary agency – actually that's a euphemism, since the work includes everything from fiction to comics – and represent Curtis Brown here. Last April I went on my first trip overseas in 25 years and met Peter. I saw all your books in his office and realized he represented you, but I was terribly late for my appointment and he very rushed; also I was depressed about my critical writing at the time which seemed to have come to a stop. So I didn't mention my interest. The letter from Twayne came a few days after that, just as I was on the point of leaving London. I wrote to him a few weeks ago, when you were busy moving, and Twayne wanted to know whether I want an extension to include the new novel. Good luck with it, I'm sure you will have good news soon.

Thanks for the information about the Congress. I had not realized that it was on their behalf that you did the Mbari and Chem-chem things. I had quite a lot of information about these organizations, though. I seem to remember a controversy in *Transition* about the backing of the latter which I couldn't quite follow. I did have your article on Negritude, both in the anthology and in Gerald Moore's book.

I agree with you about 'Mrs Plum' – it's magnificent. I like it better each time I read it. I'm not so impressed with 'The Living and Dead', though. The dialogue between the two white men doesn't sound quite right to me.

I'm busy with the essays now.

I'm trying to get hold of Richard Rive. Someone has promised me his telephone number, so I hope to be able to add the address to this letter. 2 Selous Court, Claremont, Cape Town.

I'm getting a history of Afrikaans literature for you written by a Potchefstroom professor and will send it along this week. Hope you will find it suitable.

How are you and your family liking Philadelphia?

Best regards

Ursula

1975

15 January 1975

Dear Dr. Mphahlele:

Upon recommendation of Dean Edward Lindell, I accept with regret your resignation as Professor of the Department of English at the University of Denver effective June 1, 1975.

On behalf of the University may I express appreciation for your unique contributions to the University, and wish you all success and happiness at the University of Pennsylvania.

Sincerely,

William H. Key

Acting Vice Chancellor

Austin

5 February 1975

Dear Zeke

As I promised, I presented your views and those of the other writers I talked to (Pieterse, Kgositsile and Serote) on the question of white South African participation, and specifically the participation of Nadine Gordimer as a featured speaker, in our Symposium.

I should explain that initially I conceived an event which was to be solely a Poetry Reading on the anniversary of Sharpeville and that the participants were to be South Africans currently in the United States – i.e. Mphahlele, Kgositsile, Pieterse, Brutus, Mtshali, Serote and Kunene. It was on that basis that I approached the writers and persuaded them to come to Austin, probably with no more than their expenses paid and with no assurance of an honorarium. This was the proposal which I submitted in a memorandum to Dr John Warfield, Chairman of the African and Afro-American Studies and Research Center, and which he approved.

Prior to traveling to Chicago for a meeting of the ASA, the African Studies Association, I discussed with my colleagues here the possibility of (a) the formation of an African Literature Association in the course of the ASA conference, (b) the possibility of inviting a conference of the to-be-formed ALA[1] to Austin and (c) the possibility of combining this with the Sharpeville Day commemoration.

As a result of the confluence of these plans, which are now about to be realized, the original concept for Sharpeville Day slipped somewhat out of focus but remained in my own mind, and, I am sure, in the minds of those I had invited.

After some discussion, the following resolutions were adopted:

1. The Committee was not prepared to exclude anyone from participation in the Symposium.

2. The Committee considered the invitation to Ms Gordimer to participate as a featured speaker as unwise and resolved to cancel it.

The decision is being communicated to Ms Gordimer.

In amplification of the resolutions: On resolution (1) the feeling of the Committee, which I strongly support, is that any events of the ALA will have to be open to all and that membership should be open to all. (A policy statement is currently being drafted by the ALA which will so define its own principles on matters of racial discrimination or racial domination that it would, I believe, be unacceptable to racists – whether from South Africa or elsewhere). On resolution (2): Nadine Gordimer will now (1) pay her own expenses, (2) not receive an honorarium, and (3) not participate in the Poetry Reading.

I realize that this decision only half-satisfies the concern expressed by some of our South African participants: on the other hand, it certainly only half-satisfies some of the members of our Working Committee. It seems to me that this kind of compromise is the best that we could reach without endangering the entire Symposium.

I hope that you will agree to this expression of opinion by a majority of the Committee and that you will use your good offices to persuade the other featured participants to do likewise. I indicated in the course of the meeting that I believed that you had sufficient influence and enjoyed sufficient respect among the other South African writers to persuade them to go along with your own view, which has generally been to accept the decision of a democratic majority even when you are in disagreement.

I hope that I am right in this and that you will confirm it. Please send me your comments on the decisions. If you are agreeable, I will arrange to have them reproduced and distributed to all the other featured speakers.

All good wishes

Sincerely

Dennis Brutus, Chairperson

P.S. I will also be writing a personal letter in reference to your private one.

[1] Brutus is referring to the inaugural conference of the African Literature Association at the University of Texas at Austin in 1975.

12 February 1975

Dear Teresa,

Okike is a quarterly. I'm afraid to say though, much as this is a skit, it does not fit into the atmosphere of *Okike*. It's journalistic verse, and so does not have the deep resonances of your other verse and so does not project into the future, etc. Another way of saying it's not poetry but talkative verse.

Okike is partisan, its tone is clearly anti-such 'clowns' as Amin, but it takes a view that is not focused on a single tyrant. Rather it takes in all African tyrants and anyone can find a place in the poetry who cares to see himself in the mirror. I would rather send them something with depth. On the other hand, I may be exaggerating or misjudging. So if you feel intensely about it, you may send it to *Okike*.

Love,
Ntate

Cape Town
17 February 1975

Dear Zeke

Many thanks for your letter. My trip to Austin is somewhat in jeopardy at the moment, as my husband had a heart attack a couple of weeks ago. He is making a very good recovery, and is quite determined I should go, so I haven't cancelled my booking and will decide a little nearer the time. It's a very difficult thing to decide: I'm very keen to go but of course don't want to leave him. The family have promised to look after him. Anyway, I shall let you know.

The biography is more or less finished now and I am hoping to bring it to Professor Jones who is in charge of that section of Twayne, but there is still quite a bit of checking to do. I hope you do not mind, but I am going to use one chapter as my contributing paper for the Texas conference. I was going to do something on the SA black writer and the black aesthetic, but that would take a lot of time which I haven't got, and as a large part would concern your essays anyway, I am doing the chapter on your essays and critical writing. The publishers have agreed and so has Bernth Lindfors. Seeing that the papers don't get read it won't be embarrassing for you, and there is nothing personal in that essay.

Congratulations on the acceptance of your novel. I am very much looking forward to reading it. I am of course not well acquainted with American publishing but from what I have read Third Press have become very prestigious. Since some of their books have also been done by O.U.P. in England they must have a very good name by now, which will certainly be enhanced by adding your name to their list. I had an extension on the biography so as to include the novel but I would like to finish it now. It depends on how soon Twayne would print. If it's long after your novel is published it will look a bit silly. Do you think you could let me know right away about when it would be published – just a rough indication: six months, less, more?

Thanks for the information about *Thought, Ideology Literature*. One more question. I didn't want to bother you, and so wrote to Denver to ask in which issue the essay 'The Function of Literature in the Present Time' appeared, for reference purposes, since you kindly sent me the typescript, but they didn't reply. Could I trouble you to let me know? Also please in which issue of *African Arts/Arts d'Afrique* did our extract of *Wanderers* appear?

With best regards

Ursula

Amherst

23 February 1975

Dear Zeke

I am sorry I didn't get back to you. I thought I had.

I was going to use the first half of 'Images' in *Okike* 10 which we are now putting together. Now that you have it you might as well indicate the best place for the axe. Part II will of course appear in *Okike* 11.

I saw your collective letter on Kofi in *The Press*. It was good. I had just sent a cable to Acheampong and to the Ghana Association of Writers. I notice that we are both new fellows of the GAW. A cable from you to them might help. If we are fellows we might as well put them to work.

Did I ever tell you I was moving to the University of Connecticut? I moved in September for the 75-76 academic year. Unless the military fun and games in Nigeria get much worse I plan to return to Nsukka in the summer.

Ever

Chinua

Connecticut

Dear Ursula,

I am very sorry to hear your husband has had an attack. I seem to recall that at your graduation he was laid down too, so he must have been going through a rough time. I hope he recovers satisfactorily. It would be a pity not to meet you, but can understand the anxiety.

You seem to have been putting hard work into the book and can only say more power to your shoulder!

Yes, my agent has just written to say The Third Press will publish in the Fall FS. The new title is now *CHIRUNDU*. This may be too far for your purpose. 'The Function of Literature etc' will be published in the spring issue of *Denver Quarterly*; I'm now told, if someone else doesn't come up with an expected article, otherwise it will be March for the Winter Qrt. This is exasperatingly vague, and I want to call the editor up to ask him for something definite. Then I'll let you know.

Did I ever send you three poems of mine that first appeared in the *Journal of New African Lit. and the Arts* published by Okpaku of Third Arden? Reason I ask is that you'll see two at Texas in a small publication of S.A. writing. I did 2 others for Brutus which he can't use. I'm doing my poetry phase and want soon to publish perhaps about 10 with a publisher who does little books in New York. Extract from *The Wanderers* appeared – confirm it, can't find the particular number of *African Art*. Will find out soon.

Best wishes

Zeke

17 March 1975

Dear Ursula,

I thought you would not take offence if I commented on the CONCLUSION of your dissertation. I do not know if you have since rewritten it.

Sol. Plaatje wrote in English and Tswana. H. I. Dhlomo wrote mostly in English, Vilakazi in Zulu. Where is the evidence that the ideas of these men, taken up again (you say) by Kunene and Ndebele, are based on the contention 'that ... literature'? (1st page of CONCLUSION) They did different things – fiction, drama, poetry. A person writing in an indigenous language may be logically assumed to hold such a contention. His writing is a direct product of the culture carried by his language. Like Vilakazi and Plaatje in his translations of Shakespeare. The claim about their *ideas* puts both Plaatje and Dhlomo in a questionable position not borne out by your categorical clause in para. 2: 'is sharply divided into two groups'. Dhlomo and Plaatje certainly had the highest regard for their own cultures, but the use of English and the use of European imagery cannot in any way be interpreted as a recognition of the metaphor and symbolism of their culture. And yet again the use of English was expedient for them as it is for us today – even for those you seem to approve of as continuing the 'tradition' of the Vilakazis .... They had different English models from ours. What I read into your conclusion (pardon me if I am wrong) is that because you write in an African language you acknowledge the cultural independence of your people and to do something else is to dismiss such a concept.

Ndebele and Kunene mix their idiom. Much of the time it is an English idiom, it is accessible to an English-speaking person, it is a sophisticated idiom. The tempo, particularly that of Kunene's poetry, is certainly akin to that of African speech, so is the gravity of tone, and the posture of the persona. And yet the *sensibilities* are those of poets who are commenting on the politics of TODAY, not the sensibilities of villagers and ethnic concerns. When we, whom you distinguish 'sharply' from the others, found fault with the trumped-up 'Bantu culture' the Boers were imposing on us, it was *political* protest. We refused to be locked up in enclaves prepared for us. And Kunene and Ndebele and Mtshali would themselves support us today.

I think you might have tried to see us at different times in our cultural history grappling with the African reality through various rather than antithetical techniques. The earlier writers' nostalgia about their pastoral innocence (hence the historical romances and the lyrical verse).

Followed by Abrahams and ourselves who were grappling with the urban experiences, in which the African was asserting a permanence he was being denied. The use of fiction rather than poetry to deal with this reality is *important*. We simply took our African ness for granted. We were depicting urban life, not rural life, and this was our most immediate reality. We were not consciously doing this in order to *deny* African culture. We were surrounded by it, part of it, how could we deny it? African culture to me, as is the 'African Personality', has urban and rural manifestations.

Again, fiction sees contrasts, conflicts, paradoxes, and to be authentic I would have to translate my African dialogue into un-English English, using its imagery. However urban, it was Sotho idiom. Poetry unifies sensibilities, puts things together, and a persona like Kunene's can sum up the poet's stage of mind in a way fiction cannot, as a single unit. Hence there will be a greater concentration of African idiom in the poetry of the man who uses such a device than in a novel. Our main argument would be, and again Kunene etc. agree, that African culture is not necessarily the unspoiled rural landscape and indigenous speech idiom. The place and the time make it authentic. Our urban reality is one aspect, rural reality another.

I'm afraid you speak of Boetie as if he had a formulated philosophy to live outside of European standards. Surely, if we are to believe Barney Simon, he created an ethos of his own because he had been cast out. There was nothing intellectual about the process. Angry, yes, but he found himself an outsider. You could surely not equate him with a writer who decides that African culture is independent, runs parallel to European culture and its literature and therefore has its own ethos.

You say on p. 224 'Isolated ... from tradition', 'have failed to respond to current thinking in the West'. This baffles me. Are we really cut off from tradition? Do we not depict African life in its *fragmented* state? What is the 'current thinking of the West'? Baffling also is 'their estrangement from contemporary trends'. 'Movement' sounds most misleading. I don't know if you mean urban realities are no longer the subject of literature? Maybe a reader would like to know why. Because I can't imagine that the poetry you say has gone back to traditional culture has replaced this? How cut off from 'contemporary trends' are we in comparison with other African writers?

I do find your CONCLUSION leaves a number of questions unanswered which you raise by way of assertions. The expediencies, the compromises, the protest, the urban experience and the preference of it in spite of its agonies etc. etc., the problems of audience etc. are too complex to be explained by the dichotomy you make.

I've postponed writing this owing to pressure of work, and maybe you will have time to explain some of the things. As for this man: when I criticize a novel by a white South African for not depicting black life right I would like also to concede that Whites and Blacks are more or less disadvantaged: the politics keep them apart. I want to be recognized as an African in terms of racial *particulars* and a human being in terms of *universals*. When I make no concessions, it is because I am offended by the TONE of a novel e.g. *God's Stepchildren*, *Cry The Beloved Country* and I'm offended when, as in the Afrikaans novel, I'm ignored (as a human reality, I mean).

If I am not always as clear headed as Lewis Nkosi, it is *because* I know enough of Western poetics not to apply them indiscriminately to African writing.

[Letter not signed]

Cape Town

Dear Zeke,

I was pleased to hear from you on the eve – literally – of my departure for England. So forgive me if this sounds hurried.

First of all I have pleasure in sending you Xeroxes of the two stories you need, 'The Woman' and 'The Woman Walks Out'. I have copies of both books. Balkema, who took over Julian Rollnick's stock, gave me his last two copies of *Man Must Live* many years ago, and I am sure I sent one of them to you at the time. I would hate to part with the other, but will be glad to Xerox any more you may need. They are very good stories and am glad they are being revived. I know about the work Tim Couzens is doing.

I am very sorry about the errors in the book. I asked a Xhosa and Southern Sotho-speaking acquaintance whether Puso was a girl's or boy's name and she must have misinformed me. I will write and apologize to your sister if you would please give me her current address, and send her a copy of the book. I certainly accept what you write regarding my tackling the work from outside the Black milieu. I think it is all right doing this job as a Twayne World Authors series, as to some extent this presumes readers from the outside looking in, so it is not too bad if the authors do too. I am sure there will be many more biographies from other points of view. This one is meant to answer the question: why can this writer from South Africa be considered as a world author. On the other hand something of what I personally was trying to do perhaps becomes a little clearer in the *Contrast* article I sent you last week? Richard Rive, I think, feels he must justify having made a study of Olive Schreiner, rather than a Black writer. It seems to me the Black South African writers are very very conscious of what the Black S.A. writers in exile think of them.

I would have to re-read what I said about *Chirundu*. I don't think I said that the idea behind it is trivial. I certainly don't think so, but I felt the story and characters too slight to carry it.

Please excuse the hurried note. I will write again when I return.

Ursula Barnett

14 May 1975

Dear Folks (Makhudu),

It occurred to me that in my hurried tentative letter of yesterday I must have forgotten to give you our new address. Nor do I remember if I said I'm now teaching at the University of Pennsylvania in Philadelphia? Maybe. I'm now full professor of English (in the American sense) – i.e. not head of the dept. but professor as an academic recognition. Did I say Ribs is a case worker for the blind? Maybe. Strange thing – that connection with the blind.

Bye folks, love

Zeke

Berlin

21 June 1975

My dear Ezeke,

I am very sorry that I could not return to Philadelphia as promised. My activities snowballed to the extent that even though I put off my departure from the 8th June to the 10th, I would not do all the things I had meant to do.

It was heart warming to me to be able to be with you again after such a long-long time. I realized how many of some of my most satisfying experiences I had shared with you: some experiences that have had the profoundest effects on my life. It was really great to be able to reminisce on these.

Tell Rebecca that I'm sorry that I did not take some of the turkey for *mfakgo*. I certainly would love to have some of it now – especially some of the cuts that I left untouched. It was real home cooking.

Thank you for coming to my rescue financially. I was put in a very awkward situation by the State Department. They however, decided that they would allocate 300 dollars to my traveling expenses, and this I shall get when I reach home, from the JHB American Embassy. I will then be able to pay the debts I made in the States.

I arrived in Germany on the 11th instant, after a stop-over at Heathrow's Ariel Hotel for the night of the 10th. In Germany my stay is sponsored by the German Cultural Exchange Service, an agency of the West German Government. I visit music academics at each of the places I am assigned to, to study their administration, source of funds, criteria for admitting students, methods of and goals in their teaching. I also attend concerts, visit places of interest. These are numerous at each of the places I have been able to go to. Berlin is the most exciting, even more than New York.

My itinerary is: Frankfurt 11th to 13th: Bonn-Bad Goldenberg 13th-15th: Cologne 16th: West Berlin 17th-22nd: Hamburg 23rd-24th: Hanover 24th: Munich 25th-26th. I'll leave for home at 21.20 on the 26th June, from Frankfurt.

I'll contact Pitje as soon as I get home, with a view to getting him to brief counsel. My own view is that we might as well give it a go from the outset so that the position is clear as soon as we can have it. I'll pay the initial costs – if I need help I'll let you know.

I forgot photographs of my youngsters which I had hoped to collect on my return to Philadelphia. Please keep what you think you like among them and send me the rest by post.

Thank you very much for the books. I expect to find them in JHB when I get there.

With hearty regards to you and the Mphahlele clan.

Very sincerely
Khabi

Wayne, Pennsylvania
23 June 1975

My dear Khabi,

What a spiritual uplift it was, even though we had you but a day and a half! When you left on Monday I had the disconcerting feeling that you wouldn't come back – what with N.Y. and D.C. – there's something about the life styles of these places – coupled with your own run of appointments – that couldn't allow you to go free. But because I felt so, I hoped. In all the 18 years of exile, we hadn't experienced an occasion like our reunion and I mean it. We are grateful you came.

I had a letter from Tom Karis in N.Y. in which he says you met. Says also that you were jogging one morning and met a female streaker. Was it after you left us? But for the fact that pink flesh (sometimes quite ivory) is nothing hot at a distance, I would have tripped her from behind and in Martin's words, brought up the rear! One of these days in the summer we'll visit the Karis'.

Now I've got that paragraph in, I shall seem to be rambling, because, returning to our reunion, I realized more than ever before how true it is that our lives have been intertwined in a most profound way. And I would have said the same thing about you to Norah T. How impressive your work has been these past 18 years! It's a most enviable record – the orchestras, the choirs, the other people whose individual tastes you must have shaped. And you have done more than merely survive, like so many of our people – you have done that but also found self-fulfillment. But for the academic and intellectual and literary growth I have experienced outside the whole exercise in exile can be written off as utter waste.[1] Because the self-fulfillment has only been partial, and is felt only in fits and starts. Because the feedback is not from the people who made me – South Africans in SA. For you, as for every artist among people who love art, the satisfaction has been in that feedback.

Some time ago, as I traveled through and stayed in countries in Africa, I found European music was a concern only of the elite, of a chosen few with a sense of prestige. I became disenchanted and stopped going to symphony concerts or chamber music performances. I contented myself with playing the music in my house. I even imagined that at a communal level, as distinct from a personal level, what African countries were doing was the ideal – performing African music and dances etc from folk traditions. I even imagined S. Africans (not whites) need quantities of this, with the added element of new compositions and experimentation with folk idioms enlarged into bigger productions. Somewhere in *The African Image*, carried away as I was, and disenchanted in the prestigious Western performances (organized by lonely and homesick European expatriates), I state that communally I would promote African music and let people pay for European music. Even then I knew I would rather follow my own personal inclinations as a S. African, which I know are also yours – which are towards a broader and deeper musical experience. One that can be provided by European music in addition to the indigenous. And it is this that you have indicated. And I'm glad that statement I make in *The African Image* is not wholly right. I mean your success in projecting your individual personality reflected in your (and my) love for and understanding of Western music and *your* performance skill, into communal life. So that you actually moulded people's tastes in this direction – this success makes me glow with a feeling of rightness. And the S. African will be the richer for it. The other thing you have admirably proved me wrong in is what I said in *Down Second Avenue*. Again, I projected my own anxiety on your behalf into your future – that, as you failed to get sponsorship to study abroad, you would disappear into anonymity. Of course you didn't, you kept afloat and won through, against so much hostility, distrust and sheer malice. I'm glad I was proved too pessimistic. But then I should have known you are of sterner stuff. Keep on keeping on!

Tell those fellows – Phatudi etc that I want to come and teach my own people – as long as I can feel protected. I told Phatudi that I'm not a politician, I hate politics, I couldn't go into platform politics, I am an educator and was born one.[2] So my rightful place is in the classroom. Repeat that to him if you can, if this letter gets to you before you go north. Notwithstanding what you said about Gatsha's distance from the University, tell him also this. I happen to have ideas, from the experience of teaching in six different universities, about what a curriculum for English and literature should be. I would simply want to rally support from colleagues in the dept. in the gentlest, most tactful way possible, and by stages, so that people grow with the programme.

I wish you had phoned to let me know James Baker's address to which I could always send things for you which need to be. As it is I sent off last week your records (I was sorely tempted to keep them) the photos to 7015. With them I sent three records which we meant to present you when you should return on Friday. Baroque flute music (Buxtehude, Pachelbel, J.S. Bach) J.S. Bach and C.P.E. Bach's six sonatas for harpsichord and flute. I would like to send you, when I find it in the shops, C.P.E. Bach's concerto for 2 pianos and orchestra and the other side concerto for organ, strings and coati. Just so beautiful – yes you want to go to the toilet, for fuck all! On the other hand, if you have it, you'll say so. It struck me as a pretty rare item. These things, I'm afraid, went off by surface mail. They were $11 by air and figured if you wanted them urgently, you would have phoned for me to send them to N.Y. by special delivery – off one day and you get them the next. So I packaged them strong and you should get them in 4-6 weeks' time.

I hope your trips to the north and east will be as rewarding as you could wish. I know also you will get the advocate on to the citizenship matter. Ribs should be sending you the other information soon.

Love to you and the folks at home.

Ever

Zeke

[1] See Mphahlele's 'Portrait of a man who lives in a Glasshouse'. *Era* XII, Spring 1976, pp 4-7, for a moving rendering of the experience of life in exile.

[2] This is an overstatement of Mphahlele's position on formal political involvement. In 1955 he addressed the Kliptown Congress and became a member of the ANC. Later, in exile, he became the leader of the South African delegation to the All Africa People's Conference in Accra in 1958.

Wayne, Pennsylvania

2 July 1975

Dear Tim,

Are you there? I'm so used to the mobility of academics in this country I wonder if it's the same in the old 'countrie'.

You may be aware I am working on an ambitious critical anthology of African Literature. The first volume I'm doing is poetry. Then I shall get on to the fiction. I shall in this second volume, have only short stories and narrative sketches, no excerpts from novels. I am collecting material for these two sections concurrently. Later I shall get to expository prose.

Right now, I am asking for your assistance in collecting what there must be in S.A. It's just a matter of getting me in touch with poets and prose writers you happen to know or getting *them* in touch with me. The second way you can help is to contact on my behalf people in African languages at Wits and other places who can send me translations of oral and written literature. Venda, Tsonga, Pedi are always unrepresented in anthologies of traditional poetry. Other language groups can also contribute. I'm dealing with Black Africa throughout.

Am I asking too much? I hope not. When the Dhlomo book comes out, which you refer to, would you let me know?[1] I am hoping that by December this year I shall have gathered in all the poetry I can handle.

Best wishes,

Zeke

1 This refers to Tim Couzens's biography of H I E Dhlomo, *The New African: A Study of the Life and Work of H.I.E. Dhlomo* (Johannesburg: Ravan Press 1985).

Wayne, Pennsylvania

8 July 1975

My dear Khabi,

Requests, requests, requests! Fortunately, this one may not exact so much energy. The enclosed circular speaks for itself. I have already sent it to Univ. of the North, the white universities. I try to work through people I know so we can keep personal contact. I think I shall send one to Peteni at Fort Hare.[1]

What I am asking for you is to give a copy to a trustworthy fellow who is likely to act on it at Ngoye. Where is the man who used to be professor of African languages at Wits? I think I heard he was with Shuter & Shooter in Durban – Nyembezi: he might be of some help.[2] If you need to make Xerox copies for more than the two enclosed feel free to do so, as long as you don't strain your pocket. *Any* number.

You may get to know some of the young writers who need to be noticed and I would like to get something from them. I shall be most grateful. This is an ambitious book I'm planning and I want it to be a standard text.

Love to the folks at home and yourself.

Ever

Zeke

P.S. The photos follow with Ribs' documents.

[1] R L Peteni, author of the novel *Hill of Fools* (London: Heinemann 1976).

[2] C L S Nyembezi, Zulu novelist, linguist and literary historian, was based at the time at Fort Hare, not in Durban. See *Inkinsela yaseMgungundlovu* (Pietermaritzburg: Shuter and Shooter 1961); *Zulu Proverbs* (Shuter and Shooter [1954] 1990) and *A Review of Zulu Literature* (Shuter and Shooter 1961).

Johannesburg

21 July 1975

Dear Zeke,

If I may call you that! Your letters arrived while I was in Mafikeng & Botswana trying to track down some information on Solomon Plaatje. So I hope my telegram and this letter reach you in time.

The information you wanted was a follows (this is, of course, not absolutely reliable – I found out the Wits information from the staffing office and the UNISA information from their calendar).

Wits have five 'tutors' who are black. These are all in the African languages department.

UNISA has six 'assistants' who are black. Again all in African languages.

As regards black students in white universities I have photostatted a piece from the 1974 *Survey of Race Relations* (even the Institute of Race Relations has its uses!). I assume they are reasonably accurate. I made a slight error in my telegram – I see you asked for enrolment in *English*-medium universities (I counted in the four students at Potchefstroom – also I think I left out the one at Rhodes). In my telegram I assumed you would not want the UNISA enrolment.

However, I think the table is very interesting and may give you a rather more detailed block of information for your article. Incidentally (this is only from my own knowledge – but I'm fairly sure about it) the 256 black students at Natal, I think, are largely medical students – hence the reason for the high number. Again, only on my own knowledge, black students are allowed into white universities only if they are doing courses not offered at any of the 'black universities' and only with the special permission of the Minister (of Education, I think). This was my own experience, at any rate, when someone asked me if they could get into Wits and not have to go to Turfloop (for health reasons).

If the above information is inadequate, please let me know what more I can do.

On the other request, for the anthology material, I think I can give you quite a lot. I have collected a lot of early material. It will take me a while to sort – I am busy card indexing Herbert Dhlomo's life and work – a helluva job because there is so much cross-referencing. I shall pick out material from all the early writers you might be interested in. Give me about a month to six weeks. When you say 'narrative sketches' does that include non-fiction? With what scope? Essays? Political sketches? Shall I use my own judgment on what might interest you?

Also, I shall phone and write to anyone I know who may be of help. I am very glad you are including Venda, Tsonga writers etc. They are much neglected. I have a friend who is I think one of the best poets in S. Africa. He writes in Venda so he has never been published. He is very unassuming so I may have some trouble persuading him. I think I can put you on to quite a few people. I hope *they* will respond.

As regards Herbert Dhlomo I'll certainly let you have anything that comes out. I have two tasks in hand: one is the editing of the manuscripts (there are 1250 pages – 13 plays etc.). The typescript will hopefully be completed by mid-October (whether we'll ever get a publisher, I don't know; if not, I could make a microfiche for you). The other task I have set myself is a sort of social biography of H.E. Dhlomo – I have found about 1000 pages of his journalism and I have the writings etc. of a lot of other people of that time. I want to try to write on black S.A. Lit. between 1900-1950 – to show it in context – publication outlets, relationships to social and political events and thinking, to show its continuity, its non-isolation etc.

I have just completed the manuscript of an edition of about 20 short stories (in English) by R.R.R. Dhlomo. These were written about the same time (perhaps just after) his *An African Tragedy*. They are to be published in *English in Africa* sometime soon. Perhaps this is the kind of thing you would be interested in. they may not be the type of thing English Departments with all their prejudices go for but I think they have many points of interest.

Anyway, I'm beginning to waffle. My own Department is very anti the teaching of African literature ('Not when it means having to sacrifice a Dickens') so once I get going on my work all my frustrations and enthusiasms tend to pour out. Recipients of letters and the few friends who agree with me tend to have to suffer my diatribes!

I'll get cracking on what you've asked for. I shall send you some poetry when I've got it sorted out e.g. I have some very early Peter Abraham's poetry. Also, a couple of interesting (I think) poems from the Twenties.

I hope this letter arrives safely.

Yours

Tim

22 July 1975

Dear Teresa,

We were sorry to hear about your misadventure with the VW. Somehow (Funiwe told us the whole story) I had forebodings about the engine when you left. You might have tried to contact us, because we would have towed you back here with the Volvo and had it looked at by the VW people in Wayne. Anyhow I'm glad you came through somehow. I'm sure they can bring the bug back to life, bugs are so hardy. I shudder to think of the other things that go with all towing, repairs, etc. Tell us how things are going – the car, the knee – now I mentioned them, it seems this season you are accident prone, things simply tumble down on you. But I know you'll always land on your feet, like a cat if you throw it in the air. Which is more than can be said of so many people. Only thing, of course, is that one needs to conserve energy – physical, mental, emotional.

Don't think I'm making too much of these things. It's only a father's concern and love.

You know, after you left I began to consider again this whole thing concerning your studies. It occurs to me somehow that, given the fact that you're not in a position to go into full-time schooling right now, there isn't only *one* alternative. Saving and then going in is one. Another is to consider just how much theory of communications and stuff one *really* needs to be a broadcaster and/or journalist. All this you get in the field, and indeed there are special institutions that teach it and can fit in a person's working schedule etc. So that a B.A. degree can be one with a communications major or not at all or with journalism alone or any of the humanities. You can do a B.A. because it gives you the prestige and marketability – right. To be in communications you just seek employment in that area and get apprenticed on the job. All which means I'm again wondering if you should not just hold on to your job and save only as you can, as a matter of necessity but not urgency. Then you go to night classes or investigate again the chances of a reputable institution – accredited – that may not require many class hours. Whatever. Just get a major that doesn't require intensive classroom work – I mean not like communications. Because, as I say, in the final analysis, this is what you get in the field. While you are finishing the B.A. you can, through the help of a man like Lee Nichols, sit in on broadcasting sessions, program making, etc., to get total immersion in the media you want to specialize in. How does all this strike you?

We spent a lovely weekend – 19-21 July – with an old friend of mine – a Rhodesian [Zimbabwean] – Stanlake Samkange – who wrote *The Origins of Rhodesia, On Trial for My Country* (novel). He's married to an Afro-American. A fine couple. They live in Boston, and for the first time in our lives we rode a Rolls Royce. He owns one *and* a Mercedes *and* a Cadillac (all of which he bought used from people). He just loves cars like they were toys. But he has a no-brag-just-facts attitude to all these, including a lovely big house. We trained it that way and bussed it back. Greetings to F.

Love,

Ntate

New York

Dear Zeke,

Betty and I were (and are) quite happy to hear from you and Rebecca again and Betty asks to be remembered to you both. I recall how very interested she was in talking with Rebecca as we sat together talking at Jim Cupepper's house in Nairobi.

It is indeed a far cry between speaking overseas as a Specialist Grantee of the U.S. State Dept. and being invited by the Union of Soviet Writers to visit parts of their remarkable country. And I must say that I find the latter experience much more to my liking, considering the many curious and not so curious turns the U.S.A. government's attitudes towards the Third World peoples have taken. Certainly I should think the Soviets would welcome a visit from you in consideration of your contributions to date. My suggestion is that you go directly to the source. Write to the following lady and feel quite free to tell her that we are in contact again and that I have suggested you write her.

Mrs. Frieda Lurie

Union of Soviet Writers

Foreign Commission

Vorovsky Street 52

Moscow, U.S.S.R.

Frieda is a good and close friend who doubtless knows your work. She is a fine translator and interpreter (Russian-English) and a first-rate human being whose influence with the Union is quite strong. Only yesterday I dropped her a friendly note and this would be a good time to contact her. And only yesterday a letter came to me from Blanche LaGuma in response to a message I had written. Alex has been in the USSR most recently and she was expecting him back home in London momentarily.[1] I had seen both of them only a couple of years ago when we attended the 5th Conference of Afro-Asian Writers meeting in Alma-Ata and in Yerevan. Alex is a big wheel in the organization. I don't belong to it but was invited through Frieda as one of 3 guest observers from the USA.

The enclosed brochure describes a portfolio of drawings I've had in circulation since late 1969. Since I published it myself and am in control of it I am free to send you a copy with my compliments. The yellow slip inside designates the books I've had published by Dodd Mead & Co, my publisher at 79 Madison Ave. N.Y. City 1006. Allen T. Klots is my editor if you should want to submit any of your work to him. And certainly you may say I suggested it. Though it surprises many who did not know, I've been writing for nearly as long as I've been drawing. Only recently have I been getting published. Thanks for your invitation to visit, which I may just do. Meanwhile, our best to you both.

Elton C Fax [2]

The portfolio is in the mail.

[1] Alex La Guma (1925-1985) was born and educated in Cape Town. He was a member of the Young Communist League, the Communist Party, and the South African Coloured People's Organization (later Congress), in which capacity he helped to organise the Kliptown Congress. As a journalist he wrote for *New Age* and *Fighting Talk*, covering the Treason Trial. He was placed under house arrest in 1962, detained in

1963, and went into exile in London in 1966. Mphahlele was instrumental in Mbari publishing *A Walk in the Night* in 1962 (Ibadan; later published as *A Walk in the Night and Other Stories*, by Heinemann in London in 1967). His fiction includes *And a Three-Fold Cord* (Berlin: Seven Seas 1964), *The Stone Country* (Berlin: Seven Seas 1967), *In the Fog of the Season's End* (London: Heinemann 1972), and *Time of the Butcherbird* (London: Heinemann 1979). La Guma died in Cuba where he was the ANC representative.

2 An African-American writer and artist. Author of *Through Black Eyes: Journeys of a Black Artist to East Africa and Russia* (New York: Dodd Mead 1974).

Zululand,
2 August 1975

My dear Ezeke,

Thank you for all the letters you have written to me. I have received them all.

I saw G.M. Pitje on the 22nd July and chatted with him about our case. He was hurrying to go court for some divorce case.[1] Last week I wrote to him setting out the briefing, and I stated that if necessary I would like the matter contested, because I came away after our last discussion, with the impression that he thought I was seeking friendly advice: in spite of my having indicated that I would like him to open 'a docket' – he was telling me how he thought Phathudi would help. But even that has to have someone – in this case himself – Pitje to put the case to him in legal terms. I came away feeling that my intentions did not quite register with him. When I had a subsequent chat with Josi Khumalo, he got rather chafed and was feeling that we should approach someone else – he is very impressed with Unterhalter.[2] But I will first see what G.M's reaction is when I go home next week. I touched him or rather his office last Thursday the 31st before I came here – but he was out of town.

I reproduced one hundred of your original circular, and I have sent it to all the Johannesburg English Language papers. I do not know what reaction they are now showing. Last Wednesday, Couzens who confronted you at the Writing Seminar about the *Voice*, came in at Dorkay House to see if he could not have further information about the *Voice* and the writings of H.I.E. Dlomo as well as W.B. Nhlapo. He says he has come across copies of the *Voice* and wants to know more about it. He told me that he got some copies of your letter, and he took about a dozen from my lot. He has promised to come and see me in Zululand.

Phathudi is in a bit of a spot. I do not know if this has reached you yet. It looks like that he and Collins Ramusi fell out rather badly, and he, Phathudi was forced to axe Ramusi from his cabinet. This stems, I understand, from Phathudi's visit Overseas and his participation in a symposium on investment in the Homelands. He and Matanzima were the only Homeland 'Premiers' who participated in this. It seems in the case of Phathudi, he went without consulting their political party, the party that put him into power, and Ramusi is Chairman of the said party and he, after the elections, stood down for Phathudi. Ramusi together with some vociferous elements in the party asked Phathudi some very awkward questions, and organized party rallies, which are still coming, for Phathudi to answer their questions in public. Phathudi, to avoid the apparent embarrassment, retorted by sacking Ramusi from the cabinet, through the powers that Herr John Vorster invested in all the Homeland Premiers. From Press reports Phathudi's home is under 24 hour police guard and Lebowa is suddenly in turmoil. So I do not know how G.M.P. expects that Lebowa can attend to our problem. But he says that soon after his own restrictions were removed Phathudi claimed responsibility for it, even though he has not contacted him to say so. That I consider a strange way to operate. But of course Homeland techniques are quite peculiar to the Homelands.

We are grateful that you have accepted to be one of our judges in our Creative Writing Competition. I hope something really meaningful comes out of this. You would be amazed at the amount of activity in theatre in the Townships along the Reef. And many of these productions are well supported, which factor ensures a future for this type of activity.

The setting of the University of Zululand is very much like your beautiful valley, except that the topography is more hilly. But the Winter here is not severe at all. I hope to send you pictures of some of the significant architecture here, and to tell you more about what I think of the inadequacies of the administration.

Did any of the pictures we took come out? When His Excellency, the Kamuzu Banda visited South Africa he stayed at the President Hotel, then the most prestigious Hotel in Johannesburg. The Homeland Leaders – or 'Premiers' saw him one by one. Chief Gatsha Buthelezi had me as his Aide. After the interview he was hauled over the coals for this. But at the interview itself he asked me to use his newly acquired instamatic camera. I had really never used one before, and this was during the time when a professional photographer was prancing about and taking the official pictures. I also joined the prancing and peering into the blasted camera, but I knew that I was peering into the wrong hole or lens, and I did not know what I was expected to see. So I clicked away. Gatsha gave me the films to take for development. After collecting them from the chemist I carefully opened them, curious to see the outcome. To my horror and disappointment, with some of the pictures it was difficult to tell whose legs were in the picture. In some I just caught them, their heads, at the bottom of the print. So I sealed the envelope very quickly and neatly again and delivered them to him. He was also very keen to see them. I can never forget the gradual expression of disappointment on his face that worsened with each picture. I hope that was not the case with the ones we took when I was there.

Best wishes to you and Ribs and the Boys.

Very sincerely,

Khabi

1 Godfrey Pitje, a well-known Johannesburg attorney.

2 Jack Unterhalter, a highly respected advocate at the Johannesburg Bar, who acted in many political trials.

14 August 1975

My dear daughter

Just a quicky to say hello and how's your knee shaping up? Mangoaela's death, somehow, didn't come as a surprise, although death always brings grief to those who know you. Particularly as we had been talking about such eventualities when you and F were here – remember? I guess the two girls will *now* wake up. They played no mean part in hastening the man's death.

By the way, don't ever think I was suggesting in my last letter, when I was thinking aloud, that you needn't make a try to come to Penn. After all the tuition is 100% free, and it is still the ideal way to finish your B.A. I just wondered if you would be up to the other expenditure – room and board and books, i.e. save up enough and quickly. Because you don't want to get to the age when you'll have to rationalize: 'Oh, it's not worth it anyhow ...' Indeed I would simply say that if you are determined to save up, do so and come to Penn. If you can also at the same time secure leave of absence there so you don't burn your bridges. What financial aid we can give will be determined by our circumstances and that's neither here nor there. We'd only do what we could if your mother is also working. At her age she's becoming less and less marketable for jobs. But my last letter wasn't in the least tied up with this. It's the time factor I'm worried about, what you could do in the interim while saving. Again there's no urgency to give the matter any thought in this direction.

Do what you've decided to do and I know you've the staying power and will. Just don't break your neck in the process.

Is Foday still around? Give him my greetings. Fond regards to Margarita.

Much love,

Ntate

New York

31 August 1975

Dear Zeke

Thank you for your letter of the 27th instant with which was enclosed two pieces for insertion on p.45 and at the end of the Ms. My copy is in small type and does not have both these additions in long hand. Needless to say the pieces easily fall into place, further clarify the issues, enrich and elevate the totality of content. The Ms. is informative and pleasant to read. Despite my familiarity with some aspects of the presentation I felt educated. I have also added to the bibliography the documentary histories by Thomas Karis, Gwendolen Carter, and Sheridan Johns.

I resort here to a typewriter because my handwriting has progressively deteriorated to plain hieroglyphics; it may sometimes be difficult to decipher. I have read *The African Image* and since this was sometime back I do not specifically remember reading the revised edition. However, on African nationalism, Sobukwe did stand by Lembede's 'Africa for the Africans'. We endorsed that position and understood the slogan to be the Monroe Doctrine for the whole African continent. The imperialists were to quit Africa and the dispossessed were to regain their sovereignty. I really do not know why some commentators chose to distort the PAC's stand to a point where it appeared Sobukwe wanted or favoured separatism. I can only surmise that it was their way of coming to terms with their own internally accumulated sense of guilt.

In his Opening Address to the Inaugural Convention, April 4, 1959, Sobukwe stated, among other things, that '... We wish to emphasize that the freedom of the African means the freedom of all in South Africa, the European included, because only the African can guarantee the establishment of a genuine democracy in which all men will be citizens of a common state and will live and be governed as individuals and not as distinctive sectional groups.'

Again in his State of the Nation Address, August 30, 1959 Sobukwe said: '... we shall leave all the dross of racialism and similar evils behind to emerge as a people mentally and physically disciplined, appreciative of the fact that:

'There is only one man in the world,
And his name is All men.
There is only one woman in the world,
And her name is All women.'

There is nothing in these direct quotations and in the Basic Documents that suggests separatism, let alone anti-communism. An anti-apartheid anti-imperialist anti-fascist nationalist grouping like the PAC would necessarily have to oppose at all times the ideas of separatism and balkanization of the Fatherland.

I am in complete agreement with your suggestion that whenever we speak or write we should insist on 'Boer' and not these interlopers. Webster's indeed defines Boer as 'a South African of Dutch or Huguenot descent'. We should eschew the term 'Afrikaner' as it tends to establish the Boers on the same footing as Africans in relation to the land. The translation of this word has led both Houphouët-Boigny and Kenneth Kaunda to exclaim: 'They are as African as any of us. Theirs must be recognised as a legitimate government in South Africa.'

Since Coloureds are Africans of mixed parentage we have no difficulties here. I feel you should not have enumerated them in the Ms as a separate entity. I often quote independent statistics and speak of '21 million Africans which include the 2½ million so-called Coloureds'. After all the most enlightened sections in their own ranks have referred to themselves, since 1902, as members of the African Peoples Organization. The term 'Coloured' is an imposition on these people by the oppressors who were bent on promoting their divide and rule policies. Even in the USA they avoided the obnoxious term 'coloured'. I also remember how in his *Mine boy, The Return to eGoli* and other writings Peter Abrahams felt the same uneasiness. Incidentally, as a matter of policy, the PAC made a ruling in 1959 that by reason of their origins, our traditional attitude to children whose mothers were not married, and shared historical and political experience the Coloureds be regarded as Africans. To my knowledge their most articulate spokesmen, including Sonny Leon of the Labour Party inside South Africa, have accepted this position. Quite a number of them in exile are fully aware that their African-ness is no longer a talking point; nobody doubts or questions it. They, therefore, are increasingly at ease in the ranks of the freedom-fighters and in scholarly circles and conferences where the tendency is to present a solid front against our fascist oppressors. To my mind this is an irreversible and very healthy trend.

Dikgoho le dikolobe di ntse di kopantse Iris hlooho. O re ke dumedise; ke be ke bolele hore ha lengolo la hau le fihla keha re se re getile ho tla le hlahela within the next few weeks for a week-end. Re tla le tsebisa. Madume a tswang ho bohle ba lelapa lena ho bohle ba lelapa leno.[1]

Kamehla wa lona,[2]

Peter [Molotsi]

1 'Chickens and pigs still give Iris a rough time. She sends her greetings. I should add that when your letter arrived, we had decided to make an appearance .... Will let you know. Good wishes from all of us in this family to all of yours.'

2 'As always,'

Philadelphia
3 September 1975

Dear Prof. Visser,[1]

Thanks very much indeed for your letter. I should consider it a great favour if you and Tim would send me some of Dhlomo's poems and stories. You can decide how big a range you want me to consider and send me photographs. Certainly I shall acknowledge this in the anthology and will mention your collected 'works'. I did write to Tim as it happens and he expressed the same interest and willingness to help me.

You are welcome to include anything you like from the *Lesane* stories.[2] I rather like them. They have not yet been published in book form and I have been planning to get back there, which may often have little or nothing directly to do with the racial condition. And the landscape is not being ruined at all. The young poets are nibbling at the edges much of the time. Hence my sense of desperation.[3]

I'm sure you are aware of the current trend in university hiring and firing. Fellowships are jealously being guarded for the products of each school for itself – to do the just thing by our own, as it were. The English Department of Pennsylvania has, together with the rest of the University, 'freezed' its capacity. There's even talk of having full professors teach 3+2 like associates and assistants.[4]

An idea that sits in my gullet, as I wouldn't want to do more than 2 + 2! Still, why not write to the chairman and enquire? Please ring me when you've touched base – home: (215) 293-0826. It will be a delight to meet you. Funny, when I saw your name I wondered what Afrikaner could possibly want to write to me! In a sense, you may not be a '*ware* Visser' or '*egte* Visser'! Excuse the levity.

Best wishes,

From E.M.

[1] Nick Visser was a lecturer at Rhodes University at the time and co-editor, with Tim Couzens, of *HIE Dhlomo: Collected Works*.

[2] A group of stories published in *Drum* in 1956 and 1957, featuring the Lesane family of Nadia Street in the township of Newclare.

[3] Another sign of Mphahlele's wrestling with 'the tyranny of place' and his desire to return to the country of his birth. The *Lesane* stories were deeply embedded in the intimacies of community life in Newclare and, as a writer, Mphahlele is longing for that rootedness.

[4] The American economy was going through an economic downturn and universities were not exempt from the consequences. '3+2' refers to the number of courses professors were expected to teach in each semester.

Indiana

12 September 1975

Dear Zeke

It was a great pleasure to receive your letter of August 27, and I have been most interested to read your article, or rather the transcript of the speech that you gave for your conference. It must have been extremely interesting if your speech is any indication of the quality of the contributions. It touches on such important issues and elucidates them so fully.

I am teaching a course on Southern Africa, and I am trying to inculcate some sensitivity as well as information about that area to my students. I am using films as well as lectures and visitors, and it was an extraordinary coincidence that I had just showed the film of you in the African authors series when I received your letter and article. We had talked a little bit afterwards about the strains on the exile, and I took the liberty of reading them what you had said in your last paragraph simply as an indication of the tremendous pull that South Africa has on those who were born and grew up there despite the conditions under which they then lived. I am extremely interested, even a little startled, to hear that you might want to go back to one of the 'Bantu universities', and yet it does stack up to much of what you were saying in that film. I do understand the pull to remain close to the young in the country of one's birth and to serve one's own people. Do you feel any sense of the dilemma that some of the urbanities seem to be involved in considering the universities for Africans as part of the pattern of segregation and apartheid? I feel differently about them than I do about the Bantustans, but I do appreciate the irksomeness of a segregated institution still under the control of the government.

I had not realized in fact that you had been banned from teaching and that was the major reason why you left the country. Do keep me in touch with what you decide to do, for I am deeply interested and would like to follow your progress. Of all those who have made a major contribution to this country, as well as to the international community, you are preeminent, and what you do will have a great impact on many others and on attitudes towards South Africa. All of this I am sure is much in your mind.

Here we seem to have a very lively African Studies Program. Northwestern had some difficulties in the year after I left as a natural readjustment, but I believe it is well on the way up again. Indiana pleased me very much by making me a professor with tenure with none of this nonsense about emeritus. I like it here very much and hope that you will be coming at some point when I am in residence. From the first I determined to spend only the fall semester here, and the rest of the time I go to my holiday home in Florida or else travel. It is a lovely life!

This brings you my very warmest best greetings and also, of course, to Rebecca. I hope very much that our paths will cross again before very long and that in the meantime we can keep in touch by letter.

Yours ever

Gwen

Gwendolen M Carter

Indiana

1 October 1975

Dear Zeke

What a wonderful letter because it lays out so fully for me so much of what has been in your mind during your time in this country and those urges that lead you toward the decision which you spoke of in your first letter. I think I understand much more clearly now why you are tending toward the course of action that you are considering. Such decisions are inevitably highly personal ones, molded by the experiences of the past as well as those of the more recent present. I honor you for the clarity of your thinking and the honesty of your searching for motivation and the right way to proceed. No one can or should judge one another, and all decisions of such as this or any other significant ones must be out of the individual character and understanding.

I suppose in a sort way I, too, am an exile, and yet I have never felt that I had either to cut my ties with my native Canada nor that the United States was other than a highly congenial home. Indeed for me it has meant that I had much more chance to develop and be stimulated in this country than I believe would have been possible in Canada. I do remember, however, the emotion that gripped me at the time that I forswore my allegiance to my native country and accepted that of the United States. It is a situation, and I have, of course, had the best of it. Forgive me for even mentioning my own situation in relation to yours which is so much more complex. It is only that searching my own experience I have some inklings of what it is to bridge two countries, although for me the urge to return has never been strong.

I hope that we can meet either at the ASA[1] or here in Bloomington or some place else. I would love to talk more about the South African situation itself. I have so strong a feeling that the Bantustan program is selling the Africans very short within South Africa, and I have grave misgivings about the projected independence of the Transkei and even about its reception by an all too compliant Washington, by my standards. I would love to know how you feel and where you would put your emphasis as far as policy is concerned. Recently I have been commenting on a manuscript by John Marcum which is being prepared for the *Critical Choices* volumes which Helen Kitchen is editing. I have much stronger feelings about the kind of boxing in of Africans that separate development involves than Marcum seemed to have, and I would greatly appreciate your comments one of these days.

On the chance that you would not be receiving it direct from the Johnson Foundation, I am enclosing copy of the paper that I did for the Wingspread Conference in April. I will greatly appreciate your comments when you have time to look at it. In the meantime may I say again how deeply I have been touched by your frankness and your willingness to share your thinking with me. My warmest greetings to you and Rebecca and my hopes that our paths will cross in the not-too-distant future.

Yours ever

Gwen

Gwendolen M Carter

1 African Studies Association conference.

Zululand

24 October 1975

Dear Ezeke,

Thank you for your letter. I was thrilled to hear that Phathudi had acted. I wrote him a letter that went around and around the subject – but eventually I got to make the point. I am in touch with Gatsha. The only trouble is that he is globe trotting just now. All the same, he is a very good correspondent; I am sure to get a reaction from him. My only fear is that with these Universities these chaps are as futile as ever. But of course, one never knows.

I wonder if you have heard that Njisani is now undergoing training in Pretoria for the position of Transkeian Representative in U.N.O.[1] He seems to feel that he is on a good wicket with the Transkei getting independence.

...

I have been trying to establish the Music Department. We had inauguration concerts this last weekend, they seemed to be well received. But it did involve me in a lot of planning and even achieving. The Natal *Daily News* Music Critic was very helpful in his remarks.

I am enclosing some pictures of Zululand University – taken during August. There's still winter in the air. Otherwise it is generally fertile land with lush vegetation, something like your Philadelphia-Valley.

...

Besides the two concerts, I have been asked to address the students (August) on the 'cultural role of the Black university student in our society'. And I have been accorded the honour of opening an Art Exhibition organized by the Black Staff Association (September). These were well received.

Thank you for the recordings. They reached me safely – as well as the photographs – the historic photographs.

I am hoping that the C. Baratang T. Columbia situation is now under control. I have written thrice already. Your letter reached me at the same time as hers. Her phone calls reached the Zululand University, but I was too far to be reached on the campus. Do tell her that if she should ring again – and please pass my love to her.

We are scheduled to do a recording with the university choir on Sunday. Year marks were released today. There is general gloom on the campus because some students will not be able to write some courses and have to leave the university.

With fond regards

Khabi

[1] One of the first returnees to Transkei.

Amherst

17 November 1975

Dear Mr Mphahlele

Please excuse the impersonal type, but as I said to you while your were here, my handwriting becomes illegible after a few seconds. Thank you more than words can express for sharing yourself with us at Smith. Students have flocked to my office since your visit to discuss ideas you raised and thoughts which you generated. As one student said, you were the perfect one to end our series of Cruse, Kent, and Mphahlele for you tie together the analyses of Cruse, the criticism of Kent with your very human perceptions of aesthetics and culture. You created a warmth with your scholarship – a warmth which should always be present – which precipitates praxis. Thank you for being such a dedicated, beautiful inspiring person.

When you've the chance, send us the copy of your talk, edited as you wish it to appear in our forthcoming edited work of essays.

I am looking forward to seeing you this spring at the conference at the U. of Penn.

Best wishes to you and your family ...

Fondly

Johnella E Butler

Grahamstown

24 November 1975

Dear Professor Mphahlele

At last I have a breather from the academic salt mines, to catch up on things that matter. High on the list is your request for information etc re Black contributions to *New Coin*. I have extracted all relevant poems, and enclose them, with a list of last known addresses. I apologise for the long, long delay. I asked Dr Nick Visser to get in touch with you about *Dhlomo*, which I gather he has done; and André de Villiers, who may have been able to help.

If you should meet Basil Somhalahlo in USA give him my best wishes; as also Serote and Mtshali. We teach both the latter on our English III SA paper, and the response is most encouraging. I've just marked a practical exam question calling for a comparison of Plomer's 'Johannesburg', and Serote's 'City of Johannesburg'. The quality of the answers persuades me that this component in our course is genuinely creative of increased awareness of the nature of life here: those who *know* are made also to *feel,* or at least to have a glimmering of what it must be like to be an exile in your own country. Nortje has also been a great success.

Good luck with the anthology. My own *Selected Poems* are about to appear.

Yours ever
Guy Butler

13 December 1975

Dear Zeke:

It has been a very, very long time since I met you with John Killens in Greenwich Village. Was it in the late 50's or early 60's? In any case, Zeke is a name we all know and whose works we read. Let *me* offer a clarification: I meant *only* that Western, particularly American literary criticism, does not judge black writers even from its puny traditional base. And that black writers must forge for themselves new standards of criticism which have little if anything to do with how white critics view their work. I wasn't thinking of Negritude at all. You know, I am not a critic. I hold other views, and of course, opinions.

The work you read was a paper I gave as a Regents Lecturer at the University of California at Santa Barbara in 1972. That tour was a joke. I read that paper and left, refusing to discuss it or answer questions with a mostly white audience which didn't want me in the first place.

I did a thing out at U. Colorado and the man in charge of Afro-Studies asked if I would take a post there. The English department people said it looked okay, this position, but they would be happier if they'd read some of my work. I cursed them out. Didn't want to go there in the first place, but you know all about that scene. It was to attitudes like these that I was basically addressing myself to. I still do it every day at my school.

Look, I would like to get together with you on a stint somewhere. I would enjoy it. Thanks much for the letter, book and your essay.

Cordially,
[Writer's identity unknown]

Grahamstown
26 December 1975

My Dear Ezekiel

I'm writing this from a sea-side vacation, where I am trying to catch up on correspondence and reading, as well as renewing family contacts. I have just returned from the Karoo where we buried an uncle, 81, who's lived on one farm all his life. A marvelous old fellow, who was a conservationist and anti-pollution man from his childhood. 'We must look after the veld' he said to a nephew 'so that it will be as good in 1000 years as it is now.'

Thank you for your letter and the offprint of 'The Function of Literature at the Present Time: the Ethnic Imperative'. If only I had read this a year ago my own contribution to a related field would have been wiser and better informed. I enclose an off print of 'The language of the conqueror on the lips of the conquered is the language of slaves' – really about what sort of language SA Lit is going to be written in – ethnic imperative or otherwise. (I apologize for the misprints, particularly of your own name.) In unilingual countries the 'ethnic imperative' can find its expression in variants of the *lingua franca*; but in Africa, with its many languages, we have a different problem. It seems, now, that I may have handled the English of our SA Black poets less subtly than I might have ...

I can well understand your feelings as expressed on page 34 – about white S. Africans – 'Ten years ago I used to worry that, because black and white are totally segregated in SA, we have no way of knowing each other across the wall ... now, I don't care anymore ... I shall even have the pleasure of engineering poetic justice to kill him off without as much as a tragic fret from him. That is one of my imperatives.'

It would be fine if it were as simple as that, but I'm afraid that SA. is going to be proved to be inadequate. The Afrikaner is the supreme modern example of a people who worked on 'the ethnic imperative' – partly as a reaction against the English 'ethnic imperative'. And both have now led to a black ethnic imperative. This may well be a necessary and inevitable stage, but I have a hunch that after many rejections and revenges there will be common discoveries and ventures.

For some five years now, off and on, I have been struggling with a longish poem about the African Imperative, as I see it – or at least the South African, the Azanian imperative: to find a view of our history which is acceptable to all – which is another way of saying, the discovery of the human imperative in Africa. (Make no mistake, there are White Africans.) If you would care to read it in its present form, I'll send it to you – although I realize it might sound in your ears like 'a tragic jest'!

Thank you for considering the possibility of sending something for *New Coin*. We would be most interested. If you have not been banned there should be no difficulty. (What has been banned of yours, apart from *The African Image*?) I shall do what I can to establish 'who and what are banned in SA', paying particular attention to the names you list.

What is your own legal position about returning to SA, either on a visit or permanently? Would you be at all interested in a visiting fellowship or something of that kind to Rhodes? There are one or two of these available but I think already booked up for the next couple of years. What about 1978? If you are interested, and there are no legal snags, I'll be happy to put your name forward. We'll expect you to spend most of the time here, but we could arrange for you to visit other centres and campuses, black and white.

When in UK. in April this year, I met once more Fr. Martin Jarett-Kerr CR. Do you remember him? He is as blithe and full of ideas as ever.

With every good wish,

Yours ever

Guy Butler

1976

London

2 January 1976

Dear Zeke

Of course I still remember you, and have had news of you, where you are, what you are doing, from time to time.

I didn't know you had been to South Africa. That must have been a mixed experience.

My brother, my oldest son, my daughter, are all in Rhodesia and South Africa, fervent supporters of Smith etc. Which makes family relations complicated to say the least.

South Africans seem to be much more realistic than white Rhodesians. Who all live in some mad dream world.

Anyway I posted off your book just before Christmas so it ought to arrive fairly soon. I like it a good deal. I can understand the criticisms of the structure, which does not make for easy reading. I don't know if this will strike you as absurd: I wondered how much an oral tradition contributed to that structure

– the leisurely approach from different points of view. The real trouble with the book, as you have doubtless seen, is that it criticizes African States. I have not discussed this with Heinemann, but am prepared to bet that the thinking would go something like this: hard enough to get an African series going, and to get support for it – to publish a book making such criticisms of Kaunda, it is asking for trouble. Perhaps I am wrong and they aren't thinking like this at all. I sum up your book like this: that it is every bit as good and better than some of the novels they have published. Why then is it not being published?

I have not read all the books in the African series: it sounds as if I have.

It seems to me that if you have the energy and inclination you might re-write it, making the shape of the thing tighter? The subject is fascinating. To me, at least. Precisely what might be making it hard to publish now – the criticisms of a Third World country, may be just what could make it a success at a different time, in a different context.

There is always the same problem with all novels so much embedded in an African context: they ought to be read by Africans within the country in question. Yet it is unlikely they will be read. At least now, I and other people with experience of Africa, I am talking about white readers who have enough to fill in the background. But I don't know if a white person without such an experience would be as fascinated as I am being ...

I take it for granted that you will go on writing? Another book ..., the same one, recast.

I met Stanlake on his way to the Conference; we had a pleasant lunch. Have you had opportunities to go?

It looks to me as if this particular knot can only be untied by the guerillas. The whites will only be persuaded by force, it seems to me. Perhaps I am wrong. I am very out of touch, these days; but the letters or messages I get from my family indicate to me a total blindness, intransigence. The tragedy is that a government made up of people who have successfully fought a guerilla war is not necessary the best available government.

If one were to use even the most basic commonsense to solve, the Rhodesian problem. But it seems to me that commonsense is the rarest of all qualities. It certainly is not very evident in this country, at this moment, for a start:

Anyway – I do hope you won't abandon the novel altogether.

Do let me know.

My best wishes to you
[Writer's identity unknown]

Leeds

12 January 1976

Dear Zeke

Evidently you should let yourself go as often as possible – the review article is exactly what we needed to start our new system.[1] It's judicious, it sorts out the big issues from the little ones, and it's as comprehensive as anyone could hope for.

We've had such a logjam of reviews because of the geographical extent of the field and the explosion of (printed) awareness, that we're trying to limit ourselves to one review article – an overview of the whole field – and several short notices, in each issue. Your piece will make a splendid start for the new system.

I hope very much we won't need to cut at all – only if some especially pertinent short notices would go in as a result will we do so.

Best wishes.

Andrew Gurr

[1] The journal referred to is *The Journal of Commonwealth Literature.*

San Diego

2 February 1976

My dear Sir:

Thank you for the note sent me. Here are the brochures you requested.

I enclose a copy of a recent invitation from UCLA and I'll be going there. But my request has to do with the second part of the assignment given to me and that is the DEBATE. Mazisi spoke with me at length on the phone. The debate is going to be recorded and published. His contention is that a school of thought suggests that all that is written in English or French by Africans cannot be termed African Literature rather they are part of English or French.[1] This school cites Chaucer as the only extant writer of his time because he wrote in his native tongue while his contemporaries wrote in Latin. This foreign expression is responsible for the literary death of these people. According to him African thoughts can only survive and be wholly appreciated if they are written in African Languages. I agree with this thesis in the main but not wholly. There are enormous political and social problems. The Africa condition is different from Chaucer's time. Any transition at all will have to be gradual and will take efforts and planning. Can we wholly escape some translations at any point even if we all write in our native tongues? For me to understand any works in Swahili or Sotho, they will have to be translated into Yoruba or English. Do we have the resources and personnel to translate every work into every African language? Then will all Africa buy the idea of an all-Swahili-speaking Africa? Not even modern Europe, they cannot agree on a common language among them. Only trade and culture bind them together. East Africans and possibly South Africans will have more success with a *lingua franca* than those of us in the West. And to have such or any language, it will have to be intensively used at all levels of instruction. I tend to think that writing in both African and any other language at the same time will do it. Ours is a unique condition and we must find a unique solution. Isn't there some wealth in our diversity? I want to sound sharp and reasonable at this debate because it's going to be a continuous debate till we agree on something just like those early conferences on what is African Literature. I am going to be the youngest person on this panel and I do not want to say anything now that I will regret thirty years from now. So, I need ideas from you. Whatever you can jot down and very soon too, 'cos I am writing two papers for the conf.

It's a pity to learn of Kofi's incarceration in Ghana.[2]Achebe will be here on the 21st of March for three days.

Please write soon.

Love

Tayo

1 The debate referred to is about the choice of languages in African literature, which had been galvanised by an article by Obiajunwa Wali, 'The Dead End of African Literature', in *Transition* 10 (1963).

2 Kofi Awoonor, the Ghanaian poet, novelist and critic, was arrested in December 1975 on suspicion of being involved in a military coup, an experience he would later recount in two volumes of poems, *House by the Sea* and *Until the Morning After* (both published by the Greenfield Review 1978 and 1987). He has held several ambassadorial positions, representing Ghana in Brazil, Cuba and the UN.

Bilthoven
Netherlands
1 April 1976

Dear Mr Mphahlele,

I have only just seen *TRANSITION 50* in which it is stated that you are compiling a *CRITICAL ANTHOLOGY OF AFRICAN LITERATURE* which will include poetry, short stories, expository prose and new translations of Oral and Written Poetry from African Languages.

I have an essay entitled 'Ethical Humanism as a Way of Life' which won the First Prize for Africa in the 1959 International Essay Contest organized by the International Humanist and Ethical Union, headquarters Utrecht, The Netherlands. This essay has never been published before and I should be glad to forward it to you for possible inclusion in your proposed anthology.

However, the notice in *TRANSITION* stated that the deadline begins from 31st December (1975).

Is there still time for me to forward my essay to you?

I am a black South African from Bellville in the Cape and left South Africa on a one-way exit permit in February 1967.

As an admirer of Mphahlele the writer I am glad to make this contact with you directly. I like the second edition of *THE AFRICAN IMAGE* very much. Not least of all the militant change of terminology from 'non-white' to 'black'!

Hoping to hear from you soon,

Best wishes,
James J Ravell

7 April 1976

My dear Zeke

Thank you for your letter, news of possible date for reading and enclosure today. It was good of you to send me the material from the Institute for the study of English in Africa [ISEA] (Grahamstown) and their invitation for you to join their Advisory Board together with a request for my opinion.

I will try to deal with this frankly, and will be glad to have a further exchange. On purely literary grounds it seems to me that one would be willing to assist anything which seeks to further literature; their invitation is also, of course, a tribute to your stature. But for us as committed writers and exiles from our own country, the issue can never be judged in purely literary terms – it is why most of us were, initially, in trouble with the regime. So we have to look at the politics of the issue, and the possibility of being compromised. I would say that at the present time South African academics are recognizing, belatedly, their sins of omission – ignoring black writers etc – and may be trying to make amends. Others may even be seeing literature as one way of coming to terms with the inevitably black-run society of the future. Others, more worryingly, may see in joining blacks and whites, especially the 'tame blacks' of the bush colleges, as a way of making the Bantustans more credible. This seems to me a very serious issue just now – perhaps the most serious. Pretoria will be staking everything on trying to make the Transkei look like a genuine, rather than a puppet, state for the UN sessions this October, when the Transkei applies for a seat; and failure will throw Bantustans into doubt. From all this you can see that I am doubtful; or at least cautious. I do not find it encouraging that the Bush colleges are represented. And there are other doubts, which may perhaps be more easily disposed of. In a long list of authors, the only blacks are Peter Abrahams, comfortably far off in Jamaica and Arthur Nortje, comfortably dead; and both of them comfortably unbanned. I can find no literary justification for the exclusion of Alex la Guma. If these academics and literatis really care about literature, let them set about getting literary figures unbanned and ungagged – or let that be part of their declared intent. By doing so, they would easily dispose of at least one of my doubts. (In section on topics, too, the black writers are those who are not banned; what, for instance, of Don Mattera?)

What I would do, to answer your question crisply, if I were asked to be on their panel of Advisory Editors, would be to ask them to spell out more clearly their intent and to express my own reservations and concerns – with the clear understanding that, if I was satisfied, I would be willing to join the project. I would want to know, for instance, what was entailed by 'the critic would be provided with a set of guidelines which he would be asked to adhere to as closely as possibly'. This may well be a perfectly legitimate editorial policy – it is well-known in some circles: but bitter lessons of duplicity and spinelessness by South African academics (when they are not active agents of repression at universities and elsewhere) have taught us caution; we need to know whether the guidelines will extend to censorship not only of the critics' opinion of the opinions of the subjects of their criticism. (I find the indiscriminate lumping together (under suggested names) troubling too – how much academic freedom is there at UNISA? Is 'Rand'[1] any less of a bush-college than 'North'[2]?

I am sorry for this rushed note, and these hurried comments, but I hope you will find them useful – and the fact that the outline you got was 'preliminary' is hopeful. I hope you will not mind my sharing these thoughts with others – it is one more point on which it would be helpful to have some body which could serve to get the ideas and opinions of South Africans in exile together: why don't you make a move?

Alles van die beste.[3]

Dennis

[1] The Rand Afrikaans University.

[2] University of the North.

[3] Everything of the best.

Wayne, Pennsylvania

3 May 1976

To: Sylvester and Jenny Stein

...We'll think where the two boys will begin college – we don't want to plunge them into that live crater at all.

Rebecca has just started on a new job as a case worker for an institution for teenage mothers – underprivileged. Enjoying it. She's impossible to live with when she's not employed, out there in the rough and tumble of social work.

The book. I've decided to build up a context for my own story of exile. Tell me what you think of it. As you have divined by now, I'm fascinated always by the entry of other voices, interludes that produce other resonances. So this June I'm taking a bus trip to New York and other places in New York state to interview on tape Africans who have lots to tell me about themselves. Those who matter most for my purpose live in the East here luckily. I'll then build up a composite portrait in narrative style. What I get will determine the shape. I'm going to stay away from the novel structure – my forte doesn't lie there. From now on, it's going to be the novella when I want to write fiction – and damn the market consequences. Just enjoy myself! How does the interview idea grab you?

While out there, I am also going to interview Black women. I've a gem of an idea for a novella about love and marriage between an African and an Afro-American woman.

I'm surrounded by ruins of these.

Haven't seen the [...] since that time, but we have talked on the phone. We eventually met Joe Wolpe and his charming wife Stella – here in Philly.[1] He's a psychiatrist. Somehow he is rather a weird reminder of that type of person who doesn't want to be bothered by S.A. politics, who even has old-fashioned ideas about Africans. Evidently, he was never into the life of people like you who have strong ideas against the system without being dramatic or theatrical about demonstrating this or that. Or am I fantasizing? Maybe his detachment is deliberate, a way of protecting himself. But his wife, without being a Ruth Slovo, expresses herself freely.[2]

The rains have come upon us – a standing feature in this Delaware Valley. But it's good. Love to you both and remember us to Lilly.

Love

Zeke

1 Mphahlele is referring to Dr Joseph Wolpe, a world famous former South African psychiatrist then based in the United States, reputed to be the founder of Behaviour Therapy – an approach to the modification of behaviour in psychotherapy based on the principles of learning, especially conditioning.

2 Better known as Ruth First, the wife of Joe Slovo, First was a journalist, author, academic, and activist in the ANC. She was assassinated by a parcel bomb which exploded in her office at Eduardo Mondlane University in Maputo (Mozambique) in 1982.

Wayne, Pennsylvania

19 May 1976

Dear Guy,

I have taken long before replying to your invitation to join your board of Advisory Editors for the *ISEA Series on South African Writing*, owing to pressure of work. Now that the semester has ended, things have eased up a bit.

I should like to give serious consideration to the matter. You are on to a very important project which has tremendous promise and at the same time has serious implications. To help me make a decision one way or another, would you answer the following questions:

1. Would you say that 'a set of guidelines' (subheading *Critics,* p. 2) might include political caution or might they be the normal editorial specifications for the structure of an essay?

2. More importantly: your short and longer lists have excluded the banned writers: Alex la Guma, Dennis Brutus, Mazisi Kunene, Keorapetse Kgositsile, etc. Is this political caution, perhaps necessary at the publicity stage, or will these writers never be touched? They have after all more titles to their credit than Nortje.

This question leads to so many others concerning censorship, banning etc. Indeed I think this deserves a full-fledged essay, book length, something factual and at the same time evocative without being consciously inflammatory. Such an essay would immediately indicate that the ISEA is functioning in an embattled situation, is aware of it, and cannot pretend that equal access to libraries, to periodicals, to education – to everything that is required to create a climate in which writers grow in the free world – that all these things will be available to Blacks in due time. ISEA may not necessarily make the State lift the ban – indeed I don't see it *could* – but it seems it should at least take into consideration the ideas that may come from the very Black writers whose names come under TOPICS in the short list, and others, on how the series can be of assistance.

Now, here I am telling you what ISEA should do, when in fact I am groping for answers and would like you to clarify certain things: In sum, this all adds up to the question: what is in it for Blacks to be on the boards of a publication controlled by those who have the money and power – political and numerical – unless the institution that it is is determined to acknowledge the banned and the exiled, inasmuch as expatriates like Cloete, Jacobson, Plomer etc. are acknowledged. Am I belaboring the point?

Let me hear from you, and best wishes,

Yours sincerely,

Ezekiel

P. S. I should mention that in principle I agree wholeheartedly with the scheme to provide critical materials for the study of S.A. Lit, & what better way than by producing a series under a single rubric etc.

28 May 1976

My dear Ezekiel,

Re: I.S.E.A SERIES ON S.A. WRITING.

Thank you for your letter of 1st May, and for spelling out so clearly your hesitations about joining our Board of advisory editors.

Your first question as to whether 'the set of guidelines' might include political caution is easily answered. We certainly do not visualize anything of the kind: the guidelines would be the normal editorial specifications. The only 'political caution' – which your letter has raised in my mind, but has not been discussed at any meeting – might relate to quoting banned works verbatim, for the practical, not ideological reason that this might interfere with the circulation of the work in South Africa, which is likely to be our main market.

Your second point hits an important issue right on the head – what about banned writers? Indeed. This is a matter of deep concern to me. During my speech at the CNA literary award dinner earlier this year (copy enclosed), I made the point that S.A. literature is not fully available to South Africans. The press picked this up and splashed it (cutting from *Star* enclosed). I was interested to see that one of the Afrikaans editors handled the idea with some sympathy, and that the Afrikaans Skrywerskring of Transvaal (I think) has urged that the authorities concerned should lift the ban on as many of these books and authors as possible. I am confident that I express the mind of the steering committee in saying that we would hope to extend its list as and when possible to include monographs on the full spectrum of reputable and interesting writers in English, irrespective of colour or ideology. You make a most valuable suggestion about the need for an essay indicating 'that I.S.E.A. is functioning in an embattled situation, is aware of it etc. etc'. Perhaps the first or one of the first members should be devoted to some such topic. (By the way, one of the 'exiles' should be collecting material for a study of the fortunes and misfortunes, the influence and achievements of the S.A. writer exiles. A chap called Leitch at Toronto has produced a very interesting M.A. thesis on Nortje.)

This is an unofficial and personal response to your letter. Your points will be considered when we gather to consider the responses from other invitees.

Sorry about the delay in sending the long poem. I have had another bash at reshaping it, and it is all in pieces and needs re-assembling:

Richard Rive has been Visiting Fellow at I.S.E.A. for some weeks, and has been lecturing on a variety of topics, such as 'White Lecture through Black eyes'. Tonight he is to give a public lecture on Chinua Achebe.

Another recent visitor was Martin Jarrett-Kerr C.R., who used to be at Rosettenville, now at Leeds. One of his special current interests is Non-Western Christianity.

Yours sincerely

Guy Butler

4 June 1976

My dear Guy,

Thanks very much for your answers. They go a long way to reassuring me about the intentions of ISEA, the avenues you will explore regarding banned writers etc. Your award paper makes plenty of sense and is loaded with *wisdom. Would that some fatheads could begin to shake and wake up! English in Africa: Literature and Language* – what an enriching course that could be! And more so if it were to be made compulsory at some stage in the junior degree programme. Haven't you felt, as I untimely feel, that the 3-year B.A. degree is too short to allow one to teach the growing number of areas of literature and language? In an African (Black) University for instance, I would insist that African Literature should be compulsory the whole Freshman year – for *every* student. But then one would need a 4-year structure, unless (at the old British 'A' level stage that still persists in much of independent Africa) two years could be handled as one before the 3-year period begins. I can't see the Joint Matric. Board agreeing to such a substantial chunk of matric time devoted to African Lit. Yet I didn't see why Blacks shouldn't try to push it.

I shall wait for your committee to discuss the whole bunch of queries from invitees and listen and consider.

Meantime, it looks as if I shall definitely come to S.A. for about 3 wks as a guest of the new Inst. of Black Studies opening on 14 July '76 – at Roodepoort, Tvl. They pushed from that end for a visa for me and it has been granted!! After 19yrs! I don't know what it can mean. Anyway the pilgrimage must be made and the opportunity could not be more appreciated than now when I feel psychologically I've come to the end of my tether. Will let you know more details when a foundation has assured me of sponsorship. Will read a paper on African Lit. in Eng. and Afr.

Warmest regards and thanks for writing,

Ezekiel

My dear Guy,

Thanks indeed for your letter and for the paper on the role of Rhodes. Most interesting and well argued too. Needless to say I'm glad we share – you and I – this attachment to place and particularity. Indeed we can logically go from here to one commitment to Afro-centered institutions of higher learning. I don't know if you are haunted by the idea, as I constantly am, that I don't have long enough in this earth to fritter away my time and energy trying to seek out some meaning for myself from the grand venture into world culture, often even into Pan-African concerns. I just feel all the time that I must put a stop to this prodigal imagination.

There's just so much to do – I'm appalled by the statement in your paper that South African Literature, let alone that of the African continent has such a peripheral place in literary studies over there.

I wouldn't have believed it! 'Universities (as) intellectual and cultural outposts of Europe from which we peer at a strange continent ...' A painful state of affairs.

Warmest regards,

Ever,

Ezekiel

New York

7 June 1976

Dear Ezekiel Mphahlele

This is just to let you know what is going on with The Committee for Kofi Awoonor.

Right now we have 4 things in mind: a mass mailing to college campuses in this country as part of our letter writing campaign, a benefit at Stony Brook early in the fall, a benefit fund to be used in Kofi's behalf in Ghana (we hope legal fees), and continued attempts to publicize Kofi's arrest.

A rally at Stony Brook raised about $190.00. We have an account in the name of The Committee at the Suffolk Country Federal Bank in Rocky Point.

If you can think of anything else that we should do, please tell us. We have enclosed some stationery and will be glad to send more. Thank you so much for lending your name to the cause.

Sincerely,

Peter Benson

Treasurer

14 June 1976

Dear Makhudu

Yes, the semester has been heavy for me. I have been teaching 3 courses instead of the usual 2 a semester, because Ribs lost her job and I had to moonlight, as the expression goes in this country for '*letogonyana*' to supplement income. So I couldn't answer letters.

Ga re tsebe gore nyakanyaka ea Seopasengwe e lebile kae, kamoo Muriel a re botjago kantshe.[1] South Africans get queerer and queerer as they live longer outside. I hope desperately you there and we here can maintain our sanity.

So, will you take the headship of the ABU languages dept? *You* know what you must do, but for me, I'd see it as another cause of delayance in finishing the M.A. Administration can nail you down, as it indeed has been doing with you so far. On the other hand, there's the prestige, such as it is ...

Guess what, Nimrod Mkele is director of a new Institute of Black Studies whose goals, at least on paper look attractive. They're holding their inaugural conference 14 July 76 and have invited me to read a paper on African Literature. Visa? I'm banned ... so they set about pushing that end. I applied at this end, feeling it was futile. Bang, they say permission has been granted! My British passport has now been stamped. Valid till Dec. 76. Either those Boers don't read (of course our books are banned) or else they want to test the Institute itself: Are they ready to be incited by a man like me? I don't think they would try the now worn-out window-dressing cliché with a South African. Then again they may see no danger in it as it's only a visit. I'll be able to test the ground, maybe, to size up the landscape for possible re-entry and residence. I'll report back to you. It's quite clear we'd be sitting ducks (as the American expression goes) no more or less than the radicals at home when we have returned. All the more reason for us to be among them without deliberately offering ourselves up as martyrs. Survival has been our forte as Blacks and we can still stretch it.

In haste, & affectionately.

Zeke

P.S. Ever read pp 42-43 of Revised *African Image?* – The dream. I wonder what to think of it now the pilgrimage is about to begin.

1 'We do not know how Seopasengwe's troubles will be resolved, according to what Muriel tells us.'

24 June 1976

Dear Teresa

Hope you're recovering successfully. It was good to see you and we're thankful it wasn't worse that you experienced. Your mother raves about the buba.

Have written to F., simple to repeat comments: that he act as he thinks fit, in his own interest, if he feels he has been getting a raw deal. That's his own affair.

To you I can only say you seem to have put your foot in it again! You know your Mother's response to most things is African. True, she often projects this excessively, until it refuses to fit American culture. But you should never dismiss her words. She *does* have an uncanny perception of other women. Her instincts often turn out to have been right. Her concern, which I share, has always been that you tend to invest your emotions in a lost cause – people far below your standard. The reasons are obscure to us. Remember I once wrote you from Denver warning you i.e. that it is disastrous to keep a man out of pity, unconsciously or otherwise – a man you think you need to uplift. Just doesn't work. Because eventually a man like that gets to despise himself – I think F's heroics in the decision he says he has made are at bottom a cover-up of his low esteem of himself. It's so much healthier to have a man who does not lean on you unduly – mutual respect rests on this factor. Frankly, I would not encourage F to return. The culture gap is just more than you can both correct. But be guided by your head and heart in the matter. It's *your* life. Conserve your energy for fruitful studies and as I said, adopt a do-or-die attitude and get your BA over with. The post-BA work is always more exciting because by then you have narrowed your interests and therefore focus.

Much love

Ntate

26 June 1976

SA Freedom Day[1]

My dear Zeke

A hurried note – had hoped to send you a long letter, but fear I will not be able to due to business i.e. your SA trip. I'm glad you've written so frankly. I'm especially glad to you say openly that the trip 'will be a pilgrimage' – 'a trip back to my ancestors, some of whose graves I shall visit'. It is hard to argue with that sentiment – which may well be the principal force in deciding your choice. I must say that I think on *logical* grounds there is much reason why you should not go – the graves of the school-children dying gallantly in opposition seem to me a strong reason for refusing the favors of the racists: if they give you the favor of a visa it is because they *need you* to make them appear less terrible. Let me speak to you directly and appeal to you not to go: I believe it will harm our cause – and *our fight* – if you go now when their hands and the soil of our country are drenched with the blood of our people even if it is very difficult. I urge you to cancel it at this stage: there will be other opportunities. And while you think you can use Ford, their use of you – and of black puppets – whom I unequivocally condemn is far more pernicious at this stage and far more perilous for the future than the brutalities of Vorster's gangsters.[2]

Today I spoke at a Rally on the massacre; afterwards Duma Nokwe asked me about you and an article he had heard of in *Drum* (I told him I did not know of it) in which someone says you claim never to have offended the apartheid government. I would like to know more about this as it compounds the problem: I said I did not think you would claim to be 'a good boy' and that it was probably someone misquoting you. But he asked me to write you and beg you not to go as he believed it would do us more harm than good. I had of course intended to write you before he talked to me. Well, it is in your hands; the temptation is surely great: but I believe you will be glad if you do not go and that if you do your own conscience will reproach you and you will wish that you had resolved to make the sacrifice. I know that you will not resent my speaking frankly and openly on this matter: I could expect no less from you.

Sincerely

Dennis Brutus

1 The Freedom Charter was adopted by the Congress of the people on 26 June 1955, hence Brutus's reference to 'Freedom Day'.

2 B J Vorster, Prime Minister in 1976.

Cape Province

28 June 1976

Dear Zeke,

Forgive me for the long delay in getting in touch. Since I got home I've been working very hard. While in America I wrote 62 poems and I just continued writing once I got back home. Altogether I have written about 60 impressions of America. While I am on the subject, I don't have copies of a few of those poems I left with you. You, in fact, have my manuscript copies. Can something be done about it?

I had a delightful time being a member of your family while I was staying with you and Ribs. I regret the time was so short and that I was so madly desperate to get on the way. I settle down easily in most places. But at times I am restless and want to move. The problem was only that I think I was getting a little tired of living out of my suitcase. But don't worry. I felt at home with the Mphahleles. As I said, it was like family.

I enjoyed the few days in New York ... or maybe I should say, it was an extremely interesting experience. I got to Penn Station okay. Then it was a matter of getting up the escalator with my luggage. The crowd, of course, looked at me and thought, Uh – huh, another foreigner. One fellow looked at me and offered me a hand and I was grateful. We chatted and he asked me where I was from. When I told him Cape Town, he had never heard of the place. He had heard of Johannesburg but was not certain where South Africa was. I had heard this so many times that it didn't matter anymore. I was only too glad that one person was friendly ... and helpful. I waited for Wally after phoning him. About ¾ hour later he arrived. I had the feeling he'd just got up when I phoned. I must say Wally gave me a good time. It wasn't dull and I was not bored. I saw Oswald too. Oswald and I spent one day together. He and I went to United Nations Headquarters. Via Wally I met his friends (Wally's friends). It was so crowded it seemed I had been there more than four days. I felt just a bit ashamed of the fact that in the time I was in New York, I did not see the Museum of Modern Art or any other important art museums or galleries, considering that, being a painter I should have seen those places. There just wasn't time. So I shall have to get back to New York (as I feel I shall) some time in the future and then make up for it. The one unfortunate thing about my visit to N.Y. was that I left some colour-slides there. I took seven rolls of film to be processed and was unable to get it back in time before leaving for S. A. So I made arrangements with Wally to pick it up for me. I gave him the slips and gave him enough money to pay for them and for postage to me. So far nothing has happened. I have not had a word from him even though I have sent him three letters asking him about the slides. He just has not replied. Hell, I just can't understand how some people can be so easy-going. I keep on feeling that certain people have no right to be irresponsible. I had taken those slides in different parts of the States, including the art department at Fisk University, Tennessee and Morgan State in Baltimore, for particular reasons. I don't think we can afford to say, we only travel for our own personal sakes. So I am still hoping the slides will turn up. If you see him or get in touch with him at some time, I'd appreciate it if you'd mention the fact to him that I am still waiting for the slides.

I finally got an Afrikaans-English/English-Afrikaans dictionary on Saturday and will post it to you within the next few days. I hope you find it suitable. I also hope it doesn't take long to get to you (because I have been keeping you waiting a hell of a long time, come to think of it). It made me aware of the fact that I shall have to get myself an Afrikaans-English dictionary too. I last had one when I was still at school. That was a long time ago. 1944. On the 2nd. June I was 47. My God, I'm middle-aged. Eventually I'll be going along to collect my old-age pension!

We are in the midst of Winter. But for the last number of days there has been a break in the rainy season and we have had some absolutely beautiful warm sunny days. I like this kind of craziness because it makes sense to me. Soon the wild flowers will be blooming on the hills round here. I sometimes go and stroll up the hillside and enjoy it tremendously. From up there one can see the ships going up and down the coast on their way from or to rounding the Cape. On certain days it becomes obvious why this area was known as the cape of storms. It is dark and overcast and grim and the sea is unsettled and ships pass through the storms and wind. You can see this miles away. It is quite striking.

No doubt you've heard on the news about the township troubles with arson etc. Frustration. When I think of the freedom of America, I wish we were advanced that far. So much time being wasted, so much power-madness.

They persist in going on

In such a dictatorial way

It's impossible to say

Which one

Is the true Napoleon.

I really wonder about those slides. From time to time I recall shots. There were those taken in Ayo's apartment in Philadelphia. And Washington as well. What a waste if they are lost, of film and money.

I am working hard and have been writing a lot of poetry, some composite-poems. Fragments from a poem called SUPERMARKET.

Under his little black hat,

His nearly middle-aged face

Still bearing a trace of acne skin,

I admire the way

His soft moustache arches,
As he presses his lips out
Like dried prunes
And whistles, silently, township tunes,
While waiting in line
To pay ...
Blue and white-striped uniforms
Of rather quiet butchers
Working rather vaguely
As if with things on their minds,
Handling boerewors of different kinds,
Boerewors with different flavors,
Looking, one imagines,
Like guts of well-off people
Who have always eaten
In a satisfactory way ...
The butter's expensive
And so is the bread.
When I am dead,
Put a sandwich on my grave
Instead of flowers ...
Poorly-clad black children,
Possibly undernourished,
Looking quite astonished
At a well-dressed little white child,

Acting rather crude,
Sitting crying 'snot en trane',
Being pushed by her mother
On a trolley overloaded
With a mountain of food ...

As one inspects
The limited number,
One wonders if the end of the season
Is the only reason
Why tiny insects
Have burrowed a hole
In each ridiculously expensive cucumber ...

Suddenly –
From a broken packet
White sugar pouring
Like fine white sand
Onto my astonished hand ...

The same old problem through the ages,
Different people earning different wages.
Marie-Antoinette comes to mind.
Would she be surprised to find
Bread's still so expensive,
The poor can't even think
Of eating cake? ...

And these are from a poem called SPACES

(Divers and the summer sea)

Briefly, they're seen

Passing between

Their former stationary position

And a decision.

Fingertips part the way

Into the almost-calm ocean.

Dark bodies follow.

The soles of their feet

Swiftly enter the quick liquid motion,

Leaving behind

Only the emptiness of the summer heat …

(Dancers)

Knowing it shows quite obviously

That her husband doesn't know

If he is really the father,

She rather dances with you,

Frivolously,

Curving her pregnancy

Against you

Cozily …

By the time the members of the International Writers Program were preparing to leave Iowa City, it was obvious that whoever was a poet was going to write poetry inspired by his or her stay there. It was simply inevitable. Even up to now, I am still writing about experiences there. The Japanese poet wrote to me from Tokyo to say she has been writing 'personal' poetry. I know exactly what she means because we had had a torrid and beautiful affair while in Iowa City. Fate is a strange thing. Anyway, she appears in several of my poems. Like this, for instance ...

Walking along the Iowa River,

I hold her hand.

She sings that folk-song

About the Dragon-Fly

In Japanese.

I cannot even try

To understand –

Except that we are happy ...

In the Iowan winter

The only cherry blossoms blooming

Are on her kimono ...

Love is a many-splendoured thing ... and so are international writing programs in Iowa City. It happens all the time, I believe. But I enjoyed the experience of being a part of the I.W.P. in every way. It could only enrich one, add to one's maturity.

I have been painting too. God, I am working hard. But in a few months time I plan to have some well-earned rest ... and then to hell with everything. (Famous last words.)

By the way, do you know a book called *CONTEMPORARY AFRICAN ART IN SOUTH AFRICA* by E.J. de Jager, a professor in anthropology at the University of Fort Hare? It was published in 1973 by Struik and contains illustrations in black and white and colour of works by black artists, including Sekoto. (But no works by 'coloured' artists. So I don't make it. Hey, it just came to mind now that it's been years and years since last I heard that term 'seekaffer'. Remember, I explained this term to you and Sis Ribs that night at your home while I was visiting? I really must come and visit you again. I feel at ease with people with whom I can talk shit from time to time and with whom I can laugh. A sense of humour keeps me sane). What I mean is do you have this book?

Today (2. July) is another beautiful sunny day and right now it is heading for sunset and in a few minutes I'm going to have supper and tonight I am going to drink wine and talk shit with my friends. After all it is Friday and in the Cape 'Vrydagaand' has always been taken seriously. I guess one could write a book about why this is so.

Anyway, here I stop. Don't expect a long letter for a long time. This one was due to my mood. Regards and affection to everyone. I look forward to hearing from you at some time. And don't forget about Wally. I wonder if he is still at Columbia. He was saying there was a money-complication. His last instruction to me was to get in touch with someone of the Oppenheimer Foundation.

Keep well,

Yours sincerely

Peter Clarke

29 June 1976

My dear Ezekiel,

Thank you for your letter of the 14th June, containing the wonderful news that you have been granted a permit to return to South Africa on a visit as guests of the Institute of Black Studies for about 3 weeks starting on the 14th July. This is indeed great news. The longest period I had to spend out of South Africa was 4 years during the war and that was pretty grim. What 19 years must be like, I cannot imagine. Do keep me in touch with your moves. How would you react to a combined invitation from Fort Hare and our Institute for the Study of English in Africa to visit these parts for a few days? We would naturally pay all travel and other expenses and my wife and I would be very happy if you would stay with us. I shall explore the matter with Fort Hare in the meantime.

With every good wish and hoping to see you within the next few weeks.

Yours sincerely,

F. G. BUTLER

PROFESSOR AND HEAD OF DEPARTMENT

8 July 1976

My dear Khabi,

Son of a Gun! Your letter from Deutschland came 3 days after I had sent off the photos and album. I was really tempted to keep them until I hear from you, but then thought you might need them for public relations. Now it turns out you were going to let me choose the ones I like best! What then? Would you select what you consider I'd like and send me them together with the album if it's not the last in print? We'd be most delighted. I've a scrapbook for treasures like these, picturewise.

You certainly had a whirlwind and whale of a tour, and it's gratifying you think highly of Berlin. I dig it too, much more than even Paris, let alone N.Y. London I never count among any cities I consider! And all the concerts and other musical places you were treated to – a superb re-charging!

You know, we were really ready for your return? Ribs went for a big leg of mutton and I went for 2 gallons of white wine I love so much and which we guzzled in quick time because it wasn't even a gallon. The next day, and the next day etc., I was accumulating in my mind all the things we hadn't yet talked about. Like a marooned couple will do when they haven't seen a human being for 18 years! And of course, also to re-enact your anecdotes about '*dikhoho-dikhoho-dikhoho*',[1] about Nkomo's performance, about the fellow who was so desperate not to be cheated out of a toast to the bridal party! Well, let's hope and pray to the ancestors of *Bo-Mngoma le ba ga-Mphahlele* it won't be long before we're reunited – this time, for keeps.

Thanks so heartily for offering generously to pay the initial expenses for consultation with Pitje etc.[2] Do let us know when you need help. Give our very warmest regards to Godfrey. Something tells me, as I am a believer in the togetherness of events and their significance in that interconnectedness, that your coming here was a mystical sign that it is time we surfaced from the underground realism of exile. There *must* be a design to it.

After writing you and mailing the letter, yours arrived (the next day). I immediately thought over what I said in the letter. It occurred to me how it is that all people living in exile, no matter what nationality, constantly project their own frustrations into the societies they left behind. Years ago I learned that I had also been that way, although I always had faith in the cultural survival and resilience in our people. They would never sink down under, because the white man is not interested in assimilating us, and indeed cannot, as a minority. These organizations politicking outside here continue to think they are relevant to the final outcome of events. And they feel insulted when you tell them they're irrelevant. The people back home must survive and the choices they make have nothing to do with theories trumped up by frustrated exile politics. Even though we got to know each other's strengths and sterner stuff, my own frustration at being impotent for my own people eclipsed for a moment this inner toughness you have had recourse to through the years.

Let me shut up now and say tell Grace that when we left SA it was also goodbye to asthma. I feared that as Amanzimtoti had started the rumpus, Lagos, being below sea level, would play havoc on me. But it didn't. Indeed I've been thriving in hot humid climes, in cold snow regions. Evidently emotional tensions had a lot to do with the number of the attacks. Out here, one is not really driven to solve emotional tensions there and then, as in SA, unless one has no economic security *at all*. Well, I remember gratefully how Grace propped me up with phenobarbs and because they make one feel sleepy I would swing back to Aminophylia (however the cursed name is spelled) and Ephedrine, which always drove me up the wall with hypersensitivity. And I'd prefer phenobarbs. Only thing that lingers is hay fever but I've learned to live with it. Even so, it's seasonal. Jogging has settled it for all but one season – spring, if the air is full of pollen. But a pill will knock the shit out of it in five minutes. I do wish, though, I could get the one really most effective thing for it – the S.A. Naldecol.

Enough, enough, it's just a joy talking to you in writing. I can't help it if verbal diarrhea sets in. Oh, by the way, if you see Norah T, would you ask her if she could send me a Xerox copy of a play I once wrote – a verse drama: *Shaka Zulu*. I lost the only copy I had. Someone saw a copy of it in the Harvard University Library – as a collector's item! Hi, say hello to Wilkie.

Love to you, Grace and the rest of the homestead.

Ever

Zeke

1 'chickens-chickens-chickens'

2 Godfrey Pitje, a well-known Johannesburg attorney

Wayne, Pennsylvania

27 July 1976

Dear Khabi,

How was Seshego? When is it you start at Ngoye?

Happily, last week, the Bantoe-Kommisie wrote and sent a check for the equivalent of the £200 (as it was then) Ribs put it into the purchase of the house for the old lady. I don't know what precipitated this gesture, maybe the delayed reaction to Phatudi's correspondence with them.

The last time I wrote I forgot to say how impressed I am with Senocot, even the little I used. Do you think the distributors would, if I sent money, export a supply to me? Do let me know – price, quantity etc.

Hot humid days now and they'll continue into August throughout. Yesterday I was angry, just fed up, so I jogged 8 miles. More to the point, I go to six when I'm fed up and to 8 when I'm furious. Just one of those mornings when ... I woke up in a foul mood, remembering the words of a friend who said, 'Life can be a shit sandwich sometimes'. How true. The 8 miles purged the fire out of me, though. But then one can't repeat the performance, it's so exacting, and the occasions that call for it so damn frequent!

Bon Voyage, let's keep in touch. If it's a shit sandwich sometimes, it can oftentimes be a lush and green and warm affair because of friendship.

Love

Ezeke

The pictures: the ones where I'm standing stylishly with Ribs looking down against a blue and wood background; Ribs is saying stop styling like a Pietersburg coon. You and Ribs looking down, in front of bicycle: real deep concentration on a real problem – maybe the problem why people do stupid things!

York

16 July 1976

Dear Ezekiel Mphahlele,

Thank you for your letter of 3 July and the memoir of Patrick Duncan which would be very useful indeed; this provides some information which we did not have.

I am not sure exactly what happened to the book business in 1957 except that I know he sold the stock though not, I think, the firm's name. I rather thought it was transferred to Cape Town. We have this information somewhere but I have not been able to lay my hands on it.

I have a contract with Faber for the biography so I am hoping very much that they will accept what I write. It seems to be going quite well at the moment, and certainly we are coming up with some of the most fascinating information which I do not think is at all widely known, including for instance his very close relationship with the ANC in the early '50s and some of his secret trips abroad in the late '50s and early '60s. We have been able to trace his anti-communism back to some visits he made to Germany in 1938 when he was deeply influenced by the aristocratic opposition to Hitler, and particularly by Helmuth von Moltke.

I am not sure that you will altogether approve of all of my judgements, though I am hoping to keep my perspectives as wide as possible. Your contribution will be very useful indeed. Oddly enough Jordan Ngubane has not responded to any of our often repeated requests for assistance; I really do not know where he stands at the moment at all, though it is a pity that he has not responded because in some ways I gather he was quite influential on Patrick.[1]

C J DRIVER

[1] Patrick Duncan (1918-1967), Oxford educated son of the governor-general, spent his early childhood and his school years in Johannesburg. A member of the Liberal Party and later the Pan Africanist Congress (PAC), Duncan was committed to non-racialism but distrusted the African National Congress's alliance with the Communist Party. He ended his political life as the PAC representative in Algiers. See C J Driver, *Patrick Duncan: South African and Pan-African* (London: Heinemann 1980).

Wayne, Pennsylvania
29 July 1976

Dear Nadine

I arrived back here Sunday 25 and now everything seems to have been a dream – one that accentuates the totality of the experience rather than the particularities.[1] I shall sort these out in time. I've to unwind yet. But it has been a worthwhile pilgrimage. I went up north (Pietersburg) to the village of Maupaneng where I grew up. It is still the same but far fewer houses, and deep gashes made by running water. The 'river' is now full of silt and stones and a road could easily be made on top of it, following its course. I went to the school I used to attend. The original building still stands – as a junior primary now. I went in there and stood on the floor I used to sit on. Looked at the foundation stone that says 1921. And it was 1924 I began school there. The sandy road leading there is still as I remember it! Now a secondary and senior primary buildings have been added on a nearby campus.

It was just lovely seeing you Nadine, and to fill each other in on our several intervening years. And I was glad to see the same flame in your eyes, the same glint of alertness, and to observe a calmer, more contemplative profile of you.

May I impose on you and send 7 novels and 2 plays from my African library to post to my cousin I was staying with – More Mphahlele, 1597 Dube Johannesburg, 1800. I just want to make sure they reach him. They are African reading my cousin asked me to get him to improve his knowledge of Africa. Please tell me if it's too inconvenient. I also suggested titles by yourself.

Much love to you in which R joins me.

Ever

Zeke

Remember me to Rheinold.

[1] For an early recollection of this first visit home after nineteen years, see 'A South African Exile's Return to Ancestral Ground', *First World* May-June 1977, pp 13-17.

29 July 1976

Dear Teresa

This is what I did, in addition to seeing so many people.

(1) On the advice of someone on the top floor in administration, I applied for a SA passport, to re-establish my nationality. Once that is done, all my family will be entitled to SA citizenship. So that you and the others over 21 can decide whether you want to take advantage of it or not. The thing is simply to be able to travel with national status, even if you may not care to live and work in SA. Living as we do now without documents of nationality, anyone can kick us around.

It used to be a stigma for black or white to travel on a SA passport. I now agree with Bob Leshoai that this is all bullshit, because the very African leaders who mistrust the SA document and its bearer used to travel on *British* (colonial) passports when they were moving against colonial rule. Even as exiles from their own countries they were favoured with U.K. passports. While we are still unfree, we must use every means of facilitating travel, etc. available from the oppressor. Otherwise, then, even the people who come out to visit the USA, England, etc today must be declared traitors *because* they move on a SA passport. Chew over the thing and make your own decision.

(2) Again, I was advised to apply for the professorship and headship of English at the University of the North (Pietersburg) which I did on the spot. We'll see. This and all the other 4 ethnic universities are still loaded with Boer faculty and there is pressure to Africanize. The present head of English teaches English in Afrikaans! How degenerate can you get! Again, in answer to those who speak from the comfortable position of exile and condemn the students and African faculty who make these universities, I can only say that the schools are a reality. There are human beings there and around them who don't necessarily live there by choice. They live in what used to be called 'reserves' (reservations) – entirely rural. The name 'homelands' is not theirs – it's a political term imposed by the oppressor. But they live there and need all the education and social services urbanites want. Urban ghettos themselves are a kind of 'bantustan' because the people are trapped in them. If I could teach in a ghetto high school, why should I be aloof from the rural ghettos?

The only danger we shall have to confront and know how to deal with is if and when there's a student upheaval. I shall certainly be a sitting duck, the first ready target for detention and banning etc. I shall have to know what to do. Other things to be considered are the fact that it would be unfair to plunge Chabi and Puso at their ages into that situation where they wouldn't find the style of life they're accustomed to, and where the pass is so humiliating. Just the lack of the 'little' conveniences will drive them up the wall. So we shall have to find a place for them elsewhere.

Much love,

Ntate

Philadelphia

30 July 1976

My dear Martin,

At last I got a visa to re-enter South Africa. After 19 years! A new Institute of Black Studies has been formed.[1] They invited me to come and read a paper at their inaugural conference 14th-17th July. I have just returned from it, after 3 hectic and hilarious weeks in the *ole contrei*. Everywhere I went I received an overwhelming welcome and I felt a native son all over again. It was a most happy reunion with my sister, sister-in-law and their children, with old Stalwarts like Khabi, Zeph Mothopeng[2] etc ... I smelled the old odours, the coal smoke, everything.

The conference went like a house on fire, with, of course, the security hounds sniffing all over the place. The ban was evidently lifted, as I was allowed to talk *and* write 3 articles for the *Sunday Express*, exclusively commissioned.[3]

Over the last ten years Ribs and I have been longing to return for good, feeling rather wasted in this big blob of a country, even although we function in relative peace and comfort. I visited the University of the North, made overtures for a position, met the lecturers, like Gessler[4] etc, enthusiastic and vibrant young men who want to make a go of it with the university. I feel if I could teach in a ghetto school, itself in a kind of Bantustan, there's no moral reason why I should write off the institutions in the reserves, which are a present-day reality, short of being a civil servant there.[5] So many people want me and that's inspiring, if it also satisfies the vanity of needing to be wanted.

The danger of course, hangs over me. In that insecure atmosphere where students are restless, rebellious, one can always be collected and put away. But I pray for guidance all the time.

I need a testimonial from you for my application for the chair of English. Would you be willing to write one? I should be most grateful. They need two references (I've given them the names of my department chairman – Denver and Penn) and two testimonials. One will be the University of SA, the other from you. You could write one and address it to the Registrar, University of the North, P.O. Sovenga, Tvl. Enclosed is my c.v. You can spill out everything you feel is relevant. The c.v. is to give you an idea about my sins.

Gessler is coming to Yale to do the Ph.D. Afro-American Literature.

Life is still kind to us. I'm still shaking with all the impressions that assailed me out there – so soon after the killings – impressions that are still a jumble inside me.[6] Ribs sends you her love. While we wait for a reply from the North we shall be trying to sort out the many knotty questions e.g. about our two youngest boys etc.

All the best.

Affectionately,

Zeke

1 The Institute of Black Studies, once headed by Johannesburg psychologist Nimrod Mkele, failed to survive the government onslaught of direct or indirect harassment during the Soweto uprising which began among schoolchildren on 16 June 1976.

2 Zeph Mothopeng (1913-1990) was an associate of Mphahlele over many years from the time of their joint attendance at Adam's College and their work in education. Mothopeng served three prison sentences and was president of the PAC from 1984 to 1990.

3 The *Sunday Express* newspaper was later prosecuted for publishing the articles referred to.

4 Dr G M Nkondo, at the time based in the Literary Studies Department at the University of the North, later of Vassar College in the United States and vice-chancellor of the University of Venda.

5 Mphahlele did in fact become a 'civil servant' when he accepted the position of inspector with the Lebowa ('Bantustan') government after his return from exile. The SA government had intervened to stop him from being appointed to the chair of English at the University of the North.

6 The Soweto uprising.

Wayne, Pennsylvania
4 August 1976

My dear Khabi,

I just thought to write a quicky to say I arrived safe and sound. What a time!

I am posting a letter to both you and Grace, addressed to 7015. Merely to acknowledge your reception of me in a way that won't make G. feel left out – for what it's worth. She'll pass it on to you.

My CV has gone off to Gessler, asking him to hand it over to the Registrar – to make sure it has reached the latter. I asked Martin Jarret-Kerr to write the testimonial direct and the English head at UNISA to collate my scholastic record into a testimonial if he will. Two references are my former head at Denver and the present one here. So everything's on the stove and I shall wait to see. If both nationality and the job do fall in the bag, I'm going to do *all* I can to join the North[1] in Aug '77 in spite of my speculation about Jan '78. This now seems too too far, after the reception and the assurances from my prospective colleagues. Mokgokong particularly gave me fat hope.[2] Ribs just wants to be out of this country.

I'm sending Sibongile a favourite album (for me) of Albinioni, Boccherini etc. I love it immensely.[3]

I hope you will accomplish satisfactorily all you've set yourself to do while still in recess. How rewarding to be in on the whole thing from the very foundation and see yourself grow with the programme. Did Sibongile decide to join you even at this time after all?

Take care, affectionately,

Ezeke

1 The University of the North.

2 Professor Pothinus Mokgokong, then rector (principal) of the University of the North.

3 Sibongile Mngoma Khumalo, Khabi Mngoma's daughter and an internationally acclaimed diva, has retained the family's involvement with the Khongisa Academy for the Performing Arts started by her late father. In 2007 she founded the Khabi Mngoma Foundation, whose purpose is to fundraise for the Khongisa Academy and to provide bursaries for students of the arts.

Wayne, Pennsylvania

4 August 1976

My dear Khabi and Grace,

I believe by now you have left for Empangeni, Khabi. If so, Grace'll pass this brief note on to you. Just to say I arrived safely. The whole week I've been sleeping off the fatigue I accumulated out there. The memory of so many people seeing me off, like those who welcomed me, is something to cherish for a long time. So the memory of you who confirmed in me the love between our two families. To sit in the 7015 house was to recall all those beautiful years of a generation ago listening to piano music and the sounds of Gigli, Jan Pierce, John McCormack (the spelling eludes me just now) Richard Crooks etc.

Thanks for it all, thanks again for the cap you made me, Grace. As you know, I'm a thoroughgoing, irrepressible sentimentalist, and I can go on and on with mushy reminiscences. The last night at Wilgespruit was something else (sump'n else, as they say here).

Please tell Sibongile that I'm sorry I did not have time to talk to her, Linda too. I'm sending *her* a beautiful record. I know if she's made of the same stuff as you she'll love it. Especially Boccherini's and Albinioni's organ and strings work. Pachelbel ought to be heard in slow tempo to be appreciated. But the whole album is powerful sweetness itself. What else? Simply that it has been a wonderful 3 weeks beyond my wildest dreams. Ribs laughed to hear me recount the episode of a man loaded with stuff going to the plane and trying desperately hard to wave an unfree arm to the crowd. She says you can take the nigger out of the country but you can't take the country out of the nigger.

Take care you-all and let's keep the lines of communication aquiver.

Love as always,

Ezeke

Johannesburg

6 August 1976

Dear Zeke

Of course I shall be pleased to post on or deliver in some other way to your cousin books you want to send. One small problem about the first two parcels (which I gather you've already dispatched); out of the blue, since I saw you, I am now coming to the States early in September, and shan't be home again until some time in October. This means the books may arrive while I'm away. But don't worry, I'll make some arrangement for someone to drop a note to your cousin and suggest that she pick them up if she's in a hurry for them. If not, they will be safe on my desk until I return.

The reason for the trip (Reinhold is coming, too; first time in the U.S. for fifteen years) is our son's sudden decision that he'd like to go to Columbia University. Frantic rallying-round of friends in New York to make a late application for him; equally frantic efforts at this end to get a student visa in half the usual time. Thank heaven Joe Segar, whom you met that night, is in charge of that department at the U.S. Consulate here and has been most helpful. If the London consulate can be stirred out of its long hot summer torpor, the child may be on his way in a few days. I am full of trepidation; no-one knows the peculiar alienation of life in America until he has walked along lower Broadway and passed people not only talking animatedly to themselves but also shadow-boxing with unseen aggressors.

You will have heard the dismal sequel to the conference – Fatima Meer banned, Nimrod harassed by the S.B.[1] And since yesterday the horrors of June have begun again. Communications – such as they were – between Johannesburg and Soweto have never been properly restored in the interim. Perhaps they never will be. All is more complex and tragic than it looks, even in the newspaper pictures. Winnie's position, for example: she is accused by some Soweto parents (I had this view from one of them today) of 'using' the children; others accused her of collaboration because she and fellow members of the Black Parents Association yesterday tried to mediate between the young marchers and the police, to avoid violence. Peter, doing his job as a press photographer was man handled but carried on – extraordinary man.[2]

You know that I feel as you did – it was a joy to see you again, dear Zeke. And with all the quiet surety and strength you have gained. Exile destroys many, tempers the rare few. You are one of steel. And shining brightly.

I shall be in the US about two weeks (to France and England on the way back) and don't know whether I'll get to Philly. But should like to very much, and shall try. I'll phone you from New York, in any case.

All the best from Reinhold. My love to Rebecca and you.

Nadine

P.S. You can contact me c/o Alan D Williams, Viking Press, 625 Madison Avenue, New York 10022. On second thoughts – if someone at the P. O. should get curious about the contents of a letter addressed to *you* and thus be on the alert for books addressed to *me*, you might never receive them anyway. For that reason I shall send this letter under cover to New York.

1 The security branch of the South African Police.

2 Winnie Mandela and the photographer, Peter Magubane.

9 August 1976

My dear Ezekiel,

Thank you for your letter of the 28th July. It is a great pity we did not manage to meet during your visit to South Africa. I did try to make contact with you and so did Professor André de Villiers of the Institute for the Study of English in Africa, but to no avail.

I am in a whirl of work at present and not able to write as fully as I would like. I enclose a paper which I recently gave at a Symposium on the future of this University in which I quote you to make a very important point. If you have any criticism or comment on it I would be most grateful. I have written to the *Sunday Express* for copies of your articles.

I do hope your application for a South African passport is successful.

We live in agonizing times but not without hope.

Yours sincerely,

Guy Butler

Pennsylvania

16 August 1976

Dear Tim,

It was good seeing you, even for a brief moment. Thanks for the Dhlomo stuff, and thanks indeed also for the inscribed copy of *Mhudi*.[1]

I'm fighting to find time – make it really – to sort out all the material I've received. It's formidable, but gratifying that the people responded the way they did.

My mind is still teeming with my 3 weeks' experiences and I'm trying to sort out the realities from the dreams. I shall be thinking of what you proposed re: a gig at Wits. Meantime I must wait and see how my plans work out for the re-establishment of my nationality and for the North;[2] the former being of course the crucial thing for the moment.

Villiers was supposed to contact me when he comes back to this country. Maybe he did when I was down there. Maybe he'll still come through.

Best wishes,

Love

Zeke

1 Tim Couzens and Stephen Gray were responsible for a reprint of Solomon Tshekisho (Sol) Plaatje's novel, *Mhudi* (originally published in 1930 by Lovedale Press), published by Quagga Press in 1975.

2 When the time came to leave the United States Mphahlele left with Rebecca and his youngest son, Puso. He came home with only a promise of a job.

Voice of America

31 August 1976

Dear Dr. Mphahlele:

On behalf of the Voice of America, it is my privilege to thank you for your participation in the VOA program series, 'Conversations with African Writers'. Mr. Lee Nichols, Special Projects Officer for the VOA African Service, has told me about his meeting with you and how generously you contributed your time and talent. You may be interested to know that, in addition to being aired over VOA, tapes of the series have been played on many African radio stations and have been requested by the libraries of a number of universities in Africa, Canada and the U.K.

In presenting this series of programs it is our aim to focus international attention on creative writers of this decade who are playing such an important part in modern Africa. We firmly believe that such effort in cultural communication will be beneficial in advancing the role of African literature throughout the world. We also hope that our presentation of these programs will help express the ever growing interest Americans have in the cultural development of Africa.

The broadcast on which you appeared was the first program in the series and set the scene in general terms for what was to come. We think you will be interested in knowing that an impressive number of our overseas posts and many African listeners have commented specifically how pleased they were to hear you and follow your remarks.

Another series of 'Conversations with African Writers' will be aired over VOA in 1977.

Thank you – and all good wishes.

Sincerely,

James H. Logan

Chief, African Division

International Broadcasting Service

Nigeria

17 September 1976

Dear Zeke

You can't imagine how bad we felt about not visiting you in Philly. It was not at all easy for us. First, Mary did not finish her work for the M.Ed until well into June (1st period of summer school); and then we had to get into the hassle of shipping arrangements, plus struggling to get Ibadan to pay our freight, etc. You know too well how slowly the administrative machine here grinds – so you can imagine what it all took. Please forgive us. We just couldn't help it.

I also feel ashamed I haven't been able to come up with a short story for your anthology. Believe me when I say, Zeke, that I find it difficult to write a short story. I really did sit down to compose one for you – but my mind works much better in a broader compass, i.e. a full length novel. I have started my third novel, and I feel much more at home with a big subject (this time I'm doing a historical novel from Nigeria's 19th century jihadic history). I really do fear that I may not be true to my promise after all, and I thought it may be less discourteous to warn you at least about that. Once again, please accept my apologies.

How is work? Your tireless hand must be on to something new – and it's always a joy to read your mature refreshing and well informed [...]. Few African writers/scholars give me the joy that I get from reading your writings (and I don't mean any empty flattery).

The Last Duty has finally been published by Longman – a beautiful production job. We spent 6 days in England on our way back, helping to promote the work: a lecture at the African Center, 5 interviews with the BBC's various departments; etc. I hope things turn out well.

Love to your family. Please write.

Isidore [Okpewho][1]

[1] Nigerian novelist and literary critic.

28 September 1976

Dear Teresa

Thanks for the books. I shall read your friend's poems when I can get a few moments. Am afraid it will have to be on my return from Dakar. It's going to be some fanfare there – academic gowns, presidential protocol, the works. Sounds a good idea – for the joint anthology, with your friend, but let me read the stuff first.

For the big concern – your intended move. Yes, it's a stunning blow. Margarita's certainly going to flip over. *Eso es la vida*, as the Spanish say. You realize of course that $800 is nothing in these parts. Nothing! I asked Beverly Sanders (215)243-7541 of Minority Recruitment to send you the registration and admission literature. She is the best person to answer your questions about late admissions, when you can enter, all the academic requirements and minimum period one's allowed to stay at Penn. You might as well mention that you're the daughter of a prof (although I told her) so that she knows what kind of case she's dealing with. There's talk of phasing out the tuition privilege for faculty 'children', so you must know what is expected of you financially now. Ask her what she can do – no, what prospects there are for a work-study programme. I should imagine, though, that if the privilege still holds for faculty offspring, it's not likely that they would offer work-study advantages as well. Remember, also, that there is a fee of some $400 (General Fee) paid each semester (or year, I'm not sure) that must come out of the student's pocket outside of the free tuition. You have to act fast on these mechanical procedures so that you know by December what credits you have, what you still have to work for, what money you have to work for at least.

As for my staying in Penn, that depends on how soon I obtain a passport and the job I applied for. I'm ready to go any time after July 1977 – the sooner the better. Which means that if I get the two things wrapped up and secured before August, I must move out in August 1977, which is the beginning of the last term of the year in South African universities. I just couldn't wait around ....

Do the best you can to establish your academic standing at present and its relationship to the Penn requirements. Come and brave it, for a job, for schooling, etc. One thing I will do, though, if it will work, is that I shall take leave of absence for a year – the first year in SA, so that you could at least have 1977-78 on me. I'm hopeful they could grant it.

That's about the size of it. We have arrived at an age now that we must concentrate our energies on Chabi's and Puso's schooling and on our retirement status finance-wise, and cannot afford a single dime.

Love, and cheerio for now,

Ntate

Wayne, Pennsylvania

11 December 1976

Dear Stuart,

The University of the North, where you sent a testimonial about me, wrote last month that my application was unsuccessful. Just like that. They did not even write to my other two referees. It now turns out that they were high-handed, because they *took it for granted* that the Government would not let me in to settle for good, of course the perverse logic is that Black universities in SA are directly under the government, and the latter screens all candidates.

I wrote to some big Black nobs to protest and they are taking up the matter with the government. Meantime, the government has replied that inasmuch as I was allowed back in July, they can give me a visa to re-enter. Which only partly solves that political problem. Because I want a *passport*. A visa would only allow me a limited time to stay and how can I take up a job on that basis?

So we are still corresponding, and my man on the spot assures me that we shall overcome.

Just thought you should know that your letter cannot have been all for nothing.

I have made other contacts – in international circles – UNESCO. I have now applied for a position as its seconded academic who will work in an African University (not SA as she never ratified UNESCO's declaration on equality etc). I wanted to give them your name for reference but feel abashed. I went ahead and gave it anyhow. Hope you won't mind – indeed I know you won't, you hound you! We shall see what UNESCO gives.

Love to Jean, you and the lads from us both.

Ever,

Ezeke

13 December 1976

My dear Khabi,

I thought to wait before I write, until I should have something tangible to report. I have. Early in Sept. The North wrote a curt note saying my 'application has been unsuccessful'. The head of my dept here says they never wrote to him for a reference and in reply to my enquiry from UNISA, Prof Beeton wrote a letter marked *Confidential* saying he was never written to! Gessler suggested I write to both Mokgokgong (Poth.) and C.N.P. to inform them. Poth says the appointments committee he's on was never called to discuss *any* applications. CN was most roused and he subsequently sent me a copy of his letter to the Commissioner-General saying he was astounded by the twist The North had given this matter. This, because the Rector had written to him to say he had been given to understand that Interior wouldn't allow me to return. This, again, in spite of the promise by Mr Muller that he would give my application to return his consideration; this, yet again, in spite of the letter from Interior to the Comm-Gen. Which says I can be given a visa to return. The C-G explained to CN that The North acted with undue haste and should have consulted *him* first. He would then have told the Rector that I'm allowed to return. He's most respectful towards CN in the letter. Someone goofed, as the Americans say. Poth says the matter of my application is receiving attention at a high level and all is not lost. CN made it clear to the C-G that the two things – the university job and my re-entry – should be treated as two separate things.

I've now written to CN to say in practical terms it's important, between ourselves, to recognize the inter-relatedness of the two. I must be coming home to a job, not to look for one. But if he thinks I can risk it he should tell me, so that I go ahead and apply for a visa. Which brings me to the passport matter. Interior holds that I surrendered my citizenship when I returned the SA passport in favour of a British one, which makes me a British citizen. I immediately wrote to CN to explain I could not become a British citizen since my father was not born in England, nor did I file naturalization papers as I would have to live in England for that and I did not. A British 'subject', which is what the passport says, is not a British *citizen*. The passport facilitates my travel anywhere, where the SA one only gave me Nigeria and Ghana. I am eligible for American citizenship, but I never applied and don't want to as I did not intend to give up my original citizenship. So I hope to hear from him what the next move is. Indeed it will have to be explained how I can just enter by a visa which has a time limit, if I want to age and die there! Maybe, as Ribs thinks, it will be like a forever entry permit as an exit permit is a forever thing for leaving.

I hope things will sort themselves out, as I'm desperate to come home in August at the latest. Did Sibongile receive the Adagio record? I hope so.

I did not know whether to send this letter to Kwadlangezwa, not sure if you'll have come home for December. I'm certain that the closing has given you time to work out your programmes and iron out those super-sub frictions you told me about. That's something I last experienced at the University of Ibadan 1959-61 and finally caused me to accept the timely invitation to take the Paris job. So I have had a good 15-years' run, with never a sour note in my relations with my dept head. I've been lucky that way.

You should let me know where to write to while you're still on vacation – an extended one!...

Affectionately,

Ezeke

14 December 1976

Dear Makhudu & Muriel,

I hasten to reply to your letter about your need for books. I'll be happy to buy them for you. I shall this week make enquiries at our School of Education to obtain a bibliography, then order what I think would be major representative texts. I shall also see about abstracts from these. I promise to go expeditiously about it.

I was also going to write to say thank you so much for the lovely shirts Phooko sent. They are the proper size and give aesthetic pleasure. The grey tone is most soothing.

Chabi is 17 now and is due for college next Sept. Puso is 15 and is still working his way through senior high. I am applying to Roma for Chabi. We are still exploring possibilities for Puso's schooling. Something tells us to try Salisbury too for Chabi. One way or another they must get the hell out of this sick society while they still remember it for its vast educational opportunities.

The first part of your letter came. It was followed by part 2 a day later. I began to write before I realized there was still another part coming. Hence the above sentence about enquiries at the School of Education. I'll set about borrowing in the library for the dissertations etc and find out what the bookstores have.

You'll probably remember back in the 50's some of us were constantly preaching against our people allowing themselves to perform to segregated audiences? Part of that fight was against white sponsorship and what it does to ruin our artistic expression as Africans. But our folks wanted a name plus outside recognition. They went abroad. We sympathized with them because, shit, there's enough suffering without adding an item like crisis of conscience. That the groups collapsed in exile was a logical outcome. The stuff their white promoters told them was saleable if streamlined for external audiences was after all not durable material. Then we had the more sophisticated and superficially more profound patronage – that of Athol Fugard.[1] He is simply using these players for his own reputation and has not apprenticed anyone to write plays. *Ipi Tombi* is but an extension of the old patronage. We have refused to go and see the Fugard plays here because the thought of it chokes one.

No, we won't go to FESTAC [the Second World Black and African Festival of Arts and Culture]. First, the cost of it, second, even if I receive an invitation I shall be thrown into fierce moral debate with myself. Years ago I decided not to have anything to do with these big circuses: the prestige of the host country, the big spectacle while the day-to-day programmes for artists, writers etc have a tough time surviving; the flock of white Africanists trooping in to enjoy it all, feed on it all, turn it into academic fodder eventually etc. Whom does this kind of circus really benefit – the taxpayer? That's my debate. It came home to us like a bombshell in Dakar early October. Ribs and I were invited by the Senegalese govt to attend the weeklong celebrations of Senghor's 70th birthday. We really went because there was to be a colloquium on culture and development in Dakar to mark the event. The pomp and circumstance! So many of us were asked to contribute papers. Ribs and I worked on ours and delivered (in a literal sense). She on the changing role of the Black woman in SA and I generally on culture and government control. She and many others never got to read their papers. I was given 15 minutes to present mine – because so many people had papers. The damn thing was organized by the session. There were lots of Frenchmen who read papers. In an African country, on an African topic! It gradually dawned on us that the colloquium was an excuse to have a birthday party at the expense of the taxpayer so that the colloquium would appear to be the chief event, to which so many people were invited and had their fares paid for, housed, fed, watered, wined!

So much for that. It would be good, though, to see that concentration of African arts. Maybe I should not sound so self-righteous and moralistic. Maybe I should use the occasion for self-edification if for nothing else. I don't know.

Your letter takes a dramatic turn from the intent to finish the M.ED to the desire to do the M.A. Does this mean after the M.ED? Because you say 'So M.A. it's going to be'. Do you mean abandoning the other or an additional Master's? Anyhow, there is unfortunately almost nowhere you can do the M.A. purely made up of African Literature. Not even in an *African* university – as neocolonialism will have it. Except maybe Nairobi, which recently created a Dept of Literature (instead of Eng) which purports to be African centred. Another possibility is the University of Wisconsin in Madison. In all universities (even in Leeds and the others in England) you read conventional English courses and then can do an M.A. thesis on African literature. When I get the Wisconsin brochure, I'll send it to you. I do know they have a dept. of African languages and Literature – the only one in this country. What I'm doubtful about is whether you could do exclusively African Literature altho' you can do a graduate dissertation in it. You'll hear from me on this point.

I'm sure you're right when you say with a TESL M.ED you can go places. The Academy of English in SA has an office that deals with TESL as a research unit.

Love to you both & the clan.

Ever Zeke

1 Mphahlele is referring to the collaborative work Fugard did with John Kani and Winston Ntshona, to produce *Sizwe Bansi is Dead* and *The Island*.

1977

14 January 1977

My dear Guy,

Things have been happening – others refusing to happen – since I last heard from you, after we had missed seeing each other. When I was back there, I took a shot at the Chair of English vacant at the Univ. of the North. The head is supposed to be on his way out for retirement. I also saw Dr. Phatudi – Lebowa's Chief Minister – to continue our dialogue about the political mechanics of returning for good. I have always thought of my coming back in relation to a position preferably equivalent in rank to the full professorship I have in this dept. (without being head of a dept. necessarily) at the North.

What should happen but that the Registrar of the North should write in Sept. (the application was handed in in July) to tell one my application 'was unsuccessful'. I discovered that they had not even written to my referees, one at UNISA and the other my present Chairman. They had had two testimonials etc. Dr. Phatudi on hearing the sad news from me, set about investigating the thing. The Minister of Interior had already given him his ruling that I may return for good and the Rector was saying that he turned down my application because he had had it on authority that I would not be allowed to return! Now the matter, I'm told is being reviewed. Incidentally, the Commissioner General was upset – or so his letter sounded – that the outgoing Rector should have failed to check my political standing with him first before arriving at his decision not to have me.

I had now made up my mind that, as the re-entry problem no longer exists, I move back to S.A. next August. I shall go straight to Pietersburg to set up house, whether or not I shall be employed by the University. How ironic it will be if I find it necessary, nay imperative, to ask for a job in your university or any other 'open' institution when I told you I should consider it morally indefensible to teach in an institution that excludes Blacks! Maybe my indignation then would be so overwhelming that I should act with a sense of vengeance, without any qualms. Who knows?

Did I hear by the way, that the English Academy runs a project in English as Second language? Would you tell me what is being done in that quarter?

The statement made by retiring Rector Boshoff, as produced in *The Star*, was pathetic. The Schizophrenia operating down there is beyond belief. *Mais, que faire? C'est enverant à la fin*![1]

I met Visser at the big MLA (Modern Language Association) circus in New York last month. I was presenting the enclosed introduction for a panel discussion on African Lit. I'm reminded of your plea in the paper you read – the one you sent to me – on S. African Lit. We shall have so *so* much to talk about and I hope, to work together on when I'm back. But you'll need to educate me on S. African education – if there is any such glorious thing, even as an *idea*, in a fragmented culture. We didn't have time to talk with Visser, but it was good to meet him at last.

My warmest wishes & may 1977 be a beautiful year for you & yours,

Zeke

1 'But what can be done? It's back-to-front to the end!'

8 February 1977

Dear Teresa

Just a quicky to say we're excited for you and the new prospects, the new job at Spellman. Well, I can't say I'm bashful about the kind of clout my name seems to possess! Congratulations.

Yes, just this morning I was writing to accept the invitation – which all resulted from the fact that the new president, Donald Stewart, was a colleague of mine at Penn. We first met in Paris where we had him for dinner at du Montparnasse. I'll arrive on the 13 April and stay till Wed. morning. Will sure see you both.

Your Mum's still at work and we'll talk about Atlanta, a possible trip etc.

Good you received the cash, and it helped out.

Here's p.2.

Love

Ntate

Benoni

28 February 1977

Dear Uncle Zeke,

I have tried to reply your letters. Thrice I did so but every time I had to post a letter a kind of upheaval would take place. And I would ask myself whether it was worthwhile to write about the weather or risk some consequence with the detailing of another crisis. By the way we lived through countless crises last year. Then we had the Xmas morning which was a bit of our own show after the spate of detentions. Then there was the Carlton Centre incident which seems to have sent out ripples that are hard to settle. There is a new spate of detentions. There is a new clamoring for an enquiry into the deaths of those that die in prison. Our situations boggle the mind; it is a life of frightful experiences; the people are going out of their minds. Can you imagine a woman carrying an unborn child for nine months and then get so upset with her husband that she dips the child in a bowl of hot oil, straps the child on her back to walk 1 mile to the local hospital where the child is certified dead on arrival? I don't wonder at these things. Only yesterday I was speaking to a woman whose husband has been detained since August last year. Answering a query about her life she said: I am hanging onto my sanity.

I have begun to despair about the magazines. My excuse for delaying a new edition has been that the demonstrations took a toll of our readership. Now I ask myself: how relevant are they? I am aware the White readership may be keenly awaiting the next issue of *New Classic* or *Sketch*. My uncertainty arises from a concern with the Black reader. I don't seem to have the courage to publish what he wants. I have a nagging feeling that the magazines are going to be snuffed out of existence as soon as I show the shift in the thinking of the black man. There is a stainless mood among the kids which shames so many adults around here. It is painfully lamentable that the adults don't seem to have learnt how to build on their own experiences – this would have made the effort of the kids so much easier. How do you think we feel to witness fathers disowning their children? The one snarls, the other smiles before the white man. You should remember the 'mopping up operations' of yesterday. We are living through those days all over again.

I have not written before because I can't seem to separate the various feelings impinging on my body. They are such a strong pressure that the one sensation I've come to know well is numbness. I was able to escape from it all for a short period at the beginning of this year. And in that period I had to produce a record of my current mood. Hopefully that record will soon see daylight from abroad as *ASH URNS IN SOWETO*. I am hoping that you have been receiving the magazines I sent out via Lesotho and my new book via Swaziland. But your silence over these has made me wonder whether or not you did receive them.

When I had finished what was to be my first novel late last year, I declared it unfit for daylight. It had elements that were seen in abundance last year but because they came from an earlier experience they looked pale against the present day light. And so I must look at it again. And I was very fortunate to see *EMERGENCY, THE WANDERER* and *NATIVE SON*. For me these works represent the tragedy of my life – its emptiness more than anything. A crisis in my life has been forcefully brought to the fore. I must decide to continue life here living a reflected existence or go to Botswana or Swaziland or Lesotho where I might live perhaps a rung or two below the level I know but with the satisfaction of writing as FREELY as I am capable. It is painful to be stopped between home and point X and have one's car boot opened for one reason or another. I've gone through this experience too many times not to know what it is doing to me. And I know life is going to be pretty tough for me once my third anthology comes out.[1] It was inspired wholly by the experience of June 16th. I am here writing unashamedly as a historian. And have more to say along these lines. I need to burn out before I can stop. What concerns me is what will remain of me at that point. While here I seem to have a strongly suggested picture.

New Classic No. 4 should be out in a few weeks – 2 to 3. But I am terribly short of cash so much that I will be owing the printer some R250 when he delivers. I don't have fears about paying up at the end of 3 months. But this is provided the magazine's is not banned – there's always an even chance for that sort of thing to happen. *New Classic* & *Sketch* are seen by the authorities as part of the Black Consciousness Movement. And I personally have spoken publicly in favour of that cause. Consequently. I shall have my fingers crossed from the day it comes out.

I summoned the energy and guts to write this letter only after I got to know that Sally Motlana would be leaving the country and therefore able to post it OUTSIDE home.

Please accept my apology for being so terribly irresponsible about my correspondence. My whole body is a sore that seems to be hard to heal.

Best wishes

Sipho Sepamla

1 *The Soweto I Love* (Rex Collings 1977).

Wayne, Pennsylvania

Dear Tim,

It was very kind of you indeed to respond to my letter so promptly, first by cable and then by letter. Your research fascinates me immensely, your subject infinitely intriguing. I'm excited too because you are generously going to send me material for the anthology. By all means let me see Dhlomo's short stories as well as H.I.E's poetry. Maybe you could do me the favour of sending me what you find most interesting – say three such stories. By a narrative sketch I am thinking of a narrative piece which may not be fiction of the short-story breed but is an account, well written and with abundant feeling. Something also different from the essay. A political sketch, as narrative, would be fine. I want to put together under one category sketches as a genre in its own right. To hell with what English depts think! Which reminds me of Wits and its attitude to African Literature. I'm not surprised, simply amazed. Makes me marvel at what would happen if in their enthusiastic posture of the 'open university', they would take in Africans to pump them with Dickens only most likely the Black colleges don't teach AL, but there would be a fighting chance for it there.

The Venda would be a treasured addition if your friend's poetry turned out well in translation. I hope desperately you can persuade him to crack out of his shell.

The information about the student enrolment is most helpful. Indeed the table clinches my final statistics for the article. Again I was keen to know what Blacks teach at Wits and UNISA.

Thanks again for all this.

Yes, please use your judgement as to what you think is worthy of an anthology such as this one. And when the Dhlomo MS is launched, I shall consider it a great favour to be allowed to see it. Who publishes *English in Africa* and where does one write in for subscription?[1]

Best wishes,

Yours Zeke

1 *English in Africa* is published by the Institute for the Study of English in Africa at Rhodes University.

Wayne, Pennsylvania

4 June 1977

Dear Nadine,

We are getting set to move, even though we do not yet have definite clearance from the Top for re-entry. But Phatudi said to me on the phone back in Feb not to worry about that. I told him my return should not be contingent on obtaining a job at the University of the North, which he has been trying to negotiate for. Somehow I get the impression that he wants to secure *that* first for his own self-esteem. If I return & wander about looking for a job he will feel bad & he must fear that the people of Lebowa may conclude he doesn't have clout after all. Someone passsed through here on his return to J'bg, who told me that he frankly thinks either the man doesn't know what pressure he can exert on Pretoria or else he's timid, because people who had come out in flight are back in the Transkei. I came out on a passport.

So we're still waiting for some travel documents whatever it is they'll think up for people who surrendered their SA passports but did not take out alien citizenship even when we did qualify.

Meantime, we had to sell our house here – summer is the time to do it – or else be snowed in & have to wait till next spring. It was bought last Saturday. End of July we must vacate it, when my resignation from the University of Penn also takes effect. Summer teaching ends mid-Aug. & we're fixing to be on our way out. Where to? That's the adventure we may have to negotiate. If we don't make it direct to Pietersburg/J'bg (we're determined this, & not the job should determine our return) we'll wait it out at Gaborone. I have just cabled our man in Lebowa to acquaint him with the latest. We have applied for our youngest boy to finish high school at Waterford (who say they're full & must wait & see if someone else drops out) & for the older boy to begin college at Lesotho. We're hoping we can find a house in Gaborone to rent for as long as it may take before the old Savannah chug-chug stops by to pick us up, so to speak. We're actually more optimistic than this may sound, & I thought to let you know the latest. Looking forward to seeing y'all, y'hear?

Love

Zeke

Wayne, Pennsylvania

4 June 1977

Dear Khabi,

We're feeling forsaken these days, with not a soul writing from the ole country, just when we need all the courage we can muster – guts it should be, more than courage.

In Feb I phoned CN to ask why the silence since the application for the passport, and what should we expect? He said not to worry, it'll be all right. Still nothing, since, except a letter from him asking that we postpone leaving till end of the year. I then wrote him a long letter spelling out the problems. If we don't sell our house this summer – the only time people buy and sell as the weather is perfect for moving and relocating children in school etc – we'll be snowed in and will have to wait till next summer. Reason being that he has to bring the new Commissioner General into the picture, the former one having collapsed and died. Strange reason! He also says Kgware is sympathetic to my intention to join the North, and the job will be readvertized in September.[1]

So we put the house up for sale and it has been bought. We vacate it end of July. I tendered my resignation as from that date. We simply decided to do all this as an act of faith. If the worst comes to the worst, we'll go wait in Gaborone, rent a house there for the duration. I told CN that it's the re-entry mechanics that are more important than a job for now – I can negotiate for a job – any job – on the spot. I finish teaching 15 August and we'll be on the move almost immediately after that. One can't keep imagining the worst – a long process of attrition in a state of siege in Gaborone. And yet the spirit of my ancestors keeps whispering to me to keep cool because it will turn out well for us.

That's where it's at these days, as the Americans say. Baldwin was here for a long afternoon last weekend. He was on his way out. Promised he'd go up specially to meet CN and tell him he actually saw the For Sale sign here with *both* eyes – no *manga-manga*. You know his bald diction! He says CN is too timid, because he really has the clout to tell the biggies up there that he wants me back home. Sorry this letter is all about us and I haven't asked how you're faring ...

Cherio,

Ever

Zeke

[1] Mphahlele did not secure the post at the University of the North and, on his return, had at first to accept employment as an inspector of schools

in Lebowa. As Chabani Manganyi puts it in his biography: 'The optimist had not planned for this kind of political humiliation. The trap was set and [he]walked right into it' (*Exiles and Homecomings*, p 296).

7 June 1977

My dear Ezekiel,

Thank you for the copy of *Africana Studies* and *Research Centre No. 4* which I look forward to reading in the near future. I am writing immediately because your note accused me with justification, of a sphinx-like stillness. I wish to assure you that this stillness does not indicate a lack of activity, feeling or thought.

You will be pleased to hear that a second year course called English in Africa has been approved in principle by both Arts Faculty and Senate. It now goes to Academic Planning Committee, University Council and then to the Minister of Education for his approval. If all goes well the course will be offered next year. I will arrange for a copy of the curriculum to be sent to you when it has been worked out in greater detail.

My wife and I are leaving for the United Kingdom on some study leave on the 23rd. We shall be at Clare Hall, Cambridge, for three months. Our moves after that are uncertain. If you are in Great Britain during this period, please get into touch with me. It is time we met and talked.

Yours ever,
Guy Butler

10 June 1977

Dear Professor Mphahlele

It is my great pleasure to inform you that you have been elected (again) to membership in Phi Beta Kappa. Founded just two hundred years ago, in the first year of the nation, Phi Beta Kappa is the oldest and most prestigious academic honorary society in the United States. Congratulations on the outstanding achievements in liberal scholarship which have qualified you for election. The Chapter investigated and found that your eligibility to join by virtue of your previous election had lapsed, was sympathetic to your reasons for not heeding our call then, and was anxious to have you as a member – so we elected you again. (We find some cause for rejoicing in that this may never before have happened in the Society.)

At a meeting on 20 May the chapter initiated you into the Society *in absentia*. I enclose a copy of the citation which our President, Stuart James, read on that occasion.

I was particularly pleased to have the University of Denver Chapter elect you because I was initiated by the Delta of Pennsylvania Chapter at the University of Pennsylvania, long years ago as an undergraduate. There is a symmetry there, which pleases me.

I enclose a page for the Chapter's Roll Book. Will you sign it and return to me please? And fill in the membership card and send that to Washington. Many thanks for taking care of these details.

Again best congratulations from me, from the Gamma Chapter of Colorado, and from the many individuals who remember you with pleasure here at the University of Denver!

Yours very sincerely

Dennis Barret

Secretary

Wayne, Pennsylvania

20 June 1977

Dear Nadine,

Thanks a lot for the express letter and clipping which arrived on Sunday 19th. I appreciated v. much your deep concern on our behalf. Indeed when Jean le May rang me up in May to tell me there was to be a hearing, I thought there must be an error, and that the issue would be resolved in our favour. Now this! It's just so depressing.

Something tells me that in the process of pleading my case, Dr Cedric Phatudi struck rock and this must be it; on further investigating my political standing, someone must have discovered the 'banning' record. I fear now that it may harden the hearts of some of the biggies ...

It is certainly something Dr P. will need to confront. Right from the beginning it became clear that mine wasn't a straightforward case. This is just part of the rubble. Dr P., I am told, is overseas for some weeks. When I wasn't hearing from him since he told me things were 'moving', in May, I went to Washington last Thursday [...] It's evident that he'll find the banning record. Your letter came after my visit. Dr P. is not likely to know unless he's told during his travels, and I don't know if he has left someone on this assignment. Maybe you could ask the lawyer to look into it, although it would have been better politics if he were to consult with P. first.

NADINE/On second thought I have decided to enclose this aerogramme in an envelope to enable me to put in a sheet of information to show the lawyer. Who knows, there may be some precedents, and when the signal reaches you to ask him to move on it, he'll know. A few of these chaps who returned to the Transkei had after all left the country *without p*assports, and I reckon theirs was a tougher case.

Ezekiel Mphahlele: Age 57

Rebecca: Age 56

Left S.A. 6 Sept, 1957. Rebecca followed with 3 children on her passport.

Our passports were endorsed for Nigeria & Ghana only. To facilitate travel, & because S.A. had no consulates in these two countries, I took out a British passport, Rebecca followed suit, in 1959. This was on the strength that S.A. was in the commonwealth, & we had lived in colonial Nigeria for more than a year. I sent both our S.A. passports back to Pretoria (the folly of the century!)

But we did not naturalize as British, we were only protected for travel.

A fourth child was born in – in S.A. when R. returned for a visit. The fifth was born in Nigeria, which was then independent (1961). He got into his mother's passport.

1970 we came to the U.S. on immigrant visas, & so obtained permanent residence. But we didn't naturalize, because we *always* wanted to return to S.A.

Rebecca's British passport expired & she didn't trouble her self to renew it. I still have mine, & travelled on it last July to S.A.

When R. & I were invited to Senegal by Senghor she used the re-entry permit in lieu of a passport – which permit immigrants are given for outside travel.

Every member of the family has the green immigrant card. But only three sons want to accompany us to S.A.: ages 16 (the one born in Nigeria), 18, & the oldest, 30. The other two are on their own & prefer to wait here.

In 1972, we expressed our desire to return when Dr Cedric Phatudi was in the U.S. He promised to look into the situation and was delighted to hear that I wanted to come and teach at the University of the North. But each of us understood that my re-entry was *not* to be contingent upon employment in the University of the North.

In March he sent me a copy of a letter from the Commissioner General, Bezuidenhout, now late, alas. The letter categorically states that the Minister of Interior is willing to allow me to re-enter & that I would find no difficulty in looking for employment. All I was waiting to hear from Dr. C.P. was what travel documents we should use. Should we wait for S.A. passports? (I submitted to him application for one when I was there last July on his advice). Or whether we should use the foreign documents – first for the purpose of re-entry. His silence ...

[Letter not signed]

20 June, 1977

Dear Makhudu,

Your letter says nothing at all about the stuff I sent you, way back in April: copies of abstracts, of pages from books and two fat brand new, hardbound books – from the part of the list – those you said you wanted to own copies of. And I wrote, too, explaining what I found or couldn't find. Now I'm scared all these things may never have reached you. *Say* something about them – although one can't *do* a shit about them if some monkeys descended on them from some palm tree perch. *Daai ouens kan 'n man se twee balle steel ba lebeletje. Net om daaroor te dink laat my twee balle onveilig voel en begin te jeuk.*[1]

I'm so happy you got the Stats. business together. In no time you should whip up the dissertation.

No word yet from Phatudi. The ball is in his court because, having secured the Minister van Binnelandse Sake's consent to let us in, he has to get us travel documents. Anyhow, if it still hasn't come through, we'll go wait in Gaborone. Meantime, Mokgokong (Poth) managed to influence the appts. committee to hang fire with a replacement for Boshoff the retired ox until they're sure they've someone really qualified. They'll readvertise the job in Sept. But whether or not I'm employed there, we're determined to go in and I can look for another job. We leave this house 30 July and I finish summer school teaching 12 Aug. Posting the parcel from Britain will be too late, unless it were by air, which will be too expensive. Hold on to them till we let you know.

Our plan is to leave the country on or about 14 Aug.

Love to you

Zeke

1 'Those blokes could steal a man's balls. Just thinking about it makes my balls feel unsafe and they start jerking.'

8 July

Copy sent to I Ayob

Dear Nadine,

I now have a letter from the Commissioner General in Seshego (dist. Pietersburg) in which he states that the Minister of Interior permits me to return. I must, however, apply for a visa as my possession of a British passport and return of the South African one back in 1959 should be understood to signify that I have surrendered my S. African citizenship. The C.G advises that I go ahead and apply for a visa with the stipulation that I want to immigrate and have my S.A. citizenship restored. I have applied for forms from Washington. I have also written to Dr P. to draw his attention to the *Express* case and ask him to press for the removal of my name from the banned list. Without this I couldn't teach.

Whatever the situation, Nadine, I must return, and Rebecca feels the same way. In any case, we have burnt our bridges and must move forward. I'm not deeply apprehensive, because in the last five years I have thought about our return so intensely it became an obsession and when that kind of decision is made, come hell or high water, things must move. If the worst comes to the worst and I am gagged indefinitely, that's the way it will be. I must simply devise *some* means of livelihood, as so many others have to. It *is* a damned nuisance, and I should be glad if your lawyer friend went ahead now that I have official sanction, and ascertains my banned status.

It is strange that I should be regarded as being non-South African when I have taken no other citizenship. When I went to Washington to see the minister (as he is peculiarly called) about my not hearing from Pretoria, he said that the law states that a person who uses a foreign passport without the knowledge of the S.A. govt. is committing an offence, but that as S.A. was still in the Commonwealth in 1959, Pta might concede something. He was, however, going to try to help me. Then came the CG's letter. I don't know what the relationship there is, if any, between my citizenship status and the ban.

Best wishes.

Love

Zeke

Philadelphia
17 July 1977

My dear Khabi,

I used the above address as we are vacating the house in Wayne. We'll be staying with a friend till 12 Aug. We fly out of Philadelphia on 15 Aug and arrive at Jan Smuts on Wed 17 ex Frankfurt on Lufthansa 540 at 10.55 a.m.

I have written to Rex in Atteridgeville to meet us and take us to Pretoria. We should stay there a day or two and be highballing north from there. We'll 'do' JHB later. C.N.P, through Phankge (remember our volatile and gracious host at Mphahlele?), or better still Phankge himself, with Mafori's help, under the eagle eye of CN, procured temporary accommodation near Seshego – at Lebowakgomo where the new 'capital' is being put up. It's about 50km out of Seshego as I recall.

The Commissioner-General, successor to the one who collapsed under the heavy responsibility of caring for our people, wrote a fine letter to me. He quotes the Minister of Interior's words that Mph – (they always write it 'M'Phahlele'!) is permitted to return. But as I took out British citizenship (I have only the passport, not the citizenship) I must apply for a visa. The CG advised I go ahead and the machinery will be worked out for reapplying for S.A. citizenship. At this point, all we are concerned about is to get home, even if later they rule I should be a Lebowa citizen. You and I know that when the shit hits the fan (as the Americans say) it may not matter anymore what citizenship I have. I'll be home and dry.

Hau Baba 'nduna!
Siza buya si bonane![1]
Zeke

[1] 'Greetings honourable chief. We'll meet again.'

Johannesburg
2 August 1977

My dear Zeke,

Of course I understand very well how you and Rebecca feel; there is no going back, at this stage, on a decision so momentously made. We must just do everything we can think of to make you as free as possible to do your work and live your life here as you would wish.

I thought Rebecca's statement, given prominence in the press here, was excellent.

A copy of your letter went to the lawyer the day I received it, last week. This was Ismail Ayob, in the absence of Ismail Mohammed. To-day I telephone Ayob to see if he had any news, and was told that as Mohammed is now back, the matter and correspondence was referred to him yesterday. I've phoned his office and left a message for him to ring me. If there *is* any news, I'll add a note to this letter.

In the Transkei I bumped into Nimrod – didn't know he was living there at present .... Naturally we talked of you; he said you could certainly get a job at the new university going up in Umtata. Well, I don't know how you would feel about that. Transkei struck me as somehow a tragic place. A people having to deal with something that should never have been accepted in the first place. A very few people are enjoying head-long the most obvious benefits; for the rest, life is wretched, and made more glaringly so by the new status under which it looks like being perpetuated.

Newspapers here keep telephoning me for information about you. I tell them nothing except to confirm that you are coming home; I understand you are considering several posts; that's all.

Please keep me posted if you leave your house before quitting the U.S. and have another address at which you can be reached by letter and phone. Have you decided on a date of arrival here?

Love

Nadine

6 September 1977

Dear Nadine,

It is 20 years today since I left for Nigeria! What a journey to come full circle like this! We got our visas two days before we were due to fly from Phila. I received my passport to Nigeria a day before I was due to fly from J.S. Sweat it out, that's the point.

But the welcome was just so heart-warming one forgot all about the tension preceding our departure. Indeed all the 12 months since I left the country in July '76 it has been one moment of tension after another.

We're home and dry now, and have taken a temporary house in Lebowakgomo, 50km from Pietersburg (S.E.). I'm hoping the Univ. of the N. job will materialize, the chances are 90 to 10 that I shall move into the chair of English. Dr C.N.

and I are going to see the Commissioner-General this week to get things in motion for the removal of the ban & to get through the immigration formalities for permanent residence. Will keep you informed.

Rebecca's sense of euphoria about being back home is matchless. We're trying to get Puso into Waterford, as he can't speak Sesotho, among other things.

I jog every morning, and the birdsong in the woods & in the mountains takes me back to my childhood. I can retrace the goat routes I used to take, recognize the same red soil I knew so well.

I try to search in my mind for the logic of these disparities – gross disparities – between the calm & peace in these valleys & the turbulence & pain that surround us ...

I'm using a temporary address, which will always be useful as my cousin is a very fine man:

c/o P. O. Box 120

Mphahlele, Tvl.

Love,

Zeke

7 September 1977

Dear Teresa

It has taken us this long before we could write. Folks in cities can phone through better. We stayed two days in Atteridgeville, then moved to Mphahlele, the district that claims the postal address Mphahlele. Rather than being a town in the orthodox sense, it is a complex of villages. Phoning from there was a task too huge to contemplate! Then we moved to Lebowakgomo, a new developing town. Here there'll be electricity. The longest distance I've phoned from my cousin's house is Swaziland. Lebowakgomo is going to have a parliament house, administration buildings etc. It's 50 km from Pietersburg (S.E.). Think of a small southern cracker town and Pietersburg is it. When I get the job at the University of the North, we shall move into a Univ house. The facilities there are superb. It's 30 km from Pietersburg. (There are 5mls to 8km so you can work it out). This is a pretty house. Can you imagine a house with 3 bedrooms, sitting-dining-room, two out rooms at the back with garden worth R4426 ($5090)? After paying a deposit of R2000 we pay R20 ($22) a month. No mortgage nightmares, taxes on property, etc! Although the toilet is detached from the house (so is the bathroom), improvements can't cost much more.

Your Mum is happiness and peace of mind personified. Puso is making friends with people who can talk English to him. He's excited because on the 20 Sept, I've to take him to Swaziland to write the Entrance Test for Waterford school where Zola was. He drives our Peugeot 504 very well, although we only go around Lebowakgomo and about 10mls out. Driving age is 18 here, and they don't fool around with fines. He's enjoying the car – right-hand steering with a stick shift (upright). The mountains and valleys here are a gift of the gods – just beautiful. I jog up and down them and can recognize the trails we followed with our goats and cattle when we were boys aged 6-12 years. I can recognize the precise spots where dramatic things happened to me. The birdsong of my childhood is all around us. I'm trying to probe the logic of the disparate forces at work – between the peace and calm and the larger pain & cruelty of the times dramatized elsewhere in this land. How's Betty? Give her our love. And you and F.?

We have been most fortunate to find the kind of welcome and hospitality all round. By permission from the top I was able to address a packed meeting of teachers by invitation – about a teacher's life abroad. No fire-eating stuff, just facts. So we're back in the mainstream. Can you imagine that in 20 years we were never able to stake a claim for this or that because we didn't belong? We were given 3 months visiting visas, during which we had to file immigration papers. So I'm shutting up and keeping my eyes on nothing but the post I'm gunning for. Besides, my days of activism have passed. I must conserve energy for my fiction and poetry.

Much love to you both.

Affectionately as ever

Ntate

Johannesburg

17 September 1977

My dear Zeke,

I was so glad to hear from you at last. Your final letter from the U.S. took 15 days to reach me (by airmail!). So I had already read of your arrival in the papers before I knew you were on the way .... At once I tried to track you down; but you had disappeared: I was told you had gone to lie low in Pietersburg pending various official decisions. For this reason my welcome is belated, though just as warm as it would have been if I had known in time when to meet you at the airport.

The logic of the disparities you are experiencing: it is to be found nowhere except in the obstinate affirmation of life, *in spite of everything*, and for god's sake don't let anyone make you feel guilty about your joy in feeling your own earth under your (jogging) feet. Brecht wrote about a time when it seemed a sin to talk of trees; it's that sort of time here, now. But I don't think men like Biko die for people to deny what is live and positive in themselves, but to refuse what is deadening and negative.

I'm keeping fingers crossed that you'll be sitting in that Chair of English soon, and that there'll be a Chair to sit on. Waterford-Kamhlaba would surely be a good idea for Puso. He'll enter more gently into his heritage than you could hope for him to do here; whatever we do for ourselves, we have to look for the least bewildering circumstances for our children.

Here is a letter I received from Mr Ayob. I don't imagine you'll want him to make any move now, when you clearly have a more hopeful avenue of approach. Would you perhaps drop him a note, anyway? I also enclose a round-robin I'm sending out – self-explanatory. Do let me have your reactions. It is tantalising to have you and Rebecca so near and yet so far ... I do so much look forward to seeing you.

With love,
Nadine

Mphahlele
11 October 1977

My dear Nadine,

Thanks so much for your heart-warming letter. I treasure your phrase very much – 'the obstinate affirmation of life, in *spite of everything*'. It's good to know that you have your fingers crossed that I should find a Chair to sit in & acquire it. There certainly *will* be one by all accounts. They *could*, however, pick someone else. I'm optimistic, though.

I have written to Ismail Ayob to explain this whole song & dance about the ban & the stipulation from Interior that I should teach at the University of the North! I have also told him that I have never received a restriction order. We'll wait and see. Somehow my reflexes seem to be changing gears accordingly without any 'difficulty' – or shall I say surprise? Particularly with regards to this age-old activity of waiting, waiting for the bus, in some cases the driver of which has already decided he's not coming one's way or he's going to zoom past; and of course one doesn't know it beforehand.

The issues you suggest a non-racial PEN could tackle are most compelling indeed. Yes, a PEN club should not have to degenerate into a recreational club, with so much around to reach to, to act upon, to affirm, to challenge, etc. And your sentiments against a racially exclusive body are wholly mine too. Your decision to withdraw from the existing institution, so characteristic of your personality, bespeaks nothing less than the true artist.

I may be misreading events, such as I have tried to keep *au courant* with over the 20 years I've been away. Am I right in thinking that on so many occasions when the Godfather has clamped down on non-racial institutions, the Blacks have suffered more in the way of individual banning, detention etc? Of course even when there's an effort to regroup & assert a nationalistic character they suffer anyway. And I suppose the white element in the union of journalists that led to the formation of UBJ [Union of Black Journalists] is just a pack of dwarfs whose stride could never take them beyond the confines of traditional privilege. I wonder if an 'integrated' PEN would not find itself landed with such an element, so that the Blacks would in turn find themselves doing more work in the building of the bridge? This also seems to be a traditional trend. So much suffering has attended the Black man's endeavour to come across.

It's a bitter irony that you, I, lovers of enlightened Black opinion, should have to retreat into our little enclaves when we have the most human message for this country. I am trying to say that it appears the time is not yet, for a most timely proposition like yours. Just at a glance, I would not say that the Black man's mood is that of withdrawal, on the same scale as that of the American Black. It is the cruelty of the times, rather, that urge our people – at any rate those who institutionalize a black consciousness – to choose to suffer for something more tangible if negative, as against the painfully positive sacrifice for what seems unattainable, even criminal.

I'd like to have your reactions to all this, Nadine, as I am also trying to get things clear in my own head. Let's keep talking about it.

I hope we can make the trip to Jbg before long, & I shall give you a ring.

Love from both of us

Love

Zeke

PS. Sorry, *my* fault. Just want to say that the idiocies like duRand's at P.E. would be funny if they didn't reflect the academic monstrosities that creep & crawl in some of these institutions.

Z

14 October 1977

Dear Teresa

I should have given the above zip code, which then makes 'Transvaal' unnecessary. Transvaal being a province (almost the equivalent of an American state – 'almost' because the provinces are not independent entities). It's a miracle Motswiri's letter arrived at all, having been addressed 'P.O. Box 120, Transvaal, S.A.' – no town! But the name must really be famous – that of the town or mine – Mphahlele.

Your letter came when we were beginning to wonder if things were ok there. Now it comes and brings lots of news and a moving account of your emotional life and of the equally turbulent lives of the 2 musketeers. I just can't get over your beautiful description of the couple – 'All big and brave words – can bat off anything that comes their way … ' Each time I remind your Mum about the letter we just can't control our laughter. About them, later.

The letter you wrote just before we left Philly touched us as deeply as you can imagine a 'child's' sense of self-discovery should do to parents. Yes, those were painful days – indeed years – when it seemed to us that your Mum and I were destined to lose our children to the culture of the Great Society, that you were gone, in the most profound sense of the word. But I have never been the one to indulge in the middle-class sentimentality often expressed in terms like 'Oh what did we do wrong?'. Because, as I have always emphasized, I don't consider my children owe me anything, they owe *themselves* a lot. Yes, they deserve to come out better because we have never denied them anything we thought might advance their chances of self-fulfillment as adults. And when you and P seemed to be borrowing so many years in advance from your young adulthood, I could have wept. The rupture was violent and painful. I'm merely confirming your words about your realization of what it must have been like.

Still, the one consoling factor I always reiterated to your mother was my faith in your resilience – I mean *your* personal ability and capacity for taking matters in hand, taking care of business. …

So when you wrote that you cried on your way to Atlanta, I was glad of that moment of self-realization, the glorious rediscovery of where you've come from. That's sufficient, my child: the rediscovery of an identity. Nothing more need be said. My belief is that my children do not have to settle for less than they deserve, considering their upbringing. The environment everywhere we stopped in the 20 years offered no genuine roots, and we moved only when I was assured of better prospects and a higher position. But I'm sure you're spiritually the better for it, your personality has realized its deeper springs.

It is in this light I also view your decision to cut loose from F. It's as it should be. The discovery or realization that a love relation is more than the mechanics of functioning as a couple is most valuable. And when even the level of mechanics is not satisfied or executed, as between you and F, things become pretty bad. And all the love sentiment in the world isn't going to provide what's missing. It was always a one-sided effort – yours. Again you saw through the whole failure – maybe in time, before you started destroying each other. I'm happy the whole episode ended the way it did.

We are of course disturbed by the fact that you have to start job hunting and apartment crawling all over again. The consolation is that you've seldom stayed long before landing a job, inflation notwithstanding. Keep us informed please.

...

Swaziland decided to give the one empty place in Form IV to a Swazi national. There was a toss up between the two. Puso was most disappointed. He loved the landscape so much when we drove out there. So we're trying Lesotho High in Maseru, where I once taught for a short time.[1] Also Rhodesia (Zimbabwe) and we've written to Edith Sikabi to enquire for us. Meantime I'm working his ass off with English exercises and composition – on a daily schedule. He'll be hollering with piles at the end of it all. There's a cousin here who takes him out taxiing – sometimes even to Pretoria, and he's met more people than we have. He can greet in Sesotho, but tries frantically to discourage or avoid prolonged talking from the other side.

Am still waiting for results of my application for the Chair of English.

Let's hope you find a job and an apartment to your taste. Let us know what gives in that direction.

Much love from us all.

Ever,

Ntate

1 Mphahlele is referring to a short teaching stint at the Basutoland High School in Maseru (1954-1955).

Johannesburg
25 October 1977

My dear Zeke

Thank you so much for your good wise letter. I share all your misgivings about the hope of forming the kind of group one would like at this time. I would say only one thing: of course, there would be the possibility that a certain kind of white would want to join, but the issues to be dealt with and interpretation of purpose I have in mind would send them scuttling off in alarm, I assure you. Anyway, I have received a number of letters in reply to my round robin, and there are more to come. The reactions have been everything you might expect: from derision and rejection to something close to enthusiasm. One I wrote to received my letter the hour he heard of Steve Biko's death. When I think I have all the response I'm going to get, I'll send you photocopies.

That is likely to be early in the New Year; at the beginning of November I am going to Columbia University for the rest of the semester to hold some writing seminars. This gives me a chance to visit Hugo – that's why I accepted – and on the way home to spend Christmas with Oriane, my daughter who is married to a Frenchman (once more out of work, I learn from a letter this week) and lives near Nice. I don't suppose there's much hope of you coming up to JHB before I leave, alas. But in January, if you can't come here, I'll get down somehow to the family seat at Mphahlele. Please keep me in touch with developments about the academic Alan D Williams, Viking Press Inc, 625 Madison Avenue, New York 10022.

The Du Randt thing fills me with nausea. But in the present climate I can't let it pass, so I am advised by everyone. I am going to sue him. Litigation is something I've always shunned, before. Suppose I lose? Lawyers cost a fortune.[1]

In the shock of October 19, I don't know whether you noticed that Sipho's new book of poems has been banned. October 19: it surely will be the name of a street or public square some day. I still can't get used to *World* not being for sale on every street corner. One of the side effects of the banning is that my friend Peter Randall can no longer act as honorary secretary administrator of the Mfolo-Plomer Prize. He was about to write to remind you that you kindly accepted verbally last year that you'd be one of the 1978 judges. I hope that you haven't forgotten and are still willing. The job isn't as onerous as it sounds; usually only 4-6 manuscripts are good enough to get as far as the judges. There has to be some weeding out of hopeless stuff, and this you are not troubled with. We are not worried about your legal status, if you are not so do please confirm that you are going to be a judge. Would you write a note to that effect to Ad

Donker, Mofolo-Plomer Prize Committee, Craighall Mews, Jan Smuts Avenue, Craighall Park, Johannesburg 2196? He will be standing in for Peter Randall.

If there is anything I can do for you in the States – contact family, publishers, friends etc – let me know. I leave on November 6.

Love to you and Rebecca

Nadine

[1] Professor Humphrey du Randt, then head of the Afrikaans department at the University of Port Elizabeth, wrote in a set work for Afrikaans university students of literature that she (and Athol Fugard and André Brink) advocated violent revolution. The matter was settled with Du Randt publishing an apology.

Mphahlele

31 October 1977

My dear Martin,

Thanks immensely for the very impressive testimonial. It's just so heart-warming. You addressed the envelope simply Box 120, Transvaal, S.A.! It was lucky you also wrote an alternative address – Registrar etc. Box 710 and the province. But then my son in Denver did the same and my surname gave the P.O. a clue – it was forwarded with 'Try Mphahlele'. A former colleague at Univ. of Denver sent his to Box 126, Pietersburg. It took a month to reach me, with 'Try Mphahlele'. They're becoming intelligent here aren't they? You see, Mphahlele district was ruled by Phahlele, whose name so many of us fear, related or not. Like so many Masemolas etc.

Still waiting for the bureaucratic machine to grind over the last lap of its course and maybe early in Nov, we'll be interviewed, if ever.

I'm maintaining a low profile mean-time, and enjoying the feeling of being back home.

Ribs gives you her love. I shall keep you informed about the outcome.

Take care,

Affectionately,

Zeke

6 November 1977

Dear Teresa

Good to receive your letter in which you say you find it gratifying to be back in D.C. We're mighty glad you have found companionship and congenial working conditions.

The Jewish colonization doesn't surprise us, as we saw it in full force at Penn plus in the Mental Health and Retardation racket in Philly.

It's good also to hear you have found a companion you can depend on, and that's a wholesome start.

No fear, we are maintaining a very low profile, as if we hear nothing, see nothing ...

Lesotho High is our next bid for Puso. Just now we want to get him out of this local small-town element of folks who set their sights as far as a midget can reach or even a centipede. Then he can go to Swaziland for his A-levels – which is equivalent to Junior College.

Will you deposit the enclosed in your account and then buy me with money packets (500 pkt boxes) of Sweet and Low sugar substitute. We just cannot find it here and the saccharine jive sugar is distasteful. Use up enough so that you have left money to post the stuff in a neat carton by air parcel post. Mark it 'medicated sugar substitute' if you have to fill in a parcel slip. Find out what rate you can best send it airmail.

Our goods arrived at last – in a huge truck from Durban – unexpectedly! The house we're in, although it is a 3 bedroom house wouldn't contain them all, so we decided to keep them intact like in a warehouse. We live in the 2 bedrooms and kitchen, the rest of the house being packed ceiling-high! We don't want to unpack if we are going to move to the University soon. But nothing is getting us down, in spite of candle-and-gas lighting etc. Electricity will come here when we're gone, may the gods be on our side.

This is but a hurried note, we'll keep you informed. Continue to use the above address.

Much love as always,

Ntate

Mphahlele

25 November 1977

Dear Peter and Dawn [Thuynsma],

Here we are and writing at last. Three months already gone since we arrived here – 17 Aug! We came up North soon as we had landed. No press or social funfare such as greeted my home-coming last year. Largely, because the *Sunday Express* was fined R300 for quoting me last year. They had asked me to write three articles for them, and that, after being told that I was not banned – by some biggies in Justice. They'd been misled. We are now working at the removal of my name from the list. Indeed, we are still going through the process of regularizing our stay. The conditions of the visas were that I reside in Lebowa – the Northern 'Bantustan' and that I should seek employment at the University of the North. I applied for the Chairmanship of English and am still waiting. It's quite clear that the Rector (black) doesn't particularly relish the idea of having me in there, hence the delay, (I hear said that I've only one competitor – a white). It would be history in South African higher education if I got in, and if they don't take me, someone's going to stand on the mountain top and holler. All this doesn't go anywhere to dampen our sense of euphoria – the homecoming euphoria. The University job is not the end of the world. As for the insistence that we reside in Lebowa, this is where we always wanted to return to. Soweto and Pretoria townships are just unlivable. More and more houses have been erected without any consideration of facilities and services. The ban (they say it has been in force since 1966) doesn't restrict my movements, though, once I get a job as a teacher, which is what the biggies want me to do, automatically the order must lapse.

We are in a new town 50 km (i.e. 30 mls) south east of Pietersburg – Lebowakgomo. (The University is 30 km (i.e. 20 mls) north east of Pietersburg). The town is on land which used to serve as a cattle post when I was a boy – 8 mls from Maupaneng. I made several pilgrimages to Maupaneng and retraced the cattle and goat trail I maintained those days in the '30s. The landscape hasn't changed much. The school I began Sub A in still stands (since 1924 – it was actually built 1921). An overwhelming experience. The mountains and valleys here are simply superb – not like the monstrous Rockies!

Rebecca just can't get over Blue Cross and medical care that costs so much in the US, high electricity and phone costs etc.

Chabi, who made a bolt for it to Denver just before we left, is now with Motswiri – remorseful, we learn. Puso is adjusting, although he confessed he didn't want to come in the first place. He'll still learn the magnitude of what we were saving him from in the US. We hope he'll go to Lesotho for high school in January.

About your dissertation: I don't know how you want to go about it, now I'm so far away. Whatever you propose I shall be glad to fit into your scheme.

I sincerely hope you're both in good health. Funny, whatever little nostalgia I feel, it's all connected with Denver. We made solid friendships there, unlike in Philadelphia. Tell us what y'all doing – I mean the Thuynsmas of Littleton.

Peace affectionately,

Zeke

Peter, sorry my address book is in unpacked boxes. Am asking Sonia to forward this.

Mphahlele

6 December 1977

Dear Bernth,

Just a brief note to make contact again. Arrived here 17 Aug., & have been waiting for the results of my interview for the chairmanship of English at the University of the North. It's still formidably staffed with whites even though it's a Black University in a *black* area. So are all the other 4. When the councils can be predominantly black, we'll see progress. If I'm taken, I shall be the first African head of English in the history of SA. university education. If they don't, there's every indication that from the community's standpoint, it won't be the last we shall have heard about it.

It's just an overwhelming experience being back & being welcomed with such enthusiasm among the Africans. We are in a small developing town called LEBOWAKGOMO, planned as the future capital of LEBOWA if & when it does opt for 'independence'. At the moment there's abundant resistance, like in Zululand. 'Lebowa', incidentally, is Sesotho for 'north'. We are 30 mls S.E. of Pietersburg (N. Transvaal) & if I'm appointed we shall go to a varsity house – 20 mls N.W. of P'burg. Mphahlele, as above, is a large postal district, named after the man who ruled the land & died in the forties. He established the first community (ie non-denominational) primary school in the country – in 1921. That's where I began – in 1924. It's just 7 mls from here, and Maupaneng, our village, is in another direction from there. I revisited the school – it still stands solid. Retraced the road to Maupaneng, across the river. I've been jogging a lot & retracing the goat-and-cattle trails of my boyhood – 1924-1931. It's powerful therapy for me. Down south – Soweto, Pretoria etc breathes turmoil & the cruelty of the times, but here in these valleys is a more serene affirmation of life. My next odyssey will be the search for the logic of these disparities.

Do continue sending me the *African Research* journal. If I need to send money for it, please let me know how much.

Best wishes,

Ever
Zeke

Nigeria
11 December 1977

My dear Zeke

Your letter of the 13th December came through, and since I've been included in the official Ghana delegation to Festac, I had postponed response till I am in Lagos. Been here almost two weeks now taking part in the literacy encounters with old friends, Wole, Okara, Nwoga etc.

The whole Festac is a bizarre nightmare, thousands of black people 'wallowing' in their 'blackness'. The Arabs have discovered that they are black and their participation is shrill and arrogant.

I am glad about your beautiful response to my decision to stay on in Ghana. I know you will understand it, not as an impulse to glory in my recent ordeal, but a recognition that we have work to do here, and if we must die, let us at least die on the native soil.

This brings me to your desire to go home. I support it a thousand percent. There at least the issues are just, the battle lines clear: The kids of Soweto, like the little child of the New Testament have led. You must not hesitate. Do I understand there's a University position? Where better to plant your seeds of real subversion of a monstrosity? In America, you are always going to be on the periphery, a curiosity of some sort. But at home with all the problems, you are in the midst of the struggle you once begun and now need to return to order. My only worry is the other ones – the boys. Will they be ok? But of course they will, if they must taste the South African reality. Perhaps Rebecca will hesitate, because she is a typical mother and wife – ever concerned, sensitive to past and future pains. Assure her that there is pain *always*. What matters is what we do with it, how we endure it that others may not undergo as much as we have.

I've come out less angry, more patient. That is why I can still talk to people like Wole who have suddenly found a grand stand. He gave a paper at the end of which he paid tributes (glowing, permit the cliché) to Senghor. I pointedly asked him a number of questions concerning Dakar. But of course I should expect the self-serving answers I got.

Well, Festac is over. I go home on Sunday 13th· Write soonest. And when I die, don't weep because you have already done your duty by me.

Give my love to Rebecca and the kids.

Salute you.

Kofi

P.S. Kgositsile is due for ANC, Mission is here, oh everybody is here. It's nice to see everybody.

1978

Mphahlele

5 January 1978

Dear Tim

The council of the University of the North has unanimously proposed my name for the headship of English to M.C. Botha.[1] I believe he's still on vacation. So any day I should hear from the University. I was interviewed at the University of Pretoria (head of the English Dept. there with a strange-sounding name – like 'Sebaga' – Sotho phonetics!) + head of RAU's English Dept + Kgware + Dean of Arts at the North + the latter's Venda head. They were also unanimous in proposing my appointment to the Council. But the interview was on the 1st December. They pushed it to the very edge of the cliff because they were trying to seduce someone else, from England, for the job. So it was quite plain they did not like to take me in the first place. Things didn't work and they had their backs to the wall.

We'll see what kind of institution it is, if something does not go wrong between M.C. and whatever/whoever ...

You can thus see that I shall be pressed for time before the University reopens – what with setting up house and preparing for the year. It just seems the 3-7 February will be too much for me to negotiate so that I can take part – 'negotiate' i.e. to manage. Had I been given Nov-Jan to plan etc knowing that I have been appointed, there would be no problem. I wish I could say 'yes' right away.

The way I see it, from the day I am appointed the ban should automatically fall away, as I couldn't enter an educational institution otherwise. But Phatudi told me some paper work will be needed after everything, in order to clear me officially.

Hope things go well for you with the workshop.

Best

Zeke

note new address

[1] Then Minister of 'Bantu Administration'. Soon after M C Botha's retirement this government ministry became the department of 'Plural Relations', later to be changed to the department of 'Co-operation and Development'.

Dept. of Education

Chuenespoort

Dear Tim,

You've heard the worst, and I'm still stunned. Meantime I'm Circuit Inspector in charge of English. I'm trying to work up enthusiasm, and who knows, I may yet become one of the inspectors. There are of course good men in the dept., men with sense of mission. I miss the classroom madly, but they give me a sense of purpose.

Helen Suzman wrote to say she went to see 'the Wheelbarrow' in Cape Town about me. He told her he wasn't going to reverse his decision in respect of Sovenga (Univ. of the North), in addition, he'd veto any appointment I may obtain in any school or university *under him*. In a Bantustan I'm free to work in a school etc because education depts. of these areas run their own affairs.

The good news is that I'm not banned, only 'listed', since 1966, so I'm not restricted to any area. For work purposes, I suppose that, since I was allowed back to SA on condition I reside in Lebowa, which I'd planned to do anyhow, an employer in the urban areas would need to speak up for me to be permitted to work there. I see little difficulty in that quarter. As I want to embark on a collection of Sotho, Venda and Tsonga oral poetry with parallel translations into English, I don't want to be outside the province. I'm having to decline an offer from Natal University in Durban to be in their Eng. Dept. *or* Extension programme, which ever can be worked out. I'm also having to say no to U.C.T. who has offered me a proposition for African Studies. *Que faire? C'est toujour la lutte, hein*![1]

What bedevils the situation is that if an employer offered me something in say Johannesburg, the mechanics of finding accommodation boggle the mind, and somehow I was frightened off by smoke from Soweto – the smoke from coal stoves, and something told me I wouldn't want to live in Soweto.[2] I guess I've become too suburban in the 20 years I've been away.

If there were an extension system at say Wits, that covered northern Tvl, I might organize English classes here, from Matric to degree level. It would work splendidly – there are just too many people in need of assistance owing to shortage of universities or colleges and the stagnation at Sovenga. UNISA might not like the idea as they might think their students were being lured away. I could of course broach the idea of tutoring *their* students without committing them to a residential set-up.

I'm rambling and thinking aloud. Would you please find out what's possible at Wits, accommodation aside? I'd be grateful. I hope your workshop went off satisfactorily. I'm glad I don't have to miss such occasions in future as I'm not prevented from attending gatherings.

Cheerio for now,

Sincerely,

Zeke

1 'What can you do? It's always a struggle, not so!'

2 Little did Mphahlele know that he would ultimately have to live in Soweto after accepting a position as a senior research fellow in the African Studies Institute at the University of the Witwatersrand.

Johannesburg

9 January 1978

My dear Zeke

I have a little present from Ellen I think might go bad in the post – is there anyone from here going your way soon who could bring it to you personally?

She was very pleased to have first-hand news of you and your family. Oswald also sends his best. He is having a tough time, financially; a tiny grant from U.N. pays tuition fees for the teacher's training course he is now launched upon – difficult indeed for him, since he has had so little formal education. He is having to take many undergraduate qualifying courses, such as biology. A mystery he had never penetrated before, except in the living out of his own life! He is cheerful, and writing fine poems.

I spent a good month as the (paying, paying) guest of my student son in New York. Ditto (two weeks including Christmas) with my daughter and French-speaking grandchildren in their medieval village near Nice. Unfortunately my beau fils is once again out of work .... Compared with what has happened in my absence here, and since my return last week, these are minor matters. I am anxious for news of you and what your plans are, or rather how they are working out academically. I heard from Stephen Gray some interesting and surprisingly encouraging things about the attitude of the profs from white universities who conducted the official university post interview with you. Please brief me?

Depressing that two black writers were detained while I was away. Gwala was one of the people who wanted PEN revived; Mqayisa's only piece of work that I know, a naïve play, was already banned. What can one do to help – to feel helpless is a poor excuse. Mqayisa's wife has a two-week-old infant and a child of two. Food has been provided for a month or two, but in the long-term?

With love and warmest wishes that all things may go right for you both, and the boys, in the New Year.

Nadine

Mphahlele

February 1978

Dear Noel [Chabani Manganyi],

Thanks for your letter. It is gratifying to know that you are forging ahead with your project – at least with the preparations.[1]

It seems your dates will fit well into my schedule – or what there is of it. It has been shot by Sovenga's rejections of my services – psychologically, that is. I'm trying hard – desperately so – to plan for the future, having dismantled almost all the schemes I had planned would be university-based. I find I can't even sit down to read. *Mashangu's Reverie* is still staring me in the face, telling me it's next in line. I can't, I hope you'll bear with me and let me sort things out first. To make matters worse, without electricity here, I can't read at night. Frustrating and irritating.

I should leave for Vendaland on the 23rd March.

Best wishes,

Ever

Zeke

[1] The reference is to the research for *Exiles and Homecomings* and the first edition of the present volume.

Mphahlele
March 1978

Dear Adrian,

Nadine has asked me to write and say whether or no I still want to be a Judge in the Mofolo-Plomer Prize contest. I would certainly love to be one of the Judges.

What sad news about Sipho's book of poems! Outrageous!

I forgot to say last time when I wrote that the instructor who took my place at the University of Pennsylvania is teaching South African literature and is using the consignment that arrived from you for black poetry. I was happy my leaving did not cause a cancellation of the course.

Best
Zeke

12 March

My dear Teresa

Just a quicky to ask you to do one thing. Hope Puso arrived all in one piece .... I asked the bank about Exchange Control as one has to be permitted to send money out – like in Kenya, Zambia, etc. they will require a letter from the school where Puso will be attending – on its own letterhead – confirming that (a) he's attending the school; (b) in what grade; (c) what moneys he has to pay re: sports and other levies. Then you should type a letter saying you confirm that (a) you are Puso's sister and guardian (b) you require so much a month for his boarding and lodging. Calculate these on the basis of a business deal considering the cost of living, even if you won't charge lodging (although if you think this is an imperative item you should say so). You can then in a letter to us say how much we should pitch in with. Head the typed letter 'To Whom it May Concern'. The reason for quoting it in a business rate is to allow us to send money whenever my ship comes home. I shall earn less than at University, but your Mum is seeking employment.

Puso must understand, we told him, that our maintenance of him depends on whether or not he stays in school – the sky's the limit if this condition is satisfied. Also he must know you're the best person to look after him and he'll be standing to lose our sympathy if he wants to cut out from your guardianship. By the way, state another item in the business letter – medical care and insurance.

Much love, and thank you for your willingness to give my brat a chance.

Ever

Zeke

Please return the clippings for my scrapbook. I'm now a civil servant – how ridiculous! It's in the Education Dept. – to look after the teaching of English from elementary to Teacher's College.

Chuenespoort

Dear Teresa,

Your letter put us at ease about Puso's trip. Glad he came through. We can appreciate his desire to work and resume with the new semester. Hope his longing for school doesn't flag. Tell him please to keep the fire burning inside himself. He'll probably also be doing some re-thinking. He needn't feel sore for the loss of a year. He can put the break to good use. Think of the whole experience – something American kids would only be too eager to share.

Your report about Lee's letter and yours is most disconcerting. I have no doubt in my mind at all that I enclosed in a large envelope, addressed to him by *registered* post, a traveller's cheque signed by Puso to the value of $180. And then for your letter to turn up like in some cloak-and-dagger act. Could it mean that the man/woman who signed the slip for Lee couldn't resist the temptation. If Puso still has the white slip with the cheque numbers on, he should claim the $180 as lost.

You haven't said if you ever received two cheques I endorsed over to you for money to wait for Puso's arrival so that it would tide you over a period before the T-cheques should arrive.

Please send the cutting about me to Prof. Gunnar Boklund, Dept of English, D.U., Colorado 80210; a copy to Kathy Legnini, Dept of English, Univ of Pennsylvania, Philadelphia – Pa. 19174; a copy to Bob Pawlowski, 1113 Adeline St., Hattiesburg. Mississ. 39401 (He's at Univ. of Southern Miss.). Did you know the Pawlowskis moved, last August? I'll write to them. All you need to write on the copy is 'for your info'.

I have been given a job as Inspector of Education to look after the teaching of English in the whole region's schools and teacher training colleges. The Civil Service? – Bah. But it'll keep the wolf from the door. And the content of the job isn't far out of my beat. I regard it as temporary though. Seems I'm going to take on short-term professorship in some 4 universities consecutively – they're inviting me. But who knows, the Univ. of the North may yet come to its senses, what there are of them .... Otherwise we're taking it easy. Your Mum isn't perturbed unduly and we're happy.

Hope your studies are coming fine. It's something to hear of an apartment being $340 – close to a mortgage installment on a house as big as the Wayne one ($470)! Incredible!

Much love,

Ever,

Ntate

Johannesburg

23 March 1978

My dear Zeke

Forgive me for not having written before. The delay is not as long as it may seem to you, because your two letters written on the 25th and 27th February took 12 days to reach me. I thought there might be something sinister in this, but careful examination of envelopes and numerous post offices stampings have persuaded me that it was nothing worse than the pace of the ox as maintaining in rural and suburban post offices. From Chuenespoort to Pietersburg, two days; from P-burg to Jhb, three to four days; then the letters went to the Parkview P.O. whereas registered letters for Parktown should go to the Braamfontein depot, so another 3 days went by to achieve that transfer: finally, twelve days later, a slip from the P.O. in my box. Shall we buy some pigeons?

In the meantime, your 14th March letter has turned up fairly promptly. (I'll try sending this one by express instead of registered, however.)

Some of the questions you ask I could answer immediately, for others I have had to seek expertise. The easy one: about your royalties. It is true that it is forbidden to have assets abroad, as a South African. One is not allowed to have a foreign bank account or any property. My position as a non-resident alien of the United States, earning money there, is that under South African law I have to bring back all royalties and also payments for any outright sales of work (articles, etc), to South Africa; under American law 30% non-resident tax is deducted from these earnings at source, by the publisher or my agent, and is payable to the US and other earnings abroad in the usual income tax returns statement in South Africa, and the amount of tax duly paid in the US. I then do not pay tax on such earnings here. The 30% US 'withholding' tax (as it is called) applies to earnings up to $10 000 a year, if earnings exceed that amount, the tax rises. In Britain the withholding tax is a (staggering) 45%, and it varies in other countries – for example Germany is 25%. When your agent gets royalties for you, now that you are living here, she must deduct the US tax and send you a dollar cheque for the net sum. You are then in the happy position of earning foreign currency for SA. Your bank will welcome the cheque in Pietersburg. You write across your deposit slip – royalties. And you carefully retain the accounting of the amount as marked by your agent – showing the withholding tax has been paid.

There are various other small matters I'll explain when we see each other.

Now, about the business of being 'named' not banned. I have been to see my friend Advocate George Bizos about this.[1] A named person:

is not admitted to the Bar or Side-bar

must give notice of any and every change of address (to the police)

may not communicate with anyone on whom a *banning* (known in the legal sense has been placed)

usually can obtain a passport only under very special conditions

cannot be quoted, cannot publish

cannot attend meetings of a political nature but is not barred from gatherings; (there's an incredible circumstance, however, arising out of the fact that a named person can't be quoted: suppose you were to found and become chairman of the Lebowa Oral Literature Society – your utterances at the meetings would have to be omitted from the minutes!)

may meet other *named* people.

That's about it. But I suggest you write and ask Ayob to send you a copy of the Act, so that you may study it in full. I offer the most important provisions phrased in something less precise than legalese.

During the past week, I have had two telephone calls concerning you. First, Barend van Niekerk, Prof of Law at Natal. He has, of course, been in touch with you. Now – he is eccentric and flamboyant, has a pretty high opinion of himself, but is a bold and brave man, nevertheless. So one must not dismiss any suggestion from him. He tells me that Cruywagen has no jurisdiction – of course not – I mean *Koornhof*, since we're talking of 'white' areas, has no jurisdiction over the appointments at 'white' universities. Therefore if Natal invites you to come and teach there, K can do nothing. Secondly a rather more concrete and carefully-worked-out idea from André de Villiers, of the Institute for the Study of English in Grahamstown. He phoned to ask me if you were named or banned – the bewilderment over your status, dear Zeke, is countrywide. He was relieved to hear it was the former, as he, André Brink and Guy Butler had made a plan to get Rhodes to offer you a fellowship (of short duration, due to money problems) to come to Rhodes for about three months. The thing that pleased me was that they had the forethought to arrange that the invitation would include a staff house on the campus. (Apropos your remark if I applied to Wits, Rhodes or Unisa ... living quarters would present a problem.) I feel encouraged that here may be the kind of offer you may feel able to take up; I understand they have written/are writing to you. At least you would be in reach of libraries etc. and perhaps be able to get on with that part of your research that will have need of the written word.

I know, of course (though perhaps the others do not) that it has not been at all your intention to come back here to teach on any permanent basis in any of these universities – indeed that would be a defeat of your purpose to give your talents and energies to your own people, first and foremost. But it could be a way of asserting your status (of another kind than the one we've been looking into with lawyers) while H.S. and Phatudi *et al* are working on getting you off the gagged list. I shall be interested to know how you feel about these offers. I think they would be followed by others, by the way. And I think, personally, that the Rhodes one is much more likely to become firm than the Durban one.

Since Rebecca found Doreen Levin unusually sympathetic (for a journalist) I thought you might like to have the full text of her article, as it was before cutting and editing over which she had no control. You'll notice a number of opinions and sections of opinions did not appear. For her sake, the text is confidential?

I also am sending a rather idiotic letter that appeared in the *Star*. What on earth does the man mean by 'politics will never be the same again'?

Of course you did right to send your son back. Thank heaven nothing happened while he was here; the pressures must have been unbearable for one so young, and without any memory of this country to prepare him. But it's sad to be without one's children. When I think that we sent Hugo to Waterford because we didn't want him to go to a segregated school, and that meant losing six years of his childhood; and now he is in the US and again we are losing the pleasures of contact with his young manhood – but then I tell myself I am lucky *not* to have him here.

It is relief to know that the Lebowa post isn't too unpleasant for you, and indeed may give you a chance to work out some of your ideas on education. Apropos the raising of funds for a communal college, you are quite right that you will find difficulty because of the reluctance – based on fear or opinion – of trusts and foundations to give anything to Bantustans. But the persuasive eloquence and original argument of the P.S. to your February 25 letter make me think you might succeed if you put these forward in person. You will have to come up to town and interview these people yourself.

Forgive this ill-typed thing. I am working very hard and am also rather harassed by the ordeal of that censorship panel the other night. That judge – you have to meet these creatures in the flesh to realize what we're up against in self-righteousness, crass stupidity and time-serving morality.

Love

Nadine

[1] Advocate George Bizos acted in many of the major human rights trials of the apartheid era and subsequently acted for the ANC during the post-1994 constitutional hearings.

Hillcrest

10 April 1978

Dear Professor Mphahlele

First, welcome back to South Africa, if welcome is the appropriate word. I was disgusted by the decision of the Minister to overrule the University Senate and Council. I thought that the whole purpose of appointing an African Vice-Chancellor was to give a certain measure of autonomy to the University, but it did not turn out like that at all. I am not sure where you are at the moment, and am sending this letter care of Mrs Turbeville at *The Star*.

I am doing for *The Star* sixty two-hundred word biographies of prominent black (African) personalities in our history, beginning as far as back as Ntsikana, Dingiswayo, Shaka, Hintsa, Sekhukhune etc. Each biography is illustrated by three cartoons portraying three important events in the person's life. I would very much like to include you as a representative of literary achievement, and am writing to ask you for the favour of giving me a very short biography of yourself. It should include the date and place of birth, a word about parents maybe, education, and your writings with dates. I should also like to conclude by mentioning the decision of the Minister not to appoint you. Am I right in supposing that such an appointment would be recommended by Senate to Council? Is it necessary for Council then to refer it to the Minister? Or in this particular case did Council inform the Minister, and then he decided to reject it? I assume also that the decision of Council was to appoint you as Head of the English Department, or some department of African studies or literature?

I forgot to mention in the above summary, that I would like some details of your career during your absence from South Africa. It does make things easier for the cartoonist if the events lend themselves to his particular art, and it would help me if you would suggest what three events are most suitable for this purpose. Please do not go to a great deal of trouble over this. The most important thing is that I should not be guilty of any inaccuracy of mis-statement.

With good wishes to you

Yours sincerely

Alan Paton

Chuenespoort

18 April 1978

Dear Martin,

The enclosed speaks for itself. Certainly got the papers, including those of the Establishment, babbling and babbling. The new Minister simply sat like the Sphinx – no comment. The *Star* and *Mail* both had editorials deploring his decision to block me, when Interior allowed us back on condition that we reside in Lebowa (N. Tvl.) – which we wanted to do anyhow, Johannesburg being now simply unlivable – and that I seek employment at the University of the North. *Mais que faire? Mon Dieu!* On being interviewed the two professors – Pretoria and Rand Afrikaans universities – English Departments – said they found my academic standing and response to questions at the selection committee stage unimpeachable.[1] Your reference letter was just superb. Someone, it is firmly believed, wrote confidentially to the Minister to overlook the Committee and Council decisions to appoint me. Who dun it? Maybe we'll never know. *Sunday Times* carried comments from Paton, Fugard, Jack Cope, André Brink, Etienne Le Roux, Nadine Gordimer etc., which were most elevatingly indignant.

Meantime Helen Suzman raised the matter with the Minister after a question in the house. He said he wouldn't change his mind and he'd veto any other appointments I may be offered in any of the Black Universities under him (all are).

But as the 'homelands' Education Departments are autonomous even when the governments are not independent, I may be employed in the schools of Lebowa or in administration. So Phatudi gave me a job as Inspector specially in charge of the teaching of English in this whole region. As you will imagine 25 years of Bantu education brought incalculable ruin for English in the schools and teacher training. I must re-evaluate texts, teacher qualifications, which are extremely poor, challenging and yet the classrooms call; Natal, Cape Town, Transkei Universities have invited me for short-term lectureships. But why should I go and teach white students where only the privileged blacks are allowed? So says my instinct. My head tells me to be more realistic and think of the rebuff the other side.

I find I was 'listed', among a whole bunch of writers, who were outside, in 1966. Not banned. But Phatudi is working on a plan to have me 'unlisted', so I can write. This job requires a lot of that.

Meantime there's a new act that gives councils autonomy, which allows them the final say on appointments. There's talk the new council of the North (they change every 5 years) will review my 'case', as the chair is still vacant. Dare I hope?

But Ribs is taking all this philosophically. Her sense of euphoria dwarfs everything. Just being back home, even where there are smoldering ruins, gives us strength.

My warmest regards in which Ribs joins me.

Affectionately,

Zeke

[1] It is indeed a sad commentary on South African higher education that a man of Mphahlele's standing should have had to be subjected to the kinds of interviews he went through upon his return. This shows the institutional resistance to the recognition of black talent and the extent to which such recognition depended on the good offices of whites.

Chuenespoort

April 1978

Dear Adrian,

Thanks for your letter.

The civil service? Well, well! But I'll survive. I've not returned to my MS since November '77, at which time I was frantically waiting for the University to reply to my application, then had to wait for the interview, for the Council, and no one in the whole fucked-up bureaucracy decent enough to tell me how long I was to wait. The sadism! And of course the bus wasn't coming at all ...

had decided even before the post was advertised that it was not going to arrive at *my* stop. So how could I even summon up the guts to continue with a *personal* essay?

As soon as I can establish a rhythm of work, I should return to the MS.

The banning? The Chief Minister here is taking up the matter with the Minister of Justice and the other biggies. We'll see, of course if it is lifted, you could easily do *Down Second Avenue* – and more perhaps. I'll send you a copy – the American edition (paper) which has an introduction. The original Faber edition doesn't have an introduction. I think myself it can be omitted here as it was meant for a foreign audience.

It would be just great if you could come up. Now I'm in the civil service, my mobility is restricted somewhat, because I could only drive down south on Friday afternoon. If you came up north, you could either go to Pietersburg (Holiday Inn) and come to *Lebowakgomo*, 50 km south-east (all tarmac). This is the 'town' stated to be the capital – it's still being built up. Or you could shake down in a Potgietersrus motel and drive NE to Lebowakgomo – through Zebediela – 70 km, all tarmac. We've a small room we pretend is a guest room. It has a comfortable ¾ bed. We use paraffin lamps and candles, but we're better situated for space and cleanliness than our brothers and sisters in all municipal townships in *any* urban area. So if you don't mind, you're welcome. We don't have a house phone, the office is Chuenespoort 66. I'll be out to the schools everyday except Fridays the rest of April and all of May. The week of 8-14 May, however, I'll be home as I'm running a course here. Weekends, including Fridays, I'm home. I only travel out weekdays. Take your pick.

Warmest regards,

Zeke

Chuenespoort

Dear Tim,

Thanks for your letter. The interview was impressive, serious, open. Nothing like the burlesque I attended at Pretoria for the Sovenga interview: A barbed-wire burlesque, that was (to coin a phrase). The Wits one was really elevated. I was invited to state the things I want to do and am doing. I was also asked if I would like to lecture in the Comparative Literature programme. I jumped at it. In the English Dept? I said yes, although not as enthusiastically.

In the African Institute? This was taken for granted. It gave me the idea that they could use me in both Comparative Literature and African Institute.

D asked if I would settle for a 3 year contract or so. I said yes, but would hope for something permanent later. I explained the mechanics of living (for myself and Rebecca). We wouldn't go into a municipal box and wouldn't want to. Physically impossible. C asked if Dube would fall in that category. I said no, but didn't press the point that I still find Soweto unliveable – Dube or no Dube .... A fellow in History – I forget the name – asked what my attitude would be towards teaching in a university where most Africans are excluded. I explained that when Guy Butler first asked me, before we left Philadelphia, I wondered if it would be morally defensible, even though Wits does not uphold that policy. But I could arrange an accommodation within myself whereby I could teach and compensate by doing research that is based among Africans.

Also if I felt that Wits was seriously involved in extra-mural teaching among blacks, that would also be a compensation. But I left them in no doubt that I'm keen to teach at Wits .... C asked, by the way, if I wouldn't feel it was worthwhile bringing my experience and culture to the consciousness of white students and faculty at Wits .... My reply was that it depends on how many years one still had in one's life: it's a long-term mission – that of educating the white community, 'Well I've been doing that all my life,' he remarked (sic). Let's hope for the best.

Apologies for imposing on us? Crap!

We were just too happy to have you and to get to know Kathy. Rebecca has the talent to whip up anything at short notice and think nothing of it. Anytime you drop in and we're going to eat, we're going to feed you too. What pity, though Tzaneen didn't yield a duck. Rebecca is superb in preparing *canard à l'orange*. But Tzaneen! But then, why not? It's a neat little cracker town, and damn it, even a duck they should have. There goes my myth about Northern hospitality!

We'll keep in touch. When we're next in Johannesburg, we should drop in on you, if you give us your home address and directions.

Warmest regards to K. For now Cheerio, and thanks for everything.

Zeke

P.S. Hooray! Just after I had enclosed your letter in an envelope, a letter arrived from Rhodes. The Registrar says they are offering me a Fellowship for 3 calendar months in the University's Institute for the Study of English in Africa, 'to enable me to initiate, pursue or complete research on a topic of your choice in the field of English in Africa'.

Tenable at Rhodes, where an office and secretarial services in the Institute will be put at my disposal. Furnished accommodation available on campus if I desire it. One public lecture on African Literature and possible contribution I 'might wish to make to the English Dept's 2nd year course *English in Africa* in form of seminars or discussions or lectures would be greatly appreciated'. Well, since I'm a thoroughgoing romantic, I can't possibly be bruised by taking the offer. Romantic in the sense in which I spoke of 'morally defensible' and all. By which I also mean that my romantic mind is so overwhelmingly thus that I can afford to make these adjustments and accommodations, I hinted at ...

So now I shall write to them tomorrow to say yes, – but explain that it will be next year. I should imagine that when the Wits offer (if any) does come, they can wait for me to return from Rhodes. On the other hand, this might clash with other conditions I'm not yet aware of since I don't yet know Wits' mind: to begin with the 1979 academic year? I don't know. I've to take the Fellowship at Rhodes before the 1st August 1979, according to the Reg's letter. I could open the academic year at R and then start at Wits, which so far seems to promise the longest tenure.

Thought I should let you know of this.

Tennessee
10 May 1978

Dear Dr Mphahlele

I met you in 1976-77 while a fellow at the Moton Center in Philadelphia. Recently, I read of your decision to return to your country and some of the events which have occurred since your return. This letter is to say I admire the stance you have taken relative to your responsibility to your people, specifically your position on the transcendence of work over self-involvement and self-pity. Much too often, we hear of persons who allow the sun of social responsibility to be eclipsed by their self-moons. It was encouraging to read of your decision to enter the camp of those who live by their convictions. Undoubtedly, your work will add to your people's struggle.

It was a pleasure meeting you and I hope our paths may again cross someday.

Unity and struggle,
Dorothy Granberry-Stewart, Ph.D.

Canada

23 May 1978

Dear Zeke

I was terribly pleased to receive your charming letter a few days ago. It meant a great deal to me, and I was most interested to hear about your recent activities.

I returned to South Africa for the first time in fifteen years this past Christmas. It was a strange experience – a combination of trauma, sentiments, remembrance and longing. Seeing my parents again, after all this time – old friends – the places of one's childhood and youth – the beauty of the country. I am sure you know the feeling. The trauma came when I discussed the country with these people I knew and loved – and experienced their prejudice and fear – not all of them but sufficient to make me realize that I would never again be able to live in that kind of society.

During the one day I spent in Cape Town, I visited Ursula Barnett (to my surprise, she lives only a few blocks away from my brother). We had an interesting discussion on South African literature, and black writing in particular. I had corresponded with her a few times during the months preceding my visit, prompted by her book about you, which I had read with great interest. She told me that you had moved back to South Africa, which rather surprised me at the time.

I have always been interested in writing, although I have never produced anything worthwhile, due mainly to laziness and a lack of imagination. However I had planned to produce something from my trip, a sort of personal narrative, recounting my impressions after an absence of fifteen years, about my past attitudes to South Africa's problems – along the lines of an introspective 'return to Goli' – perhaps to be titled 'Confessions of a white South African'. But I don't know if this is going to be possible, as I tend to be a bit *too* introspective about myself and about my feelings for and attitude towards South Africa.

I would really like to continue corresponding to you, views on a variety of subjects, and learn about your current activities.

And also, if any of your children ever find themselves in our part of the world, we would be delighted to receive a visit or a telephone call. [...] is just across the river from Detroit, and the manner in which people move about in North America, it is quite likely that our paths could cross.

Yours very sincerely

Conrad Reitz

Johannesburg
30 May 1978

Dear Dr. Mphahlele,

A friend of mine is compiling a dictionary of writers in the English language, for a series to be published in Paris by Laffont, and has asked me to give her a hand with South Africa, 20th Century. Not very much space will be allotted to each writer, but I am anxious to submit only accurate material. The series is intended for wide middle-brow circulation.

I hope you won't mind my asking you therefore if you would supply some information. For each writer they need a short biography (date and place of birth, schools attended, further education, degrees, prizes, awards, travels, professional career). There is a 2nd section dealing with his/her place in SA (and where applicable, world) literature, innovations, experiments, noteworthy aspects, and the themes the writer is involved with. Thirdly a complete list of published works is required, with publisher and date for each, and a very brief indication of what each is. In the case of major works, an outline of the content as well. It is not necessary to list contributions to magazines, journals etc.

In your case, as you know, there is quite a lot of material available. I'm not too happy with Janheinz Jahn, who purports to give comprehensive information, in those few areas where I think I can judge. For example, was it ever possible to 'prepare for one's matric' at Unisa? I take it your 2nd degree at Unisa was a BA Hons. This isn't said. Therefore I wonder if the rest of his information is reliable. The names of schools you attended before Adam's Mission are not given. Could you also fill in the gap between 1972 and now: biography and publications.

Considering my own ignorance in matters literary, I feel you will very likely prefer to vet your own entry, as it were, which is why I'm taking the liberty of asking you.

With French readers in mind, I have a couple of questions. I know that *Down Second Avenue* was translated into French. Is it correct that its title was *Au bas de la Deuxiéme Avenue*? If any of your other works has been translated into *French*, could you give me the title it received?

Since you have written short stories, essays, criticism and at least one novel and an autobiographical work, what do you like to be called? We have categories, namely poet, novelist, playwright, essayist, polemecist, critic and writer. Do you like just writer, or a combination of some of the others?

I'll be very grateful if you are prepared to help. If you don't want to be involved, or haven't the time, could you send me a post card to that effect, and

I'll do the best I can with what I can find. Naturally if you're going to be in Johannesburg in the very near future, and would be prepared to see me, I'd like that. My phone no. is 642-3554, and telegraphic address Malaprop Johannesburg. Unfortunately I have to hurry with this and won't be able to work on it after the end of June.

Yours sincerely,

(Mrs) Verna Hunt

Hillcrest

30 May 1978

Dear Ezekiel

It was a great task to compress your biography into 200 words. I am sure that *The Star* has no conception of how long this work of compression takes. I picked out about 30 facts from all the material that you sent me, and I am enclosing a copy of the final result.

After re-reading *Down Second Avenue* and listening to your lecture, I am convinced that a book on exile and return would be something worth writing. It is quite clear that you have a deep feeling for the country to which you went at the early age of five.

With best wishes

Yours sincerely

Alan Paton

PS & tit for tat. Any chance of my being able to read the piece you did on Higher Education in South Africa?

Johannesburg

14 June 1978

Dear Dr. Mphahlele,

I do appreciate your taking the time and trouble to reply to my letter. Your c.v. is the greatest possible help, especially in providing data on the last three or four years. I'll put you in, as you say, as P(oète), CR(itique) *et* R(omancier), & possibly as NOUV (elliste) though my friend dislikes this term in French, and that isn't an order of preference or judgment.

Thank you for the explanation of your Unisa matric. Restores some of my confidence in Janheinz Jahn, a good thing as for some of the lesser known writers he's the fullest source I've found so far.

With what I've got now, I'll have no excuse to phone you or to say I need to see you if you come to Johannesburg. Needless to say, I'd like to meet you, just for my own pleasure, and the more so after your remark about John and your running argument. You may well imagine that your next comment, 'why should I bore you with that' made me smile because I know that you know that 'bore' could hardly be the word. Things about you and your thinking interest me very much, and the fact of that personal contact with John only adds to that interest, jointly and severally as it were. The trouble is, I have really nothing stimulating to offer you in return, which is why I won't try to press you into a meeting if you do come to Johannesburg. BUT I'd like to leave it to you to see whether you have a spare evening or lunch-time if you come, and if so, to give me a ring. *La vie,* as you say, *est difficile,* and I'd better say right now that it's possible I couldn't ask you to come to my flat, because I have given it up to my daughter of 21, who has had a sort of psychological breakdown and during more or less lengthy periods can't accept my presence in there at all. I have moved next door for this reason, where I can't entertain as I'm not *chez moi*, except maybe for tea or something. So I might have to invite you to a restaurant, if you didn't object. On the other hand, my daughter could be better quite soon, and then we could sit around comfortably in my place. I don't normally trot out lengthy explanations about all this, I simply don't invite anyone around. My address and phone no. still hold, and if you leave me a message I can phone you back.

You won't want to see the dictionary. My Parisian friend insists it's going to be horrifying to the scholarly. The entries will be alphabetical and not segregated nationally, so I could ask her to send me the volume you're in – but you won't get an idea from that of all the horrors I'll have perpetrated on SA writers, or what she's done with the rest of the world. Perhaps we should tell the Alliance to get the complete dictionary!

Thank you especially for fitting a letter to me into your tight schedule, and for answering all my questions. And I do hope we will be able to meet, if it suits you, and whenever it does.

Yours sincerely,
Verna Hunt

15 June 1978

Dearest Zeke

So good hearing from you and so sorry that it has taken me so very long to answer. It has been a rough semester – a lot of writing, traveling and teaching. Also some expected personal confrontations with this gov't (more about that at a later date).

I miss you and Rebecca so very much. And I hope you two let me know if I can help in any way. I'm quite serious about the latter.

The children are out of school now. Growing, Getting quite 'bad'. They had a fine school year. It's a struggle to keep them in that school. So expensive.

I've just finished 3 books. Am looking forward to a fall publication. Will of course send you copies.

You sound strong Zeke. Your last letter tingled with electricity – a recharging of juices and life forces. I know it's a struggle for you and Rebecca. But I for one am so proud of your stance. No matter for how long. It is a dance/walk of courage you and Rebecca have been doing!

George Lamming stayed here for 6 months – from Jan to June 12th – he's just recently returned to England. He's a brilliant man.[1] And our house grew accustomed to his walk. We miss him already.

The children and I will be traveling to Barbados from June 26-July 11th. We look forward to our first vacation in 12 years! We'll write you from there.

Now for some gossip – what little I know – Houston Baker was in California for the year. He'll be back at the University of Pennsylvania in the Fall – then again in the spring semester (He's a Guggenheim [Fellow]). I haven't heard from him at all. Cheryl Payi, his assistant has left Penn. Further I don't know. Mayor Rizzo has decided to run for a 3rd term – means a revision of the charter which he is pushing for. Phila remains a southern town located on an eastern shore – supporting her middle class Blacks and her white/racists at the same time. Doing very little for the poor. I'll be teaching 3 courses in spring, women in literature, […] or writing poetry, contemporary Black Poets – more later.

Love

Sonia Sanchez

1 George Lamming, author, inter alia, of *In the Castle of My Skin* (McGraw-Hill 1954) and *The Emigrants* (McGraw-Hill 1955). Born in Barbados in 1927 he taught in Trinidad before moving to England in 1951. He returned to the University of the West Indies in 1967. In addition to his visiting

position at the University of Pennsylvania in the United States he spent time in Denmark, Australia and Tanzania.

Mphahlele
26 June 1978

Dear Prof Hodge,

I have for a long time been wanting to write and respond to your kind letter and English programmes at the University of Transkei. Field work prevented me, and I'm sorry for this silence. I'm back to my desk now and yours is the first of the pile I must tackle.

Thanks very much indeed for the syllabus and for making me feel that I'd be welcome in the Department, that I could contribute something to the ideals you have set for yourselves.

Your comments on South African universities and their obsession with the journalist approach – the worst side of the New Critics – strikes a chord in me that tells me that you and I would make a formidable team for pulling our students towards the more rational approach to literature (and art in general – or rather the arts). Your views excited me to the point that I decided at once to respond positively to any invitation to come to University of Transkei. I myself began with UNISA, so that I was apprenticed in journalist criticism. I should say that in all fairness my late professor, Edward Davis, did encourage me to relate the literary image to life, although the history of ideas, culture, were never adequately confronted. David's ideas of 'life' in this context were the general ones that concern 'literature and morality' or 'literature and belief'. 'Moral' was always an elusively defined value. My contact with African literature and with those American critics who go beyond formalism – to ontology (which embraces culture, social focus etc) corrected my squint. I'm with you all the way and find your Honours programme simply the most fascinating, the most liberal and forward-looking I have seen in this country.

When Manganyi first spoke to me about the possibility of coming to the Transkei, I wasn't sure if I'd like to do it. But after reading your letter and seeing the programmes, I felt there's where I want to be. Then, alas, we met on Saturday 25th and he told me the sad news that the authorities have instructed the University not to proceed any further in trying to bring me out south.[1] Wild questions are beginning to plague me: Did I return home to be a prisoner in Lebowa (where I am)? What's the sense of it all? But something deeper also tells me this is where it's at – and 'where' takes in all of the land called South Africa.

We'll wait and see, maybe reason will yet prevail.

Best wishes and thanks again,

Yours ever,

E. Mphahlele

[1] Chabani Manganyi comments, 'This was the one occasion in the early years of the University of Transkei known to me on which the Transkei government intervened directly to stop the appointment of an academic approved by the Senate. It was too soon after the University of the North episode for there not to have been a connection between the two non-academic decisions!'

Benoni

5 July 1978

Dear Uncle Ezeke,

This letter is somewhat late. I've been thinking of sending you a telegram to apologize for the fact that I did not show up for the Pretoria meeting. There were too many forces against my attending it. I didn't receive your invitation until the following Monday evening when I returned home from work. Believe me, this is the second time this happens to me. 2 years ago I was invited to a farewell function to take place on a Saturday evening. Someone was leaving the country to study overseas and possibly live outside the country for the foreseeable future. I read the invitation at the time he must have been checking in at Jan Smuts. I don't seem to be winning with our postal system!

How did the whole thing go! I've tried to get hold of Gedumizi Buthelezi because I noticed you said you had invited her. But I've not been so lucky.

There have been developments around here. I was co-opted to a body charged with the duty of founding a black-orientated organization for artists. We've gone so far as to name it the 'FEDERATED UNION OF BLACK ARTS (FUBA)' and it seems I'm going to work for it full time as soon as funds became available. Our first project has been put down tentatively as a festival of black arts to be held in September. Soweto has been suggested for the venue. But more about this whole thing later. We are trying to secure premises as well and if the Dorkay House trustees agree to step down, we want to make that our base. We are at the point of talking to various parties at the moment.

I cannot claim to have studied your memo thoroughly but I do believe your aims and ours this side have much in common. Much as I have already indicated a willingness to work full time for the cause of black arts, I am worried about its funding. If I had to judge it by the frustrations of *New Classic* and *Sketch* only, I wouldn't want to touch the job. But I do have a certain faith in this matter. Guys who are able to go overseas and talk English, as the people say, paint a very rosy picture of fund raising. I suppose my own handicaps related to the passport make me skeptical.

At last I've received a bit of cash for *New Classic* and *Sketch*. I'd be glad to receive anything from your contacts around there.

Best wishes,

Sipho

Natal

24 July 1978

Dear Zik,

Further to my recent telephone conversation with you I may just mention that I subsequently saw Gatsha Buthelezi and he informed me that his government had officially applied for your de-listing following upon my representations. I have not again heard from the Bophuthatswana government and I shall in the near future drop them a line again.

The university is still presently on vacation and I shall take up the matter of a visit by yourself with the people concerned in the near future. I am very sorry that nothing will apparently develop along the lines proposed previously but it was simply impossible to get the people in the English department to show a bit of dynamism much as they support the idea. I believe, however, that there will soon be a vacancy for a senior lecturer in the department and I would strongly urge you to apply. I am almost certain that you could walk the application. It may perhaps be a good thing if you were to write to the Registrar about vacancies in the English department.

Hoping you are keeping well and hoping especially to see you again soon,

I remain,

Yours sincerely,

Barend van Niekerk

30 July 1978

Dear Teresa,

Here's the money for Puso's medical bill. I am sending by the same mail a bank draft to Matt Black Jr. for $411 – $200 of which is for you. I've told him in a covering letter to ring you and say the money has arrived. You can arrange how you can collect it. ... Soon as I receive your statement of maintenance costs, notarized, we can send out something equal to what you propose will meet the cost of keeping Puso. Remember that the statement was to approximate $450, which the bank can allow for without prior application to Exchange Control .... You should, in a covering letter to me, say what you will settle for as subsidy to maintain that fellow. ...

Just now we want you to recuperate and get back to your state of fitness. So let us know what has been done in hospital, and how you are etc.

I've reverted to the old address, as you'll notice. The Education Dept one is still ok and looks more innocent. Continue to use it (on second thought).

The University of the Witwatersrand (Wits) is going to offer me a lectureship, most likely in Comparative Literature + African Studies Center. The sooner I get out of this service dump the better for my sanity. Meantime, a man visited us yesterday – from Lesotho, on a mission to ask me to head an institute of Southern African Studies that National University of Lesotho is setting up, with UNESCO help. I told him I'm interested and felt quite flattered when he said it would be worth it for a group from down there to come north for further discussions. So they'll come. Will see which is more appropriate. Meantime your Mum says *Zilch!* – she's not leaving from here to become an expatriate again, but says I *should* take the offer for my own peace of mind. I appreciate the attitude immensely. Also, we must not lose this house, and she has just started working at a job that will only be meaningful if she operates it herself. And here she's in the right milieu for the job. We'll keep you informed. Luckily Roma isn't far from here and I can easily come back once a month. I've long been gunning for UNESCO connection, and it seems *this* is where it's at. Wits has the advantage of a milieu – I'll be among home folks – and cultural activity is simply a jumping joint – lots going on. Whatever way I choose that will be as it should be.

Have just accepted an award from Rhodes University in Grahamstown, Cape Province (one of the English-medium universities) to take up a two-month research fellowship. I'll teach some, and work on my new book I started soon after arriving here. Should be able to finish it then. This will be Feb-March '79. Will take leave from this job, although I feel it in my bones that come Jan '79 I shall have landed a better job – a campus operation – either Wits or Roma.

Hey, take care,

Love you,

Ntate

P.S. By the way, you once asked me where a certain classical tune came from (in Wayne it was). You thought it was from a record. Right. I knew at the time it was from Mozart – what of his wasn't sure. I was playing a record when the tune hit me. Well, here goes: the record has two symphonies by Mozart, and wherever I've seen an album, they are always a pair: Symphony 41 ('Jupiter') and Symphony 35 ('Haffner'). The names in brackets are commonly used among musical people to refer to the Symphonies. When you say Mozart's 'Jupiter' they know the number of the Symphony.

Johannesburg

2 August 1978

Dear Professor Mphahlele,

Mr. Kirkwood of Ravan Press has asked me to look over your novel *CHIRUNDU* and consult with you over emendations before going to press. I send you herewith the first two pages of my suggestions and queries. I must explain the conversions I have used to indicate the place and the alteration I am suggesting. I number by page, paragraph and line, using Roman numerals for the paragraph (e.g. 26ii5 meaning Page 26, second paragraph, fifth line). Where I have counted lines or paragraphs from below, I have used a minus sign (1-ii-1, i.e. Page 1 second last paragraph, last line).

I use an equals sign (=) to mean 'should be replaced by'. To indicate the deletion of a word or passage I use the symbol 'x'. To indicate a word or phrase to be inserted I quote the immediate context with the insertion marked, beginning and end, by the symbol '^' (e.g. 'over him ^after^ the two years' means that 'after' is to be inserted between 'over him' and 'the two years').

Finally, for my own comments I use capital letters to distinguish them from quotations, and in cases where I am only half hearted about my suggestion I follow it with a bracketed question mark.

I trust this explanation is not confusing. It may be redundant anyway.

I wonder if you remember meeting me many years ago when I came to see you at the offices of *DRUM* magazine to ask you for permission to publish a story of yours (or was it two?) in the *PURPLE RENOSTER*.

I almost forgot to say that I shall be waiting for your responses to my suggestions. We shall take it that where you make no comment you accept the alteration.

Yours sincerely
Lionel Abrahams

Minister van Onderwys en Opleiding
Ministry of Education and Training
Pretoria
7 August 1978

Dear Prof Purcell

APPOINTMENT OF PROF E MPHAHLELE

With further reference to your letter of 19 May 1978 I wish to advise you by direction of the Honourable WA Cruywagen, Minister of Education and Training of the Republic of South Africa that the sentiments you have expressed on behalf of Dr Mphahlele, who has been a former colleague of yours, are understandable and are also appreciated.

I wish to assure you however, that the decision not to appoint Dr Mphahlele to the position for which he had applied, was motivated solely by a sense of responsibility to the people concerned after careful consideration had been given to all the information and facts at my Minister's disposal. I have no doubt that the University has accepted my Minister's ruling in that light.

Yours faithfully
PRIVATE SECRETARY

Benoni
9 August 1978

Dear Uncle Ezek,

Many thanks for your letters. What a pity we have to resort to paper in order to communicate even the essentials of our lives. Other people would have had no problems catching a plane or hiring a car at this hour.

I feel hemmed in by a sense of urgency: so much seems to be happening that I wonder if I'll manage to remain on course all the time.

I think your second letter should be considered point for point. And to help myself, I am sending herewith a copy of the press release. I do hope it will throw a bit more light on some of the issues you have raised. Further I might add:

1. We want to cater for both the professional and amateur or beginner. Hopefully in the next 3 to 4 wks we will be starting our schools project which will entail our men conducting workshop classes in drama and plastic arts for a couple of months. We shall be concentrating our efforts in Soweto. Then we will move to the East Rand and then the West Rand. Because we have had inquiries from the Vaal Complex, we might have to investigate the possibility of outlets there sooner than we would have done. If we had the money things would move faster. Although we cannot claim to have highly qualified personnel in some of the things we want to do, we believe some of our people are well qualified to tackle some of the problems we encounter in life and they can give enough light until the better qualified people are available. I am encouraged by the spirit that prevails around us. We have our teething problems and detractors but these seem to count for naught. The men want to carry on.

   I shall forward to you a copy of the constitution as soon as it is ready. We hope to call a meeting for its approval sometime next month.

2. We have writers already in FUBA. We are going to establish contact with PEN International (JHB branch) as soon as it comes off the ground. I see FUBA providing a lot of facilities to organizations that will not be in a position to have such. I'm hoping that the workshops on creative writing will rest heavily on PEN while the journalism classes will depend on WASA [Writers Association of South Africa].

3. FUBA will always have an African Stamp. To say we are non-racial seems to me to be an accommodation for Indians and Coloureds.

I think I've covered a lot of the FUBA ground. I want to raise another issue with you. Last Saturday (5th) I was invited to a meeting which appeared to have been initiated by the Afrikaans writers Guilds. Present were several writers including Nadine, Lionel Abrahams, Essop Patel, Ahmed and André Brink (in the chair). The purpose of the meeting was to find out if writers belonging to the Afrikaans and English writers Guilds and PEN (JHB) could work together toward a conference which would be held in Gaborone next year. The reason for holding it in Gaborone was so that exiled writers could attend. Because I was slightly late for the meeting, I kept quiet for a while and allowed others to say their say. I was feeling something growing within me although I couldn't say what it was. After a while I realized that I was suppressing a feeling to scream. At this point those who spoke were debating whether it should be the Afrikaans body or PEN to call the conference. By then I couldn't contain myself and I spoke up against meeting exiled writers when local black writers have not been heard. The upshot was that I was asked to investigate how black writers would react to a conference in Dec/Jan in JHB. I thought of you and Richard Rive. Please let me know how you feel.

Sipho

Johannesburg
27 August 1978

Dear Zeke

Thank you for your warm friendly letter. It made my day, the day it arrived. Over the years you've grown into something of a legend, and that was why I addressed you so tentatively in my first letter – and after all it's been a long long time and you may well have forgotten our one brief meeting. The story you gave me for *PR* was 'The woman walks out', which afterwards found its place in *Down Second Avenue*.

The regeneration of the JHB PEN centre has produced hectic activity for writers here over the past couple of weeks, and I blame this partly for my slowness in completing my notes on *CHIRUNDU* for you, but here the rest of them are now – and somewhat less of them than I estimated there would be. I must say, I find it a fine, substantial, original novel. I am particularly engaged by the characterizations – so clear yet so richly complex. Among other things, my political education has been palpably advanced. I am reminded how deprived we have all been by that pernicious, idiotic gagging clause, and I certainly hope it is not going to obstruct present publication plans.

In my notes I have not recorded every instance of American spelling, so if you agree to de-Americanise, someone will have to hunt through the text for the words that need correction. By the way, Mike wanted me to ask you whether you would be marking the accepted corrections on a copy for the printer, or whether you would have us make the corrections on the copy I have here.

I ought to tell you that during the past year your name came up in a crucial way during a controversial correspondence I had with Ursula Barnett over the place of the white writer in South African literature, and that I intend publishing this debate in an annual anthology I edit called *QUARRY*. I hope you don't mind.

Perhaps we will meet when you come down here to run the workshop for PEN.

Hope so.

Warm regards.

Lionel

Chuenespoort

5 September 1978

Dear Tim,

Still waiting with bated breath. I keep hoping that I'm not being betrayed by my idealism – that Wits University will see me as other institutions don't ...

I should be sending you a proposal for Ford Foundation which I spoke to them about a few months ago and they indicated that they would consider a small grant for transport across 3 territories. I am asking you to write a letter to back up the value of such research. Ford usually wants two persons who know the applicant to (a) say how well they know him as a human being, in his professional capacity, as a writer (as in my case) as one whom you consider most capable of handling the relevant research with more than a reasonable possibility of his producing commendable results; (b) say how essential and valuable the research is in the field or discipline the person is working in. You could mention that you have heard me lecture blah blah blah – that sort of testimonial.

Please direct it to Mr William Carmichael, The Ford Foundation, International Division, 320 E 43rd St., New York, NY 10017, USA and mail in the enclosed envelope.

It will be helpful to mention in what capacity at Wits you are recommending me for a grant to execute the research (put this latter part concerning the grant in these general terms).

I reckon that even if Wits should employ me, I shall need that extra assistance to supplement what the university allows (if at all) for promoting a research scholar.

The enclosed cheque: from the sublime to the narcotic and celestial. Would you kindly buy me tobacco? Johannesburg is the only place where I can buy it. It's *Capstan* (Medium) tobacco, and they sell it at Mickey Bass, Market St., off Harrison. Buy as many tins as is possible, leaving an allowance of so much for postage.

Thanks in advance for all this.

Rebecca joins in sending you, Kathy and the kids warmest greetings.

Love,

Zeke

8 September 1978

Dear Teresa,

It is a relief to hear that the cheques arrived – I was so worried, as I posted them here on 31 July! Disgusting the time a letter takes across the Atlantic. The average used to be 9 days.

I hope you sort out your study programme, and the financial arrangements. We are really thrilled to see you set your mind on the degree and even setting your sights higher. Why not? You've the drive, motivation, courage and ability. You certainly have plenty of hours to take, let's hope the strain won't be a set-back. We had hoped also to hear brighter news re your health.

I wrote in my last letter that the IIE is looking for candidates to sponsor at university, and suggested you try them.

...

If you have occasion to speak to Chabi tell him I'm waiting for a reply to my letter – he should tell us what he wants to do education-wise and we'll help, but he's got to come clean and be on the level with us.

The Ns came through here. Actually slept in our house. But M is neurotic. Scared of the dark, uneasy all the time, like he's waiting for some enemy that's laid a siege on him to knock at the door. Yet J is so self-confident and didn't mind the inconveniences. Your Mum gave them your dress, whatever you call these things. Pretty stuff.

Much love,

Ntate

P.S. What have you decided about your address – should we use the Univ one or your apt? I asked my agent in N.Y to send you something whenever it's due at the Univ address, so keep checking there. Thinking further about the man N, he must have been a bed-wetter.

17 October 1978

Ma chère Teresa

C'est bien ça! Un petit mot en Français – parfait! Avec de la patience, tu ne trouverais pas les leçons trés difficiles. Je comprends bien ceux que tu dis – la traduction d'une langue étrangée est beaucoup plus facile que parler et écrire.[1] Speaking it must come from being surrounded between mass media and society and its theoretical basis on the one hand and your actual writing for broadcasting on the other do not surprise me. And also it's exasperating, as you found it, to have to do a double-think and double-feel when you separate your real self from the significance deeper than the surface lead. As long as you are able to sense the distinction, and are able to see through that silver-medal woman and her dramatics, you're on the right path. You'll eventually think it through if you are persistent enough. All in all you sound happy and stimulated in the programme. Maintain, maintain!

Puso wrote from Denver. Doesn't say much. Simply that he wants to go to school, he's working at M's former joint ...

Still waiting to hear from Chabi again in Wayne. His last letter from there was full of hope and determination. And he's very articulate, too. I asked him, as I also did Mr Webber, his host, to send me a notarized statement of his college fees, etc. etc. Told him he must contribute half of his keep ($100) each month by working part-time. After starting this letter I remembered that I wanted to send this Internal Revenue cheque. Please keep it until we hear from Chabi and we'll tell you what to send him. But please *right away* send a cheque to our Tax accountant for $75 – Harry Hufendick, 5925 E. Evans, Suite 109-B, Denver, Colo. 80222. Say it's his Income Tax Returns fee. By the way, instead of sending 4 aerogram letters, which come on different days – 4, 2, 1 & 3, in that order, why not also save money by writing 4 airmail sheets from a pad for 31c – in an envelope?

Love from us,

Ntate

[1] That's good. A little word in French – perfect! With patience you won't find the lessons very difficult. I quite understand what you say, translating a foreign language is much easier than speaking or writing.

Claremont

31 October 1978

Dear Zeke

No doubt this will come as a major surprise. The intention is to shock you out of your wits. Yes, it is Richard Rive writing after years of silence. Actually I have been in purdah for longer than I care to remember. Somehow I have kept abreast of your movements, so have not been cut off entirely. Since last I saw you (in Paris?), I went to Columbia for an MA, returned to Cape Town, taught and did a B. Ed, then to Oxford where I did my D. Phil. I am at present head of the English Department at Hewat Training College (where incidentally I qualified as a teacher initially).

I was unwilling to go to UWC when I returned as feeling is very strong down here about staff joining the University. I share this. Cape Town University wanted me to teach *Middlemarch* and *Lord Jim* to white first year coogles from Constantia, a fate worse than death. No African or South African literature. The same old fight. All literature died with Hardy. *Hoe sê hulle? 'Dieselfde ou parcels net different labels'.*[1] So I opted for Hewat where I took over the Department after two years. I teach a healthy course in African literature. My students are superb, not very bright, but on the ball. We have had sit-ins every year since I have been here, and of course they were amongst the initiators in 1976. During a period of three months I tried to teach 'L'allegro' and every day was interrupted by something being burnt down, or teargas or police taking pot shots.[2] It wasn't much fun and played havoc with Milton, but he'll survive.

I am supposed to rewrite my Olive Schreiner thesis and edit the letters for Donker, but have no stomach for it.[3] Olive was fine while she lasted and strangely enough fitted in well with the twilight of Oxford, but she is somewhat out of place in robust, 1978 Cape Town. Also Donker is as tight-fisted as anyone I have yet encountered. He has reduced this to such a fine art so that no writer is safe. I wonder whether Sipho is on the dole already.[4] I must wriggle my way out of his clutches. Be careful of cultivated accents, even Dutch.

How's the family? I read *The Wanderers* I think in England and wondered as it wandered. I presume that you are writing at the moment. I have written two short stories this year, a helluva output for me, one I sent to *Drum* (remember? It was a magazine once) and the other to *Staffrider*. *Contrast* has gotten too precious for me.

Incidentally I have a grant (still getting them at ripe old senility) to do research at Texas. I presume your ghost still breathes there and they speak of

Mphahlele in muffled terms. (This is no joke. I have met people who feel that you must have died decades ago as you've become a legend. You know, Shakespeare, George Eliot and Zeke.) Don't worry, it is rapidly happening to me. People ask, have you met Achebe, Soyinka and Okigbo and you're still living? Be that as it may, I am going to America in January-July, to do some research at Texas and then a helluva lotta traveling in the States to the African literature departments wherever they are, bringing a breath of oppression and much goodwill.

I hope that when I return in July, I can come via Johannesburg, and then may be we can have a reunion 'And when that time comes which is the beginning of our end ...'. In either case, desultory as it is, I am extremely glad that I have renewed my correspondence with you. I am not married yet and now unlikely to be. The last before one, married while I was at Oxford (thank God, what a close shave) and the most recent, a buxom wench who cooks well, is at the time hoping to get political or marital asylum.[5]

When next I write I shall be in a more serious vein. By the way, where is Cosmo teaching? And Dennis. If you have addresses I shall appreciate them.

Love to Ribs, whatever kids are still at home and most of all yourself.

Richard Rive

1 What do they say? 'The same old parcels, just different labels.'

2 'L'allegro', John Milton's famous poem, which begins with the banishment of melancholy, written in 1631 or 1632 when the poet was a student at Cambridge.

3 Rive completed his doctorate as 'Olive Schreiner (1855-1920): A Biographical and Critical Study' (University of Oxford 1974). *Olive Schreiner, Letters 1871-1899*, co-edited with Russell Martin, appeared in 1987 (Cape Town: David Philip).

4 Sipho is Sipho Sepamla, known, by this stage as a poet, having published his collection *Hurry Up to It!* with AD Donker (Johannesburg 1975). He would later publish a novel about the Soweto uprising, *A Ride on the Whirlwind* (AD Donker 1981). One might speculate that Mphahlele's letter to Donker a week later, withdrawing *In Corner B and other stories*, was influenced by Rive.

5 In retrospect, Rive's concern not to disclose his homosexuality to the Mphahleles is worth noting. While his letter assumes solidarity on several fronts, this issue was clearly still beyond the pale.

Mphahlele

9 November 1978

Dear Adrian,

Hi! I thought I might be able to call you on the phone when I was in JHB last week running writers' workshops for P.E.N. but simply could not find the time to take breath.

I have been thinking a lot about my work, my writing etc and unless I do something drastic, I shall never be able to organize my time. My return may be just a retreat into futility.

I am slogging on with *Exile* but I will get it done. Meantime, I have decided that, as this listing is hanging over me like a swing axe, I should publish the *Selected Works* abroad *first*. By the time I'm unlisted, I hope, I shall have finished *Exile*. So would you please send me back the MS + copy of *In Corner B & other stories* – the package I proposed for *Selected Works*. I'm going to send it to my New York Publishers. When we return to a humane existence here – who knows? – there may still be some slot where Ezekiel Mphahlele can fit in on the SA literary landscape.

Will be glad to have the stuff back.

Meantime, cheerio for now.

Ezeke

Adelaide

14 November 1978

Dear Professor Mphahlele,

I am writing to you as Chairman of the Writers' Week Committee for the Adelaide Festival of Arts, 1980.

In past Writers' Weeks we have had notable writers such as Allen Ginsberg, Lawrence Ferlinghetti, Yevgeny Yevtushenko, Michael Frayn, John Updike, Anthony Burgess, Nadine Gordimer, Edna O'Brien, Andre Voznesensky, Sumner Locke Elliott, Hans Magnus Ensensberger, Leon Garfield, Ted Hughes, Adrian Mitchell, Wole Soyinka, Robie Macauley, John Rowe Townsend, Galway Kinnell and Margaret Atwood.

The Committee would be very pleased if you could let me know whether you would like to be our guest at Writers' Week in March 1980, if suitable arrangements can be made to cover all costs of your air fare and expenses in Australia.

The climate in Adelaide is perfect in March. South Australia grows some of the best wine in the world and Writers' Week is not bogged down in formalities.

I do hope you can let me have a favourable reply soon.

Yours sincerely,

Rosemary Wighton,

Chairman, Writers' Week Committee

Johannesburg

19 November 1978

My dear Eskia,

What fun to have a new name![1]

I like the idea of your book very much. Standard 5 always presents problems because children of this age can be so very mature or so very immature. I think the work you have chosen should be stimulating. Some of the things I did not know and enjoyed reading.

I am interested in your grading of African poetry in standards 5 and 6; African and English poetry in standards 7 and 8; and mainly narrative and descriptive work for st 8. I have been thinking of trying to do an anthology of narrative verse but wondered how to begin. So much good narrative verse has been used again and again and I feel that I lack the energy these days to start hunting for new things. Over to you ... With my blessings!

Thank you for mentioning my Longman anthologies. They were done when Frank was first ill in 1964 and they have been selling steadily every since. They are out of date and should be redone but Longman is not prepared to do anything about them. Books 1-5 appeared together. Book 6 was a wash-out. The cover was bad. It was not well printed and the choice of material left much to be desired. But the real reason for its failure was that it did not belong to any particular part of the school structure. I'd like to re-do it to fit in with the new structure. I wish Longman would let us do it together sometime.

By the way there is an error below 'The song of the Engine'. Book 4 is *People and Poetry* and Book 1 is *A Poem Today*. As a matter of interest Pat Lee was one of my old pupils – as were many of the people whose poems appear in the books. Today she is Pat Devenish and her husband lectures in law at the Coloured University in the Cape. She is a splendid girl and did wonderful work with speech and drama at the Indian Teacher's Training College here.

Sheila and I go to Qwa-qua to give a course next week and I hope to go to England in December if I can finish the work I have still to do for Via Afrika.

All the best to you both

Love

Norah Taylor

Let me know what happens about Wits

1 Mphahlele changed his given name, Ezekiel, to Es'kia when he returned from exile.

9 December 1978

Dear Teresa,

Haven't heard from you for a long time. Are you ill or just too busy with term work. Hope the latter only.

We haven't heard from Chabi ever since he indicated that he wanted to pick up the threads where he left off. You haven't said if you ever received the US Treasury cheque I sent. I asked you to keep it against a request from Chabi to start him off on college, and to pay Harry Hufendick, the Income Tax accountant (Denver). Sent 18 Oct. by registered mail.

I wrote to Motswiri and he replied. It seems tempers are sleeping once more, although he succeeds in making such a rattle and razzle when his temper's high that it echoes long after, throughout a truce. He should try a part as *Hunchback of Notre Dame*, swinging on the bell he's tolling continuously, with vengeance.

We are enlarging our house – the master bedroom, dining area, putting up a new kitchen so that the present one becomes a bathroom + toilet (our toilet & tubbles bathroom are outside!). When you visit us, you will only tell what it was from the existing pattern of a number of families. We're spending less than we would if we built a new house from the foundation because our houses are subsidized, so that for ours, actually worth R12,000 (c. $13,800), we paid a third of that and even pay instalments without mortgage interest! We are also putting up a huge study and pantry. We reckon we'll have a house worth some $21,000 – 3 bedrooms, lounge + dining, 2 bathrooms, storeroom, large kitchen. A fine deal. Your Mum is in charge of building operations and she is efficient. Knows what she wants, and can still draw on her experience as a girl watching her father getting houses up for renting.[1]

Will you be going in for treatment this winter? Hope the time is not intolerable for you. You'll have closed by the time this reaches you. Take care and much love from us.

Ntate

[1] In Sophiatown, where her family lived before she married Mphahlele in 1945.

Chuenespoort
9 December 1978

Dear Chabani,

It was good of you to send a reference letter to Ford Foundation. Thank you for it.

I am still trying to disengage from this Department, as it's a dead end for someone who wants to *do* things and not just talk about them. All kinds of obstructions are put in the way. But let me not gripe, there are people – several thousands, nay millions – who are doing jobs they don't derive an iota of inspiration from. At least I am earning a living.

I am asking you another favour and please bear with me. I was at NUL [National University of Lesotho], Roma, in mid-November, to give a lecture and at question time a student read publicly a statement, which was for me a moving tribute: to plead that I teach at NUL. Would I please accept if an offer is made? Signed by 103 English Department students. All this is in the presence of the Head of the Department and staff! I said I would not dismiss such an offer if it came.

The Head has followed it up and wants to know if I'm interested. I presume it would be a professor's rank (*à l'American*) I've said yes. I shudder at the nerve and wonder if I'm saying so *because* I was deeply moved by my reception and the students' tribute when my own country – or rather those who run our country are rejecting me. We'll see. My request: that you serve as a referee. I have two – Denver, Philadelphia and they want three. I've taken the liberty of giving your name and hope you don't take offense. They'll write.

I laugh at myself when I speculate on being an expatriate all over again, with expatriate allowances and all – colonial style! And I smelled the blood of retreaded expatriates spat out of Zambia, Kenya, India – when I was there. Lesotho, Botswana and Swaziland are the last catchments of the sediment! And I may be one – wow! But I must go back to the classroom, no matter how, as long as it's not a humiliation, and this will not be.

Warmest regards,

Love,

Zeke

29 December 1978

Dear Teresa,

Are you ill, in hospital or just too busy? Hope only the last possibility. This is a hurried note to send the enclosed exciting piece of news. It means those books of mine that were prohibited here because I was listed as 'unpublishable' will now be made available. Those banned under the Publications and Entertainment Law will stay prohibited. These come under the censorship law that applies even for unlisted persons.

Would you please send xeroxed copies to Cyndi Kahn, 2345 Leyden St., Denver, and to my agent, Ellen Levine, at Curtis Brown Ltd., 575 Madison Ave, New York NY 10022. Will be grateful.

Another piece of good news. Am starting work at the University of the Witwatersrand ('Wits') as Senior Research Fellow in the African Studies Institute. January is my notice month here. The National University of Lesotho has offered me a job, even possibly as chairman of English. But I just don't want to be an expatriate in an African country any more. Wits will put me closer to cultural activity – writers' workshops, the lot, and I must do intensive research. I shall look for single accommodation somewhere and come up here every other week – your Mum wants us to keep here and she'll continue in her present job. Besides the house extensions are still going on. We see the Wits job as a step to still greater things which are still vaguely defined in our minds. When you visit, the house will be sump'n else, I can tell you that.

We're boiling here, the rains will be in any time now. Out there – blizzards I guess, or how? Hear anything about the boys? Chabi has never come back to us since his solemn declaration he wants to go to college, to which I replied favourably. Boys, Boys!

Take care,

Much love,

Ntate

1979

Grahamstown

[Undated], early 1979

Dear Bernth,

Thanks for your note. To my shame I haven't been able to settle down to the review of Lewis N's book.[1] The request came when I was in the throes of moving from the US; then I was unsettled waiting for the inanities of life in this country to take their course, culminating in the giant inanity concerning the University of the North. When I realized there was a conspiracy, in which the *African* administrator had no mean role, to neutralize my presence, I wondered if my idealism had betrayed me. Things picked up when I was invited to Wits to become Senior Research Fellow in the African Studies Institute, (Tim Couzens', now headed by Charles Van Onselen – both v. fine guys). I shall return to Wits end of April, & will unpack my boxes to fish out Lewis's book to review it. Please be patient; it shall be done.

My address now will be African Studies Institute, University of the Witwatersrand, 1 Jan Smuts Ave., Joburg 2001, for all correspondence & RAL.

I was given a 2-month fellowship here which I took on after my first month with Wits (Feb). Am finishing a memoir on exile & return which I had started in Phila. André [De Villiers] invited me, which I think was v. sporting of him.

Say Hi to Richard [Rive] & say he's a lucky bastard to be able to make trips in & out, like he has summer & winter cottages abroad. Often I long for those stimulating American encounters, but I always come back to the basic conviction that it was the right things for us to return here, no matter the inanities. And our people's reception – more important than anything else, has been most inspiring. The elite fringe that sees us as ghosts return to challenge or upset their emergent-Africa comfort – the counterparts of the Addison Gayles – one can dismiss as petty.[2] Actually one doesn't even have to deal with them in print like it was with A.G.

Warmest regards,

Zeke

[P.S.] Ravan Press in Jbg is bringing out my novel *CHIRUNDU*, which *no* American house that matters would accept. Some of their reservations, outside of the economics, are well taken.

1 Lewis Nkosi. Mphahlele never did find time to review Nkosi's *The Transplanted Heart: Essays on South Africa* (Benin City, Nigeria: Ethiope Publishing Corp 1975).

2 Addison Gayle Jr had published 'Under Western Eyes', a negative review of Mphahlele's *Voices in the Whirlwind* in *Black World* 22(9) 1973, pp 40-8. Mphahlele had responded in *Black World* 23(3)1974, pp 4-20, the same issue that carried Gayle's rejoinder, 'A Note to Ezekiel Mphahlele', on p 21.

Italy
17 January 1979

Dear Sir,

Let me first of all introduce myself. I am a last-year under-graduate at the Faculty of Modern Languages of the University of Udine. Since I spent most of my childhood in South Africa, I have decided to prepare my graduation thesis on a South African author. While looking through some books I happened to come across your poem 'Exile in Nigeria' which raised my enthusiasm; shortly after, I bought your autobiography, *Down Second Avenue*, and I thus decided on the author of my thesis. So I now have a few problems and questions to put to your kind attention.

The first is that I hope you have nothing against my carrying on with such a work, which would entail using excerpts and passages from your novels and poems.

Secondly, I don't know how and where to get hold of some of your books and articles. In this part of Italy there are no Departments and Schools of African Studies; moreover the biggest bookstores are no longer able to find your first books or those published in Africa. So do you perhaps have the addresses of the publishers of the list (of books) here with enclosed or have you yourself got copies or photocopies of them (for which – needless to say – I shall pay)?

Another problem is that my bibliography is still rather small; do you know of any critics who have written reviews, essays, dissertations or articles of criticism on your literary production? I would be most grateful if you could let me know, since a bibliography is always important, as you well know, and even more so in an Italian thesis.

Would you be interested in having *Down Second Avenue* translated into Italian in the not-too-distant future? If so, what are the conditions set down by you or the publishers for the translator? I would very much like to undertake a task of the sort.

Lastly, I hope you forgive me for disturbing you and for taking up so much of your time, but a thesis is an important part of a student's academic career. I hope also that, if the problems I have pointed out find a positive solution and I finally start working on my thesis, I may be allowed to keep in touch with you.

In awaiting your reply,

I am,

Yours sincerely,

(Flavio Urizzi)

The books I have not been able to find are:

1) *Man Must Live,* African Bookman, Cape Town 1946 (or 47?)
2) *The Living and the Dead*, Ibadan
3) *In Corner B*, Nairobi 1967
4) *Voices in the Whirlwind*, New York, Will and Wang 1972
5) all the poems scattered in various magazines and reviews.

Johannesburg

18 January 1979

Dear Houston,

Yes, I have myself felt bad about not writing when you were still at Stanford and since you've been back to the east I think it has something to do with my temperament. Whenever I'm spiritually down and don't find a sense of equilibrium, I tend to withdraw – away from friends. Because I feel friendship is only worthwhile when I can contribute buoyance, euphoria – generally a sense of well-being. So I failed to write. I could have written to Sonia [Sanchez] too, more than a single letter or so telling her about things. Now you've broken the ice and I am better placed than in the last year, I don't feel the need to skulk. Your request unfortunately, comes when I'm in the throes of changing jobs and when my residence in this country is not yet resolved. You see, I'm being treated as an immigrant, because it is argued that when I returned my SA passport on the acquisition of a British one, I was automatically relinguishing my SA nationality. All this means that I can neither use the British passport, which has expired and would in any case be invalid, as I'm trying to re-establish my SA nationality, nor can I be given a SA travel document until residence is made permanent. It's a long process. I'm sorry I cannot make it to the English get-together. Indeed, I would have loved to contribute something concerning literature this side of the Atlantic.

Sorry, too I did not cable, because I felt I should write a letter. A cable would be more worthwhile if it were not negative.

Having hung around for 7 months without a job, because I was waiting for the University of the North to reply and even employ me as head of English (that was crap that one), I found asylum in a booby hatch called the Department of Education, as a loony Inspector of Education, involving myself in the teaching of English in schools for the mentally sane. *Now* I have been appointed Senior Research Fellow at the above university. It's one of the English-medium 'open' universities, which are trying to plead with the government to open doors to African students. They have permission to employ the likes of me (mentally rehabilitated, *bien sûr*). I start 1st February. We'll keep our home base in the North – 350 km from here and Rebecca will keep the fires burning. I'll visit her weekends. She has a job as community social worker with the local government. I'll be back in my element at 'Wits', as it's called here (Witwatersrand) and am looking forward to it: research and lecturing. Rebecca's sense of euphoria never flags, you should know, and even when speculation about returning to Pennsylvania came up, she just put her foot down. 'I've returned home', she proclaimed. So, kind though, ... to keep the Pennsylvania slot open for 2 years, it seems certain we'll stay and make a go of it. There was a toss-up between Lesotho and Wits eventually and I decided not to be an expatriate again, unless I had my back to the wall. I am writing to Stuart [James] to let him know the latest developments.

Believe me, I feel sorry for myself that I cannot come to your get-together, but next year, maybe.

Love to you and Charlotte.

Love,

Zeke

Ljungby,

2 February 1979

Dear Mr. Mphahlele

You have perhaps already received a letter from Solveig Ryd, Växjö, Sweden. It was sent away to USA in December last year. Inspired by a series of lectures presenting African literature she started to write a paper about your autobiography *Down Second Avenue*. As I am very interested in African literature, too, she kindly invited me to be her co-writer. That's why you see a new name at the bottom of next page. Both of us are studying literary science at the University of Växjö.

Per Wästberg, Stockholm, has now informed us about your address in South Africa. He also sends his regards to you.

In *Down Second Avenue* you tell us about your thesis 'The Non-European Character in English Fiction'. We have chosen to study *your* description of the non-white man only – and if *you* are sermonizing (like Paton?). We want to find out, if you manage to transfer your thesis on your own work. We really mean that you have described characters of universal application. We are going to show that in our paper. But there are other problems. In the foreword of the anthology *'Afrika berättar'* Per Wästberg writes how difficult it is for an African author to reach his audience. What is your opinion? To which audience did you write *Down Second Avenue* and did it get through?

Your style reminds us about the style of the Russian Gorkij (perhaps about that of Dickens, too).

Did you write the book to a literary untrained audience? We then think of your short sentences; the language sounds more like spoken English than like written. Is it perhaps written for Jenny (the dedication)? – In the 'interludes' you use another style: Why? Has the book appeared in South Africa? And if so, what did/do they say about it? (We realize that there are twenty years between 1959 and 1979 ....)

We have got information about your biography till 1974. Would you please give us such information about your life and activities that you yourself think may be of interest when we complete your biography up to 1979. (Please, don't find our appeal impertinent). If you allow us, we are going to use your answers in our paper. It will be put before our teacher, university lecturer Jöran Mjöberg, Växjö, and his students. We want them to meet the man, the woman, some people in Africa's real life described in a close and thorough way – the good and bad points at the same time. We don't want them to meet the African as the primitive barbarian nor as the noble savage but as a human being like you and me.

It would please us very much if you answer our letter. Solveig Ryd and I send our kindest regards.

Yours sincerely,

Vivi-Anne Linderos

PS. If you answer, please tell us how to pronounce your name. DS.

Afrika berättar = Africa tells

Växjö and Ljungby are towns in the south part of Sweden.

Just now we have a white and beautiful winter with lots of snow.

It is so lovely that we hardly long for spring ... (Well, when you are clearing the snow away you have perhaps some other thoughts in your mind ....)

Lesotho

23 February 1979

Dear Professor Mphahlele,

Thank you very much for your letter. Let me say at once that I was hoping against hope that the reports of your appointment to Wits were not true and that you would be able to join the English Department here at NUL later in the year. Now I understand your position and I congratulate Wits on their exceptionally good fortune ... may be able to alliance you to Lesotho when the situation in the Republic has changed.

I'm sure I understand very well many of the implications for you of what you called 'the tyranny of place', and I surely do appreciate what returning to South Africa means for you. I regret that some of the more radical students here showed so little appreciation of your positions, they do tend to see things in very simplified terms and so some will learn in time that life does not present us with simple situations.[1]

As you will have guessed, the other members of the Department, particularly Njabulo, are all very disappointed that it has not been possible for you to join us. If I may speak for myself, I feel particularly sorry about it, having the responsibility of leading the Department here is an on-going process of development and response to the heads of modern Africa. I would have so much appreciated your advice and guidance, especially in the area of African Literature – not only in the planning and teaching of the courses, but in the whole field of African writing – just talking about the novelist, dramatists and poets and all the very important issues that young African students should be familiar with our concern about their studies. I sincerely hope that you will be able to visit us from time to time and help our students to appreciate more deeply their special heritage.

In the meantime I wish you many blessings in your life and on your family and I hope that one of the results of your presence at Wits will be that White students will come to appreciate the wonders of a world from which they have so far been excluded.

Yours sincerely,

A Tushy

[1] Elsewhere Mphahlele gives an account of this lecture at the University of Lesotho, at which he received sharp questions from young South African exiles about his return to South Africa (*Afrika My Music: An Autobiography, 1957-1983*. Johannesburg: Ravan 1984, p 250).

Grahamstown
March 1979

My dear Gunnar,

Yes, I'm afraid it won't be possible to take off for a stint so soon after joining Wits. I feel sorry for myself; because so often a wave of nostalgia sweeps over me and makes me feel as if I were choking – just thinking of solid hearts of gold like you and Vanja *et al*. Whenever I long to be back, it is Denver that is uppermost in my mind. *Mais, que faire?*[1] Tell John that I would have deemed it a great honour to fill his place, to sit on the maestro's very chair. And I dare say he would have felt greatly honoured too, to know that no better, no greater person than Zeke was keeping his seat warm! No, I really should say 'no other than'. Still, thanks for responding positively to my query, Gunnar.

I'm here at Rhodes for only two months – March and April. Will be back at Wits on 30th April. I was granted a Research Fellowship here and am finishing a memoir on *exile and return*, which I started in Philadelphia. I will certainly finish it. Today my publishers in Johannesburg phoned to say my novel will be out this afternoon – *Chirundu*. It's set in Zambia and I finished it in Denver, just before I left you. It has been on the road in the US all this time and my agent has been flogging it high and low, without success. The market, the market and all that sensible crap. It had to wait for me to return to the old country ...

Much love to you and Vanja. Say hi to Anna and Barn.

Love,
Zeke

Ribs has just phoned to say hold it and don't close the book on the visiting professorship, in spite of what I say inside. We might negotiate with Wits yet. The banning on my works here which also prevented any writer or speaker to quote me, has been lifted – after 12 years. Rejoice with me.

[1] But what is there to do?

Växjö

12 March 1979

Dear Mr. Mphahlele,

I am very happy to write to you and say I have got your letter. When starting with the paper, I looked in *Who's who in African Literature* and *A Readers Guide to African Literature*, but I could only follow you to 1970. So I called the African Institute in Uppsala and they thought, you were still in Denver (I think you have to visit Uppsala one more time and tell them certain things, Mr. Mphahlele). After sending the letter to Denver I did what I should have done immediate: I wrote to Per Wästberg, a man, who knows everything, and he was so nice and gave me your address.

I had an opponent to my paper, Vivi-Anne, but she asked me to be my co-writer, so that's the reason we are two now. Vivi-Anne followed this African course last year in Växjö together with me, and we both now know that we ought to know *much* more. I followed some series of lectures of African religions, geography, social conditions and so on; I think that is necessary for the understanding of the African Literature.

You might be interested in how we work with the paper? It is important to say at once: It is not a political paper but a literary paper. I have never been in Africa and know too little to write about – you know what I mean (I cannot use this awful word). Your opinion about negritude is quite o.k. for me too. As a matter of fact, I don't like saying *African* Literature, *Russian* novels etc, An author is an author for me, where ever he lives.

I began comparing the situation in Africa in the '50s with the situation in Sweden (and elsewhere) in the '30s, where we have so many autobiographies (perhaps you have read the autobiographies by Harry Martinson and Eyvind Johnsson, Nobelprizewinners in 1970's?). They were all inspired by Gorkij and so I compare you with Gorkij too. That is the starting-point.

After that we present you (thank you for helping us with the years after 1970) and give a summary about D. S. a. Here in Sweden we have to reply to a question when writing a paper, so we gave this question: Has Mr. Mphahlele succeeded in writing about people in D. S. a. without idealizing or making them barbaric? We also look upon the environment and the style.

As I was first, I took the best parts of course. I start with an analysis of the women: your grandmother in Maupaneng, your grandmother Hibila, auntie Dora, your mother Ma-Lebona, Rebone and Rebecca. It was a great pleasure to work with this.

Vivi-Anne has written about the men: your father, Dinku-Dikae, Boeta Lem,

Old Riba and Old Rametse, Big-Eyes, Kuzwi (you can be sure there are still Kuzwis in mathematics, I had one) etc.

With joint forces we then dissected you, that is to say, how you write about the person called Ezekiel. We took your words (in *African Writers Talking*, the interview with Pieterse, discussing the difficulties with writing a biography. Well, then Vivi-Anne wrote about the environment and I am still working with the style. (Thank you for replying my questions). In my way, writing the paper, you must understand that I compare you with other authors, to see, if there are any striking similarities between you and them.

As you said, I find the language direct; that is why I say some words about Gorkij and his autobiography trilogy. You have managed to write a humoristic novel and I suppose you have been inspired by Dickens way of writing – of course without Dicken's awfull sentimentality (for American export?). I go so far that I write that perhaps you have taken a little of the technique of the realistic sketch, so common in England in the 1830's.

When writing so humoristically, with ironic (sometimes sarcastic) commentary to all people, even to yourself, we find your novel more effective than for instance 'Paton's sermon'. For me it's one of the most critical books I ever read, because of your writing in this way. I hope you understand what I mean, – English is not my language.

I think, I found the key of the interludes: In a commentary by Michael Millgate to Steinbecks *The Grapes of Wrath* he says: 'Steinbeck's technical problem, like that of Theodore Dreiser, John Dos Passos and other American social novelists, was that of combining a story of individual human beings with a large body of social documentation. His solution was to present the fate of the Joads as a specific example of a general situation ... Throughout *The Grapes of Wrath* chapters telling the story of the Joads are juxtaposed with chapters evoking the larger story of the dust-bowl, the mass movement to California, and the problems facing the migrants once they had completed their long journey. The Joad chapters are linked with the "inter-chapters", as they are usually called, in a variety of ways ...'

I cannot explain your interludes in D. S. a. in another way. As a German teacher I taught for a while of Brecht with his 'Verfremdungseffekte', but no, Steinbeck must be right? You see, I have read no commentaries to your novel, but Per Wästberg told us, there is a monograph by Ursula Barnett in World Writers Series. We have ordered the book from the USA, but as usual one has to wait for weeks. Because we have no essays to work with, we work like happy amateurs, and I must tell you: it is much more interesting to be your own Columbus.

Last autumn I went to Germany and made an interview with a German lyrical poet. He is quite unknown (as almost every lyrical poet, if they don't have names like Senghor or Maozedong) and he told me, with a big sense of humor, that he did not know he was so interesting until a girl student began to analyze his poems. 'I taught a lot of things in my poems,' he said sarcastically, 'perhaps I taught this, but I didn't know it.' That is the point: perhaps, when making an analysis we make too much about it, thinking things which are not born. That is also the reason why I wrote to you and write again.

Finally we say a few words about Peter Abraham's *Tell Freedom* and Bloke Modisane's *Blame Me on History*. I call Abrahams the Author, Modisane the Journalist, and you the Debater and Cultureworker. (To be a culture worker is very good in my eyes) as an appendix we have taken (in English) your short-story 'A ballad of Oyo'. In the foreword to 'Lawinos Song' Okot p'Bitek says: they have clipped the eagle's wings (by the translation from Oculi to English and then to Swedish) and as we don't want to clip your wings (we work with the Swedish translation of D. S. a.) I insisted on taking an appendix in original. I play the violin myself and for me the ballad of Oyo has a very musically language, so similar with our ballads. It's a wonderful rhythm in your language. I have already written too much. Thank you again for helping us. About your jogging I can only say: Et tu, Ezekiel Mphahlele

Greetings from a snowy Sweden (we will never have springtime this year).

I have got a nice letter from Mrs. Mphahlele. She thinks I am a man. Shall we tell her the truth I am a woman? You can find my curious name in Ibsen's play *Peer Gynt* 'or Grieg's sonat, 'Solveig's song'. Sorry to say that I have no similarity with the wonderful Solveig in *Peer Gynt*.

Solveig Ryd

20 March 1979

Dear Zeke and Ribs,

I've owed you a letter for so long I'm becoming ashamed. I think I wrote last before Christmas. Well, well. That should give me more news to write, but actually the importance of many things recedes with time and what once seemed necessary and even urgent now seems stale and meaningless.

The biggest news is domestic, I guess. I had to go to Minnesota in December. My sister died and I wanted to attend her funeral. The morning we stood beside her grave waiting to inter her, it was 12° below zero farenheit. Even the elements conspire to embitter us. It was sorrowful as hell for me. She was my only sister. She had lost her husband some years ago – ten I think. She had nine children, two of whom are still legally minors – one fifteen and the other seventeen. But it was a kind of blessing. She had suffered greatly from the King Crab, Cancer. Well, it's now over for her.

Margaret continues to thrive in her unemployed status. Bob graduates from high school this Spring. I don't know for sure what he will do – no, let me change that. I'm pretty sure he will try college but I don't know where. Vince continues his growth to the stars. He now stands about 6'5" and is awkward as a crane. I hope the rest of him catches up soon. He becomes a junior next year.

Bill Zaranka has stepped into the creative writing job at Denver. He's even been kind enough to invite me out there in May for a reading and to judge their poetry contest. Now, how's that for scratching my back? I look forward to the visit. I like to look at our old neighborhoods and let the images form. I like, too, to see the old bastards we left behind (alas, for new and mighty ones here in many cases). I will like, too, to find my sausage companies and bring back some good Polish and Hungarian sausages. Sheit – these rebels know nothing of sausage. It's greens, greens, greens – no thanks. My Polish soul has its own demands!

I've been writing some lately. Not much, but enough to encourage me. It was a fleshing six weeks but interrupted by the necessity to prepare four hours of lectures for a junior college in Meridian (you'll remember that town from civil rights days). I finish up on Thursday. Meridian sits buried in the depths of Mississippi. About 70,000 live there. It resembles a small city with a downtown area that is till alive, i.e., the 'malls and shopping centers' haven't yet closed it down. I have the impression of isolation, of an American town in Australia or perhaps even England. I don't get the impression they want many visitors. But I'm sure this is all after-the-fact impressionism.

I put out for a few jobs this year – one near Seattle in Bellingham and one in Virginia just outside Washington, D.C. Nothing came of them. Sooner or later, however, I will move. I know I don't wish to retire and die here. I think I'll opt even for the 12 below zero.

You once mentioned something to the effect that a place could be self-fulfilling at least in an academic way. I agree but hasten to say it ain't this place. If you found Penn cold, cold, cold with arrogance, self-assurance and indifference; you would find this place heated with petty spite, small-mindedness when not empty minded, and totally, totally dull. I wonder to what end some of these people live their lives. It's amazing. Baptist church service on Thursday nights and Sunday mornings, church choir practice on Wednesday nights, meet their classes, think and speak of nothing (I don't believe many have read a book since grad school, if there), breed a couple of kids, drink a lot of coca cola, demand their rights, deny others' rights, pompous, pompous, pompous without the decency of merited pomposity. The administration is interested only in middle-class images – glossy publications depicting bright-faced, healthy youngsters in various poses of work and play, and statistics, statistics, statistics which bear no relevance at all to education. That is what they are interested in, that and problem solving. For instance if decent programs demand larger numbers of faculty, the way to solve the problem is to create programs that don't need so many staff despite the inferiority of the new programs. And they are slick. One method is to buy off people in key positions. I suspect I am one of them. They pay me a handsome salary and in return want no trouble from me or my faculty. Oh, they are old tactics, old tactics. No, this isn't a university. The students, like everyone else in the South, when not espousing the kindness of Jesus, are intellectual slugs who want from life nice clothes, coca cola, fucking (noiseless fucking that is), big cars, the Baptist church, and each other. Well, they are welcome to themselves. And the politics here are nothing if not corrupt, and the goddamned people are proud of being fucked by the fat cats. They BRAG about the corruption and rottenness of their political world. Alas, they've seen too many 'B' movies.

Well, that minor tirade to get us going. No, to get us to the end. A visiting lectureship at DU? Hop to it! I hope it works out. Then we'll surely get together. If not, then I just may have to come to Africa while on one of my many trips to Rome ... via Iran and the Khomeini.

All love to both of you,

Bob

Johannesburg

21 March 1979

My dear Zeke,

You have the blessed instinct to do the right thing; to write to me, since we've been within half-a-mile of each other all through February but not so much as exchanged a word. I've been feeling much worse than you about it, believe me – after all, I'm the one long installed in this city and would have wished to have you come round for a dinner, a talk. I had been looking forward to the idea of your being within reach. But then short February went by with my mind distracted by petty nonsense, people staying in the house, the problem of getting time to myself to work or see my friends. I was beginning to think, by the time I get hold of Zeke he'll be so offended he won't want to see me. And even to think: well, perhaps he doesn't – why hasn't *he* got in touch?

Well, now we forgive each other, don't we? There remains the fact that there's something amiss with life if one doesn't see the very people one wants to spend time with. I look forward to Grahamstown, quite truthfully, because you'll be there. When I did phone Wits (to ask you to come to a play at the Market with me) you had left that day.

It is reassuring to hear your impression that the institute is genuine in the way the university (I suspect) can't be. By that I mean that none of our universities can be, while education continues to be the discriminatory privilege it is in our country. For myself, to come to Rhodes for the Institute is my chance to prove my good faith to those people who certainly don't believe in it. A few years ago I refused an honorary doctorate Rhodes wanted to confer, giving my reason that I felt I could not accept any honour stemming, even indirectly and from a 'liberal' university, from a government education policy based on segregation. My action was much misunderstood, or if understood, regarded as wrongful. I stressed at the time that, although I wouldn't take an honour, I should be pleased to take up any opportunity to contribute to the broadening of minds among the students – I would talk to them, lead a workshop etc. So here I come to the Round Table.

I think you need have no qualms or distaste about talking to the *Skrywerskring* crowd.[1] They have long passed the stage of the traditional, churchy hypocrisy of their people. They have even (the best of them) passed the indulgence of breast-beating in guilt. André Brink, Ampie Coetzee, Rosa Keet – they are honest people who know that (in the eyes of blacks, at least) the sins of the fathers are branded on their foreheads. They buoy themselves up on no mystique of the *volk*. They don't even delude themselves with the vanity of belonging to the only white African tribe, Jan Rabie style. And they are aware that no matter what they say and do – short of the Sartre dictum B.B. [2] followed – they are less likely to be accepted by black fellow writers than English language white writers are, although some of those English language writers retain secret attitudes they themselves have abandoned.

Talking of the first Afrikaner you ever got to know in a personal way: at present a group of young people are giving a play at the Nunnery which is a sort of inquiry into the meaning of B.B. as a phenomenon of our society in general and the Afrikaner in particular. It is marred by the use of old Danny the Red 1968 rhetoric – some of the dialogue, chanted, seems straight off the famous posters. And in other parts the rhetoric is that of the pompous white establishment they are attacking. But the production is imaginative and rousing, the acting exceptionally good. At first I thought we were in for a romantic eulogy; then it became clear that this was not going to be the easy way out for young people to deal with B.B. There is a real attempt to deal with the two vital elements in considering the man – the failure (self-aggrandizement, messianism, plain stupidity and Myshkin-like saintliness); and the failure of the rest of us (whites) to have the guts to risk that kind of failure. I wish you could see the play. I don't think it'll have a long run or will be likely to be revived, alas.

Sipho phoned me yesterday. He wants to leave on an exit permit, now.[3] What can one say? He asked whether I knew of anyone who could help him to get a job abroad. Perhaps you may have some advice; but it will probably be not to go.

I gather that you had to sacrifice the Australian junket because of Wits and Rhodes. Adelaide must have been disappointed. Anyway, no doubt you have had enough of suitcases for a while. The house problem is a terrible one, particularly when you want to settle quietly to your research and writing. Wits *must* find a suitable place – it is wrong to expect you to buy one of those jerry-built costly houses going up in Soweto. Frankly, I can't see you and Rebecca tolerating the particular kind of isolation, even if the house were to be offered on a plate. I wish I had a garden cottage; or knew someone who had, and who was willing to have (very) long weekend guests – that would be a solution.

Much love. See you on the 17th.

Nadine

1 Gordimer means the Skrywers Gilde, the Afrikaans writers' association.

2 Breyten Breytenbach.

3 Sipho Sepamla considered following his predecessors into permanent exile.

22 March 1979

Dearest Teresa

I am here for March-April and will be back at Wits 30 April. I was given a Fellowship to finish my book – something I had started in Phila. Will certainly finish it. This month my novel *Chirundu*, about Zambia, is coming out in Jo'burg. Will send you a copy. No publisher in America would touch it, for different reasons (economic, market considerations and all that crap) than the British, who are scared it may lead to libel suits. Their laws against libel there are ridiculously strict: if one suspects a novel is referring to him, in a bad light, he can sue!

How are your studies coming on? I hope fine, and that you can feel the distance shrinking between yourself and the finishing post. Hang in there, baby!

Your Mum has been rather hesitant to come south: hates Jo'burg now and prefers the slower life up north. For my part, I always feel if a job is interesting and engages my intellect and heart and my colleagues are cultured, I can adjust to a place. Seems she will make a concession, because we both feel the strain of being apart, as you guessed we might. She is trying for a position at the School of Social Work at Wits.

Quaint little town, Grahamstown is. Dates back to the 1820 British Settlers, and has never forgotten them. Everywhere is some British Settlers object of commemoration. And the British are racist in their own weird fashion. Rhodes was started on an endowment by that top banana of British imperialism, Cecil Rhodes, founder of Rhodesia [Zimbabwe]. Pretty campus indeed, but as conservative and comfortable as any Victorian autocrat. The students could be the inmates of any Mormon university over there.

I decided to write to Motswiri early this week, but took a chance to address the letter to his Humboldt St. address. I gathered you said he had moved? If he does phone, warn him of the letter. I'm merely asking him – indeed appealing to his humanity – to tell me about Puso, as he is near him. It's so silent in that quarter. We're most anxious. ...

Much love and a belated birthday message of fondest wishes. I woke up to the 12th on the 20th! This change of setting ...

Ntate

Grahamstown

My dear Khabi and Grace,

Morocco intimated that you might make it to the North soon. I arrived here on 28 Feb for my March and April stint. I flew to East London and then on to P.E. from where I was fetched by car to Grahamstown – 85 miles. The folks in this institute are decent and solicitous. I have been given a lovely flat, furnished, with linen to boot. An electric stove, fridge, the lot. The stove stares at me and tells me 'get off your arse, chum, and fend for yourself'. Have never, since I've been married (33 years), had to cook for myself, so I'll settle for breakfast and a modest supper which does not require more than 2 pots at a time. The price one has to pay for intellectual pursuits! – a meatless life in *all* senses of the phrase. Incontinence suddenly threatens to be a virtue.

I spent an easy, relaxed February month at Wits. I've a nice office, and the Secretary of the African Studies Inst., which is where I'm at, is a white woman. She comes in my office at least twice a day to ask if I want coffee or tea, and she brings it in. Is always ready to help, to telephone on your behalf. She'll ask me if I want something to eat from the cafeteria in another building next to ours some floor down and will go especially for the item. And you wonder what fuss this whole master-race to-do is all about when people can respect each other. The director of the Inst. is Afrikaner – van Onselen, but emancipated. Spent 8 years in England, where he got his PhD in Social history. Outstandingly bright, married to Bozzoli's daughter (Vice-Chancellor and Principal). A veritable deviate! He has taken up the matter of housing for us with the big chaps at Wits ... This will be fine as Soweto is really unlivable ...

I dropped in on X and wife to say Hi! He was pleased to see me. I'm sitting there and listening to echoes from his pa's 'Yes ... of course ... yes ... oh no ... it can't be ... yes ... ye-e-es'. And then I look at the man's face and I see a replica of his Ma's – soft wet-looking eyes like those of wounded pride, only you don't sense a brittle, cactus interior behind those eyes the way you know lurks behind the mother's soft eyes. What makes it worse with the mother's is that her soft eyes are belied by the facial skin that is too close to the bones to exude warmth and the eyes become a fake. No, the young man's eyes are genuine and he is all gentleness. I think the Senior is also, but the old guy has never been able to keep out of the clutches of those who love domination. He's the kind of fellow, I think, who *must* simply be governed, ordered, punished or praised, otherwise he'd fall apart.

There may be some small particle of that in Junior – who knows? But he talks more profound stuff than Papa ... Ribs now feels she should join me, as I've been urging, as it's senseless going up north so often, and because she's going to be using the car, it will have to be by train, something I wouldn't like to look forward to, couldn't relish, at all.

I was looking thro' my files the other day when I found a letter from you, Khabi, written in Sept. 1959, when Ribs was back in SA for a spell. You comment on *Down Second Avenue* – most flattering. But you also say some newspaper reviewer thought I was a racist. You mention Mooki and say he's still as slippery as ever. You say you both motor-cycled to Durban! You two needed your heads to be examined, Grace perched on the saddle for all those miles! The hips, 'marago', the spine – how was it in all those parts? Ever heard of cyclositis? The buttocks vibrate in such a way that the anal muscles get quite confused, not able to discriminate between what wants ejection and what should not come to the gateway ... it was fun reading the letter and will keep it for future generations who come to study my writings.

Grahamstown is 'Sleepy Hollow', so British it's not funny. The ghosts of the 1820 Settlers are all over and I think even reside in the spiders that abound in the houses.

Love to you all,

Ever Zeke

Grahamstown

3 April 1979

Dear Charlie [van Onselen],

It was good to hear you the other day.

Have been chewing over some things – herewith – for what they're worth. Shall have your reactions when I return. Will shoot straight to the north and come tumbling down – no lumbering up – to Johannesburg about the 1st.

Cannot wait to be back. This place is fine if one wants a cloistered life – crap raining down all the effing time, clouds hovering about as if they were being paid for it, 1820 cobwebs getting onto your eyes – a town lying in state; Rhodes liberals drooling and farting all over the campus.

Warmest regards to you, Tim and B. Tell Tim that he's an institution at ISEA. I think they're ready to commission a sculptor to make a bronze head of him. Fine, as long as it doesn't stay out in the open. Grahamstown's pigeons seem to have come straight from Trafalgar Square or Piccadilly the way they whitewash statues. Tim's the last person I would want to treat like that. No, but seriously he has unearthed a hell of a lot during his researches – promising work that is gold.

Best to y'awl.

Zeke

Grahamstown

9 April 1979

Dear Tim,

Just a quicky to say Hi and ask about accommodation. Tomorrow the Institute is holding a launching party for *Chirundu* on behalf of Ravan Press. 'Twill be fun, I think. Returned from University of Transkei in Umtata. I addressed a jam-packed hall and the reception was tremendous. Next day I was asked by the Education Dept to address teachers and inspectors at the Town Hall. They wanted to know what's doing in education in N.Tvl. and what kind of education I think Transkei should develop! I told them it's naïve for them to think of adopting white education, which is as defective as Bantu Education. That they have to establish a permanent commission on education to evolve a system and monitor its operation, etc etc. Encore, encore! André and I then headed for Coffee Bay for Saturday. Returned yesterday. Had to zigzag thro' to avoid border control as this native son has no travel document!

It was comforting to hear you on the phone just when I was in the middle of this letter! Pity the house has no study – I'd hate to think that outside of the books in the Wits office I'd have to travel to Lebowakgomo to fetch a book I need! Maybe I shall need to ask someone in Johannesburg to keep the rest of my library. Would you suggest to Rebecca, if she should think Frankenwald is an attractive proposition, to consider asking Norah Taylor if she could house the third of the library I would want within reach? Say to her whatever she decides, I'm with her.

Please ask Barbara to send this letter to Exclusive Books, as I don't have their address. Thanks.

Can't wait to be back up-country.

Take care!

Ever

Zeke

P.S. Please ask B also to forward the information sheet to staffing.

23 April 1979

Dearest Zeke

Please forgive this paper. Am out of stationery. So very happy to hear from you. I had written you a couple of times but had gotten no response – thought you were either busy or perhaps you had forgotten about us. Glad to hear that you're teaching again although not where you wanted to be. I cherish your words. Things are worsening my brother. The disturbing sounds emanating from some of our brothers' mouths would frighten you indeed. I am ready to leave this madhouse now. Have enclosed my latest book. Hope you like it.

Am/Poetry/Review became uptight about some of my articles. They said that they were too different – not of the mode they expected. Asked me not to write a column for them – wanted to elevate me to a contributing editor status – so that they'd continue to work as if they're truly integrated. I told them to shove it and that indeed they were a bunch of little racists hiding out here in Phila. Chrisman sent them a copy of my book – they'll probably try to attack me there. We'll see.

Houston Baker went to California for one year. Came back home and got a Guggenheim. He'll be off. George Lamming is back in England. We all miss him very much. Let me hear from you Zeke. I promise I'll write more often now. This is our last break in school. Do you and Rebecca need any things? Please let me know.

Love

Sonia [Sanchez]

16 July 1979

My dearest daughter,

Today's Chabi's birthday and I'm going to try send him a cable. I say 'try' because life has been crowding me and I'm ashamed I have not written to you for a *long* time. I go from one thing to another, but I should be getting my shit together soon. I thought to write briefly for now, to say your Mum phoned me about your disturbing letter. I think a lot about you and the pain that is making your life so miserable.

You should not, I beg, give up now, just when you're almost over the hump. You *must* proceed to the M.A. Martin Kaunda and his wife came here a month ago, for him to be examined for his blind eye. Blinded by hypertension. When we told him about your aspirations in Communication, he readily said he'd offer you an appointment (with the M.A.) in his new dept. – more an institute – at UNZA, which he's heading.[1]

I am a consultant for Ford Foundation in the arts in this country. I mentioned to the director in charge of Africa and the Middle East that you want to do the M.A. in Communication if you can find the sponsorship. Nothing more than that. It wouldn't hurt if you wrote to him fully, stating your needs and your intention to come and work in Africa. Say I suggested you write to him. Ask if Ford would sponsor you. If not, would he suggest what other source to tap. But please don't think it's all hopeless if the reply is not helpful. We are quite prepared to help to a considerable extent. We feel you have jacked yourself up and courageously put everything you have into the present project. I should not say you *now* deserve help – you've deserved it all along, but for our own deficiencies. We shall be better placed once your Mum has joined me at Wits (she's due here 1st Aug). She and I agree that you need not – should not – bother to refund the money you used which we thought Chabi would have. Write it off. We can't wait to see you next month, baby.

Much love as always,

Ntate

[1] The University of Zambia.

Johannesburg
16 July 1979

My dear Khabi,

God, jy's 'n moer van 'n correspondent![1] Don't say it – life is hectic for you running a dept. and thinking *for* other people like those you work with.

Just wanted to touch base, as it were, and let you know we're still thriving. This is an exciting place to be. The Institute is about the only place that makes it possible for Wits to reach out into the African community. They let me continue to run writers' workshops and we should soon be mounting art exhibitions. All this, in addition to research projects. I shall teach a term in Comparative Literature, which is in German Studies – Black literatures being my field.

Ribs is still in the north, but has been appointed Senior Social Worker in Community Health projects – part of Wits but funded by Urban Foundation. She'll join me end of July to start in August.

I've rented a house – one of those built by Urban Foundation – Selection Park, which is really Pimville extension. Adequate for our needs. We have a guest room, with ¾ bed, so you should (must) stay with us when you're up-country.

What is the news about your application to Ford? I hope I didn't raise false hopes, as I'm sure you'd have told me if the results were in the affirmative. There's so much to do, so much backlog to make up for in our education and arts. I shall wait with baited breath. I should be going north about mid-August or end of it to record poetry in Vendaland at the time of its festivities. Who knows, I may be seen on the front truck in the float raising dust in Sibasa streets.

I hope Grace's health is bearing up. Met T – weird ideas he's got about education. Love to both of you. Hey, write man and get your shit together.

Zeke

[1] God, you're a bad correspondent!

Lesotho
23 July 1979

Dear Zeke,

It's been a long time! I hope you did receive my last letter. It was an air letter. I posted it just the day after the bomb blast in Maseru at the post office i.e. I did say in the last letter that everything has worked out well in Denver. I have a teaching fellowship and complete tuition waiver. However I am applying to AAI for either additional expenses (books and living expenses and family allowance) or complete sponsorship, such that if the load (teaching) makes my work too heavy, I can drop it. I am planning to spend not more than 3yrs in Denver if I can help it. The call of Southern Africa is too great!

I am already beginning to wind things up. I am hoping to leave on the 20th of August. I want to spend a few days in New York with some friends there. Everybody, except me, in the Department here is on leave. So I am acting as head. This has made the task of winding up difficult. There are so many petty administrative chores! I am quite clear that I will not be forced into this position when I return.

We have missed another good person – Lewis Nkosi. But the circumstances are slightly different from yours. He had applied and accepted, but decided to go to Zambia instead. Said something about being confined in Lesotho.

I read and finished *Chirundu* a fortnight ago. I have reviewed it for the local press. I found it revealing, moving. I loved the portrayal of the community of feeling between the exiles, Moyo (the representative of the new working class), and Tirenje, the enlightened rural sensibility. I liked too the historical dimension which is the anchor of Moyo's vision. The new national hegemony must be seated in an indigenous sensibility. It is an extremely positive, hopeful novel which is, at the same time, encouraging. *Chirundi* is a definite advance on *The Wanderers* for it is a crystallization of experience embodied within a profound, timeless aesthetic maturity. Here is a work of artistic wisdom! Much more can be said, but I *should* point out that I place *Chirundi* in the same generic slot as Betis' *Mission to Kala* in terms of the two novels' success in portraying the entire process of life in its most appealing vitality. I'm talking about life in social change. Thematically there is similarity with *A Man of the People*.... Beti is an aesthete. I've always loved him!

So much for now, you will hear from me from Denver. I can't wait to get there.

Please do me the enclosed reference. I shall be most grateful.

Thanks for the enclosed bibliography.

Yours sincerely,

Njabulo [Ndebele]

P.S. I am reading Boccaccio's *Decameron* right now. I am laughing to tears throughout!! I think I'll go on to re-read Chaucer again immediately after. These were great men![1]

1 The intellectual preparation Ndebele was undertaking in advance of his studies in creative writing at Denver is revealing. His collection of short fiction, written at Denver, *Fools and other stories*, expresses the indigenous sensibility he speaks of in this letter, but it is interesting that his range includes the medievalists – Giovanni Boccaccio's *The Decameron* and Geoffrey Chaucer's *The Canterbury Tales.*

Grahamstown

2 August 1979

Dear Zeke

I've been meaning to write to you much sooner, but I've been tied up in the production of a play and that keeps me busy morning, noon and night: *ek is besig om my gat te sien*![1] It was good to see you again in Durban; what a pity that Grahamstown is tucked away so far in the bundu, as I'd love to spend much more time with you. I haven't even had time to discuss *Chirundu* with you yet, which I found a moving and disturbing experience with its constantly shifting perspective on what is so essential to the whole of Africa today: the clash of cultures, and the situation of the individual within it; the need to define loyalties; the need for integrity.

Even this isn't really a letter. Just an urgent note to ask how the planning of the writers' conference is going? Please send me the dates etc as soon as possible, as I really want to attend but will have to make arrangements for leave well in time. And please remember that I personally and the *Gilde* in general would be only too happy to help with any organization you may require.

Incidentally, I'm sending you a copy of the *Gilde* constitution as you requested. As you see, it's phrased in a pretty neutral way: the point is that the organization arose out of the need to combat censorship on an organized basis and to explore the common ground of all writers in the country. It is NOT tied to Afrikaans literature – people like Athol Fugard are also members – and personally I feel it has the potential (largely unrealized so far) of becoming a really significant unifying force among writers in the country. I feel it has more than enough of a *raison d'être* of its own alongside of PEN, which offers the important international window above all. It would be wonderful if you would decide to become a member. Please give it some serious thought.

Tim sends his love.

All best wishes, en *hou die blinkkant bo.*[2]
André Brink

[1] Totally exhausted. Literally 'busy enough to see my arse'.

[2] 'look on the bright side'

E Transvaal

Dear Professor

It is so long since we met that I do not dare call you by your first name – more especially as I have read in the papers that you have changed it! It is a long, long time since we met at Rosettenville but I have always followed your career with great interest and much relished some of your books. I confess I have not read the latest one, but I promise myself the enjoyment of reading it in the very near future. The point of this letter is however this. If you are able at any time on your way to or from Lebowa to visit me here, you will be doing an old man a great favour. I would love to have you to stay here: perhaps we could talk about things as they were / or as they are.

Yours sincerely
George Harwood

Note by EM: George taught me some Latin in 1935 at St. Peter's Secondary School Rosettenville, Jbg.

Johannesburg
24 August 1979

My dear Khabi,

Just a hurried note to say thanks for the newsy letter. Your wire certainly missed us. Ribs joined me at the beginning of August. I almost had to prise her out of the bog down there – she was psychologically resisting because she couldn't accept the fact that much as she loves the serenity of Lebowakgomo etc, stagnation goes along with it: add to that the petty-mindedness that possesses 'educated' rustics, petty jealousies, white prefects in the civil service, official indifference to the job they had appointed her to, etc.

Hope mother and daughter *et al* survived their own whims and those of the vehicle they drove. How I feel for you in the predicament that has been imposed on you. To even have to dive for cover in some corner of your premises. One always needs that kind of corner. As I get older I realize I develop an attachment to a private nook which, as you rightly put it, must express one's tastes and personality. The way these youngsters behave wears you out, they want to trample you down and pass on to leave you smarting while they enjoy themselves in their youth. Your refusal to finance X's lethargy is most commendable. So sorry to hear the not-so-cheerful news re Ford. I shall be writing to them.

For my part, I am heading North – Venda – to search for and record oral poetry, and then come back thro' Gazankulu and Lebowa. I leave here on Monday morning. All hotels out there are booked up, so I shall be adventuring. Baldwin will of course be there and I intend to sit on his conscience. All you need to do to attract positive attention is to noise it around that you're going to sleep in your car, and observe how people bump into one another in the effort to prevent such an indignity! Cynical, eh! Just playing with an idea that tickles even me.

You're stuck with a farting repertoire, I see. We two are always arguing about who done it the next day. On the other hand I have the strange whim, when I'm alone and can't possibly embarrass anyone, including myself, to let go like a well-fed horse. Especially when I'm jogging. The silences that occur, though when one or the other has farted seems to be the beginning of the silences you find between two very old people. Just as if they are beyond caring, indeed weary of caring what wastes the body releases.

As there's a large golf course adjacent to us in Pimville, I have not yet tried the Wits facilities. But I'm going to when it's warm enough to swim. On our side of Pimville the coal smoke is rather sparse, a good thing. Will you be going to Lebowakgomo? I intend to do Venda and Gaza over two weeks or so beginning September 10. Let me know, and we can romp together.

Love as always,

Es'kia

Crawford

[Late 1970s]

Dear Zeke

Thank you very much for your kindest invitation of all. I am more than willing to come up to Johannesburg, but the dates fall towards the end of my quarter. I officially go on vacation on 19 September until 1 October.

I am unable to break away unless my lecture for you is over a weekend, i.e. between Friday and Sunday. The two weekends most appropriate are Friday 5-7 September and the following one, Friday 12-14. It could be so arranged that I can arrive late Friday afternoon (but this would mean shuffling lectures around where I am: although for your sake this could be done). However, I depend on your intellect (albeit slow about constitutional matters) to work it all out.

I would like, if it is at all possible, to speak on 'Forty Years of Black South African Writing' or even better 'Being a Black writer in South Africa – personal essay'. I have just finished my 'Memoirs' and this could tie up with a reading from it. I read from this two weeks ago in Durban and it was a roaring success.

Lots of memories about how it first started etc.

Let me know. Fit me in but in such a way that I don't lose my job down here. My students have been boycotting for six weeks and now need me desperately, but they can give me up for a weekend or a Thursday after, Friday-Sunday.

Love to Ribs

Richard

Zululand

25 September 1979

My dear Ezek,

I hope your Vendaland exploits were fruitful. How was the circus? as Nathan called it.

About the poetry – I had hoped it would be easier than I am finding now. I have spoken to each of two people who are very good at composing this type of poetry. Eliakim Mthiyane, a lecturer here – he is in the Dept of 'Bantu' languages (Nkabinde insists that the 'Bantu' be kept) and Knowledge Simelane who works as reporter for *Ilanga*. I met him again on Monday and he asked me to ask you to call him at Durban (code 031) 68165 so that he can give you an idea of what he has, and between you, to decide what he should send you.

If you should want to contact Eliakim Mthiyane our phone is 93611 (code 0351) our exchange will put you through to where he should be found. They are all so cagey about the stuff.

I'm up to the eyebrows in work and managing. Grace is in Soweto to Nkosi's funeral (Guzi's father). He died last Saturday – cancer. The cortege will leave Guzi's house on Saturday at noon (29th instant). We'll be coming up for the funeral. She'll be staying behind after the funeral. Sorry for telegraphic letter.

Ever

Khabi

DAEDALUS

5 October 1979

Dear Ezekiel:

DAEDALUS, the Journal of the American Academy of Arts and Sciences, has long been interested in publishing an issue on contemporary Africa. While this interest reflects in some degree the importance of the subject itself, it derives also from the Journal's continuing when they are reflected on by men and women who approach them with distinct and different professional, disciplinary, and ideological perspectives. *DAEDALUS*, now in its twenty-second year of publication as a quarterly, prides itself on what it has been able to accomplish through planning procedures that draw on diverse talents and interests and that show a concern with something other than the perpetuation of established orthodoxies. Our policy has always been to spread our net widely, to ask questions that are not conventional.

So, with our proposed issue on Africa, our hope is to avoid producing a compendium that will largely resemble others that already exist. To achieve such a purpose, however, implies a willingness to entertain bold proposals, to convert such ideas into concrete and specific writing assignments, and to find authors willing to reserve time for thinking about issues that transcend the daily preoccupations of the mass media.

Only a planning Committee composed of men and women prepared to conceptualize what a unified issue on contemporary Africa might reasonably include, and how its divergent segments could be made to cohere, would be in a position to organize such an intellectual effort. I write you at this time because I am anxious to involve you in such a planning effort. Through the generosity of the Rockefeller Foundation, its study and Conference Center in Bellagio, Italy, has been made available to us for our planning sessions for the period

December 14 to 19, 1979. It would mean a great deal to us if you could arrange your calendar so as to be with us during those days.

Let me tell you more about how our proposed Planning Committee would operate. First, we will be a company of no more than twenty-six persons. Our membership will be markedly international – African, European, and American. Many in our group are 'Africanists' who have made Africa their principal field of study for the whole of their professional lives; others have interests that relate to Africa, but they would not claim to be principally expert in the affairs of that continent. A good number are social scientists – historians, economists, sociologists, anthropologists, and the like – but the humanities have in no sense been scanted. Indeed, we hope that interest in scientific and technological matters will also be much in evidence at our meetings. Many of our members are academics; others, however, are not. The group is intended to be diverse, and every effort has been made to assure that it is.

The meetings will be closed; papers will not be read. Instead, every effort will be made to encourage the kinds of oral exchange that will serve to indicate why certain themes ought to be pursued and why others might be reasonably set aside.

It is important that we understand that our purpose is not principally to prepare a manual on a geographic area (Africa) in the late 1970's. Rather, we meet to determine which matters of long-range significance are most susceptible to serious and substantial inquiry, and how they might best be treated. Some have argued that we could do nothing better than analyze Africa's relations with the external world, doing this in an imaginative and novel way. What parts of the external world are 'dependent' on what parts of Africa, and what is the nature of that 'dependence'? In what ways can it be said to be political, strategic, economic, cultural? What is the reverse 'dependence' like? Who in Africa 'depends' on what parts of the external world, and why? How are relations with the former colonial powers evolving? What other states have substantial 'interests' in Africa? What are these? Ought we to consider also relations that are not simply state relations? How much is Africa, for example, linked to other parts of the world by religion, shared intellectual and cultural interests – by concerns with education, health, and other social purposes? Can we learn a great deal about the continent by dwelling on these mutual 'dependencies', or ought we to strive for a quite different kind of inquiry? Should we be emphasizing intra-African relations more? What patterns of development – political, economic, cultural – can be discerned as emerging within Africa? Would such an approach serve to illuminate what might otherwise be obscured? It is important that we dwell on Africa's 'distinctiveness', on why it cannot in most respects be compared with other continents and regions.

Those who have discussed the issue to date – in the *DAEDALUS* offices and in numerous conversations abroad – have been immensely helpful in suggesting yet other ways to organize the issue. Their recommendations will of course be communicated to the Planning Committee. However, it is the Planning Committee itself, in its Bellagio deliberations, that will set the larger agenda for the *DAEDALUS* issue, recommend authors, and establish priorities as between the various approaches that we might wish to take to realize our principal objectives. The Bellagio meeting is, for us, an absolutely crucial encounter. It would mean a great deal, therefore, if you were able to attend, giving us the benefit of your counsel.

Through the generosity of the Ford Foundation, we are able to meet all your travel expenses (economy class) to and from Italy. Most members of the Planning Committee will be coming by air to Milan; ground transportation will be arranged to take you from the airport to the Rockefeller Foundation's Villa Serbelloni in Bellagio, where lodging and meals will be provided for the duration of your stay. Conference participants are asked to plan their trips so that they arrive on December 14. There will be a short meeting that evening, followed by all-day (and occasional evening) sessions on December 15, 16, 17, and 18. We will be departing the Villa on December 19. Additional information about the conference and the facilities at Bellagio will be coming to you just as soon as we know that you have accepted.

Enclosed you will find a 20-year index of *DAEDALUS*. It will tell you something more about the Journal and its aspirations. Needless to say, we would be delighted to send any issue still in print to you if you indicate your interest.

I so much hope that you will be able to accept this invitation. Do let me hear from you just as soon as possible.

Sincerely yours,

Stephen R. Graubard

Editor

P.S. It is much too long since we last met. Can we hope to see you soon?

Johannesburg

20 October 1979

Dear Teresa,

I phoned Pretoria yesterday and the Department of Interior told me that 2 weeks ago they instructed Washington to issue you a passport. So I wonder what's holding up the works. Your re-entry arrangements, perhaps?

Schooling for '80?

I enquired at the travel agents what your status will be now. You see, S.A. Airways has an excursion for a visit of minimum 14 days; maximum 45 days, which is about $100 less than your regular ticket. Regular because we were expecting you to stay more than the 45 days. Now it seems you may have to decide (if that is in your power!), whether you're likely to bear the maximum 45 or settle for less. If the latter, we have to cancel your Pan Am ticket, get a refund and get you the S.A.A. excursion. Only, S.A.A. doesn't come through West Africa. It's Rio. If you feel you'd still want to go through West Africa to visit your friends, no sweat, let it stay at the Pan Am deal.

We are being invited to New York, as of 9th-15th December. I'm one of three educationists – we'll be coming to talk with corporation and university executives to inform them about the state of education among Africans, needs, priorities, finances etc. Am still applying for a passport – *that* must make you feel envious of the stimulating time I shall have of it, waiting for a passport! I know just what state you'll be by now. September 6, 1957 – my passport came (no, I fetched it) the day before flying. August '77 – I fetched the visa in Washington the day before flying. That's the pattern. Why some people enjoy other's pain and anxiety I can never tell .... By the way, if you do have the SA document, let the school that wants to take you for January '80 give you the students visa form – 'I' – something, which you have to present this side for re-entry.

...

Lovingly,

Zeke

Johannesburg

22 October 1979

My dear Khabi,

Back to square 1. G. has been fired ... and so he has to leave in Dec. Result? He wants his house back. Poof! goes the 3-4 year arrangement. No lease, just a gentleman's word! Can't go to his parents' house because Ma-in-law – daughter-in-law relations are *kakvol*. So he says. Who can't believe him?

So we're hunting for a house. Burns us both up when we think of the extra furniture we bought – R1 070 – to fit into the house. So we *have* to look for the same size of house at least. And houses are not plenty for the picking.

Should you hear (even at that distance) of anybody who's selling – even the municipal box, we're prepared to take a plunge. At least we can effect improvements at a reasonable price compared with a fat loan involvement for an Urban Foundation house. I say at that distance because goings-on in Soweto somehow reach Cape Town, Durban, P.E. So why not Empangeni!

We're still waiting for Teresa. Interior says they have instructed Washington to issue her a passport, so we don't know where the hitch is.

Much love,

Ezeke

11 November 1979

Dear Ezekiel and Rebecca,

Since I have had no letter from you for is it a year now? I cannot respond to the things you would tell me. Alas, such friends that leave a fellow embedded in the old south, in Mississippi and moonlight and magnolias, such friends. Occasionally a word will drift down from the fjords where the old Viking remains, golf weapon in hand, but such news is elliptical and tentative. Alas, alas. Then to /news of my own, such as it is.

Bob is at the New Mexico Institute of Mining and Technology which is in a small town in New Mexico called Soccoro. From what I can gather he's doing well, but he misses his friends and chafes against the small town (about 8,000 population) and the smallness of the school (about 1,000 students) but realizes he's getting a decent education and that the social limitations of the town are temporary. I hope he can make it through and do the work he seems to enjoy, i.e., some aspect of physical science. Right now it's geophysics he's leaning toward.

Vince is in his junior year at the local high school and is keeping active and doing well enough. Doing well enough, I say, considering he is living this year without his mother. Margaret has gone off to school herself. Yes, she has left home and hearth (only temporarily) and is attending Texas Woman's University in Denton, Texas, and pursuing a master's degree in library science. The long and the short of it is that the program here is not accredited by the American Library Assn. nor is any other program in this state so accredited (they're a fussy bunch and very political; for instance, in all of Texas only three program are accredited, and two are in the town of Denton, one where Margaret is and the other at her alma mater, North Texas State U.). She considered going to Louisiana State U. at Baton Rouge or to the University of Alabama at Tuscalooa, both about three and a half hours away, but the TWU is in something called the Academic Common Market which allows one to attend a school for in-state tuition if a program is not available in your own state. Participating schools in fourteen Southern states make this possible. It's a great saving in tuition, but difficult for the domestic life. However, perhaps in the long run it's good for her to be away from me while studying. I think you can guess the reason I say that. We get together, so far, about once each month. I must go into New Orleans to pick her up on Nov. 20 for Thanksgiving vacation; then a month later for Christmas. After Jan. 1, however, it may be a bit longer between visits.

That much for family. I go on as I can and must. I will be fifty in June. Will you believe that? I remember you sent me a fine letter, very thoughtful, speculative, philosophic, and the like when you were coming to your fiftieth. You were in Zambia, I believe. Do you remember? But I have no speculation, thoughts, or philosophic turns for you. I seem to miss the environs of my youth a bit. Certain tugging comes with the thought of the hard graveled shores of our lakes, of the snow swept fields and golden, cold light of late afternoon December, January, and February suns. Oh, how I long for it, but I could not bear the entire winter again. About one month would be well, but not four. I spoke with my mother yesterday (yes, she remains; will be 83 next month) who told me the snow was there to stay; that they awoke to an absolutely frosted, snowed world. Not only the ground was covered, but every branch of every tree was white. Maybe you remember mornings like that from Denver. And the clouds of breath coming from the mouth. That weather made one move! Margaret would, of course, kill me if I were to return there.

Well, this is more than you deserve, not having answered my faithful correspondence. Try this time to bring us up to date.

[Writer unidentified]

Cape Coast

6 December 1979

Dear Zeke

Its sometime when I wrote to you in response to your letter of the 19th May 1979. Your silence bothers me. I hope you received the letter, and are also well.

Let me know all about you, Rebecca and little (big) ones.

I thrive and go on from strength to strength.

Do you spend Xmas? I don't anymore.

I don't know why a Jewish lad should linger on conscience for so long.

Write.

Love to y'all.

Kofi [Awoonor]

Johannesburg

13 December 1979

Dear Professor Mphahlele

Please accept my hearty congratulations on being made an ad hominem professor. I am only sorry that our administrative machine is such that the decision could not have been taken more quickly. Because we regard it as such a high honour the rules and procedures are complex and time-consuming.

You have joined a small group of very distinguished academics at the university who have been awarded this title. I hope that you will be happy at Wits and can continue to make your academic contribution as you see fit.

Best wishes

Eric Glover

Johannesburg

14 December 1979

Dear Professor Mphahlele,

Just a brief note to let you know how delighted I am that the proposal concerning your ad hominem appointment had a happy outcome.

I am only sorry that our procedures did not allow for faster action, but I imagine that we are not unique as a university in having difficulties of that kind.

I hope your association with Wits will prove to be both happy and fruitful. Compliments of the season and a happy birthday.

Yours sincerely

Noel Garson

1980

California

11 January 1980

Dearest Pasha and Ribs,

Mon dieu: I've been waiting for what seems like years now for word from you. You promised to send me your new address ... eh? Anyhow, I called Charles Larson the other day, and he said to try this address, so here goes. I do hope that you receive this. If not, it has been an exercise in typing: You have been on my mind ever since you bade farewell to these western shores, and if winds can speak, you have heard my thoughts. So much news. I don't know where to start. First off, I am still at Chico State teaching more and more Freshman composition, as is everyone. Are we really raising a generation of illiterates? Anyhow, don't ask me how I like it, 'cuz I don't particularly. Once in a while, I get to teach a graduate course in Comp. Lit., or in African lit, and that suits me just fine. Palmer and I had a little boy in September of 1978 ... adorable, I might add. His name is John Edward, and he's literally 'all over the place'. Imagine me chasing a little one around the house: I shall send a picture if I hear from you so I know that this is the right address. I saw Anne Fuller last summer; she is still 'deaning' at Scripps, but has resigned effective June 1980. We spent an evening reminiscing, and, of course, you shared most of our conversation. She sends her love. I haven't talked with anyone else from Denver recently. I think Boklund is chairman now; and Chambers is editing the *Denver Quarterly* and, from my point of view, is doing a fine job of it. I know that Jerry had a Guggenheim fellowship and spent some time in England researching materials for a biography on Burke, but that's about it. Oh, unless, that is, you remember Mike Holland. I also saw him last summer at a meeting, and he is still teaching at Fullerton. Looks o.k., but was drinking a bit too much at the time. Anyhow, he, too, sends love. And now, since I have covered 'pictures from the past', what about now? I finished the translation of *Le Pagne Noir,* and have been sending it out to publishers. Johns Hopkins gave it a good going-over, but decided against publishing 'the charming and interesting' translation, largely because their Atlantic culture series has not yet branched out to include works of fiction.[1] Heinemann rejected it also: a good translation but, apparently, not a strong enough collection. I have sent letters of inquiry to Chicago University Press and Oxford University Press, but no response from either as yet. Also, I sent a copy to Mr. Donald Herdeck, editor of Three Continents Press, and this just recently, so I am hoping that he might just say: 'Let's go'. Do you know him? Zeke, if it is possible and not asking too much, could you write to him for me, saying that you are familiar with my work and that you feel Dadié should receive more attention in this country? Address of Three Continents Press: 1346 Connecticut Avenue N. W., Washington D. C. 20036. I would surely appreciate it. Just a few minutes ago, I wrote to Bernth Lindfors, asking for his advice as to a possible publisher. I do hope that he will answer. I'll be glad to send you a copy of the translation if you would like one. Anyhow, whatever ideas you have would be welcome as you know. And so, what are you up to? What are the latest creative enterprises? Who's publishing them? Surely, surely, you've now written the GREAT AMERICAN NOVEL about 20th-century life in a colonial town? in a cattle town? in the flighty West? What possibilities: if only I had your perspective. I finally got around to reading Soyinka's *Myth, Literature, and the African World* last week, and I must admit that it was a bit rough going in the first chapter; the rest is marvelously lucid. (Conton's *The African* does seem of another world, doesn't it?) Zeke, what, supposedly, did Ouologuem plagiarize in *Devoir de Violence*? I've read the novel but have not kept up with the 'scandal'.[2] From what I read lately, the folklorists have taken over the literary journals in this country. *Mon dieu*: what Levi-Strauss has done to the study of literature: I keep looking for that refreshingly *human* look at literature ... the one with a sense of humor and a knowledge of human values. Enough lamenting. How is Ribs? Is there family around? Are Terry and Tony in this country? Is there something you want from here that I can send you? (I'm asking all these questions, expecting an answer, you know ...)

More soon. Meanwhile, please, please write and fill me in on your news. Tell me what to do with *P. Noir*, and tell me, please, that you are well and happy.

My love, as always.

Karen [Chapman]

1 *Le Pagne Noir* by Bernard Dadié, translated as *The Black Cloth*.

2 Yambo Ouologuem's novel of 1968, *Le devoir de violence* (translated as *Bound to Violence*), won the Prix Renaudot. It later produced a lively debate when it was later discovered to have plagiarised the work of a number of authors, most notably Graham Greene.

15 January 1980

Dearest Terry

I am enclosing the cable, which is puzzling, as you indicated it was all in the net and now?

Nice to hear your voice the other day. We keep thinking you're standing at the kitchen sink or will soon come out of your bedroom – weird! Missing you, there's a hole in our lives.

Am rushed. Hoping things dovetail as you planned. Write. Am writing to Puso at long last.

Much love,

Ntate.

P.S. Yesterday morning at dawn, Puso phoned. Gave us a thrill, his voice sounded so mature.

Denver

6 February 1980

Zeke, you old, so-and-so,

Time again for a major contribution to our sporadic correspondence – the two-month interval seems to be standard. This time there has been a special reason for my delay: I've taken over the chairmanship from Stuart and landed in the midst of budget preparations, tenure and promotion affairs and more muck of a similar sort. But this horrible elevation has also made it more necessary than ever to write to you.

When Manganyi was here, I mentioned to him that if he had time to sit down with Stuart and me in the office, we could elucidate quite a few things about your disreputable life by referring to the official English Dept files. I also said that there should be documents there which specified the terms of your appointments, what courses you taught and what lectures you gave, and that I could possibly have some of them copied and sent to him. Now he writes to me and enquires about them, whereupon to my amazement I find out what the actual state of the Mphahlele file is: very little that is official and above board and a lot that is personal or concerned with immigration matters, letters to and from senators, state department officials, ambassadors and the like. While I understand that your biographer should receive what aid we can give him, there is a line that has to be drawn, and you are the one who has to tell us roughly where to draw it. That the University may have something to say on this issue too goes without saying. But, dear Zeke, what information do you want released at this time?

Since I didn't hear from you in December, I assume that your visit to the United States did not take place. Too bad for you and also for us, since we would have loved to see you even for a very short time. I've tried to get in touch with the 'wayward boys', as you call them, but so far without any luck – Patrick is no longer in the phone book. Anything you want Vanja or me to do?

The big and bad news from here is that John Williams is ill and will go into hospital this month to have part of one lung removed. He went to the doctor in December and was told what was wrong – was also told to stop smoking, which he can hardly be said to have done. He is rather cavalier about his prospects in other ways too, but we can feel how serious the situation really is and definitely keep our fingers crossed.

The big Pole came through on one of his pilgrimages a couple of weeks ago. He's applying for assorted administrative positions, and this time he was on his way back from his first real interview. He hasn't changed much: to judge from his description of what took place it was Pawlowski who spoke out in judgment of his prospective employers rather than the other way around. He still leaves big footsteps. He also complains that he doesn't hear from you.

Which brings me to a touchy issue. Zeke, some of your friends have the uncomfortable feeling that you're deliberately limiting your American contacts to a very few people. I believe I can understand you if this is so – I'm after all a dumb Swede *'jenseits von Gut and Böse'*, as one of the good/bad Germans once expressed it. Could you give me a hint? I could then relay it to the parties concerned, or at least some of them.

Our swimming practice is in a bad state of repair nowadays. Chapman, Richardson and I try to keep it up, but the limit seems to be thirty laps rather than seventy-five. Too much time spent talking and not enough exercising. We started to go downhill when Jerry fell ill last spring. Mononucleosis for heaven's sake – the 'kissing disease'. He has been recovering from it very slowly and is of course more susceptible to any bug, real or imaginary, than anyone I know. In Texas even the hypochondriacs are Texas-sized. He has been living in what used to be known as sin with a very talented twenty-six year old. Only young girls seem willing to mother Jerry, and not even they last very long. He is still his old unhappy self, with an unpredictable and sporadic interest in matters outside him, still believing in his conspiracy theories on the local, the national and the international levels. Henry Kissinger, who used to be his prophet, has now been elevated to godhead. I can hear your noncommittal 'Is that so?' at this startling piece of information.

And on that note I think I had better end this letter. the typewriter doesn't agree with me any longer, as you can well see.

Best wishes from Vanja and me to Ribs and you.

We think about you frequently.

As ever

Gunnar Bokland

Johannesburg

25 February 1980

Dear Norman,

You must think me a cavalier kind of person who never answers letters. Actually I do, and unanswered letters bother me, nag my conscience to exasperation. Field work has kept me busy in the last 5 months. Where to begin? Although I told you verbally that I appreciated your wisdom and insight as shown in your critique of 'Mrs. Plum' I should re-iterate the kudos in this letter. Your empathy is something quite rare in people who come to writing that deals with a culture outside their own. Every bit of what you say displays reason and warmth.

I'm sure you cannot imagine that I would decline an invitation from you to be external examiner for your Honours students!

Themes? Ideas? Modes? I rather prefer collision (conflict) and reconciliation (compromise) than simply 'cultural collision'; seems to add a dimension to the argument. You might add *satire* and *comedy*; 'Black Master, Black underdog'.

From the lyrical to the dramatic – the poetry moves from lyrical expression of Africaness (including negritude) to the apocalyptic (dramatic) – later Okigbo and Soyinka, Clarke, Ngugi, Achebe, Laye; the oral tradition and modernism and so on.

Met Hilary yesterday. We promised each other lunch. I must conserve time: Would you say to Chabani that I have heard from Boklund (Denver), who wants to know what records (re. E.M.), he would like. Says 'I find to my amazement what the actual state of the Mphahlele file is: very little that is official and above board and a lot that is personal or concerned with immigration matters, letters to and from Senators, state department officials, ambassadors and the like. While I understand that your biographer should receive what aid we can give him, there is a line that has to be drawn, and you (E.M.) are the one who should tell us roughly where to draw it. That the University may have something to say on this issue too goes without saying. But Zeke, what information do you want released at this time? …'

If Chabani would like to ring me at Wits (we have no phone on the Wits estate where we are squatting temporarily) – Ext. 8154 (secretary's), 8287 mine – we can straighten this out.[1]

We are lodged at Frankenwald Estates (Wits-owned), where they have flats. We are in a one-bedroom flat, all jammed, but breathing. It's open country around for a stretch – a Turf Research Station. My eyes sweeping across the landscape, I fancy myself the squire of Frankenwald, listening to the perpetual complaining of doves and smart-assed talk from the winged extroverts. All I need is a game-keeper, except that he mustn't be naughty.[2] I don't want to have to write a novel about it!

Warmest regards,

Love

Zeke

1 This correspondence, housed in the English Department at the University of Denver, was subsequently made available to Chabani Manganyi.

2 Mphahlele is referring to the gamekeeper in DH Lawrence's novel, *Lady Chatterley's Lover*.

10 March 1980

My dear Pete,

How good to hear from you! I had begun to despair of it when Chabani told us the exciting news that you were planning to return. And just before your letter arrived he phoned to say it was all in the bag. We are simply thrilled. It is unbelievable that your odyssey began 10 years ago!

One year more than we were in the US, excluding the abortive Zambian adventure.

It is a wise decision, at least you'll be able to size up the dimension of your American ties and know better when they stopped to be meaningful, if ever, and if your destiny lies there.

Funny about C.D. – she was out of mind until you revived her image; with quick bold strokes you put her in front of me; the image of the hog between her thighs clinches it so beautifully. Forget the lapse in communication. We kept wondering, but only yesterday my thoughts stayed with Thuynsmas, and indeed I was going to write again to ask if what Chabani told us was for real. So your trial return buries all 'sins of omission'.

Congratulations in anticipation of your defence.[1] I'm most happy you decided to have a final bash at it. I'm not surprised to hear about G. She's a dead-end. I've been told that she hasn't published a thing since her PhD dissertation.

I think academics are only a job to her. And anyhow, most people would be out of their depth with your theme. Any other readers? Carry it away and come and put it to good account where learning is still appreciated – in Africa, where nothing is ever stale.

[Teresa] spent a lovely 2 months with us – her first return since she was 7, when we left the country. She was given a S. African passport, which all of them use, entitled to except Puso (born in Nigeria with a right to a British passport or if he prefers, to a SA one when our nationality has been regularized here).

Umtata isn't much of a town, but after big city life you may find, as we have, pretentious urban living hard to take. But then maybe this heart's becoming disenchanted with lots of other things, although in the vortex of life.

It's heartening to learn Dawn and Heather are really looking forward to the move. *That's* the spirit.

You know, your handwriting touched off some nostalgia for Denver and its folks – I seem to *hear* you talking. Remember me to Njabulo, say I'm waiting to hear how he likes the grind, how his writing ... etc. Give Dawn and Heather a bear hug for us both, and let your homeward preparations prosper.

Affectionate regards,

Zeke

[1] Mphahlele is referring to Peter Thuynsma's oral defence of his PhD. As it turned out, Mphahlele happened to be at the University of Denver for the occasion and joined the panel of examiners.

Florida

12 March 1980

Dear Zeke:

I have now had confirmation that the books on your order form were sent off to you book post on January 21. They have been charged to my account here so you got the 40% discount. The total is $35.04.

What I hope you will do instead of trying to get the money out of South Africa is to send an equivalent amount to my bookseller in Johannesburg: Ms. Fanny Klenerman. Her address is P.O. Box 4563, and her phone number 728-2287. I am sending her a copy of this letter so she will know the arrangement. She keeps me up to date on what comes out that will be of special interest to me and we have done this for a long time. She used to run the Vanguard Bookshop but now does all her business by mail.

Its great to be in touch directly with you, and I also enjoy reading your pieces for *The Voice*. I'm delighted that Wits is developing an African Studies Program on an interdisciplinary basis and even more pleased at your role in it. My greetings to Charles van Onselen and his wife, and her parents if you see them.

Also very best wishes to Rebecca whose great energy is no doubt transforming the community health services of Wits. Medical school as well as to yourself,

Yours as always,
Gwen

Denver
28 April 1980

Dear Chabani,

Your letter reached me immediately. He asked me to look at the bulky file myself & select according to my discretion. I seem to be destined for preservation in fat files. The SP. of 1957 showed me a fat one when I was applying for a passport – just to show I have a heap of sins blocking my way & wherever. I'm sure WRAB [the West Rand Administration Board], after that house-hunting expedition, will already have constructed a formidable one. Tell Charles I keep wondering how big he will make mine. Why, why – a simple harmless heathen like me.

But there I have had the lot I think are relevant photocopied – at 5c per page – that's a heap. I fear to tell you. I'm sorry to have to do this to you – charge you for it – it's the cheapest rate as it's a dept. machine. I've paid $9.50 which you could make out to Ribs – approx R7.50. Tell her to save it for me because Mack the knife will be back in town, as the song goes.

I'm having to send the packet by surface mail, which means 6 weeks for April 28. Postage in the country has run amok in rates.

Kind of calm here, & my teaching load of 2 courses is pretty light. It's just good to be back in the grind – regularly & working to time. I was ahead, rustically a bit. I'm only now unwinding & flying free of the Jbg mould. Gessler made contact 2 weeks ago. He's teaching for a month at Colorado College in Colo. Springs – some 50 miles south of here. He's going to visit me for a weekend – the 1st in May. I'm amazed – I thought he had written me off.

Dennis Brutus was here three weeks before me, invited by the School of International Studies on campus. He was to read his poetry, instead of which I'm told he spent about ¾ of the time berating Africans who came to the US on S. African passports & are being used by the SA Govt. to bring our people to study in the U.S. The audience should beware of this. Several people interpreted him to refer to me as I've to do with screening of students there for scholarships. So he's now against people who come & study here. The futility and frustrations & impotence of exile ... the same old story.

I'm sending you in the packet a copy of a statement I made at the request of Lawrence Still & Co. who are publishing *CHIRUNDU* to answer questions about the 'compromises' I had to make to be allowed re-entry into S.A. He'll publish this in the book. Maybe it is no wonder I breed in fat files. Everything I touch sets off sparks. Re-reading your talk 'The Censored Imagination' is a thrill.[1] There is so much sound thinking in it – as usual so precise & incisive. I brought it along in case I need to refer to it if I'm asked to talk about the subject. I was asked, & it served me admirably.

Take care,

very sincerely,

Zeke

1 'The Censored Imagination' was published in *English in Africa* 6(2) 1979, pp 24-32.

6 May 1980

Dearest Teresa,

Arrived safe and not as exhausted as when we arrived in N.Y. from JHB. Found the house almost complete. We moved in on Friday 2nd. It's bigger than that coon's. Three bedrooms, one of which I use as a study. We wonder what the coon feels to see we're back here to haunt the life out of him. Took 2 months to build and the coon could have waited without losing a drop of blood – idiot! Your mother is still busy packing stuff in its proper places, and she feels most relaxed. She and Carrie went to Lebowakgomo while I was over there! Can't keep those two down! Can't wait to play your gift records – we're still waiting for electricity to be connected. Will tell you how I find them when power is in.

How's your health? We hope you're doing more than bearing up. Still thinking of changing to AU? [1] It bothered me no end to think that I was leaving the US while you lay there, immobile, in pain.

Your Aunt Girlie called me and your Mamma this last week.[2] She told us one eye was totally blacked out – diabetes and hypertension. The other one was feeble. Had to be laid off work at the factory because she couldn't thread a needle any more. Has to be operated on the bad eye soon. Told your Mamma that she has no money for rent, R17, and is fearful of the worst. Your Mamma was pissed off on account of G's habit of always touching base only when she needs help. She came when we moved house to help. I told her straight in your Mum's presence that she has been responsible for much of her misery: allowing B to bring a school girl home and sleep with her without bothering to go and report to her parents and driving B out of the house. The man she kept who gave her 4 children, the three following B are still too young to look after themselves and now where's he? A no-count nigger who does nothing for his own progeny. She admits that she has been holding on to the wind. We told her about your visit and her not coming to see you. She says cryfully she wanted to throw a welcome party for you but had no support (material) from her children. Parties were not a gesture of love, I told her – her presence would be. I reminded her that the relationship between us did our mother no credit. That's where it ended.

Still waiting for the boys to write: I took them to Arapahoe Community College to register and they were to apply for new green cards for the purpose.[3] Also told them the house they lived in with the Walter guy was not worthy of habitation. They were to find an apt. near the college to share, like it or not. Chabi's more adjusted to the idea of sharing than P. M's freelancing is paying off, and he's comfortable. Stayed with him 2 days, the two boys kept in their place. Am still trying to hustle money for your car and it's tough. Am still hoping, now with the boys coming up for assistance.

Tons of love from us,

Your loving

Ntate

1 American University.

2 Girlie was Mphahlele's only sister.

3 This happened during Mphahlele's first visit to the United States since his permanent return from exile.

Cape Town

9 May 1980

Dear Professor Mphahlele,

You probably don't remember me but we met twice – once in Philadelphia years ago when you were coming for an interview – and then on your visit to Inter-Group Studies last year. We also corresponded before you went to Wits as I was trying to get something at UCT organised for you.

The reason I'm writing is that I would like to have Ravan do a book of essays on *Literature and Society in South Africa,* and would like to have (1) any comments or suggestions you may have on the subject-matter or some of the essays. (2) An indication of whether you'd be willing to give permission for a section of *African Image* to be printed. (3) Your sense (if you're still with me up to here!) of how your publishers would be likely to respond to a request, probably unaccompanied by any money, certainly not by much!

The other people I'd thought of including include Jakes Gerwel (whose work on the portrayal of the 'Coloured' in Afrikaans fiction you may know), Tim Couzens, Nic Visser, Jacques Berthoud, John Coetzee, some graduate students like Isobel Hofmeyr and Stephen Watson. Mike Kirkwood suggested Adrian Crewe at Sussex and I would be very grateful to have any other suggestions. One of the aims of the volume would be to encourage further publications and to give a model for students who at present find the models offered in literary studies rather limited.

Here the boycott seems to be ending with a more positive achievement (not yet in material terms) than seemed likely to me, I must confess. UCT got in on the act a week late (we were on holiday when the boycott started) and produced some [...] very good street/guerrilla theatre.

We still hope to have you teaching here soon (if only for some relief from research!). Ursula Barnett is helping out this year.

Keep well. I do hope you will feel able to support the project.

Yours truly,

Ian Glenn

Johannesburg

9 May 1980

My dear Zeke

Thank you so much indeed for sending me a copy of 'Zeke's View' as published in *The Voice* of April 30-May 6.

I was delighted to have this written version of the address and even happier to have been able to hear you deliver your Graduation Address last week.

Your sentiments are as always forthrightly and lucidly expressed and provide most thought-provoking reading.

I am so pleased you are able to give of your time in the planning of the Senate Lectures for this year and look forward to many more happy meetings with you on Campus and off.

With kindest regards,

Yours ever,

Phillip V. Tobias

Massachusetts

26 May 1980

My dear Zeke,

It was wonderful to see you in March and renew our friendship. If anything is to come of your project and Smith is involved I shall *certainly* expect to play a part from this side of the ocean, a part which would emphasise South Africa's interests, needs and wants rather than America's. Of course, *ideally*, one would want both to coincide, but if they shouldn't South Africa's *must* come first. Dire said this to members of our faculty, and they understand.

As you know this is commencement time in the States, so I've been running to exhaustion. And I'm not finished yet. The youngest of my three half-sisters will graduate from college at the end of the month before going on to Law School in the fall. So I must go to that for the commencement and on to California to see my mother. Also, May is the anniversary of my parents' marriage and the 6th anniversary of my father's death, so *emotional* I've been drained. But I'll be my old self after visiting my mother.

I'm arriving in Johannesburg on the 9th of September from London via South African Airways. Could you suggest a hotel there where I might stay upon arrival as well as one in Gaborone, Botswana when I go there later in the month? I'd like to have the matter of accommodation settled in Johannesburg before I leave for London on August 19th.

Please, let me know what I can do to further *your* project here at Smith. Oh yes, what kind of weather should I expect there in Sept., Oct., and Nov? Spring or summer like?

Affectionally
Walter Morris-Hale

18 June 1980

Dearest Teresa,

Why so quiet? Haven't heard from you since my last letter. Have you had the time/courage to think about the things I mentioned? And how's your health – physical and psychological? We worry about you so much, and your letter was most unsettling.

M.M. called yesterday to say she spoke to you, when she was calling her brother. She told me you sounded fine. She wants to come to the US, incidentally, but her high school status is in doubt. Like a trusting fool, I spoke to an administrator at Oberlin[1] when I was in Denver and recommended her. Purely on the grounds of my acquaintanceship with her articulate manner and level of understanding. I simply assumed that no-one would aspire to University without a high-school diploma. IIE now writes to say she didn't finish her O levels. Am meeting her for further clarification.

We're enjoying the new house, and your Mum speaks less and less about her Lebowa house. I've always believed that if you're happy in your job, the physical setting fits in. The reverse does not hold. If there were good jobs in Lebowa, the rural dullness and inertia would not matter a damn.

You're not saying anything about your illness, about the account no. at the bank, and we don't know what is afoot at the Howard end. Are you hanging in there!

It's still possible that I shall go to Spelman Dec-May and then D.U. Sept-Dec with the summer thrown in *somewhere*. We'll see. Your aunt Girlie didn't have the eye op after all. They say that won't save the eye, so she might as well carry a non-functioning eye. Visited O and G the other day for a short while. For the first time ever I had a cup of tea there! What a life! We had a straight talk with your aunt and told her how heartless she was not even to come and see you. She starts crying, saying she wanted to do 'something' for you (a feast) but her 'children' wouldn't pitch in with money help. I told her you didn't want anything of the sort. It's love that matters, which drives a person out to visit. This is too high for her to appreciate ...

Enough! Do write. We're anxious.

Much love from us both,

Ntate

1 Oberlin College in Ohio.

July 1980

My dearest Teresa,

I had just mailed the aerogram when your letter arrived. A most painful letter to be sure. I'm sorry I had to tell you the distressing news about your aunt G when you can least tolerate bad news. Sorry about that.

You know best how far your capacity goes for carrying the things that bother you. At least you know when you're pushing yourself too hard. I don't know if it's insecurity – material and moral (in the broadest sense of the word), or more of the one than the other. If it's material, you need to prune your lifestyle even more than you have done, austere though even *that* is. A bedroom-living room affair, although the neighbourhood may not be right. Spending less, although you're far from a fancy eater. But all this may be a mere papering of the cracks and you need to make a *bolder* decision, more radical.

Yes, it would be rather good if you obtained the M.A. before decamping. But I suggested to your Mum, which she agreed with, that you don't need to continue under those conditions of stress if you feel your tolerance level, physical and mental, has reached the maximum without solving your problems, or else has stayed at a low point too long to rise. If either is the case, you should not tax your constitution further. You should just pack it, say thank you to the UN, and return home. Here you can do the M.A. at greater ease, although lecturers can drive you around the bend. White lecturers, as you won't find any blacks in your field. I don't know. You have to grind your brain cells over the matter. Maybe the greatest challenge here, even more than racism, is the *mediocrity*, the *inanity*, that keeps coming at you. There are various dodges and on-and-off switches one can operate to deal with racism: it's stark, visible, etc but mediocrity is sump'n else. I'm learning to keep my cool in its presence, because to rave and rail and shout only breeds ulcers. But damn it, it may be, indeed I believe it *is*, something one can deal with better than the more complex, barbed-wire tangle the American thing is.

Back here you would need to do the M.A. in order to sell your labour to the highest bidder. You would need to do a year B.A. Honours, which is the equivalent of M.A. course work there, followed by a thesis. If you came to Wits, you would be entitled to a remission of fees. For under grad. children of faculty pay 25% and the rules are being revised to include grad. students. Another possibility would be to find employment and study under the Univ. of SA (UNISA), my alma mater where I did all the degrees but the Ph.D. Whatever is offering, whatever mediocrity one sees, is matched by the demands of the professions in SA, which suits the country. You can survive it. Maybe you *need* a homely environment. But weigh the whole thing carefully. You said you might transfer to AU, where the M.A. is a year or maybe 18 months. Let us know. Meantime I hope you can bear up with the pain and maintain it at a tolerable level if it has to be borne.

Take care now, and lots of love to you,

Your Ntate

London

9 July 1980

My brother,

you don't know how good it is to hear from you. i've been back to philly once or twice since you left and we often speak and always think of you and wish you well it so happen that yr letter of 5 June, addressed to i at uwi had to get sent on here since i am at present on study leave until end of august which means that if i can make it, we ought to try and have everything settled while i'm that much quicker away: even though you'd have to fetch me from Jamaica or as if i was there (i will probably be in Venezuela as a matter of fact)

the first thing i'd like to know is: how wd i get a visa. i am Bajan and carry a barbadian passport. can you begin to have that checked from your end? i suspect and fear that it will be quite a business but all being equal, i wd like to respond positively to you personally: i mean it would be lovely to see you at home, kind of; and of course the opportunity you offer of a second week to meet some of our writers is something i very much appreciate and can only thank you for the subjects i think emerge from discussion with you. i mean i need your guidance on this. The Arts in the caribbean today seems to me a fair working title; esp since i'm pretty sure that many people won't know much more than that we exist/somewhere so let this man hear from that man and forgive the poor typewriter which though perhaps less literate than i, is much more illegible, mek I tell you.

One love

Edward Kamau Brathwaite

DAEDALUS

25 July 1980

Dear Zeke:

We missed you greatly at Bellagio. Indeed, we hoped till the very end that you would show up and that you would be able to participate in discussions that were immensely important and significant for us. We have moved slowly in preparing this issue because we wanted to have a maximum input from Africans, Europeans, and Americans. However, I now feel that I ought to proceed to commission essays for the volume and I am very anxious to do so now. I write you at this time because I do want to involve you and I hope very much that it will be possible.

I am very anxious that we should develop some scheme for indicating which African hopes, after independence, have in fact been realized, and which ones have not. The political, economic, and social evolution of Africa has been a very different one than anyone anticipated. The story is not necessarily and not wholly distressing, but it is a story which is very different from the one commonly told. In this connection, I think that there is a lot to be said both about how Europeans, Americans, and others misperceive African problems, but also about how Africans themselves fail to take into account certain developments.

In any case, such themes are going to figure prominently in our volume. Because so much has turned out so differently from how anyone anticipated, there are many conditions in Africa that are almost unique to that continent. Thus, for example, in talking about Africa during the meeting, many referred to the large number of exiles from that continent who now live in Europe, America, and elsewhere. Indeed, the exile is a contemporary African figure in much the same sense as one might say that the salesman is a characteristic American figure. As the group at Bellagio reflected upon African politics, on why it is as it is, we thought increasingly about the whole phenomenon of exile, of the difficulty of Africans finding their way at home after they have once enjoyed power and lost it. However, it is not only political leaders who are in exile, but also a vast number of students, professors, intellectuals, and the like. It occurred to us that an essay from you on the phenomenon of exile in contemporary Africa could be an immensely exciting and important contribution. Indeed, it would tell us a good deal not only about the political climate of contemporary Africa but also about the social and intellectual climate. Also, it would suggest the ways in which ties to the former colonial powers remain, even as they are vastly transformed. It would be no exaggeration to say that in London today one has a greater collection of Ugandans than in any other place in the world. The number of former high officials from Benin who congregate in Paris is immensely impressive.

The idea of an article from you on the phenomenon of exile, particularly as it expresses itself in contemporary African life has enormous appeal for us. Is this something that would have interest for you? Is it something that you would like to do? Or, is it something that you think takes you away from other of your major preoccupations at this time?

I am sorry that we have not been in closer touch these last months. I can only say that my failure to write was caused principally by my overwhelming concern to be sure to develop a set of themes that would have interest for individuals like yourself. We need a good number of essays from men and women who are still in Africa, who are very aware of the struggles that are going on in that continent. I hope very much that you will consider this invitation seriously. If this is not a theme that has interest for you, but there is some other that would interest you more, I need to know that. Our greatest concern is to involve you.

As you know, our practice at *Daedalus* is to commission essays, to have these essays reproduced and discussed in a closed conference. For this issue, we are asking authors to submit drafts of their essays of approximately seven thousand words to us in Cambridge by March 1, 1981. We would then hope to meet in April in some convenient place for discussion of the essays and we would look forward to their publication later in 1981. Through the generosity of the Ford Foundation we are in a position to offer you an honorarium of $500 for such an essay.

May I say in closing that the theme has been selected by the planning committee, but that the development of this theme is entirely for you to determine. You must make it whatever kind of essay you think would be most useful at this time. Also, may I say that we have never been too strict about word limits, and that we do not propose to begin being that way now.

I so much hope that you are able to accept this invitation.

With warm regards.

Sincerely yours,

Stephen R. Graubard

Editor

Johannesburg

29 July 1980

My dear Gunnar,

I need not tell *you* how speedy the administrative grind is in Academia. Application for leave; how long? how much does it weigh? how many sq meters? who's escorting you across the Atlantic? – the lot.

Now, at last it's Yes, you can go west old man!

I suggest the Spring Quarter 1981. Then I can take the Fall semester at Spelman, Atlanta – 1981. Does this make sense?

I meant to ask if they would help with part of the air fare, as Ribs will want to come for a study 'tour' for about half a semester some time during my stay there. They, you (DU) might pitch in for the other part of the fare. If there is any such possibility, would you call President Donald Stewart of Spelman and make a proposition on my behalf? – like the swell Swede you are.

Life is still treating us well in this hemisphere. I hope you and Vanja are flourishing. Let me know your thinking, so that my chiefs here can be informed how long they'll miss me.

Love,

Zeke

New York

11 August 1980

Dear Prof. Mphahlele,

By now you should have received six of the papers for the Bellagio conference on 'African Cultural and Intellectual Leaders and the Development of the New African Nations', as well as travel information and travel forms. I hope that it will still be possible for you to join us in Bellagio on September 17.

Ali Mazrui's essay is, as you will see, perhaps a bit discursive, and Robert July and I have been discussing ways to keep the group discussions that follows it from being too unfocused. Perhaps you have some ideas in that regard. What we would like would be to begin the general discussions for that session by putting one thesis or question before the group at large.

I promised in my last letter that I would eventually get in touch with you with regard to my own research, which considers the relationship of magazines to intellectual and cultural movements.[1] I have begun doing research now on African magazines, including *Black Orpheus*, *Transition,* and *Drum* – largely, I should say, at Jack Thompson's suggestion. I wonder, in this regard, if you would be willing to spend an hour or so, one evening at Bellagio, talking with me about African magazines. We could record our discussion, and a transcript could eventually be sent for your review. Please excuse me for proposing to intrude thus upon your time. I know that you must get many such requests.

I look forward to hearing from you, and to meeting you again at Bellagio.

With all best wishes.

Sincerely,

Peter Benson

Visiting Research Fellow, Humanities

1 Peter Benson was to publish this research in *Black Orpheus, Transition and Modern Cultural Awakening in Africa* (Berkeley: University of California Press 1986).

Johannesburg

20 August 1980

My dear Khabi,

Thanks very much for the copies of the letters concerning the Chair. It is quite clear what's going on in the mind of our man, die *poephol van*[1] *Kwadlangezwa*. I can't imagine how he could act negatively and thus fly in the face of such overwhelming evidence of academic integrity and wisdom. It would amount to lack of faith in some of the very people he has placed in high positions by virtue of his esteem for them. There's a guy who's fond of saying of someone whose intelligence he doesn't think much of: *o tletse masepa ka sebonong*[2] (as if the stuff could be any other part of the body and furthermore, it's always on its way out with the fellow). I would say if our man made a false judgment this time, he's really in that kind of trouble.

I must say I admire the stand of the academics who are supporting you. For once we see integrity prevail in an area of our life that's been fouled up for so long – for a ¼ of a century that one could never believe that there could be a small pocket of fresh air in our musty life – where the Ballantynes, ... exist. Note 2.2 in the letter from the fellow is classic and the letter should be framed as a pre-historic item. That an academic can suggest that whatever is African can't make a 'department', and this in 1980, is mind-boggling even while it infuriates me. A letter like that shown to your grandson when he will be 20 will be a clear reflection of what it was like with Africans ... of this period. We'll keep our fingers crossed, even if it will mean more and more administrative work for you. Still, it will mean you will be entitled to a secretary. Above all, you will be able to shape the department the way an *African* university should *truly* have it, and you'll not have to be working under some other asshole who'll subject you to intermittent spurts of crap, something much worse than a downpour.

The Council of Black Education and Research is now in motion.[3] We have offices (3) at Abbey House, 51 Commissioner St. A building where there are about 2 African and one Indian lawyer. Carnegie Corp. is giving us $15,000 for the infra-structure: furniture, rent, etc. and then we shall have to ask for grants for ad hoc research projects. Will send you a Press Release.

It's like this: when the Carnegie representative and I talked last July and I proposed the Council, he asked me to draw up a memorandum, (which led to the one you have). I told him I would have to talk to people who have been on the scene all the time about the proposition. Who, better than the Teachers Action Committee? I didn't want to have it said Mphahlele has come again and is meddling with things he has been away from for 20 years – blah-blah ... So I met the firebrands ... (alas, we came full circle!) – the fixtures. They liked the idea and asked me to elaborate and spell out my ideas, which are in their final form in the copy you have. They ratified it. So we were automatically a steering committee. As time went on, they kept up a steady inconsistency in attendance. Eventually we would only be three, until Fanyana was banned.[4]

I thought 'Fuck them, we're not going to call them again.' During the earlier discussions I just heard N announce to me with a straight face that so-and-so is now secretary. The not-so-young Turks, alas.

I knew better than to quibble. Meantime we had to set up a Trust, so that it can collect money by contract. The new law forbids soliciting of public money, unless it's a Welfare Organisation and it's become as difficult to register as one today as it is to kiss your elbow. A Trust can, on the other hand, be registered as a company and thus be able to take money in return for services like research or supplying teaching materials – *spaza* kind of stuff.[5]

A lawyer has drawn up a Deed and submitted it for registration. I and a white lady are Trustees and we can augment the Board. It only means the

Trustees control the funds. I, on the other hand, can be and am on the Executive. I decided as a Secretary was foisted on us, it will be politic to retain him and make him Organizing Secretary. Because a Secretary would make a Director imperative and we wouldn't have the funds for *him* – the [...] didn't think of it. I have assumed on my own the role of honorary director. They like platform antics, our guys, but call them for *work* ...

Carnegie will come in soon as the Deed has reached them and the contract procedures can be worked out. The Organizing Secretary is ... an ex-teacher.

I must augment the Executive to no more than 14. I've thought of writing now to invite people across the country. This is also a formal invitation to you. The Executive can meet 3 or 4 times a year and fares will be paid and subsistence to those coming from outside.

The Executive will give *direction*. I'm thinking at the moment that we should have a projects committee that will stay on the job of supervising and monitoring research projects. One that will meet more often. Let me hear from you. I am also inviting Temba Nhlapo in Durban. Can you think of one other in Natal who thinks seriously about education and research?

The Executive should meet soon, maybe in October to discuss a conference of educationists – black, across ethnic lines.

Love to you all,

Zeke

1 'the arsehole of Kwadlangezwa'

2 'he is full of shit in his arse'

3 An educational organisation founded by Mphahlele in 1980.

4 Fanyana Mazibuko, a teacher at Soweto's Morris Isaacson high school, was banned after the 1976 uprising.

5 *Spaza* is township slang for red herring.

19 September 1980

Dear Gunnar,

Thanks so much for your letter. Refreshing indeed, brings me good news.

Certainment? Mais bien sur mon vieux![1] Spring quarter 1981 would suit me admirably. The courses will be just right for me. I long to sink my teeth into it all! Throw in GSIS for good measure – maybe they should structure for me 4 lectures on South Africa – one a week for 4 weeks. If they are agreeable, let them write me and I shall suggest titles (topics).

I propose for Black Literature 'The Poetry of the Black World: A comparative inquiry into its major Concerns'.

As soon as your Dean or whoever invites me, I shall let you know the texts. Your suggested salary suits me, especially if I can get airfare out of it, or part of it.

Love to you,
Zeke

[1] 'Certainly? But of course my old friend!'

31 October 1980

Dear Zeke,

It was such a pleasant surprise to hear from you! Thank you both for taking time to write the English dept and for being kind enough to let me know you had done so. The process is long and convoluted, studded with the ploys of academic politics. The prestigious English department has unanimously recommended me for tenure to the Amherst equivalent of a faculty senate. The Black Studies dept is, however, much less impressed with me. My colleagues there are literal 'crabs in a barrel' and I mourned the future of the dept at Amherst last year when our incompatibility became apparent. Since two historians are already tenured, there is not much hope for restructuring that small dept. But I hate to think of leaving it in the hands of people who were not involved with the original black studies movement and have little sense of its guiding spirit.

This semester I am again teaching my course on African poetry. I began with Camara Laye's *The Dark Child* since Olney has convinced me of the wisdom of using that genre to introduce new-comers to the essence of contemporary African literature. We've done the French-speaking poets and the Nigerians. Before we move to either the Portuguese or English speaking poets of southern Africa, students will read your autobiography. If what happened last year is an indicator, they will find it informative, depressing, and moving.

According to my diss. Comm. that labor is nearly finished. (Thank you for the list of titles. I have already used *Mhudi*, but need to look at your short novel again ...). One more long, steady push and I'll be finished with the graduate work which has kept me here (and shadowed my life) for the last 3 years. I long to spend next year in Africa and will turn my attention to grants, fellowships, and jobs as soon as the ink dries on the diss. One possibility is doing an extended study on Bessie Head in Botswana. Another is teaching African-American literature at Yaoundé. Another is spending time at Ife. I long for another immersion in the 3rd world since it's been 5 years since I last left the U.S.

I have not seen Johnella recently, though we have spoken on the phone. Her diss, of course, is finished. She is still chairing the dept at Smith and still giving concerts (she did one recently called *Black-Eyed Susans in Song: Songs of Black Women Composers*). She sends her warmest regards, and I have given her your address. We're glad to learn that you will be in the States next year and are confident that some conference or other event will bring us together again with time to re-connect and share.

Peace to you and your family!

Love

Andrea[1]

[1] Andrea Rushing teaches in the English and Black Studies departments at Amherst College.

11 November 1980

My dearest Teresa,

I forgot to tell you in the other letter something about Walter M. Maybe I was too hasty in assessing his sincerity or shall I say, capacity for friendship. It shouldn't worry me, but it does, that I can be too trusting.

He asked that we bring him to Lebowa for an outing. We were not going to make the trip until this time, but we were happy to oblige: simply on the strength of the little I knew about him at Smith College when I went to lecture there. I usually demand of myself a response fitting the spontaneous expression of goodwill, so when he indicated he wanted to be a friend of the family, I breathed in the spirit in which he said it.

What does he start doing here? – first pretends he drinks nothing but sherry, and that in mean quantities. Next thing he's stealing drinks and loading himself flat out, pretending all the while the heat's getting to him. He slept all way to JHB when we drove back, having slugged down *something* early in the morning. We drop him at his hotel, after staying with H.S. and her husband ..., and for two days he's cooped up in his room, drinking. We collect him and take him to Soweto. He steals liquor, raiding the cupboard where I thought it would be out of reach! I call the Embassy to collect him. Otherwise he'd soon be a diplomatic embarrassment. That morning – only the third – he's flat on his tummy, out, when they come for him. Throughout all this, he keeps breaking into sobs and saying, 'I'm so ashamed ... what will my mother think when she knows ... I'm ashamed you've discussed me ... I'm alcoholic ... from my father ...'. It turns out a doctor ... started him on treatment against alcoholism and he abandoned the pills and slumped back to the habit ... The shitass! One morning during his stay with us he cries out and says 'I'm an illegitimate child!' Well, that puritanical crap you know sticks in my gullet. I said 'Big deal – what's so newsworthy about that!' Illegitimacy to an African ear is a hollow cry.

So you know now, as we also do, more than you did when I let on about his fleeting moment of philanthropic weakness. Think nothing of the charade. He's a 'lovely' study of mother-coddled vanity, and that's funny.

Love

Ntate

Johannesburg

3 December 1980

My dearest Teresa,

At the time of writing this, the Argus Co. which owns *The Star, Herald, Post, Weekend Post*, gave the strikers an ultimatum yesterday – to return to work or face dismissal. The deadlock was over pay during the 3 weeks strike, which the proprietors wouldn't agree to effect – not a cent. The Blacks stuck to their guns. Today it's reported that 68 have been dismissed. MWASA, the Media Workers Association of SA, includes reporters, editorial staff, as well as distributors, circulation and street corner guys – it used to be only WASA – editorial and reporters, excluding the manual gang. WASA was Writers Association of SA – only Black. Blacks pulled out of the SA Society of Journalists because the latter was predominantly white and worked for white interests. The Blacks pulled out to form WASA. SAAN is the SA Association of Newspapers – a group including the *Rand Daily Mail, Sunday Times, Sunday Express, Financial Mail,* etc.

Now we have a phone at home: Johannesburg 944-2273. It took a letter from Wits plus an M.P. to get the Post Office moving. Unlike in the US, telephones, telegrams, railroads, are run by Government.

Am sending you under separate cover a recent book on the Black Press and an essay on the subject – an historical perspective – by my colleague Tim Couzens. He has been awarded his Ph.D. and this essay was part of a dissertation on Black writing in SA for which I was one of the examiners.[1]

I shall send you more material as I receive it from friends in the media. This letter begins the way it does because I was going to send the news clippings with it – I reckoned on second thoughts to send them inside Tim's paper. So you should expect two book packages. Let me clarify certain points that will make the clippings mean something: there is in this country the NPU (National Press Union) – a white organization made up of white newspaper owners. There is the SASJ (South African Society of Journalists) – the white journalists' union. Not all black reporters are in MWASA, because it is a militant body, tending to reject white patronage in tune with the African political mood today. But all Blacks (which means Africans, 'Coloureds' and Indians) work for white-owned papers and magazines. You'll notice in Tim's paper that since 1932 when whites begin to publish for the African market (advertising was the capitalist motive), independent African papers went under. Only one emerged – *Inkundla*, subsequently run by Jordan Ngubane who lived in D.C. until recently when he returned home (you may know him). He'd be a valuable resource. He edited it – and was a first-rate editor. I remember being a regular reader of it in the 50s. He then did the foolish thing of joining White-Liberal politics full time and *Inkundla* didn't survive.[2] It was independent, probably the last of that group. So you have a crop of Black reporters, news editors and subs working for two main groups of white papers – SAAN & Argus. *Post* and *Weekend Post* (for a black readership) belong to the Argus group. The *Star* (Argus) is the main evening paper in the Transvaal Province, the *Rand Daily Mail* (SAAN) the main morning paper. Black reporters of the *Mail* are striking in sympathy with those of *Post* and *Weekend Post*, which two went out on strike in sympathy with those of *Cape Herald* (Cape Town) – the Argus paper where it all started. But the *Herald* staff are back to work after an agreement, and these of the JHB Argus gang are holding out for strike pay. It's said Argus is never going to yield on that. Meantime *Post* and *Weekend Post* have stopped production. The *Rand Daily Mail* is to the left of the *Star* in the liberal (not radical) tradition and has a much more enlightened editorship than that of the *Star*.

Back to *us*. Don't forget to use some of the money in savings for your medication. A propos of this, Kenya has finally yielded to my constant prodding to send the interest on the insurance money they blocked for 6 years to the savings a/c in D.C. They will (i.e. the Standard Bank in Nairobi) use that Washington Bank as my mailing address. Just ask the Bank to forward any such mail to you. You will decide whether it's worth redirecting to me or merely recounting the contents briefly. If it's merely a notice of Tax withholding, file with you – i.e. Kenya tax on interest.

Please send Millie Steiner, 121 So-cherry St. Denver, 80222 the sum of $8.00 and say its for the book she sent me.

Don't forget to tell Motswiri that he should recoup part of his losses with the cash he can salvage from the Community College cheque. I'll refund the rest soon.

So long for now. Love as always & take care.

Your Ntate

Enclosed cheque is for your personal use.

P.S. Tell Lee his message arrived thro'every conceivable channel and I'm working on the *Preface*. Just let him not try the F.B.I. or worse.

1 Tim Couzens. 1980. ' "The New African": Herbert Dhlomo and Black South African Literature in English 1857-1956'. PhD Thesis, University of the Witwatersrand.

2 When Mphahlele was leader of the South African delegation on behalf of the African National Congress at the All Africa People's Convention in Accra in 1958 Jordan Ngubane was a member of a Liberal Party group headed by Patrick Duncan.

Cape Town

8 December 1980

Dear Zeke

I do not know whether you have the enclosed piece from the *New York Times* which someone sent me. If not, I thought you might like to have it.

I was very pleased to see that you are giving a series of lectures at summer school here and very much look forward to attending them.

Several of my friends have asked whether it would be possible to meet you and I am sure that my colleagues whom I joined for this year to inaugurate the new African Literature course at UCT would welcome an opportunity to get together with you in an informal way. I would therefore be very pleased indeed if you could spare an evening while you are in Cape Town so that I can arrange this at my place. If you are agreeable I would appreciate it if we could fix this before you come, as I know that once you are here there will be many calls on your time. I look forward to hearing from you.

I hope you and your family are well. I am glad that my daughter has had some success with *Chirundu* overseas. She is hoping now for European editions as there was considerable interest at Frankfurt.

With best regards

Ursula

California

27 December 1980

Dearest Zeke,

I think I finally have a publisher for *Pagne Noir – après des ans, n'est-ce pas*?[1] Anyhow, the interested editor and press (John Gill of The Crossing Press in New York) has asked if I could find a major author to do the foreword/introduction, and I, of course, suggested you. I do not know whether you have received my last letters, but in each I asked if you would be interested in such a venture – something in the nature of the introduction you did for *Climbie*. I hope very much you will say yes – I'm pleading with you, *mon ami*. There is no one I would rather have do it, no one who would do it better than you. And I think your name would help Dadié in this country. I mentioned to John Gill that I felt sure you would, but that I was waiting for a reply. Hence, Pasha, would you let me know post haste? I shall be more than happy to send you the translation – I think you would be proud of it! Or, if you would prefer, I'll send it to you when you get to Denver, but that may be a bit long. You may wonder how I found out you would be in Denver this spring. Well, I spoke with Burton Feldman several weeks ago, and he told me. And how happy I am: Will Ribs be coming? Will you be free for visiting lectures? Would you like to come to California? To Colusa? All can be arranged – just say the word. BUT DO LET ME KNOW ABOUT THE INTRODUCTION IMMEDIATELY, eh? *Merci, mon cher*. I'll be glad to twist your arm ... or to bribe ... or to simply say how grateful I am.

Christmas came and went. My parents came down from Portland, asked about you, and when I told them you would be in Denver in the spring, they insisted I tell you to plan on a trip to the Northwest. Their house is yours; all you have to do is show up.

I received a small grant to do some research on the folktale. So, instead of the usual four classes this spring, I'll be teaching three. Must find out what those heady folklorists are doing to those charming literary tales – all that variant/motif stuff, à la Levi-Strauss. *Mon dieu*, what next? Will spend some time at UCLA. Whom should I see there? Do let me know. And that reminds me. Anne Fuller is no longer dean at Scripps. She stepped down when a new president came in, but she is busy, busy working for all sorts of academic councils centered in Washington. Anyhow, when I spoke to her last, she sent all sorts of love your way. You see, you all are still missed.

Must get this in the mail, Pasha, so I'll close. Palmer and the enfant are well. Do want you to meet them both. I SHALL WAIT FOR YOUR LETTER. Meanwhile, my love to Ribs and to you. Miss you leaps and bounds.

Sempre,

Karen

P.S. Please say *yes. Merci, merci*

1 'after all these years, not so?'

1981

Johannesburg

18 January 1981

My dear E.M.

Thank you for a very pleasant & interesting meeting:

Re the things in the library: I fancy that its beginning of Black Drama in the 50's – are mentioned in the papers in the Human Sciences Research Council & are not in those in the JHB library.

The *South African Year Book*s of '79 & '80 have articles I wrote on Black Theatre. Both articles were done hurriedly, reluctantly & briefly only because no one else would do them! Previous articles were hopeless!

I meant to tell you that I have many of your early letters to me. Sometime we should go through them together.

I have been thinking about the book of plays. I have done drama books for Maskew Miller (see pamphlet) & perhaps I can get the Via Africa manuscript back & say that it could fit into the MM drama series. I'll try to do this.

There is a need for a good book of plays now & if you can do something to indicate what Greek Drama was like we can go ahead with things. I used a condensed version of Shelley's translation of the *Cyclops of Euripides*. I chose this because it has humour & lots of action & is a story that could belong to the legends of any country. It is the length of a short one-act play.

Love you both.

As always,

Norah

Johannesburg

9 February 1981

Dear Professor Mphahlele,

Thank you for your letter of 16 January 1981. I and my colleague and co-editor, Richard Cornwell, are really sorry that you do not see your way open to serve on our editorial advisory board at this stage.

As regards your specific queries we can give you the categoric assurance that we will not allow the *Journal* to be used as 'an ideological instrument' by anybody. The editorial policy of the *Journal* will be to avoid commitment to any particular viewpoint or ideology. Furthermore, the Africa Institute as such does not hold or propagate a particular point of view, but is committed to the free exchange of ideas at the highest possible level of academic endeavour. After reading the three articles I sent you, we trust that it will also be clear that we as researchers have complete freedom to take an independent line in our writings, and therefore cannot be labelled apologists for the Government's policy of separate development.

However, we do hope that in future we will get an article from you for publication in our *Journal* (by the way, the stipulation of 4 000 to 6 000 words for manuscripts is just a guideline and articles could well be much shorter). Thank you also for putting us in contact with Dr. Richard Rive, who has indicated his willingness to do the book reviews for us.

With kind regards and best wishes for a fruitful period of teaching and research in the United States.

Denis Venter

Researcher, Africa Institute

Co-Editor, *JCAS*

2 April 1981

Dear Bernth,

Thanks for your letter. I have read the paper, & try as I might to be dispassionate in my attitude toward it, I find it impossible to evaluate,[1] Particularly because try as the writer might, he/she fails to sustain a dispassionate approach. He (I'll use this gender for convenience) is reading into motives, throws in a conjecture here & there, struts about innocently like a smug dandy with hands in the pocket, & then bang! – he comes out with it on pp. 19-20. As if he were writing a piece of fiction in which speculation is justified. He *doesn't want* to know what else I do at Wits that is fulfilling without vindicating Wits; he *does not want* to say there are books banned because one is 'listed' & others because the Publications Act doesn't like them. Because he wants to believe that some compromise was arrived at between me & the Govt. He *doesn't want* to know whether or not I would still have returned if Turfloop & others didn't exist or told me to forget it while I was in Philadelphia. He says he does not want to speculate on *Chirundu* in terms that are themselves speculation. I detest & despise such intellectual dishonesty. He could easily have stayed with the facts of censorship & left surmises (malicious & veiled) out of it. Sorry, but I can't help feeling that the guy's hunting & out for the kill, maybe to vindicate his sympathy for the S. African underdog – expecting some bouquet from the lobby?

Voilà mon ami, c'est pas la peine![2]

It now appears I shall have to return home in June, unless I can swing a grant to enable me to sit in a good folklore library for two months. I have finished recording the oral poetry in Venda, Tsonga, Pedi & need to establish a cultural context for annotating the book of translated oral poetry. Did I hear UCLA has such a library? The April date is just unsuitable for me: I have a deadline to meet for *Daedalus* (incidentally, on exile) as part of their special Africa issue. I couldn't afford to take off.[3]

Best,

Zeke

[1] Mphahlele, as an advisory editor, is responding to a manuscript on 'Ideas Under Arrest: Censorship in South Africa' submitted to *Research in African Literatures* by Daniel P Kunene and subsequently published in Vol 12(4) 1982, pp 421-39.

[2] 'So there it is, my friend, it's not worth the trouble!'

[3] This is a response to an invitation to attend the African Literature Association conference scheduled to be held in Claremont, California, on 8-12 April. He was busy writing 'Africa in Exile', *Daedalus* 111 1982, pp 29-48.

17 May 1981

Dear Chabani,

K came through here to Colorado College in Colorado Springs – an hour's drive south of Denver. He's on a month's visiting lectureship there – May. He has gotten some – shall I say permission or concession – I don't know – to invite me to give a public lecture at the College – in African Lit, which is what he is about. I have the uneasy feeling that he's bending over backwards to make me feel I'm still relevant – to what? only he knows. He spent a Saturday here, during which he recounted to me his publishing history. Again I felt uneasily that he seemed to think I had the right to know what he has been at. No doubt, nostalgia has hit him. Tried to explain why politically he would feel shut in at Umtata. He feels if he must – as he must – return he has to exhaust the home scene first before he can settle for the neighbouring countries. ...

... Harry was good enough to phone me and let me know the results of the meeting you held on the Council. I'm entirely in agreement with the decision on the secretarial position. I have written to him to confirm this and also, further, to suggest what organizations to hit for our fund raising.

The position with me is that I finish teaching June 18 here, and have asked Yale for a residency for two months on its campus – this to enable me to use its Africana library which I am told has a very good folklore section. I need to build up a context for the annotating of the translations of the poetry I've been recording.

I am today sending off a cable to Glover to request permission to stay on till Aug 14. I hope he doesn't refuse, as it would be silly not to use my presence here to exploit the library resources.

Enough for now, warmest regards

Zeke

Denver

18 May 1981

Dear Mr Aldworth

Your letter was rediverted to me by my wife.

The disturbing things about what you say are that (a) it took so long before I could have a reply to my letter of last year (Aug 7) and (b) you are making the apology on behalf of your correspondent and he remains quiet. I don't accept the explanation that there was confusion in the Africa division. No confusion can be an excuse for what I consider rudeness on the part of the person to whom I addressed a civil letter in which I was in all decency offering to clarify matters. Sepamla and I were insulted and verbally abused in public and all we can hear is that there was confusion.

If, as you say, there was 'possibly ... (an) opportunity ... grind a personal axe or two', a paper of the *Star*'s reputation should have respondend promptly to put a thing like that straight. The spate of letters continued all the same. Nine months had to pass. What kind of confusion takes that long to clear on a daily newspaper?

On the second point, I have the exasperating feeling that I'm experiencing that age-old play when they set up black against black and laugh on the sidelines. They blow the whistle for the 'gladiators' to begin and then think they only need to blow it again to stop the fight, without any consideration whatever of the leaping hate and contempt that have been generated in the gladiators. Yes, it is an ancient game that goes back to the Greek and Roman times. To see it enacted in this part of the 20th century appals me.

Yet another phase of history reveals the kind of boss who will apologise for his nigger boy's conduct while the latter remains quiet and shuffles off, confident that the master has taken care of things.

The things that were said in those letters by your correspondent display a scalding contempt for Sepamla and me, and if he says nothing to retract them, it must mean the contempt is still fermenting inside him. What am I to make of that – simply go 'form ideas of a panel of eminent writers' with 'Prof' Mtshali? What kind of panel would that be?

I certainly agree that the *Star* can promote the interest of our writers by giving them a platform that we badly need – oh, how we need it! But work with 'Prof' Mtshali – never. I was not doing him a favour by reviewing his book of verse in the *Daily Mail*. I was promoting the cause of literature, which is bigger than either him or me – mountains bigger. Because of this, I was able to swallow my own wrath and contempt, for that instant. And don't think it was a gesture of condescension, I happen to care about what South Africans read, what interests them, what their own sense is of the function of literature.

It wouldn't serve any purpose now to raise the issue in your pages that caused the unfortunate (for the *Star*) collapse in journalistic morals. You are right saying you need to move beyond the 'sterile position' now prevailing. So, good luck in your efforts. I should appreciate it if you will let Don Mattera see this letter, as you intimate his concern, because I want him to know my feelings.

Sincerely

Eskia Mphahlele

New York

8 July 1981

Dear Professor Mphahlele,

I was most delighted to hear your voice after such a long, long time. I just do not believe that I spoke to you, but that's the way it is; I did indeed speak with you.

I have been trying very hard to get and keep in touch with you. In fact when Mr and Mrs Martin M. Kaunda went down South in 1979 for his medical treatment, I was told, upon their return that they had been in touch with you. I asked if they could give me your address. I do not remember them giving it to me, even though I had mentioned to them that I had a copy of my dissertation ready for my Prof. Even as recently as last month when Peter and Dawn dropped in at our place, the first thing I wanted to find out from them was whether they were in touch with you. The answer was that you were already out here. And I had just been hoping that I would get you. And when I contacted Frank Chipasula who is with you over there, he told me that you were in fact at Yale for the summer. It really has been a great honour for me that my little dream has materialized. And from this letter, I am sure you will tell the reasons for my tireless efforts to reach, or is it find you?

Orlean and I bound one copy of my doctoral thesis and have it ready for you. I left it at home. And I hope to send it to you immediately I get back home and if I can have your address. You just won't believe this, we have kept the thesis since beginning of 1978.

As I said on the phone I am presently under severe pressure to try and get the thesis or portions of it published, ideally in book form. People at Cambridge University Press suggested that because of its rather specialized nature, it would be best to get articles out of it. This has raised some serious questions of organization, and in any case I am not very much sold to the idea. However, if that is the only way out, I will have no choice but to do so. (2) One of the members of my doctoral committee, Professor Lois Anderson, a musicologist, suggested at the time of my defence and twice after the defence that I work out three books out of the thesis. She saw each of the three portions, Parts I, II and III as constituting a good basis for three books. (3) NECZAM (National Educational Company of Zambia) which published school/academic books has finally informed me that they would like to publish the thesis as a book. They sent me a summary of what their readers saw to be important comments that must be taken into account when reworking the text. I am afraid that NECZAM, as Frank Chipasula who once worked for them will tell you, cannot at this stage carry out the job with the urgency that I have to have it done. It is perhaps my own foolishness that a) I believed that such a work ought to be published, therefore originate from the place where the research on which it is based was conducted; and b) that during my stay at home I was very much tied up with countless family problems and my own tough job of building a house. We have by the way, Prof., put up a house just a few yards from Mr. and Mrs. Kaunda's. We like the house.

[Writer's identity unknown]

Abidjan

3 November 1981

Dear Professor Mphahlele,

I hope you will forgive my writing to you in this way but I have no other means at my disposal to get in touch with you. Let me first give you the motives for this letter. I am at present engaged on a doctoral thesis on your works and on those of Alex la Guma. I had the opportunity of meeting and interviewing Alex la Guma when he came to the University of Dar es Salaam in 1976 for a series of talks on African Literature. I was at the time a lecturer in French in the Department of Foreign Languages and Linguistics. I should be glad of course to be able to meet you as well, all the more so as my supervisor has suggested that I should try and have contacts with both of you, but a return trip to South Africa is somewhat beyond my means at the present moment. That is why I make bold to ask you whether you would be willing to answer questions related to the subject of my thesis which I would submit to you in a further correspondence. Of course I should hate adding too much to your work and I shall perfectly understand if you cannot oblige me.

In the meantime I should like to give you a brief account of the circumstances which led me to study South African literature in general and your works in particular. When I had my first contact with South Africa I was a teacher of French in a Coloured and Indian High School in Salisbury (Zimbabwe). We decided with an Indian colleague of mine who had relatives in the Republic to tour the country. Throughout our journey we met Indian, Coloured and African people from different social backgrounds. Everywhere I was fed, entertained, accommodated with a rare sense of hospitality, although, as I was later told, this was forbidden by law. This short visit to South Africa made a lasting impression on me. Years later, as I was serving as a French lecturer at the University of Dar es Salaam, I came across your works. I truly enjoyed reading them. Not only did they help me recapture images and impressions with a vividness I could not imagine but they also provided me with a much deeper insight into a society I had only partially known. It was a profoundly gratifying aesthetic experience which broadened my vision of your country. As a result of this I contemplated the idea of writing a thesis for a doctorate. My project was accepted by a supervisor and I started my research for good. It has been going on now for five years with ups and downs depending on the time I could afford and the availability of research material. This research is essentially concerned with the problem of reality and that of the relationship between society and creative writing in the context of South Africa.

I shall appreciate your kindness but do not hesitate to send me a refusal if you think you can't help me.

Yours sincerely,

R Samin

Johannesburg

18 November 1981

Dear Steve [Stephen Gray]

I am sorry I have delayed so long before replying to your letter formally. Now your second has arrived. I have no objection to either *Staffrider* or *Kunapipi* publishing the interview.

Alas! Moving from one office to another has resulted in total disarray and I cannot find the form from McGraw Hill. Would you please send me another. It's okay for the *Daily Mail* review.

Best wishes, and thank you for coming to the launching.

Sincerely

E. Mphahlele (Professor)

1982

25 May 1982

My dear Zik,

I enclose some correspondence with the Poetry Society of Great Britain which may be of interest to you or people like Tim Couzens. They may have, of course, contacted you as well.

I have not forgotten our discussion about poems in English dealing with African Folklore, and will try to do something about it soon.

This evening we are having a seminar led by a young lecturer from the University of the Transkei, Dr. P.N. Thuynsma, on your desire to introduce African mythology into contemporary writing. I find this most interesting and exciting.

With every good wish,

Professor F.G. Butler

Cape Town

12 November

Dear Zeke,

I have been meaning to write for months, first of all to thank you for inviting me to attend the conference of the Institute of Black Studies in Jo'burg which I was very glad indeed not to have missed. While your brief return must in many ways have been sad for you, I am sure you must have derived satisfaction from your reception, showing as it did that you have not been forgotten and that all you have said and written was not in vain as far as the people most involved are concerned.

Could you please let me have a copy of your paper? I promised Bernth Lindfors an article on the conference. I know it's going to be difficult getting copies of papers from the Institute, but I hope to get at least a few. I'll deal only with the Literary side.

The biography is due out next month and they've promised me a copy by air and the rest of my copies by sea, but I'll ask them to send one to you. I won't say 'I hope you will like it'. There are parts I am sure you will, and others with which you will not agree, but I hope I have got across the spirit of what you stand for, so that readers can share with me what your writing has meant to me. Once again my very best thanks for all your cooperation.

I am very sad about James Matthews. I am now a member of Cape PEN, and at my first meeting heard Gerald Gordon tell us how he convinced PEN International not to chuck South Africa out. One of the objectives was lack of protest about James, and this has now been rectified. Cape PEN is multi-racial in its constitution but has no black members. People like Richard Rive are hesitant to join. Maybe there is something I can do. I know it's too late for this – the Jo'burg conference showed that clearly, but one can't very well stop trying.

All the best and kindest regards.
Ursula Barnett

1983

Somewhere on the East Coast
20 July 1983

Dear Chabani,

How are things at Wits? I hope you've settled in and housing problems have not proved to be impossible.

Ribs called me yesterday morning to tell me she has at last been given a pass. You'd think they would be just too keen to issue that kind of thing so they can more easily control niggers. One nigger more without a pass means one nigger more running loose in the country.

In passing she mentioned how impressed she is by your book. Says, however, it's wrong to say she was 'not involved with Bantu Education'. I said in return I couldn't remember the context. I later recalled that's when we were talking about the high-school era when we were fired. And maybe I meant she was not in that nor involved in the public noises the ANC was making then. As an individual gesture, she resigned to go in for social work. I suspect her gripe is that she could not be said to have been indifferent or unaffected.

Was the excerpt of the 'interview' an extension of the one *Staffrider* carried, or an entirely different item? Anyhow, I thought to mention it in case she waylays me with a brick in hand when I arrive! Although I'm aching to return, there's no other way but to hang around to wait for events (must honour a visit to San Diego, after a few days, stay in N.Y. – all in the 1st two weeks of Aug. I am more or less sure my return will be Aug 15. Harry tells me there's a man in Bonn who'd like one to come through his country and see him about the Council. He hasn't written you; so I can't say whether I shall fly to W. German on the 14th or directly back. It would only be a day's stay at most.

Warmest regards,

Ezeke

1985

19 November 1985

Dear Jan [Breitenbach],

I regret to have to tell you that I can no longer serve on the Council of the 1820 Foundation as of now.

I have given a lot of thought to this matter and can see no other way out of my dilemma. Briefly, the reasons are as follows:

(a) I am in the process of shedding membership in various councils and boards and committees owing to the mounting stress I'm labouring under. I feel utterly exhausted, and my doctor has advised that I slow down.

(b) Why should the 1820 Foundation be one of the first 'casualties?' I find myself increasingly drawn into projects that benefit mostly whites, either as participating clients or as policy makers and project leaders. I then find mine is merely a token presence. This makes me uncomfortable; as I am being asked to endorse programmes I know my people gain little or nothing from.

If the Foundation had at least three provincial offices likely to reach large communities of Blacks (African, Indian and 'Coloured') something might begin to happen that would lend 1820 a dimension of cultural relevance among these population groups. Even so, they would have to be given the freedom to plan their own socially relevant programmes, according to their perceived needs. As it is, one gets the impression, right or wrong, that the Foundation is an annual gala, a celebration of achievement without much care about the creative process (between Julys) that, among us Blacks, drains the *animateurs* who are in charge of it. Draining because of lack of facilities and material resources.

It may be argued that this was never one of the Foundation's objectives when it was first conceived: I wouldn't know. I can only imagine it is going to be uphill for the Foundation if it does not change its image, its founding code, so that Blacks associated with it see themselves as *creators* of a culture rather than merely as a subject of it or facilitator of it.

I must conserve energy for those educational programmes and projects that have their roots in Black life, and through which I directly address this life. It was good, all the same, for me to be invited into the Council and for Guy and Bozz to have thought of persuading me to accede to the invitation. Thank you for that trust. Thank you also for the privilege of meeting and knowing you personally.

Sincerely,

Eskia

E. Mphahlele

27 November 1985

My dear Eskia,

It's a pity we live so far apart, because there are many things to talk about.

First: I've just bought Stephen Gray's *Penguin Book of Short Stories* from Southern Africa, and I want to say how much I admired your contribution, 'Mrs. Plum'. I found your heroine completely convincing, and through her I got some rare and frequently painful glimpses of 'what it is like to be black in the world'. I also found myself looking at the Black Sash ladies of my acquaintance with increased admiration and unease!

Next: thank you for sending me a copy of your letter to Jan Breitenbach, resigning from the Council of the 1820 Foundation. I felt distressed about this – particularly as our INSET programme, which was founded precisely to help ease the main educational bottleneck in our country – the production of good teachers and good teaching materials for black schools – is about to start producing results. Our two INSET officers could hardly be blamed for the schools boycott which made contact with black teachers very difficult and entry to classrooms impossible; but some of their teaching materials have proved very useful, and others are in the pipeline. On the same front, we were instrumental in getting Molly Mahood to visit South Africa in order to report on the teaching of English Literature in Black secondary schools in South Africa.

I know that you and Molly had your differences in the past (you both behaved perfectly to each other during the festival), but our thinking was that a non-South African with considerable experience of English in Africa might have useful insights: which I think she has. I enclose a copy of her report. (There is a reference on p. 13 to SACHED, TURRET[1] and the University of Indiana.) There is much to think about, and act upon in it. I do hope that the Foundation's contribution in this field increases in effectiveness and volume. If you have any particular suggestions or hints, I do hope you will give us the benefit of them. Thank you for the contribution you made during your term of office.

Third: you may remember one of our early discussions – at the Glendower Hotel, Cape Town, during a U.C.T. Summer School – about South African Legend and Folklore. Well, I've continued working away at it slowly, and have assembled a considerable number of story-poems from every linguistic group in the sub-continent, and secured English translations of them where necessary. The plan is a book of poems in which South Africans of whatever origin (particularly school children) will find some of the stories of their country. A common stock of stories seems to me to be a good thing, something to share. Like you, however, I find myself overburdened with projects, so for the final stages of the work and all the administration involved, I have secured the assistance of Jeff Opland who is infinitely more knowledgeable than I am in certain fields. When we have a preliminary draft of the book I shall send you a copy in the hopes that you will like it.[2]

Jean and I send our Christmas and New Year Greetings to you and to yours.

Yours ever,

Professor F.G. Butler

1 SACHED and Turret were distance learning institutions.

2 Guy Butler and Jeff Opland (eds). 1989. *The Magic Tree: South African Stories in Verse.* Cape Town: Maskew Miller Longman.

2 December 1985

Dear Es'kia

Thank you for your letter of 19 November. I shall pass on to the Chairman and members of Council your decision to resign from the Council of the 1820 Foundation.

The contents of your letter are most disturbing. I presume that when you were first approached to serve on the Council, it was hoped that, apart from your personal qualifications to serve the national interests both educationally and culturally, you would be a contact point for the bridging of the various cultures and viewpoints in our troubled and cosmopolitan society. I must say that ever since I became involved in the pursuance of the aims of our Charter, every effort has been made to obliterate the barriers of race and colour. We have gone out of our way to see to it that opportunities are available for our projects to be truly national – and indeed that is the main theme of my message in this year's *Annual Review* of which you should be receiving a copy soon. I attach, for your interest, a copy of the latest Inset annual report, which demonstrates our endeavours into the field of black teacher upliftment in the Albany district and further afield. That is the reason, too, why over the last three years, the Foundation has gone regional and not merely confined itself to the promotion of annual cultural events, like the National Festival of the Arts, in Grahamstown. The *1820 Contact* bears witness to that in each of its issues.

If, as a member of the Council, you had these serious reservations about the role of the Foundation, I and others would have welcomed an open debate in Council – and then perhaps we could have resolved the issue, or at least have aired it. However, I must respect your decision, but would appreciate an opportunity of debating with you further the role which you believe the Foundation should play if it is truly to pursue the aims of its Charter.

I, too, have valued the privilege of knowing and meeting with you personally.

Sincerely

Jan

JJ Breitenbach

Executive Director

1987

13 April 1987

Dear Eskia

How are you? Retired, like me? What does that mean? One of the penalties of retiring seems an increase in the demands made upon one's attention by good causes of various degrees of importance. I recently saw a very nice picture of you in a glossy magazine called *Excellence*, I think, talking about your aspirations for U.B.A. I hope it goes well. Most good causes demand so much sheer sweat – particularly at this time and in this country. I try to cheer myself up with the epitaph of a young English gentleman who died young and in prison in the 17th Century; 'whose singular virtue it was to do the best things in the worst times, and to hope them in the most calamitous'.

One of my burdens is to try to get the Shakespeare Society of Southern Africa established on the right lines, and I am writing to friends for help. It is essential for the society to project an image of Shakespeare as a dramatist whose appeal seems to be universal. (Red China is the latest country to establish a Shakespeare society: they had festivals last year in both Peking and Shanghai.) He is also, for many, the literary touchstone of the English language, which in South Africa should belong to all.

What I hope you will do is to consent to be a patron of the Society. (I can hear you groan.) What does this involve? We would like to use your name on our stationery, as one of a group of eminent writers and critics, and possibly actors and producers, local and overseas) who approve of our aims, and think they are to be encouraged. So far we have got the consent of L.C. Knights and M.C. Bradbrook of Cambridge, Stanley Wells, editor of the new *Oxford Shakespeare* and John Styan of Northwestern, U.S.A. André Brink (who has translated two of the plays) has agreed, and I am waiting to hear from others. Patrons will not be expected to pay for anything, or do any work unless they have a particular desire to get involved! Their only reward will be free membership of the society.

I enclose a copy of an appeal for funds for our central administration, not in order to make you weep, but to give you some idea of progress to date. The text book project is, I think, potentially very important.

I do hope you will see your way to lending your name to this venture. I would also be most grateful if you could let me know of any friends or acquaintances who are interested in Shakespeare, either in education or on stage, who might become members of the society, or get involved in our work.

Yours sincerely,

Professor F.G. Butler

1997

29 June 1997

Bro Mphahlele,

Thank you so much for your beautiful and vigorous thought. You raise important questions and suggest fruitful approaches. Your emersion in research traditions helps to bring things into focus. When I get the time, I'll write at greater length. But I wanted to thank you for your kindness and to send you this small imperfect token of my esteem.

Sincerely

Steve Henderson

2000

27 June 2000

Dear Stephen [Gray],

Good to receive your heart-warming postcard. The pleasure was also ours when you & Henk visited.

You suggested that I compile a volume of stories and other narrative modes. I agree that it would be a task worthwhile undertaking. Problem: I'm too close to the writing to avoid a squinted take of it. It occurred to me that Stephen Gray would be the best person for the project. Would you have the time? Would it consume too much of your time, every minute of which you need for remunerative work, now that you're not on a leash any longer?

As I said, I was charmed by your anthology and critical essays (Southern Africa lit.), both of which I prescribed as class texts for my course in Columbia, SC. I should very much like for you to tackle the compilation. I would help by digging out possible entries, incl. the *Tribute* stuff, the narrative prose published in *Drum* & a bilingual journal published at Stellenbosch in the late forties, etc. Among the *Drum* stuff are a series called 'Lesane' as well as more serious pieces.

Incidentally, have you ever seen the latest novella, *Crossing Over*, same length as 'Mrs Plum' which it replaces in Ramogale's *To Kill a Man's Pride* (publ. 1999). Ravan thought 'Mrs Plum' diminishes its chances of being prescribed as a school text: their thinking is that it contains scenes suggesting bestiality (sic) – a view communicated to them by a few teachers.

Do you think you would find the time? The full number of the Lesane stories came out in a collection in the seventies or eighties (I forget the compiler-editor). The introduction to the volume would carry an imprint of a fine critic who I know for sure would place my work in proper perspective. What say you, *mon amis*? Let me say at once that I shall not be surprised nor think less of you if your answer is 'No'. I shall understand, in spite of my disappointment.

I know you are not enamoured of these new-fangled gadgets eg computers etc. But for any later use, my e-mail address is:eskimph@mweb.co.za

Warmest regards from us both

Zeke

Johannesburg
3 July 2000

Dear Zeke,

Thanks for your very welcome letter. And yes, as we drove back, taking the absolutely featureless (pot-holed) road you had so wisely advised us against ... my mind certainly was ticking over about that short story collection of yours.

By coincidence, a few days later, I was visited by the young Prof. Dave Attwell of UN's English Department at Pietermaritzburg, who had on him an actual copy of your *Man Must Live*, the first I had ever seen .... This he ran across my peripheral vision and said he was far advanced in *his* thinking about getting together a collection of your stories. He has links with University of Natal Press and would want to do it for them, I guess, and they are quite good at getting co-publications in the U.S. and the U.K.

Well, as you can imagine, I immediately more than encouraged him to approach you, gave him your phone no. (and I will give him a copy of this letter) ... and stressed that I thought he should try and get a commercial deal first (e.g., perhaps through local Penguin or another) for the money and distribution sake, and fall back on UNPress should that not work out.

I also said that I thought he should meet you to set it up somehow (I quite agree, this is the sort of project that needs being done by someone, rather than you doing it yourself – with an intro. including a statement about your standing and career, involvement with the story and related forms, for the sake of the memoryless) ... and that I would help, if necessary.

If you two get it underway, I'll give him my EM collection as well, and my huge, almost complete file of your *Tribute* columns. I said, just generally, that I thought the short story in Africa is woefully overlooked these days, and that hence that major part of your activity – including your role as an anthologiser – was unjustly scattered and neglected. I would help him as I am actively PRO pushing the short story, and also as it is quite simply my favourite part of your work.

Let's see if Dave can get this project moving ... I must say he is very well informed and very competent to undertake this kind of work. (People are getting a bit bored with Stephen Gray Stephen Gray ...) But if this doesn't work out, we'll have to think again!

All the best,
Stephen

I bumped into Sipho Sepamla, looking very elderly nowadays … and he asked after you, sending his greetings. He asked me didn't I think things were better for writers in the old days …. My jaw is still hanging: I literally did not know what to say. Still don't.

I know I haven't got e-what-what … but don't you like my Contessa MD with the proportional electronic spacing??!

Chuenespoort
August 2000

Dear Steve

It was kind of you to cast your feelers for a possible editor. Yes, we have corresponded before with Dave Attwell when he was with Unisa.[1] Didn't know he had moved. He was connected at the time with a high flight journal. I do so hope that he will undertake the Es'kia Mphahlele short story (wow! That name caused me to jump with amazement. A friend set up my initials and the land of the north Americans to come out in full at the very next tap of the space bar. The very first time in these four years that I try to type my initials! Which is why I daren't write the initials of that country across the Atlantic!).

Speaking of which, I chuckled over your pitch for the Contessa MD. You must explain to me next time what 'proportional what-what-spacing' means …. Can't say I blame you for remaining above this higher class of electronics and extended family. Luckily (for me) I still write initially in long hand except for business correspondence. You're one of the first few friends I type a letter to in the last few months: that late in my life …

I accept gladly whatever you suggest you can do to assist Dave if he requests it. I shall be a very happy old man if the job is executed (my, don't I sound officious!). And of course I shall always be at his beck and call. Tell him (not for me, for Tamarisa's sake, alas, whoever she may be!) the gods (whoever's) will smile kindly on him if he can make an old coot happy. I'm not the one to try to sport with the god's (whoever's) …

Cheerio for now, amigo, and ciao.
Zeke

PS This, by the way, is called Comic sans MS font on my computer programme! Pronounced, I'd say, what?

[1] David Attwell was, in fact, not at Unisa at the time, but at the University

of the Western Cape. When he assumed the headship of English at Wits he returned the collection of short fiction to Stephen Gray, who published it in the Penguin Modern Classics series.

2002

Chuenespoort

21 April 2002

Dear Stephen,

Sure, go ahead with the story. Good news that the anthology has another lease on life. I love the story & am happy I have your aesthetic judgment to back up my paternal bias.

I am amazed to see your address hasn't changed. Someone told me recently that you have relocated. Couldn't get it as I would expect you to inform me as one of your admirers. Indeed, the duration of one's residence in a place is a sign that person & place can contain each other, or else one will spit out the other!

There's something brewing in the Mphahlele workshop. A friend has undertaken to relieve me of a lot of papers – articles, addresses, etc – all expository stuff – and seek funding for their publication. In accord with my wishes I'm not in the editorial team he has chosen to do the selecting. Their job is all but completed.[1] I only need to give it the once-over. September is roughly scheduled for the publication, ie 2002. Just thought 'to bite your ear' (equivalent of Sesotho for 'whispering in your ear').

Keep well, good friend, prosper.

Ciao

Zeke

1 This major project reached fruition with the publication of *Es'kia* and *Es'kia Continued* (Johannesburg: Kwela Books in association with Stainbank and Associates 2002 and 2005).

2005

Johannesburg
12 March 2005

My Dear Stephen,

But of course: let's sock it to 'em. Am sending 5 copies. If you know someone in these circles, too, who can plug the idea of making Afr. Lit a teaching subject, we can get on to him. This would encourage more kids to take Afr. Lit – ie if it were to become a teaching subject. Wits does not print inaugural lectures any longer: stupid petty economies! A friend of mine who was at the lecture & works for SA Breweries as community projects adviser persuaded his boss that making copies & binding the paper was a community service! So there! I may yet become a beer guzzler (I & it don't agree) in order to keep community services going.

Best
Zeke

Johannesburg
22 March 2005

My dear Steph;

Thanks v.m. for the exciting news – wow! Who'd have thought that this dude could attract the attention of Olympia! May the gods be praised: that they are even prepared to defend a mortal like me! If I may sound a little vain: this marks the beginning of the Enlightenment in SA., two centuries after the European era. The idea of a schools edition & a gaudier cover & annotations & intro is an excellent one. David Ph … has been on to me – 'came thro' two days ago actually, to let me in on the news from you. So be it.

Thought you might be interested in the enclosed which is our publicity puff. Shd you want a few copies … nay, why don't I just put in the few – for what they're worth.

Muchas gracias una vez más,
Zeke

Chuenespoort

5 May 2005

Dear Stephen,

Thanks for your letter keeping me abreast of the progress on your side & Penguin's. I'm well aware of your expeditions & thorough habit of work – intimidating for me, alas! Let the wheels keep grinding, the good times rolling .... Sure, keep the booklet as long as you want. The contents page looks quite impressive. I'm amazed you were able to fit in both 'Mrs Plum' & 'Coming Over', the two being such long stories. Admirable!

I enjoyed your visit immensely. When the time comes for me to relocate, I shall find it easy to visit you. Who knows, I may find myself a neighbour of yours! When I realise we're already in May, it seems '06 will yet find me in Limpopo! I shan't pretend it will still be in order. There's nothing more for me anymore – here that is ... as you can imagine .... Typical of rural SA, the Bantustan patches, we can never boast to be lotus eaters – the sun kills them.

Cheerio for now, & keep in good health.

Ever

Zeke

Chuenespoort

3 November 2005

Dear Stephen,

Sorry I haven't acknowledged any of the snippets you have been pumping through the mail. Just thought you'd 'understand' ... I'm assembling the info now & should begin a skeleton today.[1]

A hurdle: most of my library is at the Univ of Venda including *Road to Ghana*. If you can, a photocopy of the last chapter or 2 will do. I can happily follow your suggestion – starting from the ending of the memoir & work backwards & forwards.

Cheers

Zeke

1 Mphahlele is referring to an Afterword he was preparing for the Penguin Modern Classics 2006 edition of Alfred Hutchinson's *Road to Ghana*.

2006

Chuenespoort

26 January 2006

Hi Stephen

Here it is. I keep feeling there's much more I should be able to say. And yet what it is I'm at a loss to say! On the other hand the linear dimension of the story is so dominant ... judge for yourself. I can't but admit that there is a grace, delicately displayed in the telling, one I cannot overlook. If the piece is unusable, say so. Don't go shy on me!

Warmest regards

Zeke

Chuenespoort

15 February 2006

My dear Stephen,

Your embellished piece is most commendable. Coming from a writer of your standing it could never be excessively dressed up! You have actually improved on my original. As I read it now (mine) it does look skimpily dressed! Who knows, with old age I may be turning puritan ...

Sincerely, you have put in essential additional information about Hutch. Thanks for that. Am pushing to be out of here before end of Feb. The expense of it may drive me back to the job-hunting queues. But as South Africans are so age-conscious, I may be back to the old days of eating bird-meat! Or maybe I can ask Cheney – Bush's Vice – to give me a few hints on bird shooting ...

Thanks again Stephen.

Love

Zeke

INTERVIEWS

LOOKING IN: IN SEARCH OF ES'KIA MPHAHLELE*

MANGANYI: One wonders how authentic the descriptions in *Down Second Avenue* are and whether important things have been omitted if they are authentic. Is there anything you could say about your childhood experiences?

MPHAHLELE: Every so often when I drive down [to Maupaneng] I take a look around to see what I feel about things forty-seven years later ... I realise more and more how distant I was from my father. When he left us in Marabastad in 1932 and went back to the North we were children ... It didn't look traumatic at that time. And then, as you grow up, you realise you miss a father, you don't have a father like other boys have, right? And then later on you settle down to that kind of situation. When I look back to it now, I realise that perhaps things might have turned out differently if we had *had* a father that we could look up to and ... rely on.

My life could probably have been eased a bit. But throughout, things kept ... coming onto me: living with my grandmother and

* An edited version of an interview published in 1981 in *Looking Through the Keyhole: Dissenting Essays on the Black Experience*. Johannesburg: Ravan Press, pp 4-50

aunt, my mother having to live out in the suburbs where she worked and seeing us on weekends, or we going up to see her. Whenever I drive around in the Pretoria suburbs my memories come back ... of the sort of life that was ... It was a pretty rough life and one was so exposed to so many hurts ... so many impacts ... pretty rough impacts, too. Whites ... and also just the need, the struggle, to survive. You know, you drive up to the suburbs to collect money from somebody whom they've been doing washing for at home, and then he is not there. Then you have to go back again and he is not there ... that kind of casual attitude they had towards my people who were doing their washing.

And ... I remember now quite vividly how the people my mother worked for were just so impersonal when they looked at me ... I just didn't seem to exist. I was just her son and there was no interest whatever. In fact, I hardly saw their faces ... Their faces were always a blur and I never could recognise them as people myself.

So the attitude was reciprocal. My mother, trying to hold down a job, had to behave in a certain way ... which was at once natural and unnatural. She wasn't the kind of grovelling woman who ... gets talked to rudely and then takes it. When I had gone to visit her I realised that I was in unnatural circumstances. I was always in her back room and never saw the inside of the house. Going back to Maupaneng ... I happened to meet my father's daughter, my half-sister. She was introduced to me by my aunt, who is still living in the house where we grew up.

I would imagine she must be going on to eighty now. The house is still the same. It's a rondavel. It's still there and the fireplace is still there ... and I realise how small it was now. When I was small it looked big. Now that I am an adult, it looks so tiny.

It used to be a terrifyingly big thing. Everything seems to have shrunk. The village itself is now being pressed against the mountain because of the corrosion, the erosion from the river.

When my father went back to the North, he remarried ... and had three children ... I met only two, young women, and I just felt a certain kind of revulsion. Perhaps revulsion is too strong a word. It was just a kind of withdrawal inside myself. And I had no words for them at all, and ... they had no words for me either. Even my attitude towards my aunt is very distant. She was always a harsh, tough person. She and my father were two of a kind.

MANGANYI: Paternal grandmother?

MPHAHLELE: Paternal grandmother ... the three of them seemed to have been from the same block.

There was no word of kindness ... nothing ... no affectionate word at all for any of us, her three grandchildren. Those memories come back very vividly to me and then I feel no nostalgia at all for the place – the kind of nostalgia I feel for Marabastad. And yet I keep going to the district to recollect my unprotected life as a herdboy, sniffing around for the old smells, listening to the old bird sounds, insect sounds.

MANGANYI: That is a very interesting observation ... I was going to say that when one reads *Down Second Avenue* one encounters a very grim situation ... Would you like to say something about that?

MPHAHLELE: Yes, there is, perhaps, a weird kind of nostalgia for Marabastad ... My formative years there seemed to have been more significant than back in the North ... There was a peer group, which meant a lot to youngsters as we grew up; something to rely on for moral support ... Then the school itself ... being able to go to school more regularly than ever before. We tried to make life interesting for ourselves, in spite of the conditions ... the kind of inner culture that was in the process of formation. You saw a sort of patchwork – these people were trying to make a life for themselves in a new urban situation, although some of them had been in Marabastad a long time, I would imagine thirty years or so. The jazz bands and New Year's Day festival mood when people used to go on picnics, in groups again, in clubs, and then the music of the time ... Marabi. It rings in my mind all the time ... My grandmother was a Lutheran. The Lutherans would go up and down the streets, usually on the night of Good Friday, singing and so on. I often go to the almost empty land where Marabastad used to be. I look around; recall the smell of the place again. Those are the things that I feel nostalgic about and yet they were not the things one would like repeated.

We grew up casually. I think of the boy who used to live next door to us, whom I mention. He used to sing a lot and play around in the carcass of a car, an old car that was in their yard.

Well, he died when I was already abroad. That boy's lust for life haunts me all the time ... It was the kind of death that gets to you. After we had left Marabastad I met him only once, by chance. It was a fleeting kind of meeting and we never saw each other again.

When I think of him I remember the music because there was always a group of singers that came to his house just to practise and the thumping of the piano in that house ... the loud voices – that is the memory that brings him back alive. My memory reels off things about Marabastad and there is always a pang in my heart for him.

Those are the nostalgic moments I have about Marabastad. I wouldn't want to go back to all those beer raids, which were always upsetting; to all the fights, the street fights ... women, you know, tackling each other ... and tearing each other's clothes up ... and spitting venom – just the kind of life which people were bearing up with, trying to live above their conditions ... One cannot help but contrast that with a place like Soweto, which has another kind of composition altogether, with many micro-groups as it were, or micro-sections. Marabastad was a homogeneous location. If anything happened in Fourteenth Avenue, Second Avenue, First Avenue – you got to know about it.

MANGANYI: I think that is one of the reasons why people have resisted moving to these new areas. There is something very attractive about a place like Alexandra Township, even with its filth ... because of this sense of cohesion ...

MPHAHLELE: That sense of togetherness. Something our people don't want to let go of.

MANGANYI: Yes, one would say that it was very much in line with what you sometimes describe as the humanism of the African people.

So it had the cultural background as a base, and when you move to a place like Soweto this is disrupted.

MPHAHLELE: Completely. We were disrupted and we are not moving in the same direction at all. Things tug away from the centre all the time, whereas there is a kind of convergence in places like Alexandra, Lady Selborne; that was a pull towards the same centre. People wouldn't want to leave that kind of life for an insecure and unknown situation.

MANGANYI: One sometimes develops the impression that the kind of vitality that you've been talking about, that is the basis of your nostalgia, may have something to do with what I would describe as your compassion, your interest in ordinary folk, particularly in your short stories. I think this is quite clear.

MPHAHLELE: Yes, this is really it. I am very much attracted to humanistic existence, where people treat each other as human beings and not simply as instruments or tools; where people become committed to one another as human beings without necessarily declaring the commitment; if one of their kind is in difficulties the others immediately rise to the occasion and do something about it.

... I would like to see, for instance, an adult being able to reprimand a boy even though he is not his own child – and that's something which, unfortunately, we're losing. That kind of community for me has an integrity which I'd be unhappy to see violated. I do think that compassion is a very important quality in man, which goes a long way in binding people together.

I keep going back to Tagore, who was a Bengali poet. He writes a lot about this quality in human beings – to want to reach out, outward, out of themselves. He writes a lot about how it is that we are always hungering for emotional experiences, which is why we want to read literature. He also says, quoting from some of the religious literature of India, that you don't love your son because you desire your son; you love your son because you're looking for yourself. You love someone because you are looking for yourself and this is proper. When you feel sorrow, grief and joy for someone else it is a way of reaching out; the way you enlarge yourself. You enrich yourself. I keep reminding myself of Tagore's words, because they're so very much in consonance with what I believe: people reach out because they then become self-fulfilled. That is what African humanism is about: you are enlarged and increased when you go out of yourself. And part of the vehicle for this is compassion. This is why I lay such a premium on compassion. We see it mostly in people who haven't reached a high level of literacy ... or a high level of formal education. They haven't been alienated yet. We have consciously to be aware that we have been removed from our origins and that we have to make our way back, as it were, and reaffiliate. That is very possible. I don't think there needs to be any psychological block unless alienation is complete.

I haven't found any such psychological block myself as a writer. Always I am drawn back to the people, the labourers, the non-professional people, where I see more vitality, where people still live, still feel life at its basic roots.

MANGANYI: Have you ever considered the possibility that the triumph of your aunt in Marabastad, the triumph of your grandmother, the triumph of your mother under the circumstances that you have described, and the triumph of the community, as it were, over what was basically a dehumanising social structure … could have had an impact on your own ability to survive in later life?

MPHAHLELE: Yes, I am certain of that. It has had quite an influence on my own survival. If I hadn't experienced that sort of life I would have gone on, perhaps under my own steam. But remembering all the time the lives of those people and how they survived, that has always given me a tremendous uplift.

I inherited from them the will to go ahead and grapple with life. I have been that way all my life. I always seem to be … moving inexorably, inevitably, from one thing to another; being pulled and being pulled, almost as if I wasn't controlling it myself. Almost as if I wasn't stopping and making decisions to do so … but just moving on. Yet I know I have been making decisions from time to time. But the overall journey of my life has been a kind of drive, drive, drive, on and on and on …

'Man must live' … The tenacity has come from Marabastad. The conditions in which one grew up, when there was hardly anything else outside your own schoolbooks to read, when there was nothing, nothing at all, and your parents were in no position to advise you about your educational journey … They just left you to make your own decisions, as you know, and went ahead. Yes. This is typical of all Africa … of all South Africans when you come to think of it. In Marabastad you saw the beautiful and the ugly. You had to make your own choices. The beautiful was so beautiful in the context of an ugly situation. *That* held your attention and attracted you so you wanted to move on, with the ugliness and all …

MANGANYI: To get back to your relationship with your father. This is certainly one of the most crucial experiences in your life. I have often wondered whether this compassion and devotion to humanistic values is not perhaps related to a feminine identification.

Perhaps I should explain what I mean by that. The strong people, who were the important people in your life during the formative stages, appear to have been your maternal grandmother, your maternal aunt and your mother. There are no indications really, not in anything that I have read, that there was a strong male presence in any sense.

MPHAHLELE: … yes, that's so very true.

MANGANYI: And so, I have wondered whether your sensibility is not in some way connected to that identification [with women].

MPHAHLELE: Yes, now that you say it, I feel strongly so. When I think of strong people I don't think of men, I always think of women.

I always think of women who are strong almost as if I didn't expect them to be. There are so many precedents throughout my life. I have always noticed the strong women more than the strong men. Even when I was in the United States the thing that struck me so forcibly about the whole process of survival, was not so much the men but the strong black women ... they're very resolute, they can't easily be fooled. And then again, I think of my own mother and the way she had to survive on her own and struggle through. When I hear somebody tell me that a man has been brutalising his wife I'm filled with disgust ... and revulsion.

MANGANYI: In *Down Second Avenue* one gets the impression that there was some schoolgirl you were interested in. Did you go out often with girls?

MPHAHLELE: I didn't ... I was a very shy person ... agonisingly shy. I used to feel like kicking myself on the shin for it. Because other boys just seemed to be so relaxed with girls ... I was dead scared.

MANGANYI: How did you manage Ribs [Rebecca, Mphahlele's wife]?

MPHAHLELE: I met Ribs in '42, when I was twenty-two. She came to Ezenzeleni from Wilberforce with a choir to perform for the blind. She had sprained her ankle and I was there on the spot. I told her to sit down and I stretched the ankle, twisted it this way and that. I got a bandage from our dispensary and so on ... After they left, I wrote [to her]. There just seemed to be something natural about it. I didn't have to make much of an effort at all. It was through that correspondence ... she replied and I replied. We communicated that way until I decided. She lived in Sophiatown and she had come for a vacation. A friend of mine took me to their house. I broke the news to her, about my love. Fortunately she didn't look formidable, as formidable as the other schoolgirls, who looked as if they were going to bite you if you said one single word to them ... You know the way they'll say, *tsamaya kwa* [get away]! Hell, man! I would imagine all sorts of things.

I was just dead shy. The girl Rebone was, I could feel that she was very warm towards me. I never had the courage, ever, to say to her, 'I love you' – and I knew that I did. When you get so used to each other and so close I think it becomes even more difficult, not so?

MANGANYI: I think in Ursula Barnett's book she says somewhere that you almost had a nervous breakdown at St. Peter's ... What exactly went wrong at that time?

MPHAHLELE: What happened was that throughout my school life, when examination time came, I would brood and worry ... I was always terrified of failing, because I felt my mother would have to keep on paying fees and there were two others behind me. The idea of failing haunted me throughout my schooldays. When I went to St. Peter's, the same thing happened the year I was going to write my final exams. I studied so hard, mental exhaustion overtook me.

One night I fainted and was carried to bed. I missed my half-yearly exams and that worried me even more, in the last year of JC [Junior Certificate]. I recovered from that after a week or so. I went home on vacation, came back and continued to study, then things were all right.

MANGANYI: Did you have any recurrences of that episode?

MPHAHLELE: The nearest I came to it was when I was doing my BA Honours. That headache returned. This second time ... I came to a complete standstill. I had to go to hospital.

MANGANYI: How was St Peter's? It seems to have been such an important school as far as African education is concerned.

MPHAHLELE: It was a very reputable school. It had a discipline of its own. It wasn't Spartan at all. Both teachers and students were most inspiring. We had been preceded by fellows who had taken their matric in the first class. People like ... Oliver Tambo ... Those were our seniors ... There was an open acknowledgement of students who were really good ... There were more white teachers than black, at the time ... They steered clear of politics completely, as all missionaries did. They just let things ride and people didn't feel that their views were being suppressed. When it came to open debate, for instance, they allowed anything to go. They had a very strong sense of morals, of course, like all missionaries, – in our relationship with girls, for example. But there was a climate of real scholarship – academic achievement, which was really inspiring.

MANGANYI: How did that compare with Adams?

MPHAHLELE: When I got to Adams the first thing that hit me was I seemed to have come to a jungle in comparison with St Peter's. There was order in the dorms at St Peter's. There were standards of cleanliness, standards of hygiene. Not at Adams ... There you really had to survive ...

MANGANYI: It's curious, because when one reads Edgar Brookes's account, *A South African Pilgrimage*, one doesn't get that impression.

MPHAHLELE: You never would, not with Brookes. He was the kind of principal one seldom saw. There was no contact between principal and students. When he taught us Principles of Education his mind seemed to be on other things altogether. The teachers were a miscellaneous group. Some were absolutely dumb. A few were quite inspiring. One American taught us physiology and hygiene; his wife taught us geography. A German, an impressive man, taught us psychology of education. These three were the only really inspiring teachers in the whole Normal [Education] department. The others I had no esteem for at all. There was no atmosphere like at St Peter's. Oh yes, there was a woman who taught us blackboard work and chart work. She was good. All in all, the academic achievement of students wasn't anything to talk about ... Very ordinary. Their matric results were very ordinary. There were no heroes.

MANGANYI: Would you like to say something about education in the early Fifties? That is a very important era.

MPHAHLELE: I had been working in the blind institute, I didn't feel ready to teach. That's where I spent the first four years of my working life. After two years I got my matric. Then I decided I was ready to teach. When I went to Orlando High School I knew that I wanted to be a teacher ... even at Adams, in spite of the quality of the teaching. I did a lot of my own private reading. Saturdays and Sundays I always spent in the library. I wasn't much of a socialiser. I had only one close and intimate friend at Adams. I tended to shut myself in. I did very well in my exams and came out top. When I felt I was ready to teach, I was literally stronger and more capable ... Doing matric privately gave me a sense of stability. I reassured myself that I could do other things on my own. I said to myself: even though I haven't been able to attend university, I'm going to damn well do it. As soon as I started teaching at high school I registered with Unisa [the University of South Africa]. A lot of what I was studying was feeding into my teaching ... I never thought I was doing a subject in order to pass exams. I had quite a clear idea of myself and I was sure where I wanted to go. I was then 26.

Then I became interested in the teachers' organisation and joined ... I was elected secretary.

I got married just before I started teaching at Orlando High.

MANGANYI: More stability!

MPHAHLELE: Yes. Ribs is an outgoing person – really outgoing. She hasn't my kind of personality at all. She drew me out of myself to a very large extent. So when I was at Orlando High I had really loosened up. The year I became secretary, Zeph Mothopeng president and [Isaac] Matlhare editor of the journal, we decided to launch an attack against the syllabuses of native education. We looked into the textbooks, most of which were glorifying the white man ... through and through, especially in the humanities.

Matlhare, Mothopeng and I attacked the syllabus and said what was wrong. This was in 1949. We were re-elected in '50 and '51, but in '51 the Eiselen Commission Report came out and we realised it was completely malicious. So we decided to launch a campaign against it, all over the province. We went to various areas, talking to teachers and parents, to warn them against the recommended system. It was the whole philosophical basis we were attacking. It was wrong. The architects had concocted something in their heads called Bantu culture. The African must be taught to respect his culture, they said. This Bantu culture, of which we had no conception at all ...

The implication also was that the missionaries had taught us to be rebels. Our reply was that they taught us nothing of the sort. If anything, the missionaries were teaching us the virtues of humility before the Lord. Verwoerd, of course, came to Parliament and went on with that sort of rhetoric: ... Africans shouldn't be given false hopes or given the idea that they could compete in a world which was not theirs. Things of that kind! That made it even worse. The rhetoric in Parliament interpreted the very spirit of the Eiselen report ... It clarified the whole aim of the system and made it even more objectionable than it might have been just in print.

It was when we were in the middle of launching this campaign, opening up the subject for debate, that we got letters of dismissal. This was in August of 1952. We were given a month's notice. We were told we couldn't teach anywhere else in the country. We left. But the circumstances surrounding our dismissal went further than our attack against Bantu Education. It involved also our work at school, our positions at Orlando High. The principal ... quite openly declared his stand on the side of Bantu Education . . .

MANGANYI: Who was he?

MPHAHLELE: Godfrey Nakene. At staff meetings and at morning assembly he expressed his certainty that Africans were going to be given good posts, high posts. His favourite phrase was, 'There is activity behind the lines' ... meaning there is a lot coming, a lot of goodies for us all. An incident that eventually precipitated our dismissal was connected with the school. He had been warning us not to go on campaigning against Bantu Education. 'You've got children,' he said, 'what will happen if you lose your jobs?' Of course, we felt we had a mission and this couldn't be abandoned because Nakene said so. We persisted. And then he decided that he was going to move against us. He accused us of causing trouble in the school. We wrote a long memorandum to the Transvaal Education Department about how the school was being mismanaged. Funds were being mismanaged, schoolbooks were bought at a discount and nobody knew where the discount went to. The school was being over-enrolled and extra students were not entered in the register, yet they paid fees. We sent the memorandum to Pretoria and Nakene got to know about it. Then he really became vicious.

He immediately wrote to the department to call for a commission of inquiry, the terms of which were to inquire into staff relations. That's all. So the troops descended on us ... It was quite clear to us at the time that the teachers themselves did not understand the full implications of what we were saying. Not at all, really. They were just not ready for the kind of stand we were asking them to take.

MANGANYI: And the parents?

MPHAHLELE: The parents were still worse. It was just too intricate for them, too involved, too philosophical for them even to understand. They had sent their children to school to learn and expected them to damn well learn what they were being taught.

MANGANYI: Where was Rebecca in all this?

MPHAHLELE: Rebecca was teaching, at primary school. She didn't join the teachers' organisation. Without saying so, I think she wanted to feel that if I was there I was representing her too.

MANGANYI: And you never had family difficulties over the stand you were taking?

MPHAHLELE: Well, at first, when Nakene was handing out his threats she felt that we three were moving on dangerous ground ... and she was ...

MANGANYI: Concerned.

MPHAHLELE: Deeply concerned. But there was never any kind of difficulty at all. The only difficulty that had arisen between us occurred when Khabi [Mngoma] and I were running a paper called *The Voice* in Orlando. Khabi, myself, Matlhare and [Lucas] Ngakane. Ngakane only joined us later on. We were mimeographing a paper of about six, sometimes eight pages. It was a paper of social and political criticism. Very Orlando in flavour. It often took a very strong satirical line against the élite who were trying to play their role in an anti-social way, we thought. Bantu Education also became a topic. *The Voice* ran from '49 to '52. It contained virulent attacks; we just didn't hold any punches at all. Nakene saw himself being satirised and made a fool of. We didn't sign our names on any article. Nobody knew the authors of *The Voice*.

Only much later we disclosed them. This was long after we had been dismissed. But even today there are many people who still don't know.

Real difficulties arose between me and Ribs when Nakene was threatening us. She felt we should give up the paper. I said, 'No, we won't.' She was absolutely uptight about it. We quarrelled about it a few times, then we made a truce and she didn't say anything about it any more. But she showed complete indifference to the thing. What made it worse was that a Special Branch fellow came to Orlando High to inquire about us. You know what a white person will do. He will go straight to the person in authority and let him know what his people are doing. You see? He won't say 'I want to see so-and-so.' No. He wants to establish his presence. It was also intended that Nakene should know that he had dangerous people in his school. That was enough to make Nakene shake in his pants.

He wanted to see me and Khabi, this fellow with shaggy white hair called Sergeant Muller. He told us, 'Well, you fellows, I hear, you run *The Voice*.' So we decided that we were going to come clean. They'd find out anyway. We said, 'Yes, we do.' He said, 'Well, I am going to send you a summons because you've been publishing a paper without registering it and without stating your names or where it's published.' We were, in fact, using a fictitious address in George Goch ... the address of a fellow called Walter Nhlapo, who had allowed us to use it. We were using all kinds of places for mimeographing because we didn't have a machine and we were always borrowing one, here and there. The summons came. Somebody took us to a lawyer. You know whom we went to see? Anton Mostert.

MANGANYI: The judge?

MPHAHLELE: Yes. He was then just a lawyer, starting to practise. He discovered that you only need to register a paper if it is appearing at intervals of one calendar month. None of the issues appeared within that interval at all. They were very irregular; sometimes less than a calendar month, sometimes more than a calendar month, never from the first to the thirty-first.

So he got us off the hook. *The Voice* affair also added fuel to the fire at school. Through it we were really trying to get across to as many people as possible the dangers of the Eiselen Report. What made it worse was that we didn't even tell our wives about it. It was only when we came back [from court] that we told them we had been to court and had been acquitted. Both Grace and Ribs were shocked by this and I think that brought Ribs back to herself. Ribs softened up and became more conciliatory in her attitude to the paper. We did continue with it, of course, until we were fired. On the whole question of Bantu Education itself, she was with me all the way.

MANGANYI: Can we move on to another important area? The area of writing, of journalism, at the time when you got involved in it, which was subsequent to your teaching. There again, we who are younger often feel that there came into being, particularly in Sophiatown, an *era* that has since passed. I mean, apart from you and a few other people it seems to have been a self-contained period in terms of creativity and writing.

MPHAHLELE: It was a fascinating time. *Drum* was founded in 1950. And it started first almost as an anthropological kind of journal, with pictures of rural life, pastoral beauty and so on. Then Anthony Sampson became its editor. He changed the whole policy of *Drum*; it became a real proletarian paper. It talked about the urban black man generally. I had already started writing and my *Man Must Live* short stories had appeared in '47. My first story appeared in *Drum* in '52 and then again, in '53. But I didn't join them until '54, when I came from Lesotho. I had just written my Honours when I joined *Drum* at the end of '54 as fiction editor. My first assignment was to go through the literary contest manuscripts. This literary contest had been an annual event since *Drum* began. Can Temba won first prize in the first contest, which is why he was immediately taken onto *Drum*. I was coming into a real literary renaissance, right in the middle of it. People were really writing furiously in a lively, vibrant style. It was quite a style of its own, an English of its own. It was my duty to encourage this literary activity, this fiction writing. There wasn't much poetry then. Fiction was the strongest medium. The non-fictional prose sketch was also a kind of social comment.

The exposés that people like Henry Nxumalo and Can Themba were writing – the exposés of the Bethal potato farms, prison life and so on – were really dynamic. Significantly, it was the black man writing for the black man. Not addressing himself to the whites. Talking a language that would be understood by his own people.

There was no appeal or pleading at all to the white man to try to understand us. We were writing about our own lives, replaying our own experiences to our own people. Ours was really a proletarian literature; people like [Todd] Matshikiza, Can Themba, Bloke Modisane, Arthur Maimane, Richard Rive, James Matthews, Matthew Nkwane, Henry Nxumalo, Casey Motsisi. We were not having meetings and talking about this. And yet there was some controlling force that made it a movement.

MANGANYI: What was it? Dedication? What put it together?

MPHAHLELE: I think it was a kind of collective consciousness. People had been suffering, and people had been living in harsh conditions without a voice. Well, they found a voice then. It was a life that had been an on-going experience, so writers began to capture it. They were ready to go. Many of our writers were not university people. I had already graduated, although I had started writing in my undergraduate days. Can Themba was a graduate. That was all. All the others were matric people … and below matric people. And yet they had a command of English.

MANGANYI: That says something about education …

MPHAHLELE: That says something about education, for sure. That the education we had had still allowed for freedom of mobility – intellectual mobility. There were things that people could unearth in the libraries, in the bookshops. There was a good deal of Afro-American stuff coming in book form and magazine form and we were reading it. Those are some of the factors that gave the literary movement an initial push.

MANGANYI: How did that tie up with the social institution in black life called the shebeen?

MPHAHLELE: In Sophiatown and Orlando shebeen life was quite a vibrant institution and it might have injected something into our literary movement. I don't think so much from the literary standpoint as from the social standpoint. I don't think anything was manufactured in the shebeen. I would consider it as one of those sub-cultures with its own quality of life. It was more an interesting backdrop than an organic part of the movement, even though it was a cult for journalists. And maybe it did something for people who frequented the shebeens. It gave Motsisi a subject for his satires. It gave Can Themba a subject also. Especially at the level of reportage, the level of the prose sketch.

At another level, imaginative writing was stimulated by education and the political climate. The political climate was a busy one in the Fifties. First there was the Suppression of Communism Act in 1950 and the riots that resulted from it; then in 1952 the Defiance Campaign of the Congress Alliance, in which whites and blacks participated; in 1951, the Eiselen Commission Report and our kind of ferment against it; the Bantu Education Act in 1953 and the removal of Sophiatown, which almost coincided. The ANC tried to get people to resist the move ... schools were being boycotted at the same time, that is 1953. In 1955 the Kliptown Conference adopted the Freedom Charter. That was quite a big get-together. Nineteen fifty-six: there was the Treason Trial. A lot was going on and the political scene was very active. For me personally it created quite a context.

MANGANYI: Now, apart from the literary renaissance and the political turbulence, one also notices, from a cultural point of view, the vitality of the music and, of course, the change in the ecology of urban black environments from Sophiatown to Meadowlands. All these things seem to have come to an end at the end of the Fifties.

MPHAHLELE: All those movements came to an end and things seemed to freeze somewhere. That's true. With the change of ecology the people just seemed to be coming to a strange land, almost as if they were exiles and had lost their voice. Things really changed. I think it is a period for very intensive study and it would yield much about African life; what happens to people when they are moved from one area to another. What kind of culture do they then develop? How do people regroup?

MANGANYI: So there is some kind of dislocation that occurs at the end of the Fifties. This is my general impression.

MPHAHLELE: Yes. There is definitely a dislocation and our young writers today know nothing about it because, of course, much of that writing has been banned. I have often felt the urge to do a book on it. The problem is that one would not be able to quote from the writers themselves. Yet it is so important for people to know what kind of writing was being published at the time.

MANGANYI: That takes us up to 1957, when you took the decision to leave the country.

MPHAHLELE: In 1957 the proprietor of *Drum* decided not to publish fiction any longer because it wasn't selling. He felt that he could sell the paper better with crime and sex.

I had, in any case, by then decided that I had to find my way out. I might just as well get back to the classroom. I decided that we had to pack up. I didn't have any conflict about it, because I didn't think that I was leaving the country for good. Both of us felt it wasn't for good. I just said to myself, 'damn it, if I can't teach in this country I am going to teach abroad'. Somebody got me in touch with a grammar school in Lagos. And I decided to apply. At the same time I applied for a passport. I waited a whole year. Then they said no.

MANGANYI: What hopes did you cherish at that time? When you say it was partly your dedication to teaching there must have been other hopes that you had.

MPHAHLELE: My hopes were that I would grow ... spiritually and intellectually. And to take my place as an educator in whatever community I would join. I would also continue to write. You know, writing to me has always been an inner compulsion which I would need to satisfy without necessarily thinking I was going to make it a career. Teaching would be the basic thing which would give me that kind of satisfaction. As I read Tagore again I find it ties up with so many things that I only dimly realise myself. I think what I was trying to do was to get out of my own self and find an extension of myself in other directions. I always assumed that if I came back to South Africa I would come back better equipped.

It really never occurred to me that I would be away forever. No, I would say that my hopes did embrace freedom for the African; total freedom for the African, without necessarily thinking deeply about how it would come about. Knowing also that there was so much resistance to what the African was offering to the white man, the chance the African was offering ... The white man would have nothing to do with it because he saw in it his own self-destruction and self-elimination.

MANGANYI: That takes us to a very complex area of experience. You yourself described it in an article as the dilemma of the African exile. I think that one can examine this area of experience primarily from two or three different points of view. One, as an exile in an African country. That, I imagine, has a different set of conditions and pressures from being an exile in Europe or North America. Then, of course, you have spoken of physical exile and spiritual or psychic exile.

Perhaps one could begin by looking at the experience of simply being outside South Africa for the first time; being not only physically distant but also psychologically distant.

MPHAHLELE: My initial experiences were conditioned very much by the novelty of exile. When I got to Nigeria I had left my family behind. They joined me three months later, by which time I was spiritually renewed. I felt – 'My word! This is a glorious atmosphere for one to live in ...'. Suddenly, something thawed inside me and emotionally I wasn't tense any longer. My asthma, which was something I had lived with since I was twenty, just disappeared. I didn't feel at the time any regrets or any kind of guilt. The nostalgia I felt was nostalgia for people. But after my family joined me it was the adventure that gripped us, just the adventure of being outside and being free of everything. So we tended not to dwell on what we'd left behind so much – until Sharpeville. Sharpeville hit us and we seemed to stop dead in our tracks, psychically, and thought about the sort of life we'd left behind, the brutality, and what people were going through. It gave us ... a moment to pause. Then the sense of adventure took over again. I was writing quite a lot. I was engaged with the writers in Nigeria, in their own renaissance. I worked with them, setting up writers' and artists' clubs and art galleries and so on. It was a busy and enriching life. I wasn't made to feel that I was an outsider. Nigerians are generous people, very accommodating. They were at ease with themselves, so they were not ill at ease with us. When we went to France we felt so far away psychologically that it started to needle us. This was compensated for by my frequent visits to West, East and Central Africa. It was Rebecca who bore the brunt of alienation.

France needled us, I think, because the European surroundings, the European milieu, is pretty unfriendly. We felt alone for the two years we were there. It was accentuated when we went to Kenya. This was another dimension of it.

It was an African country and we were not welcome really, not intimately. We were working and found satisfaction in what we were doing. I was running a creative centre under the auspices of the organisation I worked for in Paris. So I was in my element. But we did feel cut off from the people. Except for very few people they were not outgoing, so we found ourselves in the company of Europeans. That accentuated our isolation from South Africa even more. I felt uneasy about being in exile in a country like Kenya where one didn't find fulfilment of one's socialising energies. When we went to the United States after three years in Kenya the sense of adventure wasn't as strong as before. It was still there, because we were going into new territory. I was going to do my PhD and that kept me very busy, for a while. In Zambia our experience of Kenya was renewed. Again we felt a kind of alienation. But there we were thrown into the company of many South African refugees, in a way we had never been before.

... we toyed with the idea that this might be our last place of exile. After only four months we were again disillusioned. The South African refugees were in their own political camps. We were professionals who were going to teach and it was rough for South African teachers. There was no mercy at all. If they wanted to get rid of you, they just got rid of you. And yet we felt geographically so close to South Africa. I think unconsciously we were also resisting digging our roots too deep in any particular setting.

You can rely on your own inner moral resources in a situation of exile only to a certain extent. You reach a level beyond which you cannot endure it any longer, when your inner moral resources are being overtaxed and they do not have the full capacity to carry this condition of exile. Your moral resources diminish.

MANGANYI: It may well be that one survives exile to the extent that one's hopes and expectations are realistic.

MPHAHLELE: I think so. [What sustains one is] looking forward to future time. You bide your time, work and commit yourself to lots of things in the meantime.

MANGANYI: In my own case ... I went straight into a predominantly white social structure and, perhaps because of the existence of black Americans, it reminded me of home.

But one of the first things I had to contend with was the paradox that because there was so much freedom I was free to be angry for the first time. I wonder what your experience was in respect of anger.

MPHAHLELE: Yes. One was free to be angry. The things that I read in the newspapers about South Africa did make me very angry. Things that were very close to me ... living in a university community one can be very well protected; it insulates you. Some things do make you angry, but it's nothing like the anger you feel when you read about some ugly things in this country, while you're abroad. But the object of my anger was so far away. I was feeling more and more impotent to do anything about the anger.

MANGANYI: So there is a sense of futility which increases all the time when one is in exile.

MPHAHLELE: There is a sense of futility, yes. Incidentally, my feelings about commitment worried me a hell of a lot. As long as I refused to be an organic part of my new setting, as long as I resisted digging my roots in, so long I was going to remain an uncommitted outsider. You can only be committed to something in which you have immersed yourself deeply. My commitments were still here but I had no territory in which to exercise that commitment. I could never find any satisfaction in joining anti-South African movements outside because I felt that was ...the province of the people of the place. When they asked me to speak, I would go and simply give them information about South Africa ... my heart wasn't in it. It really bugged me. It also meant that I could not write about the new setting in which I was, the setting of exile. I just felt that I had nothing to say about it because I was suspending commitment to the setting this side. I even told myself that I was conserving energy for a homecoming.

MANGANYI: What about death? That worried me. I didn't know where I was going to end. Suddenly, this became a preoccupation.

MPHAHLELE: It did with me too, with me and Ribs. First the growing old in a place and dying. Nobody says they are bound to be in that sequence, of course. We always said to ourselves, 'Good heavens, if we die here, we will be buried here. Apart from our children, nobody else will care to know where we were buried.' It would be like being buried in the air, as it were. That haunted us for quite a long time, the possibility that we might just die. We even thought about the economics of dying in the United States. That's something to be reckoned with. I mean, you've got to be able to afford to die.

Now if I died, Ribs would have to move out of the house which we were renting, because she couldn't possibly maintain it. She couldn't afford the mortgage. She would have to move into an apartment and become a tenant. And then the sense of insecurity would increase as she grew older. Social security would not be enough to support her and pay her rent. If she died I would not be able to afford the mortgage on my own without her income. I would have to move into an apartment. And then old age comes, and old age in the United States is something you can't look forward to, no. A miserable prospect.

Above all was that spiritual thing about death. You feel you want to die among your own people. I mean, not to die just anywhere and be dumped anywhere.

MANGANYI: There is another phenomenon that's interesting to me. On two occasions, the first in the introduction to *Down Second Avenue*, the other, I think, in the first chapter of *The African Image*, you depart radically from your usual calm in talking about South Africa. Do you recall this?

MPHAHLELE: I recall those passages very well.

MANGANYI: What's going on there?

MPHAHLELE: I am in a situation there where my anger is impotent so I fling out wildly. I want to spill out everything that I feel deeply and strongly inside me in very plain words. I am feeling that I am away from the situation and even if I were back language would be impossible, or would place me in danger. But that is the irony of it. I think it is the feeling that I want an audience. My audience is not here. My audience is a very general outside world audience, not the audience that I want. I want the audience here. I fling out wildly because I feel that kind of distance. I am not being heard by the people I want to hear me.

MANGANYI: Have you ever considered violence as a solution?

MPHAHLELE: Yes, several times.

MANGANYI: How far does that take you?

MPHAHLELE: When I contemplate it, it goes a long way, but I often stop and wonder whether I am not contemplating something that can lead to much destruction of life. Because even while I am contemplating it, some report comes of violence that has taken place. That jolts me.

MANGANYI: I have, for my own part, one concern about violence. The conclusion I arrived at was that both rightist and leftist stands end in violence. If you become very conservative, rightist and fascist, you end up with violence.

If you move to the left because you want to revolutionise, change things radically, you end up with violence. And this is a very significant dilemma as I see it.

MPHAHLELE: Yes. Violence is the outcome of extremes ... I say, 'Why should I want violence where other people will be the participants, and not I.' This is what bothers me.

When it seems to me that the only solution is violence, I ask myself, 'Would I be the first one to pick up a gun?' and I know I wouldn't be. Why should I then prescribe a method in which I may not be the chief participant?

MANGANYI: It's a question of morality.

MPHAHLELE: Moral responsibility, without even thinking whether it's right or wrong to use violence. That worries me a hell of a lot. When the June '76 riots occurred, it went deep, deep down inside me and showed me the senselessness of it all. But the relentless tyranny can continue and waste more lives than it did at that time. This is a situation in which I've even wondered whether one dares to hope. And yet, as a humanist, I feel I must have hopes and I must be optimistic about a number of things in spite of the darkness of our times.

I hope that we can overcome and come out on top. We must be masters of our own destiny. I hope that when that time comes we will psychologically be ready to carry the moment forward so that it doesn't degenerate into some of the things we see in other parts of Africa – the Idi Amins, the Bokassas, that whole bunch. I hope our temperaments will be ready for that moment so that we will know exactly what we want to do and do it right. I used to be quite a passionate believer, given the historical reality of the white man in this country, in a non-racial society. The politicians of the Fifties offered the possibility of a non-racial society to the white man. They tried to assure him that they were sincere and that white people who wanted to lead a decent, democratic life would be accommodated in such a society. They were gunned down and they were locked up. I have said to myself, now critical of my stand for a non-racial society, 'If people refuse that kind of chance, what does one do?' A genuine humanism would be all-embracing. Therefore, it would insist on a non-racial society. But if the other side doesn't care for this, given the historical circumstances, I must reserve my humanism for my own kind and conserve energy and strengthen my own side first and see if we can stand on our own dignity and pride.

MANGANYI: I guess that is what the youth has been trying to say in the 1970s.

I see the black consciousness movement primarily as a humanistic movement ... in terms of its value system. It is working basically on the kind of model you have just put across. It has the momentum to move beyond itself.

MPHAHLELE: That is right, because our humanism has never sought to shut out anybody. It has always been a humanism that could absorb many things, influences, members. You are right. I think we need to strengthen ourselves first. I hope this can happen. Then we can pull it off. They now realise that by excluding us from South African life and putting us in an enclave they have strengthened black consciousness and our sense of self. They are scared of it now.

They realise they created it. When I was at Fort Hare recently they asked me to talk to students. I talked about African humanism. I said we needed to institutionalise our own cultural activities in order to strengthen them and that it should be an ongoing thing. There were questions like: 'What do we do if we are an urban people and we've been cut off?' I replied that we didn't have to wait for Christianity and the Bible to have a sense of morality. We have always had our own humanism. If we institutionalised our cultural activities we could also try to put a stop to the commercialisation of our culture by white people, like *Ipi Tombi* and that kind of *junk* which they export. We can work with our own African idioms in music, theatre, literature and so on. At the end of it a fellow comes to me and introduces himself as Pienaar. He is a member of the faculty. He says to me, 'Well, I've just one question. I wonder if the African will not become exclusive if he does what you say he should do; that is, have a sense of self-pride and work with his own African idioms. Will the artist not then become exclusive and perpetuate the kind of thing you are criticising among the other racial groups?' I said, 'No. There is no reason why he should if he is a good artist. Every good artist goes beyond the moment into the future. He must have a vision and there is no reason why he should become exclusive. If he does, it is because he is very local in his appeal. But there is nothing wrong with that, as a starting point.'

It gave me a hint, you see, that now the white man is scared. He sowed the wind and will reap the whirlwind.

Scared that the African will exclude him. Shit, man!

And then afterwards I said to myself, 'Who the hell is he to worry about exclusiveness?' He of all people, worried that he would be excluded from African society when he has always wanted to be apart.

MANGANYI: If we blacks are to contribute in a meaningful way to a future South Africa this contribution should include literature and art that says: 'This is where it hurts but there is a tomorrow. No black person will romanticise this anguish.'

MPHAHLELE: No fiction or poetry can capture all the anguish we feel. But starting from the given that we are in this anguish, the writer and the artist must move forward, go beyond it. That is the kind of message I was preaching at the workshops I was running for PEN last November. I was saying that what I see in *Staffrider* is real, vibrant literature. But it lacks a myth. Our myth should be that there is a tomorrow. This literature captures the agony of the moment. It has no resonance because it has no past either, no past to work on. We were saying earlier on that our present-day writers have been cut off from the Fifties. They don't even know that it existed. They think literature begins with them. So there is no resonance echoing the past, foreshadowing the future. This is what we must move beyond, and the images we use have to indicate that.

MANGANYI: This is a very important question because it has a lot of political consequences in South Africa. I have been called as an expert witness in one of the censorship hearings. I also worked with the defence lawyers at some stage during the SASO-BPC [South African Students Organisation-Black People's Convention] trial. This is where the question became so poignant to me. You read a piece of literature and you want to decide whether in fact there is a one-to-one relationship between the literature and the *actions* of the reader subsequent to reading the poem.

MPHAHLELE: I firmly believe that no poem or novel or play really impels people into political action because one is using a work of imagination which has a roundabout way of saying things. It uses metaphor, it uses allegory and it uses other devices which are meant *really* to enrich the personality rather than ... simply move from stimulus to ...

MANGANYI: To response.

MPHAHLELE: Response. Yes. To move people into action you need to speak their language, the language of every day, which is prose, and you go directly to what you want to do. As soon as you use a work of imagination, you are negating the possibilities of response from the other imagination, the imagination of the reader. It would have to be a very bad poem or novel, almost a non-poem or a non-novel, to get people into action ... Because it has then to move towards everyday spoken language. I think you are right when you say that we have to face up to this problem because so many of our young writers really passionately think that the poetry they write can be revolutionary; revolutionary in the sense that it will mobilise people into action.

It doesn't work that way; it has never worked that way. Either one has to write out a prose manifesto or do something else. It has nothing to do with political action. While at the same time it moves people and it increases one's emotional responses which is what literature and art do ... to increase us and give us a new view of an experience, of a common experience. I think this is what we should be aware of.

MANGANYI: I have always thought that we in South Africa are, in fact, depriving ourselves of an opportunity to create a vital literature and art that is not inhibited in subject or theme across the colour line. This could prepare us in a very fundamental way for the kind of synthesis and reconciliation of the various cultural and political strands that exist within the society itself.

MPHAHLELE: Yes, you are up against a formidable opposition. If only we could talk about Africans, Indians and so-called 'coloureds', as simply black ... Then you have the white people. We Africans have our own strand, the Indian another strand, and the so-called 'coloured' person, yet another. Then you have the white strand. You have a situation in which the divisions are tightly regulated and which almost forebodes doom for people who want to cross these dividing lines. The other people, for instance, will punish their own kind if they try to cross the line over to ours. Particularly the radicals. Then the liberals will play it safe on that side, as long as they think that they are crossing the line now and again, to peep into what we are doing and to read what we are writing, and to listen to what we are saying, yet conscious, at the same time, of the tough legislation that exists. I find it difficult myself to know what can be done in a situation like this where the ... legislated division is such a hard and formidable structure. Should we, as black people, try to reach across this line? It might be dissipating our energies if we set ourselves the mission of educating the other man before we have tried to educate and strengthen ourselves. Trying to educate the other man, you get hurt eventually. You run into a wall.

The other people just listen and they say they sympathise; they empathise. That's all that ever happens ... there is this inner feeling, this kind of inner slavery of the mind ... even in white academics ... who would not like to throw off those shackles, and move forward into progressive and constructive thinking. It bothers me a lot because we are now faced with a fragmented culture in this country. It is difficult to know what the future will be; what kind of institutionalised synthesis there will be. We know there is a synthesis within the personality – the African absorbing from this and absorbing from that. And at the same time, I think he very often loses balance because he really doesn't know himself and his inner potential. He has been under white rule so long that there's a number of things he mistakes for the real thing, which come from the white culture and he has no orientation. Like the urban African who has lost some orientation, because he has started off from the point where his community itself is fashioning a new urban culture, from the residual elements of memory. I'm trying to think whether we can move into a consolidation of our own side so that we emphasise the positive rather than the mere survival elements of our own culture and feel self-contained and also self-reliant.

Black consciousness comes into it, necessarily. If we can do that, we might be able to survive the onslaught from the other side, which is always coming at us; survive it in the sense that we would then be emphasising the positive element. It would also help us move towards a future in which the other man has no choice but to join in our majority culture. As we are now, it seems as if the white looks at us only as a political force and riot as a cultural force in which politics are an ingredient. He doesn't think we have that kind of culture which he himself can act out and engage in as one of us. He looks at us as an inferior people because we are politically weak, politically impotent. Not really an active kind of involvement in our culture.

Our thinkers must get together and find out how we can bridge the rural/urban gap amongst ourselves and create a sense of unity; a sense of cultural unity so that the urban man can be, in one way or another, reinforced by a knowledge of where he comes from, where he is going, and what has happened to him so far.

MANGANYI: Black memory.

MPHAHLELE: Yes. Black memory. And if we can do that I think we might be able to form a monolithic structure amongst ourselves. I don't know where the Indian would fall in or the so-called 'coloured' man. I don't know if they themselves even worry about where they belong. Do they simply see themselves as micro-communities living off the handouts they're given by the existing power?

MANGANYI: One of the things I've been thinking about which you've touched on indirectly is what I see as a typically South African definition or understanding of culture, namely the equation of culture with power and privilege.

MPHAHLELE: ... if culture doesn't have the power and the privilege then it's not worth affiliating to. Those who are in power are supposed to have the cultural stability and cultural viability which gives an exaggerated idea of its worth. You and I know that it is a defensive culture and not a creative culture; it's a purely mechanistic culture coming from the other tradition, from the 'great Western tradition'. For one thing, it lacks the spiritual force; it is spiritually bankrupt. It's a political thing. Perhaps we, as scholars, should try to mobilise our forces and talk about culture and about what we can do to reinforce ourselves and look more deeply into ourselves, more profoundly across the rural/urban demarcation line, while at the same time keeping the door open for anybody else who wants to affiliate to this bigger thing. This division is being encouraged also by the rhetoric, or the language; the terms, which the newspapers use, like the 'urban black'. The other black is never even mentioned. They're out of reckoning in the towns. I would like the gap bridged, in the cultural sense. The whites here seem so scared of really moving forward in a co-operative effort, a collective effort towards creating links with us as equal partners. I see here white people as scholars who simply take an academic interest in us, and nothing more. They still enjoy the privilege.

Nobody would want them to forgo that, but they're making no effort at all to convince us that they would like these bridges to be built which are culturally constructed and not just as an intellectual exercise. There are whites who link up with us as writers. They try their best, in the circumstances, to speak up against censorship, against a culture that creates barriers between races. But I wonder if even they think more profoundly within themselves that such a common national culture is possible. For instance, I see the Afrikaans writers as people who are attacking censorship because they are now also being affected. But I can't see them, for instance, affiliating to our culture. They still, I think, look at their culture as superior because it has this political backing.

Another group is the one whose occupation is 'race relations'; groups who try to come across, to reach across the line. They, again, are people who study problems. They're not activists. I don't see them as activists. I see them as students of race relations.

MANGANYI: Isn't it true, though, that the ultimate scenario for survival in Southern Africa will be a development of what you have described as the majority culture? If we are to survive as a plural society that eventually becomes non-racial the national culture that emerges will have to be a majority culture.

In other words, the majority culture will ultimately become the base on which any cultural additions can be integrated. This, for me, implies, amongst other things, that the sensibility of white South Africans will have to undergo a radical transformation ... in the direction of a sort of gut level conviction that they are Africans, that they are in Africa ... that the memories, the nostalgia for Greece and all those trappings of the great civilisations, will have to be abandoned in favour of new cultural heroes, and so on.

MPHAHLELE: [The identification with Africa] has nothing to do with the natural landscape. It has nothing to do with the inner core of a people's thought and belief. It's such an artificial thing, it just doesn't have roots at all. I don't see that ever becoming a viable thing of the future. How do whites begin to think African? Is it a kind of evolution we have to rely on or should the existing bridges be exploited even more? I don't know. The white man of this century is very far from thinking African. He thinks of himself as an African when he sloganises, when he wants to tell us that we must not regard him as European. He does this in order to assert his position without the responsibilities that go along with it. I wonder whether in this century the white man will ever spiritually feel he belongs to Africa as long as we are not in power, whether he thinks ours is really a culture of poverty.

I wonder if there is a possibility of our seeing a non-racial society before the political structure itself has been radically reversed.

We are in no position of strength to do anything other than consolidate our forces and our spiritual and cultural resources among ourselves as Africans. I often wondered whether Africans, Asians and 'coloured people' as a group could move towards a common culture. The obstacles are pretty stark. The Indian will be feeling that he is affiliating to a people who are impotent, without any political power. The 'coloured' man will be thinking that he is going to lose the privileges he has enjoyed as a 'coloured'. He doesn't see himself as a politically disadvantaged person in the way other black people are. He still has the idea that he's in a better position and should protect that.

In the Fifties, in the midst of real political activism, when the Congress of Coloured People was affiliated to the Congress Alliance there was a hope that 'coloured' people might affiliate with the Africans. It was also hoped that the Indian Congress would feel that they were politically disadvantaged and link their destiny up with ours. But it ... happened only at an intellectual level. The common man didn't think that way at all. Also they were separate from us residentially, so they were visibly different from us. That's what the common man thought.

Now things have been broken up even further, fragmented by the banning of the organisations and by group areas. We've grown farther and farther apart, and that hope is even more distant. I've kept wondering whether one should persevere but I realise that, the laws being what they are, we might more safely and more profitably look at ourselves as African people throughout the country. Across these artificial boundaries.

MANGANYI: That raises another very important but complex question ...the development within the black communities of an inner freedom.

After the renaissance of the Seventies, if one may put it that way, let us look at the black people, particularly the younger people. A difference has come about. Although the whole question of freedom in political terms has not, in fact, changed in any way, people have a greater sense of self-respect. They are more self-reliant and have an inner sort of energy. Some kind of liberation of the self has come into being.

MPHAHLELE: We need to teach them to know themselves better, to make even greater input into the existing beginnings of self-pride. Self-pride is an accumulation of what has been going on through the years – the black experience. The African's experience has been moving towards the point where people feel we've got to be self-reliant, to create things for ourselves – our own music, our own fun – because we are cut off from the institutions of the white man. Our people have been cut off from the literature of their own people and knowledge about their own people, by white people, by white scholars.

Nineteen-seventy-six was really a culmination of what's been happening over the decades. They need to be told now who they are, and where they come from, and what they should be doing about these things that we're talking about. That's where the scholar comes in: he must exploit that consciousness, the black consciousness, so as to probe deeper into the personality and move forward.

MANGANYI: In *The African Image*, there is a very interesting passage that has the quality either of a fantasy or a dream; it's not quite clear which. It is the fantasy of arriving in Orlando at the old house and then being gunned down by the police. It ends up by waking up and finding that one is in the suburbs of Pennsylvania. Could we see what that is all about?

MPHAHLELE: I had been thinking: what will I be coming back to, what will I be doing, what are the odds, what are the possibilities? And this is really fantasy. And I saw myself coming into a place and feeling that I might very well become a sitting duck in the sense of being exposed to arrests, detentions, the lot. That was happening to so many people.

Not because I would be politically active but simply for the views I would be expressing in public. And I wondered if it was worthwhile coming. What also kept haunting me was that I must get back and help in educating our young people, to subvert what they had been taught through Bantu education. I was quite aware then what Bantu education had done. You meet the people who were products of it. There were a lot of them in Zambia ... And if I came back to teach I'd help to purge its effects. It was almost like a dream. I sat there and thought intensely about it. But I was quite awake. This is part of the psychology of exile. Even the most benign exiles have this fantasy of having become dangerous people who may get into serious danger if they were to set foot in Jan Smuts [airport].

MANGANYI: It seems to me that people have this kind of anticipation of danger; it's quite an interesting facet of the exile's return. There's the fantasy that you might get into serious trouble. Sometimes it's not a fantasy but I think it engages a lot of people who have considered the possibilities.

MPHAHLELE: I have so often had this recurring dream, that I was back in the country, being chased, but this time by Africans, without seeing their faces at all, a kind of *tsotsi* element. I'm just being chased and chased. Sometimes I slip out of their hands and sometimes I disappear and they disappear.

MANGANYI: I think Ursula Barnett somewhere says that your major concern is people and not politics.

MPHAHLELE: My concern is certainly with people, although politics is part of people, and people are part of politics. People are politics. She's probably thinking there of my literary reflection of situation; that I'm more interested in how people react to one another than in the system in which they live, which may or may not influence the way they behave to one another. It's a question of focus.

I tend to look at how people behave towards one another, in their local social situation, instead of trying to create an idea of the system in which they live, though I couldn't possibly ignore that.

I'm very much interested in the dramas of our people – where they live, their relationships to one another – between friends, between families, between friends and enemies. I keep feeling that there's a lot that we're not documenting in our African communities because we're always thinking of literature as predominantly the reflection of a confrontation between black and white and that doesn't tell the whole story. What tells the whole story is where these people are situated, what they are doing among themselves to one another. That interests, fascinates me. We can take the system for granted; it exists, and we can reflect our people's way of life, which is determined by the system. Once you are talking to your own people you don't have to dwell on the kind of system they live in because they know it, and they're more interested in their own behaviour and conduct.

MANGANYI: Did you ever experience any pressure, either internally or from outside sources, to join the political organisations of the Fifties or the external wings of the banned organisations overseas?

MPHAHLELE: Well, yes. In the Fifties I did actually join the ANC. There was never any kind of formal joining of the ANC, you just moved in. In that sense I would have considered myself an ANC person. It was after I had given a talk at the Kliptown conference in '55. I talked on education.

I was working for *Drum* then. I remember vividly what kind of conflicts I had as a reporter and as a person who felt involved in politics. I covered the Sophiatown removal and the schools upheaval. I was intensely concerned that I should put across the real thinking of the ANC people, apart from the sensational events that were taking place. And this always put me in conflict with the editor, particularly, the editor of *Post*, not *Drum*. I covered the Treason Trial of 1956. The prosecutor ... quoted my speech at the Kliptown conference in which I said that Bantu education is founded on false principles and is meant to lower both the standard of education of the African and their own sense of self.

I also said that the main argument put across by the white politicians, especially Verwoerd, was that we shouldn't be allowed to think that we could be the equals of the white man. And my comment was that we don't want to be equal to the white man; we want to be better than the white man and this is why we're against Bantu education. The prosecutor used those passages to point out their inflammatory nature, to illustrate that they were meant to create bad relations between black and white, and to show that they advocated the overthrow of the government by violent means, which is what the Treason Trial was about.

When I was abroad I felt the ANC in exile was quite something else. The leaders were there, all right, but the things they were doing just didn't seem to me to be important at all. Trivialities like attending conferences of one kind or another, tearing across the world, you know, and getting international money. Also tribalism was pretty rampant in the exile movement: Xhosa against Zulu against Sotho. I kept saying to myself: back home there had been so much cohesion among us. I mean, nobody ever bothered about these ethnic groupings at all. But in exile, man, the thing just emerged in bold relief. You saw this happening all the time and then the refugees even had more to gripe about. They were feeling restless, wanting to go back into action and do all sorts of things.

MANGANYI: There is a kind of lament which I detect in one of your poems from the trilogy that includes *Homeward Bound*. It appears to be a lament for certain deaths that occur whilst you're in exile.

MPHAHLELE: Some of the people were quite distant but I used to think: 'People are dying and one is so far away. There is nothing one can do, or say, to console the bereaved.' But there were those who were close to me, like that boy in Marabastad, Moloi. That hit me badly, very forcibly. I never could get over it.

I'd start thinking about the whole social and political situation; of the people who were reported to have died in their cells ... that accounts for my lament ... in the poetry I express the idea, the feeling, that nobody's ever going to atone for it. It's just seen as a casual thing by those who decide where you'll be born and where you'll die.

My feeling was that assassinations don't remove the grief of the people who are wounded, the people who are hurt by it. You take away a man and you kill him, and the underdog still is faced with the grief. Which is why the lament must go on. Who will atone? What is a tyrant dead? 'The tyrant is dead' is no use to anybody.

METAPHORS OF SELF*

MANGANYI: As I talk to you about biography today, many years after the publication of *Exiles and Homecomings* and *Bury Me at the Marketplace*, my curiosity takes me in numerous directions. First, I remind myself of the singular fact that as an intellectual and literary scholar the corpus of your work has covered a very wide canvas indeed: autobiography, one thinks here of *Down Second Avenue*; short story anthologies such as *In Corner B*; essays, *The African Image, Voices in the Whirlwind*; extended fiction, *Chirundu* and many other contributions too numerous to list. A writer, literary critic, and activist all in one is a difficult act to follow. Complexity is the word that comes to mind. I could not help thinking, once confronted with this complexity, of the classic study of autobiography by James Olney, published several years ago, entitled *Metaphors of Self: The Meaning of Autobiography*. I found, and I find up to this day, Olney's idea of metaphors of self exceedingly interesting. What is more, it is even more interesting in the context of writers such as you who write autobiography and what would normally qualify as fiction. To stretch

* An edited version of an interview published in 2006 in *Selves in Question: Interviews on Southern African Auto/Biography*.

Olney's ideas a little further, how do metaphors of self, or what Hopkins once described as 'a taste of myself', play themselves out in *Down Second Avenue*, when compared, say, to *The Wanderers, Chirundu*, and your other less autobiographical fiction?

MPHAHLELE: The 'metaphors of self' is an interesting concept. Considering that one is telling one's own story and you are trying to follow the line of your life to the present maybe, which is autobiography, you are remembering a number of events. You place yourself as the narrator. It is in the first person, narrating your own life. There is no way that you are going to capture everything that happened in your life. There is no way that you can even approximate the sequence of those events in your autobiography. So, what you indeed do is to recreate yourself. It is, in a sense, a monument of self. In its becoming it's a monument and in its composition it is a metaphor. You are saying here is my life story and yet at the same time it's a metaphor rather than absolute fact.

You are [aware], [that] you have to modify a number of things because you are recreating, as in a work of art. In a work of art, you don't try to reproduce concrete life and make a concrete representation of it. But rather you present it as a symbol of something else. You are also crafting it; you are giving it a meaning that will be understood by the rest of the world who come and view it. In a way, you try to say more than one thing at a time. Because that makes your work a form of art. You are also embellishing it in many ways. In writing, you embellish it with images, symbol upon symbol upon symbol. In that way, you are striving to find that deeper meaning, and that inner meaning makes poetry. In poetry, you try to go beneath the surface appearance of things. The meaning has no finality because you are exploring. So there is the poetry and there is the telling of the story and there is the metaphor of self. The monument is in the sense that you are saying: here is my life and I am reconstructing it as closely as I possibly can. It is not a monument in the sense of 'here I am! I have qualities of a hero and here is my monument.' But rather that here is something built on memory. You compose it, you craft it and produce it as a work of art. Now, that is how I understood my mission in autobiography.

In *Down Second Avenue*, as a concrete example, I had just finished my Master's with Unisa in 1956. When I was with *Drum*, Jenny, the wife of Sylvester Stein, the editor of the magazine, said to me: 'Zeke why don't you write something about your life?' I did not think much of it at the time. I had never thought of it before. I had always just thought that I was a fiction writer. And so I mulled over it until it grew on me. I started it the beginning of 1957, and things came rolling out; memories came rolling out, often in their starkness. I went to Nigeria and worked on the second half and repolished it. I thought I was saying to the reader, the reading public: here is the story of my life and it is not unique. It is shared by so many people, those at Maupaneng and in Marabastad. Those are the people who shared my life. This is a typical story of an African in South Africa.

I was saying that this is me, but it is not singularly me. To that extent, again it is a metaphor, a metaphor of self, a metaphor of the way our people lived and the way they struggled. I try to bring out in *Down Second Avenue* the toughness of our people – my grandmother, my aunt, my mother, and the women in the street, in Second Avenue. The heroism in a sense and also the grit they had to survive.

So it is metaphor upon metaphor upon metaphor.

MANGANYI: It is interesting to me that you made the connection with poetry. I think TS Eliot recognised the proximity between poetry and autobiography. As you were speaking, I was thinking about the role of the imagination in the writing of autobiography, and I was also thinking about character in fiction. Characters have a very important role to play in the power of the narrative. That led me to wonder what your views are on the role of character in autobiography. You have already referred to some of the people who populate the pages of *Down Second Avenue*. How do you think about character if you move away from the central character, namely, the monument to the self and its surroundings or social context?

MPHAHLELE: You know, as I was working from that memory, the memory of those people under whom I grew up, I remembered very distinctly their most outstanding traits. I told myself that I want to bring these out. I wanted to paint a clear picture of each one of them according to their individual characteristics. As I was not inventing, as I would do with fiction, I wanted to represent them as I understood them. I could not write it as a fiction writer tries to do. He or she tries to use a superior voice when he or she writes fiction. The one that says I know what the character is going to think, I'm in control.

MANGANYI: The one that pronounces.

MPHAHLELE: The one that pronounces. I know what he is going to think and I know what he is leading to. With autobiography, I take them as they come. Yes, I add a few things in order to liven it up. To liven up the picture, spice it up. And I throw in a little ginger here and a little ginger there in order to fill the picture up instead of a stark character of a person. And I do it as clearly as I can and as clearly as I understand it. I also wanted to be careful not to imagine things that an adult would be expected to imagine.

I had to write as a boy growing up. And I think you see the division there between me the adult and the boy growing up. The little things that go on in my mind, the prejudices. How I interpreted the cruelty of my teachers sometimes. When I am grown up and I am talking as a person who is politically conscious of what has happened to him and what is still happening to him and other people, I take on an adult pose; I talk ideas. Not so in the latter part of the book. I talk ideas as a grown up, as a family man. Let me say after I finished it I felt I had stripped myself almost naked. I was vulnerable. It never occurred to me that this was something that could happen. But in a short time I ceased to feel vulnerable, I felt liberated.

I was determined to write this thing as I wanted to write it and embellish it the way I wanted to. It was much later after that when I said, 'My! I am vulnerable.' Everything that people will say about the book they will be saying about me. Yet at the same time one could not have done it otherwise.

MANGANYI: I think you made a very important point about the different voices. I came across this issue while I was still engaged in the serious study of biography and autobiography – the problem of an adult writing about childhood. You recognise that there are different voices that need to be used. One has to recognise this almost in a self-conscious way to avoid a cluttering of the narrative voices – the person who speaks, the person who recollects, and the person who makes interpretations. What about literary criticism of autobiography in the light of the sense of vulnerability that you were talking about?

MPHAHLELE: Often one felt that when critics were writing about it, I would say to myself they got a point wrong here. That is not what I was feeling.

MANGANYI: Some years ago at an international symposium in Honolulu which was billed as 'new directions in biography' I made the point that there was a notable surge in the publication of autobiographies, largely by exiled black South African writers such as yourself, Peter

Abrahams, Bloke Modisane, and Todd Matshikiza during the late 1950s and early 1960s. I remember saying at the time that this coincidence between exile and the flowering of autobiography was intriguing.[1] I wonder what your own thinking is.

MPHAHLELE: That is very much to the point of autobiography, the way I see it. And I seem to feel this in a way that some people don't. They thought I was overplaying the theme of exile at one point, especially South Africans and those who were against my coming back. One feels as an exile that one is out there, away from any social support systems of your native land. You are out there exposed to the elements of a new terrain. And you want to let people at home know what it is to be an exile. Being in that condition of exile you want to tell the world what South Africa is like. What it means to grow up in South Africa right from day one. As a native of South Africa, you really have a strange land of childhood. A childhood in which perhaps the only love there is is between you and your mother, your father, and within the family and ends there. As a child, I always felt that this was a world for adults because of adult bullying. As I grew away from it and became independent I wondered what it was all about? Adults seemed to gang up against children, and they seemed to feel that they display their own concerns about your growing up. It always struck me how one had to survive that adult siege. In time, you grow up and reconcile things and begin to understand your culture. I feel that in exile one wants to do this. When I started *Down Second Avenue* I wasn't in physical exile. But in a sense I was already an exile, spiritually and intellectually, being constantly in conflict with a vindictive administration. I felt I had already begun my exile and moving out was the physical exile. You hope your story will resonate in people's minds and become a meaningful text; be a stimulus for more voices. I think that is why exile brings about autobiography. You feel you have lived that extraordinary experience.

MANGANYI: What are the implications, if any [of autobiography], for your other, work, say, *The Wanderers*, other fiction, and so on.

MPHAHLELE: *The Wanderers* is fictionalised. Let me say it is mostly fiction, but it follows a mainly autobiographical line, mostly in the travels from one place to another. It has that sequence which is autobiographical. The people are fictionalised, even the ones that

1 N Chabani Manganyi. 1981. 'Biography: The Black South African connection'. In Anthony M Friedson (ed). *New Directions in Biography*. The University Press of Hawaii, pp 52-61.

are in the autobiography: Ribs; my eldest son. And also my experiences in those places. And yet again there are events that took place. I fictionalise them, place them in a fictionalised context.

Where it becomes autobiographical is when it comes to the intimate parts where I talk closely about my family and so on and the helpers who were working for us in Nigeria. Now that is a work of the imagination in a larger frame. And also again it was to show the reader what the other worlds were like to me and to show those worlds and the experiences that shaped me, that helped to shape me in later life. They are stamped in my memory. They have been there a long time. They are still alive in my memory. Once you have written a book like that, an outline of autobiography and fictional detail, you seldom want to go back and read it as a published work. For one thing, I don't know why I can go back and read *Down Second Avenue*. When it comes to *The Wanderers* I hesitate, even only to reread snatches.

The narrator in *Chirundu* is, himself, an exile. Other South African exiles in Zambia feature – those in prison and those who were not. Their concerns are about exile. Someone would come up with a story about pre-exile life, often with such painful nostalgia. And yet the central theme of the book is Chirundu and his wife, Tirenje. They are estranged, and I go into the details of their lives. All of it is fiction. I did read in the newspaper about a man who had been arrested for bigamy. I thought to myself, 'Here is something I want to explore'. It's all made up. The conversation is not anything that I ever recorded in real life. A man whose judgement I always had a tremendous respect for was the late Martin Jarrett Kerr, the Anglican priest – himself a notable critic – who was always writing to me about my writing. He was very fond of this novel. For the first time it moves away from the mainly autobiographical. It is a change since *Down Second Avenue* and *The Wanderers*. It comes after them. Then again, he wrote to me after *Father Come Home*, which he said he enjoyed immensely, saying also it was strangely beautiful.

It is this whole thing about the imagination. I wrote an article at one time that is published in an American journal called *Kenyon Review*, entitled 'Educating the Imagination'. I am here pleading for a place in the curriculum for teaching oral poetry and moving into modern poetry; showing how the very use of metaphor is intensely traditional. We have metaphors in our languages and a teacher can bring these metaphors out and have them translated from one language to another. They show how people in their daily speech use metaphor in serious situations. It's the older people I am talking about. They start using metaphor because they feel that it goes deeper into the meaning of what they are saying. And also, metaphor is memorable. People will constantly repeat it. What the English poet Auden (1935), writing about poetry, calls 'memorable speech'.

From there it's an easy movement into written poetry. There you are using images, contemporary images that make up your world. Then I give an example of my own upbringing at Maupaneng, being a child of nature, moving freely in the wilds and so on, as a herd boy. I began to learn a lot about natural phenomena without being taught by any teacher. Given that kind of educative imagination I bring it into the whole idea of how to teach poetry. You notice that very few of our teachers know what poetry is. They shy away from teaching poetry in class. It is a formidable handicap for them. And yet it is so closely related to the use of the imagination; so closely related to the traditional use of the imagination and the formation of metaphors and other figures of speech.

I am giving this example in order to move into the connection between autobiography and the fiction that I write and the poetry. I was always intrigued by folk tales. I was always intrigued by the world of mystery and the wonder they encompassed when I was a boy. That imagination grew bigger as I was growing up and getting more education. So it never left me. My imagination will move from one genre to another, even when I am writing a factual paper.

When I am writing exposition the imagination keeps working and I find myself creating images in my mind. This is how it worked with *The Wanderers* and with *Chirundu*, with *Father Come Home*, and the short stories, of course.

It never was a problem. In fact, I always had to rein it in. Reining it in is always an act of art. To create art you need to put your imagination together so that it does not run wild when shaping your work of art.

MANGANYI: What about *Afrika My Music*?

MPHAHLELE: In *Afrika My Music* I go deeper into my thinking and come up with ideas. I begin with that interview, that weird interview at the University of the North for the job of head of English. What education, what university education means to me. Along the way, in certain chapters, I discuss music. I pick up a number of things outside my own normal activities that engage the intellect in a way that does not occur in the other books.

MANGANYI: There are often statements, allusions, when people are talking or writing about what are sometimes described as the *Drum* writers of the 1950s, to resonances with the Harlem Renaissance. Would you like to comment on this with regard to your own development as a writer and the genres you took up as you went along?

MPHAHLELE: Yes. The Fifties were a fascinating time. We actually did experience a revival quite a distance away from the Dhlomos, the Plaatjes – that is, stylistically.

Drum magazine was patterned after the two American magazines *Life* and *Look*, because it was a picture magazine like them, although it was bound to have articles of investigative reporting and political articles about ANC activities, generally political personalities. We read a lot of African-American literature, which we found in good supply at a bookshop in Joubert Street – Vanguard, now defunct.

That was one stage. Before that there was Peter Abrahams. We were not yet tuned in to Peter Abrahams's writing. He had been long in exile. But we were able to get his books in the country. *Dark Testament*, his first collection of sketches and short stories, and later *Mine Boy* and others. One could see that his style had been influenced by African-Americans. We only learnt later that he came into contact with African-American literature at the Bantu Men's Social Centre in Eloff Street. There was a library set up by an American missionary called Ray Phillips.

People like Dhlomo and other African personalities also had access to it. Peter Abrahams plunged into it and read everything that was African-American. We first heard from him about Marcus Garvey in the mid-Thirties when we were in high school together. He was greatly influenced by them. His style was clearly influenced by the Harlem Renaissance: short sentences, vivid images. We took off from there in *Drum*, each on his own. We created quite a noise that had not been heard before. The strangest thing is that the white people did not bother to read that literature, the *Drum* literature. Our famous writers were largely unknown to them. It appealed to the proletariat, to the black townships. And went abroad too, to East and West Africa. So it was an institution and does deserve the term renaissance. It was certainly a revival. We realised for the first time, at least I did, that, hey, there is something more in African-American writing than we had ever created. I got hold of Richard Wright's *Uncle Tom's Children*, a collection of short stories. My! It really shook me up! I realised the style I was using in *Man Must Live* was way out. It was so unrealistic, so postured. It was just sterile. I jumped on to Richard Wright's style and Langston Hughes's in the Harlem Renaissance. So it really intrigued us. Even Todd Matshikiza, who was inventive stylistically. It was largely the Harlem Renaissance that influenced us and others like Bloke Modisane, Arthur Maimane, and Can Themba, and later, Bessie Head. The Cape Town three – Alex la Guma, Richard Rive and James Matthews – simultaneously came under African-American influence. As a literary renaissance it was also a rediscovery of a new kind of consciousness among us. An urban consciousness that used language in a way that is felt, that is heard, and that immediately strikes on the emotions; that is not highly intellectual. You could also see then that the imagination was at work because so many of us who were writing for *Drum* were writing from personal experience of the life we were living. You felt the environment impacting on you all the time. You went to bed angry with what happened to you with white folks in the city; those things that you experienced at work and the struggle to survive. You felt life physically and emotionally all the time. And the writing was bound to change in a way you would not have imagined in the days of Dhlomo and Sol Plaatje. A number of people say the *Drum* writers were not politically minded, except for a few. This comes mostly from those who don't read critically, or at all. The fiction by *Drum* writers reflected the turbulence, the pain, the police terror, generally the cruelty of the times. Alongside this is the other human drama that reveals a life of escapist activities, entertainment. People found ways to relieve the tensions.

INTERVIEW REFERENCES

Bestier, James. 1988. 'Samuel Johnson on Letters'. *Rhetorica* 6(2), Spring, pp 145-66.

Brutus, Dennis. 1953. *Sirens, Knuckles and Boots*. Lagos: Mbari Publications.

Coetzee, J M. 1997. *Boyhood*. London: Secker and Warburg.

—. 2002. *Youth*. London: Secker and Warburg.

—. 2009. *Summertime*. London: Harvill Secker.

Cullinan, Patrick. 2005. *Imaginative Tresspasser: Letters between Bessie Head and Patrick and Wendy Cullinan, 1963-1977*. Johannesburg: Witwatersrand University Press.

Ellis, David. 2002. 'Letters, Lawrence, Shakespeare and Biography'. *Journal of European Studies* 32, pp 121-34.

La Guma, Alex. 1962. *A Walk in the Night*. Lagos: Mbari Publications.

Manganyi, N Chabani. 1983. *Exiles and Homecomings: A Biography of Es'kia Mphahlele*. Johannesburg: Ravan Press.

McDonald, Peter. 2009. *The Literature Police: Apartheid Censorship and its Cultural Consequences*. Oxford: OUP.

Vigne, Randolph. 1991. *A Gesture of Belonging: Letters from Bessie Head, 1965-1979*. London: Heinemann.

INDEX